GREAT ESCAPES AND RESCUES

GREAT ESCAPES AND RESCUES

An Encyclopedia

ROGER HOWARD

ABC-CLIO

Santa Barbara, California
Denver, Colorado
Oxford, England

Library of Congress Cataloging-in-Publication Data
Howard, Roger, 1966–
    Great escapes and rescues : an encyclopedia / Roger Howard.
        p.   cm.
    Includes bibliographical references (p.   ) and index.   1. Escapes.   2. Adventure and adventurers.   3. Rescues.
4. Survival skills.   I. Title.
G525.H827   1999
904'.7—dc21   99-30992
                                                                                                                    CIP

ISBN 1-57607-032-8 (hc)
ISBN 1-57607-190-1 (pbk)

05 04 03 02 01 00   10 9 8 7 6 5 4 3 2

ABC-CLIO, Inc.
130 Cremona Drive, P.O. Box 1911
Santa Barbara, California 93116-1911

This book is printed on acid-free paper ∞.
Manufactured in the United States of America

CONTENTS

Great Escapes and Rescues:
An Encyclopedia

ENTRIES BY CATEGORY

PREFACE

There is no shortage of printed material on the themes of escape and rescue. Many well-known books have already been written that cover the extraordinary experiences of remarkable individuals in great detail. So what is the justification for another publication on the same theme?

First, very few of the existing works adopt a wide perspective that includes escape *and* rescue. Most take a narrower point of view, looking at the themes from the viewpoints of "prisoners," "soldiers behind enemy lines," or "hostages." By contrast, I have sought to take a wider angle, both historically and thematically.

Moreover, this book seeks to incorporate stories of escape and rescue that have unfolded in recent years and to include newly discovered facts about past escapes and rescues, facts that have sometimes emerged years later. The escapes of, for example, Asrar al-Qabandi, who worked in occupied Kuwait during the Gulf War; Asil Nadir, who fled British justice while on bail; and the Russian air crew who fled the Afghan Taliban are all recent events that are worthy of inclusion.

There is also always considerable room to bring out aspects of known stories that have previously been underplayed or overlooked. Such aspects include, as I explain in the introduction, the role of the sixth sense in human behavior; of national characteristics, such as the German tendency to respect all things "official"; or of the chimerical nature of "freedom."

I am indebted to a number of people who assisted me as I researched and wrote this book. But I am particularly grateful to my editor, Dr. Bob Neville, for his patient encouragement and support and for the helpful comments he has made at all stages of the editorial process.

—*Roger Howard*

True stories of great escapes and rescues have long enjoyed considerable popularity with the reading public. The existing literature is already vast and includes such successful titles as *The Sound of Music, The Great Escape, The Killing Fields,* and *Alcatraz,* which have also provided the inspiration for equally successful movies. Stories of wartime escapes and rescues continue to attract media interest long after they occurred, and those of the present day often make headlines. If, as many claim, we live in an unromantic age and in a world of near ritualistic conformity, then it is not surprising that such stories, which often blend heroism and audacity, romance and adventure, mystery and intrigue into one heady mix, can strike a resonant chord.

The primary purpose of this particular collection of escapes and rescues in history is not only to inform but to entertain the general reader, and to this end I have adopted a wide perspective upon my subject matter. I have not, for example, confined the work to a particular theme, such as the escapes made by prisoners of war or the rescues made by soldiers on the battlefield; either could easily fill several books. Nor have I narrowed the entries to a particular time or place, although most happen to have taken place during the twentieth century. Instead, I have striven to look at some of the lesser-known escapes and rescues, such as those made from Stalin's gulags or from the Japanese labor camps. I have tried also to look beyond the narrow confines of high walls and barbed wire and to consider instead the rescues of cities from capitulation, of injured civilians from terrorist atrocities, of political leaders from capture or assassination, or of explorers from native peoples.

I have also tried to adopt a wide perspective on different types of escapes and rescues. Although many stories concern escape from enemy confinement, others are about those who have evaded capture altogether. A few escapees, such as Dan Cooper or Lord Lucan, have "disappeared," others have "retreated," and many have eluded their enemies only after a desperate chase. Though most escape because they have been rescued, there are others who have had to escape on their own, and there are those who escape in order to make the rescue of others possible. A few individuals have even been rescued from escapees.

Conversely, I have omitted escapes and rescues from what might be termed (to borrow a legalistic phrase) "the vicissitudes of life," the everyday misfortunes—air and car accidents or natural disasters, for example—that regrettably though inevitably fill the pages of our newspapers and at some stage affect most people's lives. Their inclusion would challenge the extraordinary appeal of the incidents that I have selected and make the volume merely a downbeat collection of mundane mishaps. Though some readers may feel that the rescue of the *Apollo 13* crew falls into this category, I feel that it was a unique incident that seized the attention of the world and is therefore of exceptional importance.

Besides their capacity to entertain, there are other reasons why stories of great escapes and rescues merit attention. Many provide insights into the later actions of the famous, whose views and attitudes may sometimes be explained by their experiences of fleeing their enemies. The sympathy that Charles II harbored for English Catholics, for example, which was later to have powerful repercussions on English politics, was undoubtedly nurtured by the assistance some of their number afforded him while he was on the run and by the exile at the French court that he was able to enjoy as a result of his getaway. And it is likely that Joseph Stalin's paranoia, which led to his savage persecution of his enemies, real and imagined, was fostered by the relative ease with which, as a young revolutionary, he himself once slipped away from captivity under the czar.

Moreover, an awareness of how individuals are able to escape from the clutches of enemies who may threaten death and injury may prompt readers to ask questions that they may otherwise overlook. Because this book generally concerns the famous and important, people upon whom many courses of events have depended, these stories prompt some speculation: What would have happened if these people had *not* gotten away from their enemies? If Churchill had been killed on the northwest frontier, if U.S. forces had been unable to supply Berlin in 1948, or if the British Expeditionary Forces had been unable to escape from Dunkirk in 1940—these questions and others like them are implicit in many of the accounts given below.

There are a host of other reasons why the theme of this book is well worth examination. Because escapees and rescuers act under great stress, for example, a consideration of their achievements and failures offers interesting insights into the workings of our minds. One subtheme that runs through this book is the role of the *irrational*—the insights many of us have at such times that offer a clear vision into one's surroundings but that are not really based on conscious thought at all. In wartime Shanghai many prisoners seemed to sense when some of their number were about to make a break, though they had not been so informed; passengers on the *Titanic* are known to have quickly felt that the liner was doomed, even though that prospect was not self-evident. The camp commandant at Holzminden appears to have acted on his gut feeling; the captors of Mary Queen of Scots and the escapees from New Mexico appear to have been moved by

astrological prediction or, as some would prefer to put it, by superstition. At times of great stress, the ordinarily well behaved can sometimes crack and suddenly and unaccountably inflict savage violence on the innocent, as if revealing a darker side of human nature.

Seen from such a psychological perspective, this collection also offers insights into the minds of escapees and their captors. If he is to find the weaknesses of those who guard him (without such weaknesses every enterprise is doomed), a prisoner planning an escape must carefully watch their ways. Some guards have succumbed to the monotony of humdrum routine, to greed, or to excessive attention to military discipline or authority. Many prisoners have also learned the importance of hiding their true emotions, smiling as if resigned to a long term of imprisonment, feigning innocence when guilty, and appearing to be at ease when their minds are really in turmoil. For both guards and the guarded, complacency emerges as a particular danger. Many of those involved in the traumatic reality of such events later show a disturbing vulnerability to a wide variety of problems, ranging from depression, psychological upheaval, and suicidal tendencies to egotism and arrogance.

These issues quickly broaden out to prompt a more general, and highly tempting, question: What are the characteristics of a successful escape or rescue? Clearly this question has a much wider significance because these characteristics are applicable not just to escape and rescue operations but also to many other situations in which success and failure depend upon human endeavor. So, for example, the story of how a prison escapee managed to creep through a well-guarded perimeter may provide useful reading to a military chief planning to send his soldiers inside one, or a mountaineer may at the very least draw inspiration and comfort and perhaps practical lessons from the epic marches across vast stretches of territory made by some of those whose stories are related here.

Many successful escapees and rescuers have deployed an original idea or applied an existing practice in an original way, thereby taking an enemy by surprise. Most possess exceptional audacity, and a few have performed feats that seem impossible. A prisoner's ability to win the loyalty, friendship, and perhaps even the love of those around him is often crucial, and so too is the formation of teams large enough to have members with the necessary specialist skills, experience, and support but not so large that traitors or the untrustworthy are admitted into its ranks. The determination of those who work on another's behalf is perhaps surpassed only by that of the most desperate loners. Many who have succeeded have been quick to find hidden meanings in the seemingly insignificant and to seize their chance when it comes. All must know their enemies and try to predict where they will concentrate their searches.

To highlight such characteristics I have also included a limited amount of material about escape and rescue *bids*. The stories of how some missions have failed when others, perhaps much less deserving, have succeeded help to highlight the essential characteristics of a successful operation and lead to some interesting observations. Simple plans, in which there is less to go wrong, offer a higher chance of success than the complex; conversely, small, insular, and well trained forces are more likely to succeed than those that rely on the application of a massive amount of firepower. Though their architects may be reluctant to admit it, the plans drawn up by those intending escape and rescue, or of authorities who strive to detain them, are all liable to error, either through sheer bad luck or because their authors overlooked some of the innumerable possibilities that may occur when their plans are put into practice. In some particularly painful cases, they even fail to see the obvious. And technology that is sophisticated (by the standards of its day) often may easily be thwarted by a simple, though ingenious, approach. The formidable defenses that surrounded the Berlin Wall, for example, did not prevent some escapees from leaving East Germany in the same simple manner Gambetta used to escape the Prussian army in 1870, just as the sophisticated designs of the *Titanic*, the

Apollo spacecraft, and the rescue helicopters used by U.S. forces in the Iranian desert failed to prevent disaster.

This concept touches on another subtheme with which this book is concerned: the relationship between humankind and science. Viewed from such an angle, the history of escape and rescue represents a constant struggle between the application of technical and scientific know-how to repress human aspirations and the determination of human beings to conquer such restraints. Throughout the ages, prisoners have been held by authorities who have used brutal methods and devices that were, by the standards of the day, often highly sophisticated. Many technically sophisticated creations have proven far too susceptible to accident or to simple ruses to fulfill the high hopes of their designers and owners. No one has yet devised an escape-proof detention, and despite all the daily advances in technology, it is doubtful that they ever will.

If these stories expose the limits of science, they also reveal the inadequacies of human planning. Though their architects may be reluctant to admit it, the plans drawn up by those intending escape or rescue, or of authorities who strive to detain them, are all liable to error, either through sheer bad luck or because their authors overlooked some of the innumerable possibilities that may occur when their plans are put into practice. In some particularly painful cases they even overlook the obvious. Most successful escapes and rescues have been based on less-ambitious plans. Most have been very well practiced and rehearsed, allow plenty of scope for things to go wrong, are based on observation rather than speculation, and are implemented gradually and pragmatically.

A collection such as this can raise other important issues as well. One criterion among the several that have guided my selection of the entries has been an awareness of the many different things an individual can *escape from*. I am referring not to an immediate physical obstruction, such as barbed wire or a metal fence, but rather to what lies behind the rules such a person is judged to have violated. Perhaps this book acts as a reminder that every political system, every political idea, can lead to oppression, injustice, and bloodshed as readily as the ideas of Stalin, Hitler, and Pol Pot.

So however appalling the human rights record of the former Soviet Union, the anticommunist hysteria that swept postwar America also made possible McCartheyite persecution and the Vietnam tragedy. No one could possibly dispute the shocking suffering of European Jews during World War II and before, but it is also true that in their fanatical determination to establish (and maintain) a homeland in Palestine, Jews too have used tactics of terror and brutality against their British and Arab enemies. I have deliberately selected a rescue from one such atrocity, the bombing of the King David Hotel in 1947, from the many others that have been committed (by all sides) in this region. And of course, though everyone knows the injustice and brutality of the old apartheid regime of South Africa, details of the ruthless violence employed by its enemies against each other and against the former regime in Pretoria are only just emerging. Those who have fought slavery have sometimes employed means as violent as those of their enemies (and had good reason to). Most obviously, in the 1790s, French revolutionaries seized power but soon replaced the injustice and bloodshed of the ancien régime with their own. Any political theorist, it would seem, can build an Auschwitz or a Dachau with the materials of his or her own ideas as easily as Hitler and Himmler did with theirs.

This is just the political aspect of a wider subtheme that runs through the book. Escapes and rescues are about human aspiration—aspirations to find liberty and happiness or to bring it to those whom a rescuer deems worthy—but their history is almost as much a story of hopes dashed or of one form of unhappiness replacing another. Some prisoners escape captivity but are later affected by deep unhappiness. When the mobs stormed the Bastille, they felt badly let down by the true nature of the prisoners they wanted to rescue, just as Sean Bourke later had serious doubts about the man he had "sprung" from prison. Some escapees have also become reckless with their own lives, occasionally even suicidal. Others have become seriously disturbed, probably affected by the trauma of their experiences. And few criminals who have escaped captivity seem to have made the pursuit of freedom their priority; instead, they have resumed their earlier criminal careers, often to their eventual downfall. Freedom, in short, is often a chimera, an illusion that quickly crumbles in the face of the realities, self-inflicted or otherwise, of an escapee's life once he or she treads beyond the wire.

This difficulty is one among several that I have encountered in compiling the book. Though much of it has been written in the style of an adventure book, often with wry touches of humor, this tone mixes uneasily with a darker side that lurks underneath. This tension occurs partly because death and injury inevitably form part of the picture of the prison camps and detention centers that are featured. Many of those who appear in these pages have been sent to such places precisely because they are unpleasant characters, and no one could ever find the experience of detainment in such places enjoyable. But the tension also exists because the experience of escape itself is often terrifying and can sometimes exact a heavy toll from those who have attempted or been through it. This duality sometimes makes this book oscillate between lighthearted adventure and a more deadly seriousness, just as it on occasion treads the boundary between fact and fiction, or between romantic dreams and harsh reality, and just as it occasionally highlights the proximity, not the gulf, between nobility and animality of spirit.

It is often also very difficult to decide whether a prisoner who slipped out of captivity but was later recaptured really "escaped" at all. To solve this problem of eligibility for inclusion in the book, I have used my own judgment to decide whether their recapture was a likely or foreseeable consequence of their escape from the place of detainment. It seems to me that the recaptures of such great escapees as Jack

Sheppard, Walter Probyn, or Sgt. John Prendergast were more a result of their own bravery, negligence, or plain foolhardiness than a likely consequence of their escape. On the other hand, the runaway Bob Dodge, who escaped from Sachenhausen concentration camp in 1944, is not known to have invited his own recapture in the same manner and has merited inclusion because his escape bid won him freedom in an indirect way and because his story is remarkable.

Similarly, it is not always possible to know exactly when a "rescue" has been carried out. The example of Acre Castle illustrates how a rescue party may successfully free their compatriots behind bars but pay heavily for doing so. This question is also a matter of judgment, and though the dividing line is often obscure, most would agree that the Irgun at Acre did succeed in rescuing the prisoners, whereas the U.S. authorities who stormed the fortress at Waco or the German police who tried to liberate the hostages at Munich incurred too many casualties among the prisoners to be said to have carried out a rescue.

This distinction of course assumes that the followers of David Koresh's cult in the Waco fortress even *wanted* to be rescued, and this leads inevitably to another problem that confronts anyone who writes on the theme of rescue: Arguably, someone can be rescued if it is in their best interest to be taken away from their assumed captors, but this question is of course particularly problematic in a society like that of the contemporary United States, which frowns upon any attempt to enforce a particular lifestyle, or perhaps even advocate one. Hence, most law-abiding individuals may have good

reason to resent calling the springing of George Blake a "rescue" operation—not because he subsequently went to live behind the Iron Curtain but because the term "rescue" implies the existence of some form of detainment that is *undeserved*. Innocent men and women can be rescued, but not convicted criminals. I have nonetheless included this story, not because I have tried to give my theme a wide ambit, for reasons I have already given, but because Blake obviously did "escape" (a morally more neutral term), even if he was not rescued.

There are of course a host of other themes that I would like to have the space to elaborate: Was Karin Kabofski justified in using her harsh and cynical means to find the freedom she craved? Is an escapee like John Prendergast or Count Beniowski more justified in killing those who try to stop him than a prisoner who escapes in peacetime? Do some escapees, like Napoleon, flee more than just a prison camp and instead run away from some painful truth that it represents or, like the Russian prisoners in Afghanistan, from a wholly different civilization altogether? Is genuine altruism of motive really as rare a commodity as this collection seems to suggest? And is there a clear distinction between the qualities well practiced in a private life and those used in public?

It is not hard to see why this book should ultimately be concerned with all these different issues. For escapes and rescues stand at the dividing line between freedom and captivity, and there can be few things that have inspired so much from so many as has the desire to be free.

GREAT ESCAPES AND RESCUES

ACRE CASTLE (1947)

The Irgun, a Zionist terror group fighting the British army to secure a Jewish homeland in Palestine, stormed Acre Castle near Jerusalem on 4 May 1947 in a daring and dramatic bid to rescue Zionist prisoners.

The defenses of the massive castle at Acre seemed nearly insurmountable for the Irgun, and indeed for any invader. Built by the Crusaders and restored by the Turks, the castle had comfortably withstood a withering barrage from Napoleon's artillery in 1799. During the British Mandate in Palestine it was still regarded as impenetrable. To make matters worse, shortly before the Zionists were ready to strike the British stepped up security in response to the discovery of a tunnel that prisoners had started, and nearly finished, from the central prison of Jerusalem. The guerrillas storming Acre would be in the direct line of fire of more than 150 enemy soldiers using automatic weapons from several key defensive positions.

However, the Irgun leaders, hailed as heroes by their supporters but condemned as terrorists by their enemies, judged that the potential rewards were worth the considerable risks. The prison had long been the largest and most important of those used by the British, and the operation would not only free a large number of Zionist prisoners but also smash the most overt symbol of British rule.

They began by smuggling tiny amounts of explosives into the prison with the prisoners' families. Though the quantities taken inside were small, they had the capability to destroy the heavy iron bars that would separate the long inside corridor from the main assault group when it breached the wall. Once the prisoners had the explosives, they

got ready and on the appointed day waited for the signal that the attack was imminent.

During the early evening of 4 May the main assault unit moved quickly but stealthily under the cover of darkness through the British positions outside the castle. They reached the outside walls unseen, attached 250 pounds of explosives—a closely calculated amount—to a carefully selected position on the wall, and took cover. When the explosion boomed through the stillness of the night the prisoners detonated their charges and broke through their cell doors, finding to their jubilation that the walls had been successfully breached.

But within moments British searchlights were combing the chaos, and though rescuers and rescued ran as quickly as they could, many were caught by the intense British fire put down to stop them. One group ran straight into a British patrol that had heard the commotion in the distance and quickly returned to base, gunning down the enemy they suddenly found before them.

The raid was a mixed success for the Jewish guerrillas. Though they had freed 31 Irgun prisoners, they were surprised to find that almost all of the 200 others who got away that evening were Arabs, many of them common criminals. Of the nine of their number who were gunned down by British fire, six were escapees and one was a leading figure in the Irgun, a commander of near legendary repute named Dov Cohen. On the other hand, the raid's very audacity stunned the British, who had always regarded Acre as impregnable, and touched their rawest nerve—their fear of high casualties. Menachem Begin, one of the Irgun leaders of the operation, later echoed the

Duke of Wellington's remark that "nothing except a battle lost can be half so melancholy as a battle won": For the Zionist leader, too, "the feeling of mourning was far deeper than the joy of triumph."

See also: King David Hotel; Palestine
References: Begin, Menachem. *The Revolt*. London: W. H. Allen, 1979.

AFGHANISTAN: THE FLIGHT OF THE RUSSIAN AIR CREW (1996)

In August 1996 a group of prisoners of the Taliban in Afghanistan made a dramatic flight from their Afghan captors, an event that made instant headlines throughout the world.

The prisoners were the civilian crew of a Russian transport plane that in October 1995 was flying arms from Russia to Kabul, which was at that time still governed by the enemies of the Taliban militia, Berhanuddin Rabbani and Ahmed Shah Massoud. The plane was intercepted by a Taliban jet and forced to land at the airstrip at Kandahār, home of the Islamic militant movement. Its six-man crew was immediately imprisoned.

The prisoners were being held by a reactionary group famed for its indifference to the views of the outside world, and the pressure of Russian diplomats and UN representatives to secure their release came to nothing. Nor could such pressure even improve the harsh conditions in which, in true Afghan style, the men were held. Most were kept in solitary confinement after rumors of a rescue attempt surfaced in December, and they were only rarely allowed to leave their cramped quarters.

But the prisoners managed to convince the Taliban leaders that they had to carry out essential repairs on the plane once a month to prevent it from deteriorating into an unusable state. Because the Afghan radicals had few planes of their own and thus could not verify the prisoners' claims, they reluctantly agreed. So from the spring of 1996 on, under armed guard, the Russians were escorted from their cells to the plane to carry out the repair work and were marched back again immediately afterwards.

The Russian pilots then hatched a plot to find a way back home. Although there were always several heavily armed guards on the plane and many more on the runway outside, they had one weak point: Under Islamic law they were obliged to pray at midday, and they always knelt down, weapons aside, in order to do so. There were of course some guards still watching the prisoners, but if the crew members positioned themselves in just the right place they stood a chance of overpowering the guards, starting the plane, and flying off. Though it seemed a long shot, it was better than risking long-term imprisonment in such harsh conditions.

On 16 August, as the Afghan militants knelt to pray, the desperate Russians jumped into action. They started the plane's engine, claiming that it was a routine check, seized their three guards, and wheeled the giant transport into flight readiness. It quickly became apparent that the escape would be a close-run thing, for as the plane began to move over the tarmac the Taliban guards on the runway sprang into action, firing at the plane and driving into the middle of the runway to stop it from getting off the ground. But the Russians picked up speed as quickly as they could and made a perfect emergency takeoff, leaving Afghan soil only seconds before the jeeps arrived to block their path. A Taliban jet gave pursuit but could not reach the Russians before they crossed into Iranian airspace.

Though some have argued that such a fantastic escape strongly suggests that the Taliban had allowed their prisoners to leave, perhaps because they were tired of the trouble and expense of keeping them, the Taliban could have just as easily released the Russians through diplomatic channels and kept their credibility intact. Instead, the prisoners carried out a swashbuckling escape that was more characteristic of the imperial adventurers of an earlier age than of late-twentieth-century captives.

See also: Air, escape by; Kabul

AIR, ESCAPE BY

Some prisoners have made dramatic escapes in planes or helicopters, flying to freedom in friendly territory.

In recent years there have been several instances of helicopters landing inside prison compounds in order to pick up waiting escapees. In 1971 a helicopter operation took only ten seconds to lift a U.S. drug smuggler off the yard at a Mexican jail. Many different parties—the CIA, the Mafia, and the Cubans—were reputedly involved in the operation. Another such break took place from Mountjoy Prison in Northern Ireland. Irish Republican Army (IRA) members hijacked a helicopter and forced the pilot to fly to the prison and hover over the main exercise yard, where three leading members of the movement, Seamus Twomey, Kevin Mallon, and John O'Hagan, were waiting for them. All three were whisked off to the outside in an operation that took prison officers completely by surprise and led to a thorough review of security.

Another IRA leader, John Kendall, also escaped from British custody in 1987 as a result of such a skyjacking. An accomplice, Andrew Russell, hired a helicopter and forced the pilot at gunpoint to land on the exercise yard of Gartree Prison on the British mainland. Kendall and another terrorist leader, Sydney Draper, were flown off and were landed on a nearby industrial park in order to avoid being intercepted by British fighter planes. Having handcuffed the unfortunate pilot to his craft, the escapers and rescuers then hijacked a passing delivery truck, threatening its driver with violence, before stealing a car from a parking lot and escaping down the highway. Although Kendall was found and arrested some months later, Draper remained at large for another two years.

During World War II the difficulties of escaping by air were enormous, though there were some determined attempts. At Stalag XXA near Torun in Poland, two captured Royal Air Force (RAF) pilots exchanged places with two colleagues—neither of whom could fly—who were assigned to clear a nearby German runway of snow. Not far from where they were working were three Messerschmitt fighters, all lined up as if ready for takeoff. They were an irresistible target for the pilots, who, for the moment at least, were working unsupervised. At a carefully timed moment, they ran to the planes and climbed inside, unnoticed by their German supervisors several hundred yards away. Though they were unfamiliar with the plane and its controls, they managed to switch on the engine, but they could do nothing when it stalled in the bitterly cold weather and alerted the guards, who had until then still not noticed their disappearance.

Even if the pilots—wholly unaccustomed to the Messerschmitt, a very different aircraft from their Hurricanes—had managed to get the planes off the ground, their escape would still have been highly perilous. They could easily have been intercepted and shot down by other Axis or Allied aircraft in the area.

A group of British pilots who were captured in Sicily and flown to the Italian mainland were in this respect better qualified to make an escape. Not only could one of the pilots speak to his captives in fluent Italian, but he also knew how to fly the very plane they were using to take him to a prison camp. He soon began a technical argument with one of the crew about how the aircraft should be flown, and as it became increasingly technical and heated, the British prisoner simply put himself in the pilot's seat and threatened to crash the aircraft unless they changed course and went to Malta instead. Within an hour or two he was back behind British lines.

Another alternative was to build an aircraft and fly out of prison. The ingenious prisoners of Colditz managed to design and build a glider that measured nearly 20 feet long with a 32-foot wingspan. They somehow managed to hide the glider behind a dummy wall in one of the attics. It was built only toward the end of the war and was never used, even though it would undoubtedly have given the prisoners a chance of escaping.

A few escapees have used their own aircraft to fly to freedom. Not long after the

Berlin Wall was built to stop the flood of refugees crossing to the West, a Polish air force pilot, Richard Obacz, took himself and his family to the West, flying at a height of only 150 feet in order to evade Communist radar and to minimize the risk of being shot down by jets that were ordered to destroy anyone escaping in such a manner.

A number of others have escaped from Communist Europe by flying out. One was Isolde Giese, who was swept off her feet by her fiancé, a Swede named Hans Christian Cars, in a most unusual way. To take her to Sweden to start a new life together, the young Cars invested all his savings and free time in learning to fly, and when he was finally ready to undertake the journey he hired a small aircraft and found a suitable rendezvous at a remote part of the German-Czech border. Flying as low as he dared, it took him just minutes to land, pick up Isolde, and fly her back to the West. And in 1979 four East Germans made a balloon from nylon and curtains and flew over the Berlin Wall with their four young children in a manner reminiscent of Leon Gambetta's flight from the Prussians.

See also: Afghanistan: The flight of the Russian air crew; Gambetta, Leon; Kabul; Werra, Franz von

ALCATRAZ

Though other escapes from imprisonment have been as daring and well planned, few have been more famous, or more mysterious, than the story of the 1962 break from Alcatraz that was popularized by the subsequent book and film. This story, however, forms just one chapter in a much longer story of escape from the U.S. prison.

Alcatraz was originally used by the U.S. Army as a military detention center, and at that time escape from the stronghold was not considered impossible. Though it was more than a mile from the mainland, and though the currents were often powerful enough to overwhelm even the strongest swimmer, those who chose their moment well had no difficulty getting across. In 1937 a teenaged girl swam from San Francisco to the island in just 47 minutes, and for years local swimming clubs held competition in neighboring waters. One person is even known to have swum the distance wearing handcuffs.

At this time there are known to have been a small number of escapes from the prison. In 1918, while the men in the barracks were celebrating Thanksgiving, four inmates slipped past the sentries, crept down to a beach, bound some planks together to make a raft, and vanished. They were not seen or heard from again. Some years later a few others who tried the same thing fell victim to the strong currents they encountered and were found drifting a long way out to sea, shivering and afraid, waiting for someone to rescue them.

A handful made it to freedom by more ingenious methods. One prisoner who did clerical work in the prison office waited until the camp commander left for the day, typed out a release form, and forged the commander's signature on it. He boarded the ferry that shuttled daily to the mainland and was soon a free man.

Another is known to have heard of the death of a prison officer and of the fact that his widow, who lived on the island, had ordered a mourning outfit from San Francisco. On the day of the funeral the sentries at the quay saw the widow walking toward them and, not wanting to seem insensitive, let her on board without inspecting her pass. A few hours later the commander's office received a call from the dead man's wife—the real wife—asking for clues about the whereabouts of her mourning outfit.

When in the 1930s the prison was turned from a military detention center into a state prison that was to house the most dangerous and violent inmates in the United States, its buildings were fortified to an unprecedented degree. Fences, wires, bars, gun towers, metal detectors, and hidden microphones designed to pick up any efforts to dig a tunnel were all installed in almost every building. The guards were all hand-picked men who were specially chosen for their ability to deal with such a tough and demanding environment. Those who visited the prison felt confident enough to proclaim publicly that escape "was an absolute impossibility."

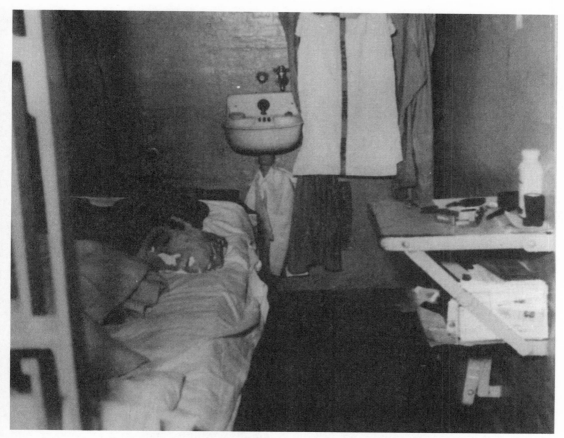

The dummy head used by John Anglin to fool prison guards while he, his brother Clarence, and Frank Morris made their famous escape from Alcatraz on June 12, 1962. (AP/Wide World Photos)

But even then it proved impossible to keep all of the inmates inside the prison, which after all housed, as one director of the U.S. prison service put it, the country's most cunning escape artists, who have plenty of time to think up ways of getting out. On 16 December 1937 a daring escape was made by two inmates, Ralph Roe and Ted Cole, as they worked in a prison shop on the northern tip of the island. Having already sawed through two bars on one of the windows, carefully disguising their efforts, they made their move as the guards' backs were turned and traveled through the thick fog, in broad daylight, to the coast. Again, nothing more was seen or heard of the escapees, though many have argued that since the current was moving at more than eight knots that day, it was probable that they failed to reach the other side.

But the most famous escape from Alcatraz took place on 11 June 1962, only shortly before the prison was closed down, by three prisoners, Frank Morris and two brothers, Clarence and John Anglin. Their extraordinary story quickly made them famous throughout the world.

Morris, a confidence trickster with a long criminal record, had been transferred to Alcatraz only a few months before he started to prepare his escape, at the end of 1961. Though his cell was no different from most others, he quickly noticed a tiny ventilator shaft built into his wall and decided to have a go at digging his way out. At first it seemed a ludicrous idea since the shaft was embedded in concrete walls about nine inches thick and since the shaft, even if the vent were pried out, was far too small for anyone to crawl through. But if he patiently scratched away at the concrete using the right tools, Morris reckoned, then he might be able to make a bigger hole around the shaft and make his way into the ventilator system inside the prison.

Using just a pair of nail clippers to get through the concrete, Morris made slow progress but realized that he would move much more quickly if he could bind the clippers together with a spoon and simultaneously scrape and scratch at the wall. Stealing the right type of spoon from the kitchens, Morris found an ingenious way of binding the two instruments together in order to make the tool he wanted: Lighting several matches and brazing the tools with the silver coating he had scraped off a dime, he was able to forge them together in just the way he needed.

Morris was also quick to recognize another obstacle that lay in his way. Since the corridor outside his cell was constantly patrolled and since the guards were able to look straight through the bars into his cell, he knew he would have to find a way of disguising the fact that so much of the wall was missing. Moreover, he knew that if he left his cell and went through the hole into the shaft, his absence would be noticed within minutes. So before he progressed far with his digging, Morris was careful to work out a solution to this formidable obstacle.

The answers he came up with were similar to those found by several prisoners of war (POWs) during both world wars. If he could mold some papier-mâché in exactly the right way, he would have a chance of filling in the missing parts of the wall and even of making a dummy head that was virtually indistinguishable from his own. Setting to work, he obtained old newspapers and magazines, soaking them in water and molding them to the right shape. When they had dried and set, he used an acquaintance's paints and discarded hairs from the barber shop to add the finishing touches. He hid the hole in the wall behind an accordion case. Morris knew that he had a chance of hiding his preparations for escape from the authorities for at least several weeks before they were likely to target his cell with a random search.

But as he made his way though the air shafts, reconnoitering the layout of the prison to gauge its strengths and weaknesses, Frank Morris realized that he would have virtually no chance of making it to the mainland alone. This problem arose not just because of the arduous task of crossing the stretch of sea back to the mainland but also because of the physical obstacles he found in making his way through the shafts, especially a bar that stopped him, at the very last stage, from getting though the shaft into the grounds of the prison, only a few hundred yards from the coast.

The two prisoners Morris approached and shared his plans with, Clarence and John Anglin, were both veterans of several escape attempts who had proved their strength and endurance beyond question. It did not take them long to find a solution to the problem of the bar at the end of the shaft: If they could find a motor, then they would simply attach a metallic spike, converting it into a drill, and probably get through the bar in hours.

The three men proved highly adept at finding the motor they wanted. Seeing a small ventilator fan in the concert hall where they gathered weekly to take part in the prison concerts, they succeeded in smuggling it past the prison guards, who were supposed to stop all outgoing prisoners to search them as they returned to their cells. Like other escapees, they took full advantage of basic failures in routine checks by prison staff. But though they worked with all their might and ingenuity, their makeshift drill simply did not stand up to the task and crumbled as it hit the metal bar that was the final barrier to their escape bid. It was to take them another six months, using wire and a small saw, to get through the bar and finally make their move.

Before setting off they were able to construct simple rafts that they hoped would withstand a strong current, using models described in newspaper articles to build them from barrels, mesh wire, and old raincoats, which gave them extra buoyancy in rough seas. They wasted no time in putting the rafts together: By chance the Anglins' cell had been searched, and they knew it might not be long before Morris's was inspected too.

For the guards on duty during the night of the escape, nothing seemed out of the ordinary. One of the prison guards noticed that Morris was sleeping unusually deeply, as he was often inclined to. Another heard a thud that seemed to come from the roof above him, but it didn't seem worth raising the alarm. Only the next morning, when there was no movement from the three "sleeping" prisoners, did it become clear what had happened.

The disappearance of Morris and the Anglin brothers can be termed an escape only in one sense because their fate, like that of "D. B. Cooper" and Lord Lucan, has remained a mystery. The discovery the next day of some of Clarence Anglin's possessions floating in the water has led some to argue that they almost certainly drowned that night. Others, however, have pointed out that this was unlikely because the current that night had not exceeded 2.2 knots (2.5 miles per hour), and no bodies ever washed up on the nearby islands and coastlines. The mystery of the Alcatraz break is unlikely to ever be solved.

References: Bruce, John C. Escape from Alcatraz: A Farewell to the Rock. London: Hammond, 1984.

ALGERIA

During the war in Algeria Bachir Chihani, a leader of the local resistance to French colonial rule, made a near miraculous escape from his headquarters, an escape that confounded his enemies.

Chihani's base, in a remote, inaccessible part of the country, was discovered and surrounded by French soldiers. Chihani unwisely ignored the pleadings of his accomplices to leave with them at night and slip through the cordon. Instead, having chosen to stay, he was trapped inside when the French dynamited its entrance. Though they thought he was probably inside, les paras (the French troops) felt sure that they had turned the base into a tomb. No one, they thought, could possibly get through the mounds of rock piled up around the entrance.

Yet Chihani proved them wrong. Somehow surviving inside for six days, he was eventually able to tunnel out, using his bare hands to perform a feat his enemies had sworn was beyond any mortal. But ironically, his escape was in vain. Having committed many errors on the battlefield and in the shady world of rebel politics, he was executed days later by his own deputies.

See also: De Gaulle, Charles; Egyptian embassy
References: Horne, Alistair. A Savage War of Peace: Algeria 1954–62. London: Macmillan, 1977.

AL-OULD (1980)

In 1980 Ian Fraser, a British citizen who was working in Saudi Arabia, found himself under arrest and facing a very long spell in extremely harsh conditions not because of any major wrongdoing—he was convicted of violating Saudi Arabia's alcohol laws—but because he was being used as a pawn in a much bigger game of international diplomacy.

The tense relations between Saudi Arabia and Britain originated in the screening on British television of a program, The Death of a Princess, that depicted Saudi justice as arbitrary and barbaric. In the tense weeks that followed the broadcast, a considerable number of expatriates suddenly faced harassment from the police even though they had never encountered such difficulties before.

After only the briefest of trials, Fraser was warned that he could face a very long period in prison. His release was dependent almost entirely upon the goodwill of the Saudi royal family, and that goodwill in turn depended upon the political situation with Britain. Soon after his detainment, in May 1980, he vowed that he would escape from Riyadh's top-security prison, Al-Ould, even though no one was known to have ever done so before.

His first plan was to take advantage of the one occasion when both guards and other prisoners were distracted: Each Friday the prisoners' friends and relatives arrived from outside to deliver parcels and letters, and the guards would always carefully search through them. At that precise moment, he thought, he might have a chance of dashing from the reception area, where the packages were delivered, through the main gates, using a knife to threaten the guards if he needed to. But when his accomplice in this extremely audacious and probably unrealistic plan was released only days before he was ready to put it into practice, Fraser was forced back to the drawing board.

But he soon found another acquaintance, Eric Price, who was willing to join him, and hit on another plan. Seeing that some of the windows in the prison were more vulnerable than the Saudi authorities realized, he felt sure that he could find a way out one of the windows to one of the side gates of the prison. The most essential thing, he decided, was to find a window that was not overlooked by one of the watchtowers and then slip through it at the dead of night.

Without someone outside the prison willing to help him, Fraser's plan would not have seemed any more realistic than his first. Using money sent to him by his family in Britain, Fraser found and paid an outside contact to buy a car and have it left on the road outside the prison, with forged identity passes and its keys inside. If they drove at a frantic pace, he reckoned, they might just have some chance of reaching the coast before the alarm was raised.

Fraser also knew the dangers involved. Though he and his accomplice planned to move in the middle of the night, the prison was brilliantly lit, making them just as visible then as in the daytime. And if they were seen, the guards would not hesitate to open up with the heavy machine guns that would be trained on the prison from the watchtowers. Moreover, even if they left at 3 A.M., just when everything had settled down, they knew that it would not be long, perhaps no more than 45 minutes, before some of the Muslims would wake up to pray. And if they did manage to get outside, the Saudi police were highly adept in the art of pursuit, well exercised by the regular practice of finding illegal Pakistani immigrants. But whether because both men were born escapers or because they just hated

imprisonment, they chose to brave the risks and go.

Waiting until the nights got longer before they made their move, Fraser and Price began their escape bid shortly after 3 A.M. on the morning of 18 December 1980. Creeping out of their cell in Block 2, they went to the bathhouse a short distance away and began chiseling at the window bars. Though their tools were primitive, it did not take the two men, driven by adrenaline, very long to force the bars open and squeeze through into the courtyard outside.

Though they had not expected it, the harsh weather came to their assistance, for there was no sign of life from any of the watchtowers, which loomed over them as they moved across the compound toward the side gate. In the bitterly cold weather the guards had moved inside and failed to maintain an adequate level of vigilance, and even when Fraser and Price attacked the side gate's padlock, at the foot of one of the watchtowers, still they saw no sign of life. In the more than 40 minutes it took them to break the padlock, they were forced several times to take cover when the metallic snaps threatened to attract unwanted attention. But each time they found, to their surprise and relief, that no one had heard and that they could continue their escape bid.

Once outside they found the car less than a 100 yards before them, and within minutes they were on the road out of Riyadh. Driving at more than 80 miles per hour for much of the way, they were desperate to reach the two police barriers along the route to Dammam, their destination, before the police were alerted. To their delight, they were not stopped en route at all; all the barriers along the road were raised and attended only by sleeping guards.

Knowing that time was of the essence, the escapees were soon able to find a small boat with a large enough motor to take them to the coast of Bahrain, some 20 or so miles away. They insisted on purchasing it there and then and on not waiting until the next day for delivery, and they took possession of the boat just before 1 P.M., a few minutes before the shop would have closed until the following morning. Their first attempt to reach Bahrain was disastrous: After several hours travel, thinking they had made it, they landed by mistake on another stretch of Saudi territory. On the second attempt they were beaten back by the bad weather. But on the third attempt they finally succeeded, scarcely believing their own good fortune and quickly telephoning their families in Britain to tell them their news.

Later they discovered why they had seen almost no police activity, even long after the news of the escape had broken out. Apparently word had reached the prison authorities that they were heading for Jeddah, a route that Fraser had intended to use for his first escape plan but that he had later changed. A massive police presence, which they would have had almost no chance of evading, was therefore concentrated along the roads and coastal areas.

References: Fraser, Ian. *Escape from Al Ould.* London: Frederick Muller, 1983.

AMETHYST (1949)

In 1949 a British warship, HMS *Amethyst,* narrowly escaped from Chinese Communist artillery that had held it hostage on the Yangtze River for nearly three months.

The *Amethyst* had been traveling upriver on its way to guard the embassy staff at Nanking, more than 200 miles away. But at a time when the Chinese civil war was still raging, the British presence at Nationalist-held Nanking inevitably attracted the disapproval of the Communist forces under Mao Tse-tung.

On 20 April 1949, as the warship moved further upriver, Communist artillery suddenly and wholly unexpectedly opened fire. The gunners were not just firing to give the crew a fright but were aiming to hit decks and cause damage and injury. Though the barrage lasted only minutes, the British were caught entirely off guard; 23 crew members were killed, including the captain, and 31 were injured. The ship was also seriously damaged and left marooned on a sandbank.

When a British delegation left the *Amethyst* and arrived on shore to talk with Communist representatives, they were accused of having opened fire first. The warship would not be allowed to move on, they were told, until the British admitted their responsibility for what had happened and paid reparations. In the meantime, several artillery batteries were trained on them and would open fire if they tried to escape.

For John Kerans, the embassy official who had traveled from Nanking to take command of the ship, the immediate object was to get the *Amethyst* off the sandbank that it had been driven onto by the bombardment. After throwing much surplus machinery and equipment over the sides, the crew was able to race the engines full bore and slip the ship off the sandbank into the middle of the river. But Kerans knew that making an all out escape from this diplomatic and military impasse would be very much harder, since the Chinese gunners had their sights trained on them and would not hesitate to open fire.

As the weeks passed the *Amethyst's* plight became increasingly desperate. Food and water supplies started to run low, and though the ship was stationary, fuel was still required to keep it up and running. Kerans knew that the ship would need 33 tons of fuel to reach the open sea, and when the fuel left in reserve had dipped dangerously close to that amount, he decided to put a plan of escape into operation.

Shortly after dark on 30 July Kerans ordered his crew to obscure the ship's silhouette with several cleverly constructed boards and to paint several sections of its exterior with dark colors. All crew members now wore dark clothing, and even the brass work on board was dulled with grease. Kerans ordered the engines to get up steam, knowing that they had some chance of escaping even though they faced suffering serious casualties and being sunk if they were seen by the Chinese gunners.

Just as the *Amethyst* was about to move, the British had an almost unbelievable stroke of good luck. By chance, they made out a Chinese merchant ship approaching them, and they realized that if they could move at its side and precisely at its pace, they would have a much better chance of not being seen.

To begin with everything went smoothly, and the two ships scarcely broke the stillness of the night as they steamed ahead. But as they passed one Chinese battery further upriver their luck changed, and the crew watched in horror as a flare soared through the night, clearly revealing their position and instantly attracting a barrage of withering artillery and machine-gun fire from the enemy positions. Since there was no longer any point in tagging alongside the merchant ship, Kerans ordered the engines to go flat out in a desperate bid to keep ahead of the Chinese fire. Though shells were falling all around them, and though the merchant ship exploded in flames behind them and sank, the *Amethyst* just managed to escape Chinese fire, probably because its lack of any silhouette and the absolute hush its crew maintained as it sailed made them extremely hard for the enemy to spot. Although battery upon battery fired at the *Amethyst*, still it sailed clear, on several occasions only narrowly being missed by the searchlights that swept the seas. It finally reached the open seas at 5:29 the next morning, just as the dawn was breaking through the darkness of the night.

See also: The Long March
References: Earl, Lawrence. *Yangtze Incident.* London: White Lion, 1973.

ANDERSONVILLE (1864–1865)

The vast stockade that was built at Andersonville, Georgia, by the Confederate armies in 1864 to house thousands of Union prisoners of war (POWs) was soon used by propagandists as a symbol of Confederate cruelty and oppression. Such harsh conditions also meant that many prisoners were determined to escape.

This was certainly no easy matter. If a prisoner missed the daily roll call his absence was quickly noticed, and the vast majority of runaways were tracked down by the sniffer dogs kept for this specific purpose and brought back to the camp and put into its jail. A great many prisoners, of course, did not reach the outside at all because their plans were betrayed to the Confederate authorities by the many informers among the POW population who were lured by the impressive $30 rewards for information.

The intelligence supplied by such informers foiled one highly ambitious plan for freedom that was launched in May 1864. The temporary departure of one of the camp's leading commanders encouraged some of the prisoners to quickly execute a plan that they would not otherwise have dared. According to the plan, when the gates opened at 3 P.M. to allow the ration wagon access, hundreds of prisoners would use the several tunnels that had been built over the preceding days to leave the camp. They would then double back, attacking and killing the guards just as all the prisoners remaining inside made their own attack. Since the guards were outnumbered by more than ten to one, the authorities took the plan most seriously and quashed it instantly.

Some plans of escape did succeed, and many prisoners—329 in all—got away while they were outside the compound working with one of the organized parties that searched for wood and other materials needed inside. A whole spate of such escapes in June 1864, when prisoners attacked their guards before running off into the woods, prompted serious concern among the camp commanders. Other escapees were paroled workmen on the site, such as Sidney Moore, of the 154th New York, who in July slipped away from his job as a carpenter at a new bakery and who after three weeks reached Union lines south of Atlanta, where he rejoined his unit.

But most prisoners tunneled their way out, usually from the Stockdale Creek end of camp, where the soil's high clay content made it easy to burrow through but also firmer and unlikely to collapse, and thus well suited to such excavation. This amenability is measured by the fact that one tunnel, discovered shortly before it was to be used, was more than 130 feet long, and by the fact that one prisoner, a sergeant major of the 16th Connecticut, was able to organize the construction of three tunnels in just ten days. One of these tunnels was

A contemporary depiction of Andersonville Prison in Georgia. (Library of Congress)

abandoned when it ran headlong into the side of a hospital wall and another caved in, but the third allowed five men to escape on 10 June.

Other prisoners built tunnels while pretending to dig wells, which the prison authorities freely allowed them to do. These tunnels, which were built into the side of the well shaft, were not only much harder for both informers and guards to detect but also allowed the excavators to discard displaced soil into the bottom of the pit, solving the problem of where to put it.

Few escapees, however, managed to evade recapture and the fate of having to spend even more time in this infamous camp.

See also: Camp Morton; Conley, Capt. Edward
References: Cangemi, Joseph P., and Casimir J. Kowalski. *Andersonville Prison: Lessons in Organizational Failure.* Lanham, MD: University Press of America, 1992.
Marvel, William. *Andersonville: The Last Depot.* Chapel Hill: University of North Carolina Press, 1994.

APOLLO 13 (1970)

In April 1970 the world held its breath as it watched the life-and-death struggle of three Apollo astronauts, John Swigert, John Lovell, and Fred Haise, to get their stricken craft back to earth.

Apollo 13 was to take its three crew members to the moon, where they planned to follow up the exploratory work made by earlier missions. The main section of the craft, which was to take them into the moon's inner orbit, was the command module (CM) *Odyssey*, and within it was *Aquarius*, the lunar module (LM), which was to take them to the moon's surface. After twelve successful earlier missions, no one involved in the space program expected any of the difficulties that were shortly to occur.

Launched, by ominous coincidence, on 13 April 1970 at 13 minutes past one, the craft began to run into serious technical problems after two days in space. Both astronauts and ground crew became seriously alarmed as the electrical system

The crew of Iwo Jima *hoists the command module of* Apollo 13 *out of the South Pacific. (Archive Photos)*

began to play up, its oxygen tanks lost pressure, and the computer malfunctioned. But the crisis really began when the astronauts saw a huge sheet of oxygen streaming out of the craft's side and then heard an enormous explosion that rocked the entire craft. It was later determined that a design fault in a heater inside the oxygen tank had caused one of the two oxygen tanks to explode.

The accident meant that the crew had to be brought back as quickly as possible, before their air supply ran out. But this was an immensely complex task, not just because the accident had happened as the craft was heading toward the moon, traveling at about 6,000 miles per hour and about 200,000 miles from earth but also because the ship had to be put back on track. Without full computer and electrical power, the craft would lose its way. The only consolation for those involved was that the explosion had not happened while they were on the moon's surface—since it would have been impossible to get the ship off the ground again—or while they orbited the moon, since to pull the craft out of lunar orbit would have been extremely difficult with limited power.

To ascertain the damage, its consequences, and its solutions was an enormous undertaking, and teams of technical specialists were called to Houston to work on the problems involved. They worked intensely, round-the-clock, and every angle of what lay ahead was examined from the limited technical data they had at their disposal. Though it was usual for new plans and ideas to be put into practice only after weeks or months of trials, they now prepared to implement their solutions after just hours of detailed consideration.

The crew's first response was to abandon the *Odyssey,* which was in much worse shape than the lunar module as a result of the explosion and the electrical faults, and move instead into *Aquarius,* using its engines to move through space. They knew they were pushing their luck in doing so, since the LM was designed only to support two men for 45 hours for their lunar landing, moon walk, and 33-hour stay on the moon's surface. But now they were trying to make it support three astronauts for perhaps double that time—perhaps as much as 100 hours—and they knew they would therefore have to live on half the amount of supplies in order to last the journey. Moreover, using the LM's engines while it was still docked to the CM had only been done once before, during *Apollo 9*'s mission, and maneuvering the craft in this way was a very difficult operation for the crew members.

Their best chance of getting back to earth, it was concluded, was to let the craft continue round the moon and then, at a carefully timed moment, boost *Aquarius*'s engine, using up an enormous amount of fuel but, if all went according to plan, effectively halving the length of the return journey to just two days. Referred to as the "PC + 2 Burn," this was one of the two key ingredients in the rescue operation.

The other essential task was to get the craft back on precisely the right path, which they had to do without all the right technical backup. Lovell and Haise determined the alignment of their existing route against the position of the sun and then, again at a carefully determined moment and using the coordinates provided by Houston, boosted the engines to get themselves back into just the right position.

One technical difficulty that they faced and that was typical of what confronted them over those few days was the problem of potential carbon dioxide poisoning. Since a great deal of the life-support system had broken down, there was a clear risk that the astronauts would become poisoned by their own exhaled carbon dioxide, which became trapped inside the craft. The solution was found by a member of the Houston team who had worked on the *Apollo 8* mission and who remembered a colleague mentioning an untested solution that might work: using items on board to build makeshift air purifiers. By putting together a plastic cover from a book and a plastic storage bag, the three men were able to make a simple device that helped to purify their increasingly faltering air supply.

By the time the craft started its approach to the earth, conditions on board had begun to get extremely difficult for the crew members. Temperatures had suddenly plummeted and were now only in the 40s, and the astronauts' breath had made the atmosphere inside extremely damp, even wet. Worst of all, none of the three men had been able to sleep during the two days of crisis, and the strain was beginning to show. At one point, one of the men entered a completely wrong computer code, a mistake that was picked up instantly by Houston and rectified but that would otherwise have caused immense trouble.

As they began to enter the outer atmosphere the astronauts ditched *Aquarius*, bidding it an almost sentimental farewell, and braced themselves for their landing in the *Odyssey*. After their last words with ground control everyone held their breaths, painfully aware that because the explosion might have damaged the craft's heat shield or the electronics that controlled the operation of its parachutes, the astronauts might be plunging to their deaths.

When, soon afterward, three orange parachutes were seen by the U.S. Navy ships waiting at the pickup point in the Indian Ocean, the astronauts' families and the ground control members who had worked so hard to save them cried out with relief and embraced each other. The happy outcome to the rescue operation was a profoundly emotional moment not just for the American people but for the outside world.

References: Cooper, H. S. F. *The Flight That Failed.* London, Baltimore: Johns Hopkins University Press, 1995.

Lovell, Jim. *Lost Moon.* London: Coronet, 1995.

ARNHEM (1944)

For many of those who survived it, the end of the battle for Arnhem bridge in September 1944 marked the beginning of another desperate struggle. Trapped behind enemy lines, more than 250 Allied soldiers fought with the same determination that they had employed in combat to evade the Germans who were now searching for them.

Most of the escapees headed for the thick woods near the battlefield, where they lay low while they tried to link up with the Dutch resistance. The story of Lt. Ronald Adams and Maj. Tom Wainwright was typical. They hid in the woods by day and moved silently at night, foraging for food and water and relying on beetroots and turnips to stay alive. The two men traveled in a northwesterly direction, narrowly avoiding the German patrols that constantly scoured the entire area in pursuit of stragglers, and on one occasion they even found themselves ensnared among gun emplacements in a German artillery park. Like many of their compatriots, they spent the next four weeks living in cramped attics and cellars or even in concealed holes in the ground in rain-soaked woods, only emerging at night for a breath of fresh air.

Some of these escapees came within a whisker's breadth of capture. During the battle Sgt. Maj. Robert Grainger had fought for possession of a strategically placed mill that changed hands seven times in 24 hours. After he had been injured by a bullet that passed through the side of his helmet, Grainger was taken with four colleagues to the nearby Wolfheze Mental Hospital, whose unfortunate patients were still inside as the battle raged outside and in a highly agitated state because the hospital had been accidentally bombed some hours before.

When the Germans began to make headway against the British forces the next day, Grainger and his fellow airborne soldiers found an excellent way of evading capture. Wrapping themselves in blankets and bandaging their heads, they danced with the patients into the streets of the town, and in a particularly wild scene they fought among each other in front of the German soldiers, who were too amazed by the spectacle to notice Grainger's army boots beneath his blanket. When this procession finally reached a small woods about two miles north of Wolfheze, one of the nurses accompanying them told the British where to flee.

But the most testing time still lay ahead. At one point Grainger was forced to hide in a small trench, only two and a half feet high, four feet wide, and five and a half feet long. Its top was covered by a lid and buried with earth, and Grainger later recalled the overpowering sense of claustrophobia that affected him every second of the four days and nights that he was forced to lie there, tortured by images of being trapped inside the hole and dying a slow and lingering death. He was eventually picked up by the local underground and taken to a somewhat more pleasant hiding place, an attic in the home of one of the Dutch sympathizers.

Many escapees were found by the members of the Dutch underground, who went to great lengths to help them and who always put themselves at great personal risk by doing so. Mrs. Edith Nijhoff, an Arnhem resident, drove around the area in her horse and cart, wearing her Red Cross gown, to look for stragglers. She would hide them on the back of her cart, covered with old sacks, in order to get through the German lines to Berkenlann. She made countless trips in and around the battlefield but was never stopped and challenged by the Germans, who thought her innocuous.

Most of the escapees were eventually able to get back to their own lines as a result of Operation Pegasus, a joint Anglo-American operation to spirit them across the Rhine. Together, two generals, one

British, Brian Horrocks, and one American, Maxwell Taylor, who had already worked together most effectively at Nijmegen, were able to pinpoint the spot where the German defenses were most vulnerable, and using their contacts in the Dutch resistance, they prepared to link up with the escapees on the night of 22 October.

The task of making their way to the pickup point was very demanding for most of the escapees, many of whom were in a physically poor state after more than a month on the run and who were all ordered to fight if they were caught en route by the Germans. When the escapees reached the far side of the river and stepped back onto Allied-held territory, emotional scenes ensued among both the British and Americans who, once again, found themselves at each other's sides.

See also: Deane-Drummond, Anthony; Nijmegen
References: Heaps, Leo. *The Grey Goose of Arnhem.* London: Futura, 1977.
Ryan, Cornelius. *A Bridge Too Far.* London: Coronet, 1974.

ASRAR AL-QABANDI (1959–1991)

The Iraqi troops that poured over the border into Kuwait in August 1990 soon encountered one enemy they had not anticipated: a young local woman, Asrar al-Qabandi, who was responsible for organizing the escape of a great many Westerners and the safety of many others.

One of her first acts, only a few days after the invasion, was to find the 15 children of the ruling al-Sabah family of Kuwait, knowing that they would be prime targets as hostages. She organized a convoy of four-wheel-drive vehicles and led the party southward through the desert toward the border with Saudi Arabia, bribing their way through an Iraqi checkpoint. Asrar is known to have helped countless Westerners to escape in a similar way over the next four months.

Though she could have escaped with those she escorted to safety, Asrar gallantly returned to Kuwait and soon made contact with the Kuwaiti government in exile, using a hidden radio transmitter. She was then able to organize the rescue of many of her fellow Kuwaitis by arranging for millions of Iraqi dinars—Kuwait's own currency had been declared illegal—to be smuggled into the country. Most of the money was hidden in cars and driven in from Jordan. It was used to buy food that was distributed to those most in need.

Most of those who knew her felt that Asrar was overly reckless and complacent, and on 4 November 1990 she was caught by the Iraqi secret police. Her battered corpse was dumped on the city streets several weeks later.

ATTICA PRISON (1971)

On 9 September 1971 a major riot broke out at Attica Prison in New York, 400 miles from New York City. The riot, one of the most infamous of recent years, ended bloodily, and it is widely argued that it was provoked by the harsh conditions and treatment that the prisoners were forced to endure. Gates and walls were torn down by large groups of prisoners who, working together, built up an irresistible momentum of terrifying power. They quickly seized more than 50 hostages, nearly all of them prison officers. They promised to hold the hostages until their demands were met, but they also threatened to kill them if any rescue attempt was made.

Any rescue mission was certainly fraught with difficulty. The prisoners were known to be armed with Molotov cocktails, and the police authorities knew that in all likelihood they would also have an array of other weapons, bombs, and booby traps at their disposal. Moreover, it would be extremely difficult to take them by surprise, since both prisoners and hostages were dispersed over a wide area and an attack on one group would warn the others.

But shortly after 9 A.M. on 13 September the rescue operation began. Hovering overhead, a National Guard helicopter dropped canisters of tear gas, while several assault teams, their members heavily armed and wearing gas masks, stormed inside. When they first opened fire they aimed at specific targets, usually those inmates who were nearest the hostages and whose movements seemed threatening, but, probably because in such high-stress situations even the best-trained can quickly lose their nerve, the shooting quickly became a barrage of automatic fire that lasted nearly a whole minute. Within minutes the prisoners' resistance had crumbled and the riot was over.

In the riot's aftermath the prison authorities were forced to ask some soul-searching questions about their decision to end the riot by force. The attack had led to the deaths of 43 people, 10 of them hostages, a casualty rate that sent shock waves of horror and dismay through the prison staff and across the United States. On the other hand, prison authorities had proven beyond doubt that they were willing to pay a heavy price to end prison disorder, which may account for the greater flexibility and conciliation that other prison protesters were to show both toward their hostages and in their protests in general in years to come.

See also: Moundsville Penitentiary, West Virginia; Peterhead Prison; San Quentin; Santa Fe, New Mexico
References: Adams, R. Prison Riots in Britain and USA. New York: St. Martin's Press; London: Macmillan, 1992.
Wicker, Tom. A Time to Die. New York: Quadrangle, New York Times Book Company, 1975.

AUSCHWITZ (1942–1945)

Although there were many attempts to escape from Auschwitz, the notorious concentration camp in Poland, only about 80 prisoners are known to have succeeded during the three and a half years the camp was operational. The three best-documented escapes were made in 1943 and 1944.

In 1943 two young Slavs, Rudolf Vrba (born Walter Rosenberg) and Alfred Wetzler, attempted escape. Both were desperately eager to break out after more than two years in Nazi captivity, and they initially looked to the camp's "International Resistance Group"—its escape committee—for backing. But they were judged to be temperamentally unsuitable and were told only that the committee would do nothing to

Only about 80 prisoners are known to have escaped from Auschwitz, the notorious concentration camp in Poland. (Novosti/Corbis-Bettmann)

stop them making their own plans to escape.

The two men drew up their own plans and approached other prisoners to help put them into effect. They were able to construct a small hiding place in a gap in a pile of wood outside the barbed-wire compound where prisoners were held, though within the much larger security zone outside, in an area where the camp was being extended. They sprinkled a large amount of alcohol and tobacco around the hideout, which, according to some of the Russian prisoners they had met, would put the German sniffer dogs off their scent when the search began.

Shortly before the evening roll call on 7 April the two men hid themselves in the pile of wood and waited for the massive search that they knew would follow. Sure enough, just minutes after it was discovered that they were missing, the Germans began combing the whole camp for some sign of their whereabouts. Fortunately for the escapees, however, they relied upon their guard dogs to sniff them out in the outer perimeter. After three days and nights of searching, during which time the entire camp was surrounded by a special cordon of SS guards, the Nazi authorities assumed that the two men had made their getaway and that there was no point in continuing their search.

Having watched the Germans carefully throughout those three days, Vrba and Wetzler now made their move, slipping past the German watchtowers late at night and heading southward for Slovakia. Though they had no documents, maps, or compasses, they persisted, moving only at night and avoiding all the roads and paths along which they assumed German patrols routinely passed. After meeting a Polish partisan who was able to point them toward the frontier, they finally reached Slovakia on 21 April.

Only a few weeks later, on 27 May, two prisoners made another escape bid. While working in a gravel pit in the camp perimeter, a young Pole, Czeslaw Mordowicz, and a Slav, Arnost Rosin, had noticed a short, narrow passageway inside the pit. Though it had been filled in with broken stones and rocks, they knew they had a chance of escaping if they could make enough room inside it to hide themselves, just as Vrba and Wetzler had so effectively concealed themselves.

Over the next few weeks the two men took turns making the bunker into a suitable hiding place, working gradually but patiently while their guards' backs were turned. On 27 May they were at last able to put their plan into effect, and like their two predecessors, they remained hidden from the extensive searches made for them until they deemed it safe to move on. Heading southward, the two men reached Slovakia three weeks later.

One other known escape was made in April 1944 by a prisoner, Siegfried Lederer, who made his way out by stealing an SS uniform and by getting to know one of the guards, Cpl. Viktor Pestek. Corporal Pestek had fallen in love with a Jewish girl and gave Lederer the necessary password to get through the outer gate. Lederer reached the train station at Auschwitz and was able to flee and join the Polish resistance in Pilsen.

Had they been caught, all these escapees would have faced a gruesome fate. Those who tried but failed were usually sent to the notorious Block 11, where prisoners were tortured to death during interrogations or shot immediately afterwards.

See also: Koldyczewo Camp; Sobibor Concentration Camp

References: Gilbert, Martin. *Auschwitz and the Allies.* London: Mandarin, 1991.

AYLWARD, GLADYS (1902–1970)

During the Sino-Japanese War of 1938, a British missionary, Gladys Aylward, succeeded in rescuing more than 100 Chinese orphans from death and maltreatment at the hands of the Japanese Imperial Army.

As a missionary, Aylward had made her way to China in the mid-1930s in order to try to alleviate the suffering of the children who were growing up in a society typified by extreme poverty and increasing political violence. Though she was only in her mid-20s when the Japanese attacked the town of Yangcheng at the start of the war in 1938, she was responsible for much of the relief work that rescued the survivors of the bombing and butchery and brought them food, accommodation, and medicine.

Her bravery became clear when, a few days later, the Japanese returned to the town and threatened to resume the cold-blooded slaughter that they had perpetrated during their earlier raid. Bravely confronting the Japanese soldiers, Aylward made them think twice about their actions; she rescued children from slaughter and many women from degradation.

However, it was not long before the Japanese began to perceive her as a threat and issued a $100 reward for her capture, dead or alive. Narrowly avoiding a Japanese patrol that opened fire on her from a distance, she knew she would have to act fast if she was to save not only herself but also 100 orphans whom she had rescued from the town. Not only would they easily be caught in the crossfire when hostilities resumed but they would probably be held as hostages in exchange for her surrender.

As the Japanese moved in, she led the children from the refugee camp where they had been staying into the mountains, heading for the headquarters of a charity that had been started by an acquaintance near the town of Sian. Getting there, however, would be immensely difficult, since it would involve crossing several hundred miles of difficult terrain.

Though all the children were under the age of 12, the party began the grueling trek over the mountains, a journey that would have tested even the fittest. The escapees had minimal supplies of food and water to sustain them and were unable to stop for prolonged periods of rest because of the grave risk of being caught by Japanese soldiers. To make matters even worse, there was a constant threat of harassment by enemy planes, which were constantly searching the area for them and which on a few occasions very nearly succeeded in inflicting casualties.

Crossing the Yellow River with the aid of Chinese Nationalist soldiers who recognized their desperate plight, they were able to make their way, partly by foot, partly by train, to Sian. They finally arrived in April 1940, nearly a month after setting off, to the astonishment of those who saw their ragged and starved bodies.

The trek was a perfect expression of the selfless determination of a remarkable woman who had gone to China to help others and who returned to Britain in 1950 with the same benevolent intentions, establishing a series of charitable organizations for those in need.

See also: The Long March
References: Aylward, Gladys. *Gladys Aylward: Her Personal Story.* London: Coverdale House, 1970.
Swift, Catherine M. *Gladys Aylward.* Basingstoke: Marshalls, 1984.

B

BAILEY, LT. COL. FREDERICK (1884–1967)

British planners knew that if they did not rule India, then some other power would. It was this that prompted their ceaseless struggle with Moscow for influence over central Asia, upon which the security of India rested. One British officer who played a leading part in the latter stages of this rivalry was Lt. Col. Frederick Bailey, who escaped from the clutches of the Bolsheviks shortly after the Russian Revolution.

As the civil war raged in Russia in the wake of the Bolshevik Revolution, the British authorities were very concerned to find out what was happening in the central Asian territories and to discover Bolshevik intentions toward the area. They had good reason for concern, for on 7 December 1917, exactly a month after the overthrow of the Provisional Government, Lenin issued a clarion call to Asia's millions to follow the triumphant example of the Bolsheviks and overthrow their own oppressors. So in the summer of 1918 Lieutenant Colonel Bailey, a much-trusted officer, was dispatched to Tashkent to try to obtain further information about the situation.

Bailey spent several weeks in Tashkent and succeeded in gathering much information about what the Bolsheviks were up to before he was arrested and charged with helping a group of anti-Soviet Muslim guerrillas who were hiding in the nearby mountains. He was immediately put under house arrest while his captors decided what to do with him.

As soon as he was arrested Bailey began to prepare to escape, putting into action a plan that he had drawn up a few days before as the net was drawing closer around him. Almost straightaway, "I tore off my overcoat, pulled on the Austrian tunic and kepi which were lying ready on the hall table, tucked the trousers into the boots, wrapped my overcoat around the civilian hat, and taking these with me dashed out into the garden" (Hopkirk 1984, 58). From there he ran into the next house's garden, then the one after that and so on until, a minute or so later, he emerged from a garden at the far end of the row of houses and, unrecognized by his Cheka guards, who had seen him as his real self only minutes before, he melted into the darkness.

As he sought to make his way from and around Tashkent, Bailey became a master of many disguises. At one point he posed as André Kekeshi, an Austrian cook who he had thought was dead and whose passport he was therefore able to "borrow." (Shortly afterward he found out that Kekeshi was not only alive but also furious that someone had taken his passport.) When a Red Army commissar unexpectedly visited the house he was staying in, Bailey explained that he was a Rumanian serving in a Hungarian unit, the 32nd Regiment, which he knew had some Rumanians in its ranks. As he related this story, he prayed that the Red Army officer did not speak Rumanian; he later spoke of the effort of hiding his relief when he found that the officer's only language was Russian. Later on he became Vladimir Kuzimovich, a Galician ex–prisoner of war, but knowing that his spoken Russian was not up to scratch, he managed to obtain another passport and turned himself once again into a Rumanian officer, Georgi Chuka. Finding that Chuka, too, was furious at losing his passport, Bailey finally became Joseph Lazar, a Rumanian-born coachman. "I could pass for a Rumanian prisoner with a smattering of German," he later recalled, "without the likelihood of a Rumanian being at hand to show that I was a fraud" (Hopkirk 1984, 77).

After eluding the Cheka in Tashkent for nearly a year, Bailey decided that it was time to escape from central Asia altogether and head back to India. His best chance, he reckoned, was to cross the remote and ill-guarded Persian frontier around Mashhad. To do this he would first have to travel by train to Bukhara, via Kagan, and then make a grueling 300-mile dash across the great Kara Kum Desert to the Persian border. But there was one clear problem: How was he, a wanted man, to get a permit to leave Tashkent and take a train to Kagan? He found an almost unbelievably daring answer: He would disguise himself as a Cheka agent on a mission against the British.

Bailey had hit on the idea when he heard that the Bolsheviks were greatly alarmed by rumors that the British and Indian armies had arrived in Bukhara and were being used to train the rulers' troops into an anti-Bolshevik force. Desperate to find out whether the reports were true, the Cheka had dispatched a succession of spies to Bukhara, and though they had all been caught and killed by the emir (the local ruler), Bailey was not deterred and seized his chance.

To arrange this mission Bailey made good use of one of the few individuals in Tashkent whom he could trust, a Serbian called Manditch. Manditch went to see the local Cheka chief, a much-feared individual called Dunkov, and said that he knew an Albanian who was willing to go to Bukhara on a spying mission. In case Dunkov wanted to interview him beforehand, Bailey and Manditch had devised an elaborate cover story for him, complete with photographs and documents, which gave him yet another new identity, an Albanian army clerk named Joseph Kastamuni. The choice of an Albanian was no accident, for they had made sure that no one in Tashkent spoke this obscure language. By luck he was spared an interview—he and Manditch happened to walk into Dunkov in the street and were given instruction there and then—a travel permit was duly granted, and they

were able to leave Tashkent, at last, on 15 October 1919.

The story took an even more bizarre turn on the way to Bukhara. An urgent coded telegram from the Cheka chief in Tashkent ordered them to "communicate all information you have regarding Anglo-Indian Service Colonel Bailey" (Hopkirk 1984, 88). The British spy, who was now being ordered to provide information on himself, sent a telegram back saying that a man answering his own description had been spotted heading for the Afghan border some weeks earlier.

When Bailey and Manditch arrived in Bukhara, they were able to introduce themselves as enemies of the Bolsheviks, rather than their agents, by cleverly producing letters of introduction that had been written for them by the Bukharan consul in Tashkent, and the emir allowed them to prepare for the last but most arduous part of their journey, a three-week crossing of the Persian desert in midwinter. Despite traveling in intense cold and blizzards that brought inches of snow, Bailey's party moved on. They had a brush with a Bolshevik patrol as they reached the border with Persia but avoided their shots. On 6 January 1920 Bailey and Manditch at last reached safety.

His story could not fail to capture the public imagination when he arrived back in Britain shortly afterwards. It was, wrote the *Times*, "A Central Asian Romance," and the *Telegraph* called it "an amazing adventure" of escape and intrigue that had put the Bolsheviks firmly in their place (Hopkirk 1984, 95).

See also: Chitral; Kabul; Kandahār; Russian Revolution and civil war

References: Hopkirk, Peter. *Setting the East Ablaze*. Oxford: Oxford University Press, 1984.

BANGKOK AIRPORT (1981)

Since its formation in 1977, the purpose of the First Special Forces Operations Detachment–Delta (SFOD-D)—more commonly known as Delta Force—has been to guard U.S. citizens from terrorist action both at home and abroad. Though its reputation was undermined by its bungled efforts to free the Iranian hostages, it has nonetheless also been involved in some lesser-known rescue operations that have demonstrated its effectiveness. Its intervention to bring a rapid end to a hijack at Bangkok Airport in 1981 is one such example.

The hijacking took place on 28 March—less than a year after the debacle in the Iranian desert—when an Indonesian airliner was forced to land at Bangkok by five terrorists who demanded the release of a number of political prisoners held in Indonesian jails in exchange for the lives of the hostages. Though the hijacking was initially a purely Indonesian concern, the shooting of a U.S. citizen during the siege aroused Washington's concern, and when, on the second day of the crisis, the Thai government—fearing the worst—asked for the direct assistance of the U.S. military, their request did not fall on deaf ears.

The next day, in a well-planned and executed operation, the Delta Force stormed the plane, killed four of the hijackers, and rescued all the passengers without loss to their own side.

See also: Entebbe; Iranian hostage rescue operation; Mogadishu plane rescue
References: Adams, James. Secret Armies. London: Hutchinson, 1987.

BARNEY, JOSHUA (C. 1758–1825)

One of the many American prisoners who was captured and imprisoned by the British during the American War of Independence was Joshua Barney, a privateer officer of the Pennsylvania fleet who had been captured in December 1780 by HMS *Intrepid*. Taken to Mill Prison in Plymouth and held in extremely arduous conditions, he was eventually able to make his escape.

Barney was driven by the conviction that his life meant nothing to his captors, and to find his way out he make great efforts to probe the views and attitudes of those who guarded him. Befriending one sympathetic guard, he obtained a British officer's uniform and bluffed his way out of the prison into the town streets outside.

Barney bought a small fishing boat and was eventually able to reach France, though to do so he had to use all his powers of ingenuity, weaving his way carefully between British warships and on one occasion slipping away from a suspicious officer who refused to believe his story that he was a secret agent on the way to visit a British admiral.

References: Barney, Mary, ed. *A Biographical Memoir of Commodore Joshua Barney.* Boston: Gray and Bowen, 1832.

THE BASTILLE (1789)

On 14 July 1789 a mob of thousands stormed the Bastille, a royal prison in central Paris, to rescue its prisoners, dramatically heightening political tension in the capital and heralding the beginning of the French Revolution.

The Bastille had long been widely seen as the great symbol of the despotism of the ancien régime and the oppression that accompanied it. Stories of the cruelty and atrocities perpetrated within its walls were rife, and when an angry crowd gathered in central Paris to protest government policies it quickly became a target for their violent passions.

The mob had several motives for wanting to seize the Bastille. After capturing several cannons and more than 40,000 rifles from a military depot near Les Invalides, its leaders had found to their dismay that they did not have the gunpowder they needed. They quickly recognized that the Bastille, one of the government's main armories, was the best source of gunpowder. But the mob also appears to have been inspired by a hope of rescuing from the prison's atrocious conditions inmates whom they saw as political prisoners, incarcerated only because they had offended a harsh and tyrannical regime.

When the prison walls fell and the mobs reached the prisoners inside, they found that there were far fewer prisoners than they had expected—only a handful. Moreover, four of these seven prisoners

The storming of the Bastille on 14 July 1789. (Library of Congress)

were quickly transported to another prison in Paris after their "liberation" when it became apparent that they were not innocent victims of tyranny but, rather, criminal forgers and confidence tricksters. The crimes of another two had been such that they had been sent to prison at the instigation of their own families. Only one prisoner, who had been sent to prison in 1757 simply because he had been suspected of being an accomplice of an individual who had attempted to assassinate Louis XIV, met the crowd's expectations.

Later on, these facts were overlooked by those who wrote about the revolution or who were inspired to write poetry or compose music about such a monumental moment in the history of the French Republic.

See also: Latude, Henri Masers de
References: Lusebank, Hans-Jürgen, and Rolf
  Reichardt. *The Bastille: A History of a Symbol of
  Despotism and Freedom.* Durham, NC: Duke
  University Press, 1997.

BELBENOIT, RENÉ
(1898–1938)

René Belbenoit, a convict at the penal colonies on the islands off French Guiana, was able to escape and reach the United States because of his almost superhuman powers of endurance and also because of his ability to appeal to a simple human emotion—greed.

Belbenoit had already endured more than 15 years on the islands when, in 1935, he set sail in a simple boat along with five fellow prisoners and slipped away from the island in a manner not dissimilar to that of Papillon. After an arduous journey the party arrived at Barranquilla in Colombia. However, the local rulers had struck an informal agreement with the prison authorities that obliged them to return any escapees to custody, so all six men were immediately put in jail, pending their deportation.

It was at this point that Belbenoit had his first lucky break. When the editor of a local newspaper, *La Prensa*, visited the prison to write about their story, he discovered not only that Belbenoit was better educated than his colleagues but also that he was something of a celebrity in the prison world, being a veteran of several determined though unsuccessful escape attempts. Knowing that Belbenoit's story could be valuable, he asked him to write a series of articles, promising to pay him well for them.

Though the facts have never been entirely clear, it appears that either Belbenoit agreed to this request on the condition that he be released—something the editor could arrange with a bribe—or else his new acquaintance simply felt a rapport and sympathy with an individual who had endured long years in one of the most arduous environments imaginable. Either way, Belbenoit was suddenly told that he would be released, and just a few hours later he heard the lock to his cell turn and saw the door swing open.

But he was still a long way from his intended destination, the U.S. border. He was in shockingly poor condition after years in detainment, a difficult escape by sea, and several days in a Colombian prison, and he knew that he would be pushed to survive the long distances he would have to travel to reach safety. But above all, he had heard stories about the savagery of some of the tribes that lived in the vast forests of Central America. He would need all his powers of survival—highly developed as they were—to make it through what lay ahead.

Once again he appealed to material self-interest to save his skin. When, after walking several days, he was approached by some tribesmen and taken to their leaders, he put into effect a well-thought-out plan. Though he had no idea if it would work, taking the risk was infinitely better than returning to captivity.

Showing the tribesmen the butterflies he had found and killed during the last few days and the net he had acquired in Colombia to give added authenticity to his story, Belbenoit explained in his elementary Spanish and through a translator that he had come to capture some of the butterflies that were to be found in the forests around them. These particular butterflies were of great value, he explained, and the trading company he worked for would be prepared to pay them handsomely for any they captured. The tribal leader reacted just as Belbenoit had hoped, his eyes lighting up as if he had suddenly glimpsed newfound wealth.

Belbenoit and the tribal leaders agreed to resume their negotiations the next day, and the fugitive was taken to a hut to stay the night. However, after waiting for the village to settle down, he crept away, found a canoe harbored on the river next to the settlement, and quickly but quietly paddled away into the night.

Hiding in the long reeds during the day and moving at night, Belbenoit was able to cover a considerable distance before he was once again stopped by another tribe, whereupon he tried the same story. In all, he was stopped 20 times by different tribes, and on each occasion the same ruse worked, allowing him to creep away into the night and continue with his long journey.

When he finally reached Panama, he knew that freedom was within his grasp. Making a careful though extremely arduous detour through thick forests to avoid local militia, he eventually managed to cross the border into the U.S.-managed area of the Canal Zone. After 22 months on the run, he was at last a free man.

But Belbenoit was not destined to long relish the freedom he had fought so hard for. As an acquaintance described him, he was emaciated, almost blind, toothless, sickened by scurvy, and fever-ridden. Less than a year after he reached the United States he collapsed and died. Liberty, for him as for many other escapees, proved to be a chimera.

See also: French Guiana; Papillon
References: Belbenoit, René. *Dry Guillotine*. London: Jonathan Cape, 1971.

BEN BELLA, AHMED

In 1949, soon after beginning his involvement in the Algerian resistance to French colonial rule, a young revolutionary, Ahmed Ben Bella, escaped from prison by using a method so simple, even theatrical, that he and his accomplices could scarcely believe it had worked. The revolutionaries baked a loaf of bread with a file hidden in it and sent it to Ben Bella in prison. The file went undetected by the guards, and Ben Bella was able to saw through his window and escape. Another stroke of good fortune allowed him to elude the death sentence imposed on him by the French secret service in 1954. An assassin crept into his bedroom, fired at point-blank range, and missed, before running off. Soon afterward a bomb that exploded in front of his Cairo office also left him unhurt, and an assassin who tracked him down in Tripoli lost his own life but failed to kill his quarry.

See also: Algeria; De Gaulle, Charles; Egyptian embassy

References: Horne, Alistair. *A Savage War of Peace: Algeria 1954–62.* London: Macmillan, 1977.

BENIOWSKI, COUNT MAURICE (C. 1745–1810)

Rather than run away from their captors, some escapees take a more audacious approach: stirring up a local rebellion and seizing control of their enemy's territory. One place where this was possible was pre-revolutionary Russia, where news of a local rebellion would take days, or even weeks, to reach the central government, and where in 1770 the Polish count Maurice Beniowski, after one unsuccessful bid for freedom, escaped from his enemies in remarkably flamboyant style.

Condemned to be sent to Siberia, Beniowski was held temporarily in a private house in Tula in Ukraine along with other prisoners, and he managed to simply slip out the front door one night. Helped by the sympathetic local population, who harbored considerable animosity toward the Russians, he posed as a Russian officer en route back to St. Petersburg and was helped along the way by local rulers, who gave him letters of recommendation to their counterparts along the route he was to take. But though he managed to reach St. Petersburg,

he was betrayed at the last minute by a Dutch sea captain who had agreed to take him back to Holland.

Sent straight back to the prison at Kamchatka, the count quickly started to draw up alternative escape plans. Using his considerable powers of persuasion and charm, he managed to find a devotee in the daughter of the governor of Kamchatka, knowing that her influence would be vital if he was to stand any chance of making his escape. Sure enough, before long he was granted considerable freedom within the settlement and even became personally acquainted with the governor.

Though he had originally planned to disappear quietly, just as he had before, the governor's daughter told him that his plans had been uncovered and he would be arrested very soon. So, quickly devising a new plan, Beniowski ordered his fellow prisoners, all trained soldiers, to storm the fort, using hunting muskets, and capture the guards. He did not hesitate to use tough tactics: He forced 700 Cossacks to surrender their weapons by shepherding their families into a wooden church and threatening to burn it down if they refused. The governor's daughter also paid a heavy price for her betrayal, since during the struggle that followed her father was shot dead before her.

Having won control of Kamchatka, for the moment at least, Beniowski sent some of his men to the nearby river Bolshoi Irgiz to see if there was any chance of absconding by ship. They found a vessel, the *St. Peter and St. Paul*, that was big enough to accommodate all 70 of them, and within a day it had been equipped with enough ammunition, food, and drink—36 bottles of vodka in all—to keep them going for some considerable time. Together with his fellow Poles and the governor's daughter, Beniowski set sail on 6 May 1771.

Their subsequent passage was not altogether easy. Lacking navigational skills, they made their way into uncharted waters and endured terrible storms at sea before landing first in Japan and finally in Macao in September. While celebrating their safe arrival, many of them made a simple mistake—excess after months of deprivation—and 23 of them died from overeating, including the governor's daughter.

References: Reid, Pat. *Prisoner of War.* London and New York: Hamlyn, 1984.

BERLIN, BATTLE FOR (1945)

When the Red Army pushed back the Wehrmacht and arrived on German soil in February 1945, they did not hesitate to employ the same savagery against German civilians that the Germans had used against Russians. And as the Red Army fought their way closer and closer to Berlin, the populace had good reason to panic at their advance.

A lucky few escaped the Red Army by air, even though this became extremely hazardous in the closing days of the battle. Hanna Reitsch, a test pilot, left the capital at the end of April with no illusions about the difficult journey that lay ahead. During her incoming flight the day before, her small Storch plane had been hit by ground fire while flying along a carefully selected route at treetop level. When her copilot was hit and fainted, she managed to grab the controls just before the plane spun out of control, and she landed it in the very center of Berlin, even though the fuel tank had been hit and might have exploded at any minute. As she left the capital, she forced herself to ignore the flurry of searchlights that suddenly cut through the sky in search of her and to brave the hail of bullets that she could see and hear all around her. Remarkably, she returned safely to German-controlled territory, even though her plane had been nearly shot to pieces.

Though a great many German soldiers, knowing the grim fate that awaited them in Russian captivity, tried their hardest to get through the Soviet lines and surrender themselves to the British or Americans, not many succeeded. A typical story is that of the 20th Panzer Grenadier battalion, which had been defeated and surrounded by the Red Army at Wannsee, a suburb of the city, on the night of 1 May. Several hundred survivors of the earlier battles tried to break through the Russian lines but soon ran into trouble, and nearly all were mown down by automatic fire. Two men, however, are known to have escaped by hiding in a fir thicket before changing their uniforms for old civilian clothes. Crawling through the enemy lines, they evaded the Russians, busily scouring the nearby woods in search of German survivors, and reached the West by posing as foreign workers.

Escapees were thought to have the best chance of getting away if they moved at night through the heaps of rubble in every street. One individual who tried to do so was a Nazi leader of minor importance, Artur Axmann. Axmann later recalled the close shaves that he and his two companions had with Russian troops soon after leaving Hitler's bunker during the night of 1 May, hearing Russian infantrymen and tankers talking, but finding to their relief that they were just minding their own business.

But as Axmann and his companions moved along one of the capital's main railway lines, he wondered if his escape attempt was over, for jumping off the bridge, he suddenly found himself surrounded by Russians. "But to our amazement and joy," he wrote, "they simply kept announcing to us *'Hitler Kaputt, Krieg Aus!'*" ("Hitler is dead! The war is over!") The Russians, it seems, had taken them for members of the German Home Guard rather than high-ranking Nazis on the run. Though for a minute the Russians' suspicions were aroused by the evasive behavior of one of the Germans, Axmann was able to slip away from the Russians when their backs were turned and eventually made his way firstly to Russian-controlled Magdeburg before surrendering himself to the U.S. Army in Bavaria.

Some of those who escaped did so only because they had the active assistance of Allied soldiers. Two of Hitler's entourage, his secretaries, Gerda Christian and Else Kruege, had crept away from his bunker a few days before its capitulation and hidden themselves successfully in a forest on the city's outskirts. Waiting there until the British arrived, they were able to get out of the city with the help of two British soldiers who put them on an outgoing train, ostensibly as "French repatriates." Soon thrown off the train by Russian and French officers who found them out, they were smuggled back on again by the sympathetic British commander. "In times of crisis," wrote Christian sardonically afterward, "only the British will still act as gentlemen."

References: O'Donnell, James. *The Berlin Bunker.* London: Dent, 1979.

Read, A., and D. Fisher. *The Fall of Berlin.* London: Hutchinson, 1992.

BERLIN BLOCKADE (1948–1949)

After the fall of the Third Reich it did not take long for the unity between the Allied powers to break down. When the Soviets began to strangle the isolated Western presence in West Berlin, surrounded entirely by East German territory, the British and Americans launched a spectacular rescue operation to save their outpost from surrender.

The background to the crisis lay in the Soviet protest at the emergence of a single West German state after 1945. By allowing the establishment of West Germany, the Soviets argued, France, Britain, and America were violating their tacit agreement that Germany would remain divided into four key sectors, as it had been when the Germans capitulated in 1945. In short, this meant that the Soviets knew that if a united West Germany existed, they would lose their influence in the West, and they wanted retribution and compensation.

At first the Russians harassed passengers and freight that was transported by road or rail through the Soviet-controlled Eastern sector of the city, imposing searches, document checks, and various other delays before letting them through. But shortly after the establishment of a new West German currency, the deutsche mark, in 1948, they began to lay full siege to West Berlin, effectively stopping all inward-bound movement of freight.

Rescuing the city from starvation and capitulation was of paramount importance to the Western capitals, for whom capitulation to Russian wishes at a time of increas-

A U.S. transport plane, carrying food and other supplies for the people of Berlin, approaches its destination during the 1948–1949 Berlin Blockade. (UPI/Corbis-Bettmann)

ing tension between East and West was unthinkable. But to do so required an immense concentration of resources and organization because Berlin, a city of more than 2 million people, needed more than 4,000 tons of supplies—food, water, and fuel—every day if it was to have any chance at all of surviving the blockade. Since forcing trucks through would have sparked a military confrontation, the only alternative was to fly the supplies in.

Over the next 11 months U.S. Air Force and Royal Air Force pilots flew round-the-clock missions to meet these requirements. At each of Berlin's four main runways, transport planes landed every three minutes with the desperately needed supplies, often narrowly avoiding collisions in midair and on the ground and imposing a severe strain on all of those involved, particularly pilots and ground crew. Though for at least the first five months the planes could not reach the 4,000 ton total, their extraordinary efforts enabled the city to hang on by a thread. In all, more than 175,000 sorties were flown to deliver more than 2.32 million tons of coal and 240,000 tons of food at the expense of 77 aircrew who were killed.

Only by the spring of 1949 were enough supplies reaching the city to force the Russians to stand down. Seeing the futility of their blockade, they lifted the siege and the Western powers retained their foothold in West Berlin.

See also: Iron Curtain
References: Arnold-Foster, Mark. *The Siege of Berlin.* London: Collins, 1979.

BERLIN WALL

From the day of its construction until the time it was rendered obsolete by the Eastern European revolutions of 1989, the Berlin Wall was a symbol not only of the Communist system and the ruthless determination of its leaders to keep its people inside the Iron Curtain but also of many people's ingenuity in trying to get out.

There can be no question of the bravery of those who tried to escape from East to West. The danger lay not so much in the prison sentences that would follow capture as in the risk to life and limb presented by the formidable array of weaponry trained on would-be escapees. An escapee had to contend not just with sentries, who were armed with automatic rifles and under strict orders to shoot to kill if necessary, but also with the land mines, guard dogs, and booby traps that could have deterred even the bravest.

There was ample evidence of what could happen if things went wrong. In November 1968, for example, a 16-year-old East German boy tried to cross into the West but quickly ran into trouble, walking over a land mine and lying, badly injured, in the middle of the minefield. Despite his agony, the unfortunate boy waited several hours before the ambulance crews arrived and could reach him safely. He died soon after he finally arrived in the hospital.

But many braved the appalling risks and made the attempt. A great many of these individuals were tempted to do so by the simplest of motives—love—and sought to join their loved ones in their own country. Others had few if any prospects in East Germany and knew that they had little to lose by trying. A few may have been motivated by idealistic motives, such as a commitment to a vision of "freedom."

Some escapees climbed over the wall, immensely risky though this was. In 1965 Jürgen Kramer, 25, read about the escape of Ronald Biggs in Britain and based his own plan of escape on it. His idea was to walk toward the wall, as if visiting the grave of an aunt who had been shot dead trying to scale it, just as an accomplice in West Berlin threw a rope ladder over it. If he could just grab and cling to the rope, then the West Berliners could pull him over the wall to safety within seconds. A bed mattress would also be thrown over the top of the wall so that he would slide over the barbed wire.

Kramer lost his nerve several times before finally forcing himself to the grave and the foot of the wall, as planned. Recognizing the go-ahead signal from the other side—a curtain being pulled in an adjacent building—he braced himself for the sudden appearance of the ladder and

Desperate to smuggle his fiancée out of East Germany, a young Austrian, Hans Pieter Meixner, hid her in his Austin-Healey Sprite, which, with the windshield removed, was able to pass around and finally underneath the barriers of the Berlin Wall checkpoints. (Express Newspapers/K 701/Archive Photos)

prepared to run the last few yards over to it. As he did so, he heard the border guards shout a warning that they would open fire if he did not stop. Nevertheless, he grabbed the ladder and felt himself being whisked to safety as machine-gun bullets rattled into the cement, missing him by inches.

Another ingenious attempt to scale the wall was made by an East German civil servant who was employed in the Air Ministry, a building that was only 25 yards from the border. At such a tantalizingly close distance, Gerhard Moessner knew that there had to be a way for him to take himself and his family across, and his inspiration eventually came when he remembered how skiers are transported to the top of mountains in ski lifts. Like Kramer, he was also wholly reliant on the cooperation of sympa-

thizers in the West with whom he was able to make contact.

One night, shortly after one in the morning, Moessner stood with his wife and children at the top of the 75-foot-tall building and threw a brick, with a nylon rope attached, to his contacts on the other side. After they had secured the rope at their end, the West Berliners blew a fuse along the wall, which suddenly plunged a whole section into darkness. That was the signal for the escapees to go, and, harnessing themselves to the rope, they slid down onto Western soil before the guards saw them.

One individual who was particularly fortunate to have made it over the wall was 21-year-old Michael Meyer. In September 1964 he tried to run over the barbed wire that divided the two halves of the city, but he was shot and injured just feet from the border. A U.S. military policeman (MP), himself of German origin, had watched this escape bid in horror, and when he saw several East German border guards approach Meyer, he knew he must intervene to help him. As the guards began to drag Meyer away, the MP trained his rifle on them and ordered them to back off and let him cross. When they took no notice he lobbed a tear-gas grenade at them, allowing several other West Berliners to dash over the border, throw a rope to the escapee, and drag him to safety. Though badly injured, Meyer survived his harrowing ordeal.

Other escapees managed to steal through the wall rather than over it. One West Berliner succeeded in rescuing his East German girlfriend by strapping her underneath his car and then driving through the checkpoint in bad weather, when he rightly anticipated that the guards would be far less likely to search the car carefully. Though the girl's face had been perilously close to the red-hot exhaust pipe, the plan worked brilliantly.

Even more hazardous, but just as successful, was the case of an East Berliner, Matthias Hoeffgen, who found a hiding place inside the engine of a giant steam train that often crossed from East to West. He boarded the train as it stopped at a siding en route and positioned himself between the engine's pistons and though temporarily blinded and scalded by the intense heat, he arrived in the West alive.

An escape just as ingenious and daring was made in the summer of 1963 by a young Austrian, Hans Pieter Meixner, who wanted to smuggle his fiancée out of the East. Carefully watching the checkpoint barrier that the border guards lowered to force cars to stop, he noticed that a very small car might just be able to drive underneath it. After subtly measuring its height as he crossed one day, he found a car—an Austin Healey Sprite—that, with its windshield taken off, might just fit, and he hired one from a West Berlin firm. As the young Austrian, with his future wife at his side, approached the checkpoint one afternoon, he drove through the first barrier and then suddenly accelerated the Sprite, taking all the border guards by surprise. Swerving around all the first barriers, which were designed to stop anyone from crashing through, Meixner then swept underneath the last barrier at 30 miles per hour, watched by the astonished East Germans.

During the 26 years the wall was in operation, the most usual form of escape was for individuals to be cleverly hidden inside cars that were then driven through the checkpoints by couriers with the legal right to pass through. One early series of such attempts was made by a professional organizer of escapes, Horst Breistoffer. Knowing that the East Germans were on the lookout for large cars that might conceal someone, Breistoffer deliberately bought a small car, which they would be much more likely to overlook. After spending more than two months modifying it to make sufficient room, he was at last ready to start transporting refugees and ferried nine escapees over the border before eventually being caught eight weeks later.

Many other escapees relied on forgery and imitation. One remarkable case was the "mystery of the missing GI uniforms" in 1965. Recognizing the potential escape value of GI uniforms, Dietrich Jensch, a professional organizer of escape, bought two uniforms from U.S. soldiers in West Berlin. Jensch walked around the city to see if any-one would stop him and found that he did not even attract a second glance wearing them; then he was ready to give them a try in the East.

Jensch contacted two individuals in East Berlin who wanted to escape and smuggled the uniforms into the capital, together with a jeep and a genuine set of U.S. Army car license plates that had been made for him in the West. After attaching the plates to the jeeps, the two escapees were virtually indistinguishable from the many official U.S. excursions that were made into the East, and they passed through the checkpoint without any difficulty. Only in the West did Jensch and the two refugees run into problems. After selling their story to a national newspaper, they were quickly arrested and fined by the West German authorities.

Other escapees went through the checkpoints using forged papers, the products of painstaking efforts and astonishing artistic skills. Dieter Rohrbeck, a professional artist, paid West German citizens to lend him their ID cards, which he then altered, adding a photograph of the escapee. Finally, he forged an East Berlin "entry" stamp and smuggled them into the East, where they were collected and used by the escapees.

When the East German authorities discovered his tactics, they introduced a new requirement: a letter of permission that was given out at the border and later collected as the West Berliner returned home. Though the form of this letter was changed daily to stop people like Rohrbeck from imitating them, Rohrbeck soon devised a way of getting round this. A first courier would cross to the East, pick up his copy of the letter, and pass it to an escapee, together with his forged ID card. When the escapee arrived in the West, Rohrbeck would forge a copy of the letter and send it back into East Berlin, where it was collected by the first courier, waiting to return to the West. It was a brilliantly designed and executed operation with a 24-hour turnaround time.

There were also many escapees who went under the wall. Tunnels were built by professional gangs, which charged would-be refugees extortionate rates to use them, or were dug by teams of idealistic students and sympathizers. One of the most important tunnels, which allowed more than 100 East Germans to reach the West, was built in 1964 by a Berliner named Wolfgang Fuchs. The tunnel, which took seven months to build, ran 140 yards from a cellar in the French sector of the city to a small bathroom in the East. By rigorously screening every East Berliner who approached them, the organizers were able to keep the tunnel in active use for several months before it was finally detected by the Communist police and sealed off.

There are many other remarkable escape stories about the Berlin Wall. One West German smuggled escapees inside a cow costume, claiming it belonged to a traveling theater company. One escapee posed as an East German policeman and waved down an unsuspecting West German motorist, demanded to see his papers, and ran off with them to the nearest checkpoint. Another individual was prevented by the West German police from carrying out his plan to herd several escapees into a water tank and lift them, with a giant crane, over the border into West Berlin.

See also: Air, escape by; Cuba, escape from; Gordievsky, Oleg; Iron Curtain; Kalbowski, Harry; Myagkov, Capt. Aleksei; Sea, escape and rescue at; Zwickau Prison

References: Gelb, Norman. The Berlin Wall. London: Michael Joseph, 1986.

Hildebrandt, Reiner. It Happened at the Wall. Berlin: Verlag Haus am Checkpoint Charlie, 1992.

Shadrake, Alan. The Yellow Pimpernels: Escape Stories of the Berlin Wall. London: Hale, 1974.

BIGGS, RONALD (1930–)

Two years after he took part in the Great Train Robbery in 1963, Ronnie Biggs followed the example of his partner in crime, Charlie Wilson, and made a spectacular break from Wandsworth Prison, where he was serving a long-term sentence.

Biggs had the good fortune to meet an old hand at prison escape named Paul Seabourne, who had already helped to organize a mass escape from Wandsworth in 1961, when prisoners attacked the warders before climbing the wall. Together the two men discussed ideas about how to find another way outside.

The plan they hit upon depended on outside help. If they could obtain a large furniture van or a similar vehicle, they reckoned, it would be possible to cut part of the roof away and replace it with a hinged platform that could be raised to the height of the prison wall and from which rope ladders could be dropped. When Seabourne was released in June 1965, he at once set about putting this plan into effect, using money supplied by Biggs's wife, and within a few weeks everything was ready.

During the afternoon of 8 July 1965 Ronnie Biggs and his accomplice, Eric Flower, went into the prison garden, ostensibly to get some exercise, and surreptitiously looked at their watches, waiting for the prearranged moment. They heard the van pull up outside the prison, saw Seabourne appear above the wall, and ran toward the rope ladders he threw over. Nearby prison officers saw Seabourne and the ladders too, and they tried to run toward them to stop them, but Biggs had taken careful precautions and had paid several other prisoners a large sum of money to obstruct the guards. Within minutes Biggs and Flower were over the wall and hurtling down the streets of London in their furniture van.

The escape did not have a happy ending for Seabourne, without whom it would never have happened. His fingerprints were found at the scene, and he was sent back to prison shortly afterward. But for Biggs and Flowers it had a happier outcome. They hid themselves in a friend's flat in Dulwich before being smuggled out of England to Antwerp in a Dutch freighter. Biggs had extremely painful plastic surgery to avoid being recognized and was able to make his way to South America, where he is still at large.

See also: Wilson, Charlie

References: Biggs, Ronald. Odd Man Out: My Life on the Loose and the Truth about the Great Train Robbery. London: Pan, 1984.

BITCHE FORTRESS (1807)

The French had good reason to suppose that their massive fortress at Bitche was inescapable, for it was built on the summit of an immensely high rock. But in September 1807, at the height of the Napoleonic Wars, Donat Henchy O'Brien, already a veteran of many escape attempts, led a successful breakout that stunned his captors. Vital to his success was his ability to detect the weak links in the well-practiced guard routine.

The first such weakness, he felt, was that the guards were likely to be far less vigilant in the early hours of the evening. He believed the guards would not expect anyone to try to escape early in the evening, and in any case in the dusk it would be easy for the guards to mistake the escapees for their own colleagues, who were still around the fortress for some hours after the six o'clock lockup time. When O'Brien and his accomplices investigated further and discovered that the night watchmen were not set and given their orders until eight o'clock and that it was most unusual for anyone to be challenged until that time, they got ready to make their move.

As the escapees climbed from their cells down the ropes and into the courtyard below, they discovered another weakness that also worked to their advantage. Passing close by the sentry, O'Brien found to his surprise that the guard did not turn to look at him but, instead, continued to stand rigidly at attention. This was not just because the sentries were complacent early in the evenings; it was also because the military's rigid code of discipline demanded such formality from sentries on parade.

Having made their way past the sentries, the escapees were able to use their rope to lower themselves more than 200 feet down the castle's massive ramparts and head for the Austrian border.

See also: Napoleonic Wars
References: O'Brien, Donat Henchy. *My Adventures during the Late Wars.* London: John Lane, 1932.

BLAKE, GEORGE (1924–)

In 1966 the British traitor George Blake was sprung from Wormwood Scrubs Prison in London and smuggled into East Germany by three political sympathizers, raising important moral questions about the right and wrong of rescues.

Born George Behar, the son of a Jewish-Egyptian father and a Dutch mother, Blake had been recruited into MI6 in 1949 after completing two years of war service in Naval Intelligence. He claims to have become sympathetic to the Communist cause while stationed at the British embassy at Seoul in South Korea after observing what he claimed was the cruelty and corruption of Syngman Rhee's regime there, but it is more likely that he was indoctrinated by his captors after he fell into the hands of the North Koreans. Returning to London in 1953 after three years in captivity, Blake quickly became a KGB agent, passing as much information as he could find to his spy masters in Moscow.

George Blake, the British traitor who betrayed possibly hundreds of Western agents working behind the Iron Curtain and who effected a brilliant escape from prison. (AP/Wide World Photos)

In 1955 he left London for a posting in Berlin, the front line of the Cold War. There, he made good use of his easy access to some of the West's most sensitive documents, such as the names of Western agents operating in the East and of Warsaw Pact officers who were sympathetic to Western interests. One of his greatest coups was tipping off the Soviets to a joint MI6-CIA plan to build a tunnel underneath the main Soviet telephone exchange in East Berlin, which would have tapped into all the conversations western intelligence wanted. Once the Soviets were aware of the plan, they could feed the Western eavesdroppers false information. Over the next four years Blake also betrayed a great many Western agents, such as Lt. Gen. Robert Bialek, an East German security chief who had defected to the West in 1953 but who, as a result of Blake's information, was kidnapped in February 1956, taken to the East, and executed. Perhaps as many as 300 other agents also died in similar circumstances during Blake's years with British Intelligence.

Blake was finally exposed as a traitor in 1960 when another double agent produced a leaked document that could only have originated from Blake's office. Sentenced to 42 years in prison after a secret trial at the Old Bailey in 1961, his fate attracted the sympathy of three other prisoners whom he met during his imprisonment. Pat Pottle and Michael Randall were both pacifist activists whose demonstrations against nuclear weapons had landed them in jail, and Sean Bourke, an Irishman, was imprisoned for attempting to kill the detective who had discovered his pedophilia. In 1966, after five years of imprisonment, the three men began to make serious preparations for springing George Blake from custody and spiriting him away to the East.

Though Bourke may have had his own reasons for participating in the rescue, Randall and Pottle later claimed to have been motivated by sympathy for the very long sentence passed on a man whom they regarded as a "prisoner of conscience," a man who had been driven by political sympathy for the Soviet system. As pacifists, both were also cynical about the claims made by the British security services and military, which they regarded as guilty of employing the same methods and tactics as their Eastern equivalents. Both MI6 and the CIA were guilty, they alleged, of assassination and of staging political coups in the Third World if it suited them. But they never explained how their pacifism could be reconciled with the violent deaths met by those whom Blake unquestionably betrayed, nor did they argue convincingly why ordinary citizens could take the law into their own hands as they did.

The plan they drew up in the summer of 1966 was simple but daring. During autumn, when the early nightfall would offer them better cover of darkness, they would throw a rope ladder from one of the streets that surrounded the prison and wait for Blake to make his way over the 20-foot wall and into a getaway car in the street below. The best chance of doing this, they reasoned, was on a Saturday evening, between six and seven, when most prisoners were usually watching a film and when there would be only a few officers in the prison block, where Blake, feigning sickness, would remain. The rope ladder could then be thrown over the wall at a blind spot at a precisely timed moment when the security patrol that passed by every 20 minutes or so would not be likely to see them.

In preparation for the escape, a radio was smuggled into the prison, which allowed Blake to communicate with his associates. In addition, a cast-iron support on a gothic window that Blake would have to pass through was broken two days before the escape was planned, and two panes of glass were smashed and removed.

When, on the evening of 22 October 1966, all was at last ready, things very nearly went wrong. Bourke arrived outside the prison at 6:30 and lingered in an adjacent street, but just as Blake was about to appear Bourke was seen by a security guard who, with his German shepherd, approached to take a closer look at what he was up to. Seeing that the guard was suspicious, Bourke took no chances and drove around the area for five minutes or so. When he returned he found to his relief that the guard had gone and the street was deserted. But again, just as he stopped his car, Bourke found himself with more company than he would have liked, for a courting couple had stopped their car just behind him, threatening to abort the whole operation. But Bourke instantly found a way to force them away: He got out of his car, turned toward them, and stared, prompting them to drive away from this unwelcome intrusion.

Meanwhile the escapee was starting to panic, afraid that the prison officers would find him missing at any moment. Bourke remembered hearing Blake's voice over the radio, blaring, "you MUST throw the ladder now, you simply must! Throw it!" Knowing that a car or passerby might happen to turn the corner into the street and see exactly what he was doing, Bourke nonetheless swung the rope ladder over the wall and waited for Blake to appear.

At 9 P.M. the news headlines were dramatic. "Tonight George Blake—serving a 42 year sentence for spying—escaped from his cell at Wormwood Scrubs in London. The Prime Minister, Mr. Wilson, who is spending the weekend at Chequers with other senior cabinet Ministers, was informed immediately. All ports and airports are being closely guarded" (Pottle and Randall 1989, 193).

As the newscaster made clear, Britain's entire security apparatus had launched the biggest manhunt in the country's history, and Randall, Pottle, and Bourke had, not surprisingly, begun to feel that getting Blake over the fence was the easy part of the operation. Moving the escapee from Britain to the East promised to be much harder.

But while Blake took refuge at the rented flat the three men shared in Hampstead and waited for the press attention to die down, a plan was drawn up that would take him to safety. Suppose Blake could be hidden, argued Randall, in a compartment underneath the seats of a van or truck, which on the way into East Germany would in all likelihood be overlooked by customs officials. Now that many assumed that Blake was already long out of the country, it might just work. Having no better ideas about how to spring George Blake to the Soviet Union, they purchased a small van and began to convert it to hide the former spy.

When, on the morning of 17 December—almost two months after Blake had made his way out of prison—the van left Hampstead for the Dover docks, it looked no more out of the ordinary than any of the other vehicles on the roads. Though Michael Randall, at the wheel, expected a check of some sort at the docks, the customs officials scarcely even looked twice at him before ushering them onto the ferry. Nor did the Belgian or German officials show any interest in the van as it sped on, virtually without a break, that December day. By the time Blake and Randall approached the East German checkpoints at Helmstedt and left Blake in the hands of the Communist authorities, they had traveled almost entirely without any obstruction.

For those involved, Blake's escape had a rather unhappy ending. Sean Bourke later appeared deeply ashamed of his own involvement, and after a sojourn in Moscow with the man he had helped set free, he even accused Blake of being "a born traitor" who "would have betrayed the KGB to the British if he had been born a Russian" (Bourke 1971, 341). Randall and Pottle made public their own involvement in the story in 1989, but their revelations were met only by an icy indifference on the part of everyone except a few antinuclear protesters. And in the same year Blake watched the regime he had sympathized with crumble under popular protest, though he remained curiously untouched by any British attempt to extradite him.

See also: Berlin Wall; Gordievsky, Oleg; Iron Curtain; Myagkov, Capt. Aleksei

References: Bourke, Sean. *The Springing of George Blake.* Mayflower, 1971.
Pottle, Pat, and Michael Randall. *The Blake Escape.* London: Harrap, 1989.

BLOUNT, FATHER HENRY (C. 1565–1625)

Although some clerics have attracted state persecution because of their pacifism, others have been regarded as dangerous protagonists of rebellion and violence, and after the Reformation, Elizabethan officials made great efforts to capture the Catholic priests who were at work in the country and whom they regarded as a powerful subversive force. But though these officials had an extensive network of informers, imposed draconian penalties upon those they caught, and sometimes spent weeks searching a single building in pursuit of their quarry, many priests still managed to elude them, including Father Henry Blount at the end of the sixteenth century.

While staying at one country house in Sussex in 1598, Father Blount and a Catholic companion had a lucky escape from two local justices who suddenly arrived out of the blue to make a search. They had just enough time to dash into the secret hiding place under the staircase. But during the week the search lasted, the two men started to run out of food and water and were forced to change their plans. Blount's acquaintance nobly surrendered himself, showing their pursuers a different hiding place from the one they had really been staying in, and Blount was able to quietly slip out of the house and flee into the surrounding countryside.

But a year or so later the local authorities were once again hot on his trail and were tipped off about his whereabouts by a disgruntled servant who had worked in the house he was staying in. Though they arrived to search the house in the middle of the night, Blount was a light sleeper and heard them approaching. Once again he narrowly avoided them, this time by disappearing into a hiding place that had been dug into a thick stone wall.

The search that followed was also a very thorough and protracted affair, but though Blount had plenty of supplies in his hiding place, he had in his haste left some of his vestments hanging through the stone wall. The lady of the house whispered to him as loudly as she dared to pull it in and inadvertently gave away his hiding place, being unaware that she was observed by some members of the search party. Before long they were hammering away at the wall, trying desperately to get inside and forcing Father Blount to brace himself against the door to prevent it from caving in.

But as night approached and it started to rain heavily, the searchers—who were not absolutely sure that he was inside the wall anyway—decided to give up for the night and start again at first light. Before long Blount was able to slip out, unseen by any of the searchers, and he made his getaway by scaling two walls, each about 10 feet high, and leaping over the moat beyond. Few other priests on the run enjoyed the good luck of Father Blount.

See also: Tower of London
References: Darell, William. *Mr Blount's Escape out of His Father's House.* London, 1598.

BONNEY, WILLIAM H.
(1860–1881)

Better known as "Billy the Kid," William H. Bonney's notoriety among law-enforcement officers of the Wild West rested not just on his banditry but also on his propensity to escape from them.

Bonney was born in New York but moved to New Mexico as a child. After the death of his mother he started to fall into a life of petty crime and before long became a fugitive from justice, using a variety of pseudonyms to evade capture. But it was not until the outbreak of the Lincoln County War—a clash between the cattle barons of Lincoln County, New Mexico, and their enemies—that he made his name as "Billy the Kid," an outlaw renowned for his sharpshooting and flamboyant style.

He proved his aptitude for escape early in his criminal career. In Silver City, New Mexico, at the age of just 15, an acquaintance coaxed him into robbing a small Chinese laundry; he was quickly apprehended by Sheriff Harvey Whitehill and put in prison. But Whitehill, probably overanxious not to treat such a young person as a hardened criminal, allowed the Kid the run of the corridor outside his cell. Whitehill left the jail for half an hour and returned to find that the Kid had crawled through the chimney, making an escape that amused the local press and demonstrated all the qualities of resource, daring, and ingenuity that were to characterize his subsequent criminal career.

This escape was curiously mirrored four years later, in August 1879, when the Kid, by now an experienced sharpshooter, was tracked down in Bonita Valley, about six miles from Lincoln. Sheriff George Kimball and 15 men succeeded in cornering him in a cabin and waited until daybreak before moving in to arrest him. But the delay gave him the chance he needed, and he again climbed up through the chimney and onto the roof and silently slipped away into the night.

But he made his most famous escape two years later, in April 1881, when he had been arrested and imprisoned for his notorious banditry since the end of the Civil War. He was taken to Lincoln Prison in handcuffs and leg irons and was always accompanied by two vigilant guards. The Lincoln, New Mexico, town sheriff, Pat Garrett, who knew almost every detail of Billy's career, warned the guards that "if this man is shown the slightest chance on earth he will effect some plan by which he will murder the whole lot of you before you have time to even suspect that he has any such intention" (Garrett 1881, 134).

But despite Garrett's warning, the Kid got the better of his guards. Knowing that his notoriety would attract a harsh verdict and inspired by the taunts of one of his guards, Robert Olinger, who had been a bitter enemy from the war, he planned his getaway. On 28 April he asked one of his sentries, James W. Bell, to take him from his cell to the privy behind the gatehouse, and as they made their way back he managed to move slightly ahead of Bell. In the few seconds he was out of Bell's view he was able to slip one hand free from his handcuffs before suddenly turning round and throwing the chain in Bell's face. The two men exchanged vicious blows, but Billy seized Bell's revolver first and shot the guard dead.

Hearing the shot, Olinger ran toward them, but he was too late to see Billy grab a shotgun, and within minutes of Bell's death Olinger too fell to Billy's fast and accurate shooting. The escapee forced another prisoner to cut off his chains with an ax and to saddle up a horse for him, and, armed with eight revolvers and six rifles, he made off into the wilderness, watched by terror-stricken Lincoln residents.

His escape caused a sensation among the general public and instantly made him the most infamous outlaw of the region in deed, not just in name. When Garrett heard the news of his escape the next day, he quickly returned to Lincoln and prepared to pursue the Kid and fight him to the death.

See also: Cody, William F.; Logan, Harvey
References: Garrett, Pat. The Authentic Life of Bill the Kid. Santa Fe, NM: New Mexican Printing and Publishing Co., 1882.
Utley, Robert M. Billy the Kid: A Short and Violent Life. London: Tauris, 1990.

BOSTON MASSACRE (1770)

One young British soldier was rescued from a large and angry crowd in Boston in 1770, shortly before his colleagues opened fire on them.

The soldier was a member of the British garrison that was responsible for the security of preindependence Boston. While he was patrolling the city on his own, a large crowd gathered and started to insult him, forcing him to retreat until he stood outside a nearby customhouse.

An experienced officer watching nearby, Capt. Thomas Preston, hoped that the problem would resolve itself and the crowd would disappear. But when this began to seem unlikely, he decided to send a group of six privates and a corporal through the crowd to rescue White. Armed with muskets and with bayonets fixed, they had little difficulty reaching the stranded soldier, who was still standing unharmed though somewhat shaken by the customhouse.

However, the rescue did have one unfortunate and unnecessary consequence. Instead of retreating back to their headquarters, the platoon formed a rough semicircle around the customhouse, and as the crowd became increasingly agitated and abusive, they fired, killing five and wounding six.

See also: Brooklyn Heights; New York; Valcour Island
References: Greene, J., and J. R. Pole. Blackwell Encyclopaedia of the American Revolution. Oxford: Blackwell, 1992.

British troops open fire on protestors in Boston in 1770 after rescuing a young soldier from the angry mob. The incident became known as the Boston Massacre. (Library of Congress)

BOUNTY (1789)

Evicted from his ship, HMS *Bounty*, by mutineers, Captain William Bligh was able to save himself and his fellow officers by using his intuition and knowledge of native ways to sense danger before it was too late.

Rather than execute the captain and his fellow officers, the mutineers on the British ship HMS *Bounty* had forced them into a rowboat, allowing them to take their belongings and a supply of food, and set them adrift to make their way back to dry land. During their long journey to safety, during which they covered nearly 4,000 miles across the Pacific, this small band had a narrow escape from the natives of the island Tofoa.

Bligh and his officers were forced to stop at Tofoa to find urgently needed food and water. Knowledgeable of the ways and mannerisms of many of the island people, Bligh at first found them friendly and hospitable, willing to trade their goods for the gifts that he was able to offer them. But as their number increased he sensed a change of mood: Their whispers and expressions, he felt, gave "some indications of a design against us" (Bligh, 1790). They had realized, he thought, that his party was unarmed and without the manpower that supported most excursions onto their territory. His suspicions were confirmed when he saw them collecting large stones, and he knew they were preparing for an imminent attack.

Bligh was sitting with some of the tribal leaders a short distance from the coast when he saw these activities, but he was careful not to let it show that he knew what was coming. He leaned over and told the Briton at his side to tell their fellow sailors, who were waiting at the coast, to prepare the boat for a quick getaway.

Breaking off the meeting, Bligh began to move slowly away from the encampment back to the boat, politely turning down the chief's request that they stay the night. But as he reached the boat the natives rushed forth, pouring down the beach toward them at a furious pace and reaching the coast just as they had all gotten in the boat.

Because the boat's stern rope was still tied to a log, a sailor bravely ran back onto the beach to try and loosen it, but he was knocked down and stoned to death by the angry mob that quickly gathered around him. Only by cutting the rope were the others able to get out to sea.

Though simply armed with nothing more than rocks and stones, the natives were well able, even at a distance, to injure the escapees. All of Bligh's men were paddling furiously with anything they could find. Bligh later wrote of his astonishment that "anyone could throw stones of between 2 and 8 pounds weight with such force and exactness as these people did," (Bligh, 1790) and when he saw several canoes, piloted by more natives, all brandishing rocks, he must have wondered if escape was beyond their grasp. Only because nightfall was descending did the canoeists, only a short distance behind, give up the chase and return home, allowing the Britons to continue their battle with the rough seas during the long journey to safety that lay ahead.

References: Bligh, William. *A Narrative of the Mutiny on Board His Majesty's Ship "Bounty."* London, 1790; reprint, 1901.

Shipwrecks and Disasters at Sea. Vol. 3. Edinburgh: A. Constable, 1812.

BRAY, JOHN (C. 1845–1900?)

During the U.S. Civil War one Union prisoner, John Bray, enjoyed the good fortune of being sent to the prison factory at Pemberton Prison, where he spent much time helping to make clothes for the Confederate armies.

He soon obtained a Confederate uniform and succeeded in hiding it as he returned to his cell by throwing a blanket over his shoulders. Taken for a Confederate soldier, he eventually reached Union lines and rejoined his unit.

References: Doyle, Robert C. *A Prisoner's Duty: Great Escapes in U.S. Military History.* Annapolis, MD: Naval Institute Press, 1997.

BRIXTON PRISON (1980)

For several weeks in 1980 and 1981, the British prison authorities were forced to make an urgent review of prison security after three Irish Republican Army (IRA) prisoners escaped from the maximum security wing at a maximum security jail. It was, as the British newspapers called it, "the incredible jailbreak," "a wooden horse escape from Brixton" that no one had thought could ever happen.

The moving force behind the break was Gerard Tuite, who had been arrested in December 1979 as a member of the IRA bombing team that had wreaked havoc on the British mainland. For some reason, he was not considered much of an escape risk, but he quickly began digging a hole in his cell wall, hiding it behind a poster. He soon realized that the steel mesh and plaster behind the cement would make his efforts futile.

By the time he was moved from this cell to the maximum security wing, Tuite had managed to get hold of several meat cutting blades from the prison kitchen and now found an ingenious way of smuggling them past the extensive checks on all incoming baggage. He hid them inside a box containing all his drawing and artistic instruments and asked the prison officer accompanying him to carry it, thinking that it had much less chance of being searched if it was seen in the arms of a member of the prison staff. He was right, and as he walked through he must have realized that he had a chance of escaping.

Once inside the maximum security wing Tuite had to find the right cell from which to scrape his way out. He quickly introduced himself to the inmate at the end of the bottom landing, whose cell bordered the outside on its left and another cell on its right. Discovering that this prisoner was unpopular with the other prisoners, he was able to persuade the authorities to allow them to swap cells, allowing the other prisoner sanctuary from his enemies and giving Tuite an opportunity to escape.

Tuite planned to scrape a hole not only through the wall to the outside but also through the wall to the adjacent cell so that another IRA member, James Moody, could also escape. Not only would the support of another prisoner greatly enhance the chances of the break succeeding, but Tuite also needed Moody's outside contacts. Before long Moody's brother had begun smuggling screwdrivers, glue, and other instruments into the prison by hiding them in his shoes, knowing that the metal detector that was passed over all prison visitors was likely to miss them there.

Tuite also found ingenious ways of improvising some of the tools he required. He found a pencil sharpener in the workshops and smuggled it back to his cell by telling warders that it needed repairing and that he would return it after a few days. The officers of course forgot he had taken it, and he converted it into a small drill by jamming a metal spike into the hole where the pencil is usually placed and attaching a metal coat hanger to make a more powerful handle.

To hide the holes in the wall, Tuite and his accomplices used a cabinet as well as the posters that had served him well before. But there was another danger to their escape plans: betrayal by fellow prisoners who wanted either to improve their chances for early release or who were jealous of what they knew was going on. But both Tuite and Moody were notorious for their ferocious violence, having been involved in the beatings of some of their IRA colleagues inside the prison as well as outside, and the other prisoners, who could hear their drilling better than the prison officers, were too terrified to inform. Tuite later praised the British police for helping to establish his notoriety.

Tuite and Moody moved at 3 A.M. on 15 December 1980, making their way out of their cells and onto the prison roof. Though they were soon within the range of the security cameras, they had found a clever way of distracting them, having arranged for one of the prisoners to switch on his cell light at a precise moment and thereby forcing the camera to zoom automatically onto its position. They then made their way to the outer wall and used some discarded scaffolding equipment to get over it.

The prison security at Brixton clearly had its weaknesses. A few weeks earlier a prisoner had been caught making his way back *into* the prison, having left a few hours earlier for an evening's drinking. Strike action by the prison officers' trade union at the time of the break also appears to have played a part in making it easier, and it is not known whether a full quota of warders were on duty during the night. Tuite also blamed the tendency of most warders to shunt responsibility onto their colleagues in other wings, all of them thinking that because others were on duty there was less need for them to make so much effort themselves.

But even though security procedures were tightened, other prisoners still managed to get free. One Sunday morning in July 1991 another IRA prisoner, Pearse McAuley, held a handgun to the head of a warder, forcing him to unlock the corridor gates. McAuley made it over the perimeter wall by putting a wheelbarrow over a dog kennel and climbing over the wall. It later turned out that the gun had been smuggled inside hidden in a hole that had been cut out of the sole of a training shoe.

See also: Crumlin Road Prison; Long Kesh Prison; Maze Prison; McGartland, Martin
References: Bean, J. P. *Over the Wall: True Stories of the Master Jail Breakers.* London: Headline, 1994.

BROAD, LT. COL. RICHARD (1910–1991)

While on the run in France in 1940, a British officer named Richard Broad had an unexpected encounter in a Parisian restaurant, an encounter from which he was lucky to escape.

Though Broad knew that his imperfect French could make him highly suspicious to any German officers or informers who heard him talk, he decided to take the risk of visiting a top restaurant with a resistance contact. By cruel misfortune, just as they unfolded their napkins an important figure suddenly arrived and sat down at the next table: the second most important leader of the Third Reich, Hermann Göring.

Staying cool under pressure, Broad and his acquaintance finished their meal in near silence, and then they hurriedly left.

References: Massingberg, Hugh, ed. *Daily Telegraph Book of Obituaries.* London: Fontana, 1996.

BROOKLYN HEIGHTS (1776)

On 29 August 1776 George Washington made careful plans to evacuate his defeated army back across the East River to Manhattan. Using all his characteristic energy and resourcefulness, he obtained a huge assortment of craft from all the creeks around Manhattan, and to sail them across he drew sailors from the ranks of the Marblehead 14th Continentals and 27th Continentals, who originated from New England fishing ports. To cover for the evacuation he selected five of his best regiments, commanded by Thomas Mifflin, a young brigadier.

The evacuation began at dusk and was hidden from British view not only by the failing light but by a thick fog that blanketed much of the area. Boatload after boatload of soldiers were ferried across the East River by boatmen who could see only a few yards ahead of them and who had no way of telling, until the last minute, if an approaching boat was a British craft or their own.

There were many anxious moments. When the wind dropped shortly after midnight it looked as though the evacuation would not finish in time, since the additional boats that might make up for the lack of wind power were not available. But, to the escapees' great relief, the wind shifted again and the withdrawal was back on target. Just two hours later Mifflin was wrongly informed that it was time for him to withdraw to the waiting boats, but when they arrived at the harbor they found a long queue of waiting troops in front of them. Fortunately they were able to return to their frontline positions before the British noticed their absence.

One of the last to leave, Lieutenant Tallmadge of the rearguard's Connecticut battalion, had a very close call. Having safely arrived at New York shortly after dark, Tallmadge requested permission from Colonel Chester to head back to Brooklyn, still using the thick fog as cover, to bring back his horse, which he had left tied to a pier. But after they got the animal onto their flat-bottomed boat and started to sail back to New York, British soldiers suddenly appeared on the quay behind them and opened fire. Though they were peppered by muskets and a few light field pieces on the quay, they managed to get back in one piece.

See also: Boston Massacre; Fanning, David; Hackensack River; New York; Valcour Island
References: Greene, J., and J. R. Pole. *Blackwell Encyclopaedia of the American Revolution.* Oxford: Blackwell, 1992.

BROWN, HENRY (1816–?)

Born as a slave in 1816, Henry Brown had worked happily in Richmond, Virginia, for a long time until, in 1848, his wife and children were suddenly sold to a Methodist preacher from North Carolina. Desperate to see them again, Brown devised an ingenious means of escape.

Brown asked a skilled carpenter with whom he was acquainted to make a wooden box, about three feet long and two feet wide. He planned to hide himself inside and to arrange for two friends, a merchant named Samuel A. Smith and his black employee, James Caesar Anthony Smith, to mail the box. The other men readily agreed to take part in the plan, and on 29 March 1849, marking the box "right side up with care," they shipped it off to an address in Philadelphia where Brown would be received by the Pennsylvania Anti-Slavery Society.

To survive the journey Brown had three small holes bored through the wood and took a container of water at his side. But the journey, which took more than 27 hours, was still extremely arduous for the escapee, particularly during the several hours he was forced to travel upside down. By the time the crate reached its destination, he was near the end of his tether.

Brown later became active in the abolitionist movement, telling crowds his story and giving an author, Charles Stearns, a full account. His white friend Samuel Smith, who had made his escape possible, was not so lucky. He was later imprisoned after he was caught trying to smuggle two other slaves to freedom in the same way.

See also: Fugitive Slave Laws; Parker, John; Spartacus; Underground Railroad

Desperate to escape slavery in Virginia, Henry Brown was boxed up in a crate three feet long, two and a half feet deep, and two feet wide and mailed to freedom in Philadelphia. (Library of Congress)

References: Ripley, C. Peter, ed. *The Black Abolitionist Papers: The British Isles, 1830–1865.* Chapel Hill: University of North Carolina Press, 1985.
Stearns, Charles. *Narrative of Henry Box Brown.* Philadelphia: Rhetoric, 1969.

BUCKLEY, EVERETT
(C. 1895–1955?)

In July 1918 one American aviator of World War I, Everett Buckley, succeeded brilliantly not only in breaking out of the prison camp in Karlsruhe in which he was held but also in crossing a heavily patrolled area of the border with Switzerland.

As he approached the border, Buckley saw three lines of guards in front of him, as well as patrols with dogs combing the area between them. But by carefully surveying the situation before nightfall, he was able to detect chinks in their armor and had worked out a way of slipping between them.

Soon after dark, Buckley tied his shoes around his neck, knowing that he would move more quietly barefooted; stuffed a handkerchief into his mouth, so the dogs would not hear him breathing; and rubbed wild garlic all over himself, knowing that it would deceive the guard dogs. Making full use of the dark and rainy night, Buckley succeeded in the near impossible and slipped across the border into Switzerland.

References: Dennett, Carl P. *Prisoners of the Great War.* Boston: Houghton Mifflin Riverside Press, 1919.

BURNS, ROBERT ELIOT
(C. 1898–?)

Prisoners who were sentenced to the American chain gangs of the 1920s and 1930s had good reason to want to escape. Besides being housed in terrible conditions at their camps and living on extremely meager rations, they also endured very rough treatment from prison guards while being forced to perform hard manual labor. But to escape, a prisoner either had to run with the

20 pounds of chains that weighed him down or to remove them.

One prisoner who managed to get free was Robert Eliot Burns, whose story became famous after it was published under the title *I Am a Fugitive from Georgia*. Like many other GIs, when Burns returned to the United States after World War I he found it difficult to settle back into civilian life. He was lured into petty crime, and in 1922 he was arrested after robbing a grocery store with two acquaintances and sent to prison.

Sent to the Campbell County chain gang, he quickly became aware of the dangers of trying to escape. Two guards were assigned to each of the parties of 12 men who were sent to work on the nearby roads every day, and other prisoners who were caught trying to cut through their chains were savagely beaten. He also found that the prison authorities had a very simple way of stopping anyone from escaping: They worked the prisoners so hard on minimal rations that they scarcely had any real wish, or the inner strength, to escape. Their thoughts were instead focused upon survival.

Burns's plan was to make his escape bid on a Monday, when he knew that only the previous day's rest would give him sufficient strength to do so. In order to remove the chain round his ankle he hit on a very simple idea: If he could get one of his fellow prisoners to strike the chain with a sledge-hammer, he might be able to slip his foot through its contorted shape.

Though he knew that if he were caught he would face serious punishment and that if the sledgehammer missed he would lose his foot, a few days later, when the guards were half asleep in the midday sun, he asked one of the prisoners to strike the chain three times. The blows contorted the chain very seriously, but Burns was extremely lucky when, at the end of the day's work, the prison guards who inspected them somehow failed to notice what had happened.

Back at the camp Burns felt his heart pounding as he managed to slip the chain off his ankle. Making his move in the middle of the night of 21 June 1922, he disappeared quietly without being seen and made his way out of the camp.

But it did not take the guards long to notice that he had disappeared, and only a few hours after he had left he heard, in the far distance, the baying of the blood-hounds hot on his trail. Fortunately, like other prisoners who have made it to freedom, he was well versed in the art of throwing dogs off his trail, and he immediately headed for a nearby river and drifted several miles downstream until he was sure he was safe.

But his flight to freedom was not over yet. The police and the public throughout the area had been alerted, and he only narrowly managed to evade a policeman whom he suddenly noticed watching him carefully as he sat in a barber's chair. But he struck lucky when he took refuge in a nearby hotel, whose owner had himself only recently been released from a chain gang and who was therefore sympathetic to escapees such as Burns.

Though he now started a new life as a respectable businessman, Burns's story was not quite over yet. Betrayed by his vindictive wife in 1929, he was sent back into captivity, again to a chain gang, with promises of early parole. But it was soon clear that the authorities were not going to live up to his promises and that he would have to serve his full term. With his savings he bribed a farmer to leave a car in the woods near where he was forced to work and was once again able to escape.

See also: Auschwitz
References: Burns, Robert. *I Am a Fugitive from a Georgia Chain Gang.* New York: Vanguard, 1932.

CABANATUAN (1945)

As the U.S. Army continued to push the Japanese back in the Pacific, a dramatic raid was made on a prisoner of war camp at Cabanatuan, near Manila, in order to liberate the Americans still held within.

During the night of 30 January 1945, three years after the camp had been opened, a unit of the 6th Ranger Battalion led by Lt. Col. Henry Mucci attacked the camp, which was far behind enemy lines. Firing as they charged toward the compound and killing the sentries before they had a chance to open fire on the prisoners, they succeeded in killing a great many Japanese and liberating 516 prisoners while losing only two of their own men.

References: Breuer, William B. The Great Raid on Cabanatuan: Rescuing the Doomed Ghosts of Bataan and Cabanatuan. New York: Wiley, 1994.
Johnson, Forrest Bryant. Hour of Redemption: The Ranger Raid on Cabanatuan. New York: Manor Books, 1978.

CAMBRIDGE SPY RING (1951)

After spying for many years against their own country on behalf of Soviet intelligence, Donald Maclean and Kim Philby were able to escape to Russia before the British police had a chance to arrest them.

The net began to close around Guy Burgess, another member of the group known as the Cambridge Spy Ring, and Maclean in the summer of 1950, more than 15 years after they had begun to pass classified material to the KGB. But as the British authorities began an extensive search for evidence upon which to base a conviction, the two spies were tipped off by Kim Philby that their days were numbered and that they would have to escape to Moscow. After getting in touch with their main KGB contact in London, Yuri Modin, Burgess and Philby sent a secret note to Maclean advising him as to how and when he could escape.

Maclean also had his own ways of finding out the best way to avoid the clutches of the British police and intelligence service. After years of working in a world of espionage and intrigue, one biographer has written, he had developed "highly fine antennae" (Cecil 1990, 200) and was quick to notice that the highly confidential documents he had long been able to browse had suddenly been put out of his reach. He also knew that if his bosses were sure enough of his espionage activities to have undertaken such a measure, then they would in all probability also be following him to look for incriminating evidence. Sure enough, in the weeks before his escape he was seen by colleagues walking briskly through London, often looking quickly over his shoulder as if expecting to see someone on his trail.

Maclean probably also reckoned that he was more likely to be watched in London than at his house at Tatsfield, on the border between Kent and Surrey. In the capital he had access to the Soviet embassy and its agents, whereas at home his wife's presence would have probably been a constraint on such meetings. It was therefore more sensible, he must have reasoned, to make his escape bid from Tatsfield rather than London.

Fortunately for Maclean, MI5, who had organized his surveillance, simply lacked the manpower to mount a 24-hour watch to keep tabs on him at home as well as in London, which would have required an extra 20 men. MI5 also felt that in a village as small as Tatsfield strangers lurking in the dark near his home would have aroused his suspicions, not just those of his neighbors.

Kim Philby, a British traitor and member of the Cambridge Spy Ring who slipped away to the Soviet Union despite the fact that he was under surveillance by the British police and secret service. (Archive Photos)

He was tipped off that he was to be arrested and interrogated on Monday 28 May, so he put his escape plan into operation for 25 May. On that evening, Guy Burgess drew up in a hired car at the Maclean's large Victorian house and introduced himself as a Roger Styles from the Foreign Office. Insisting that they had to leave at once, the pair drove off into the night, reaching Southampton docks just in time to catch the midnight sailing of the *Falaise* to Saint-Malo. As agreed with their KGB contact they were provided with forged papers while in France, which they used to travel first to Vienna before moving on to Moscow. By the time the British home secretary, Herbert Morrison, gave the order to seal the country's ports, Burgess and Maclean were already out of the country and well on their way to the Soviet Union. It was an escape that made a mockery of the

British intelligence services, which had already suffered disastrously at the hands of the Cambridge Spy Ring.

After Kim Philby, too, was unearthed as a mole, he fled to the Soviet Union in January 1963. Slightly more is known about his escape route. According to an investigation that was made shortly afterwards by the Israeli secret service Mossad, Philby simply took a taxi from Beirut to Damascus, then under the protection of pro-Soviet Kurdish rebels, and was smuggled through northern Iraq to the village of Dogubayazit. From there he was taken by the KGB, which had organized the entire escape route, into the USSR, where he spent his last, unhappy years.

References: Cecil, Robert. *A Divided Life: A Biography of Donald Maclean.* London: Coronet, 1990.
Seale, Patrick. *Philby: The Long Road to Moscow.* London: Hamilton, 1973.

CAMP MORTON (1864)

Very few inmates escaped from the Union prison at Camp Morton. The Confederate soldier John Montgomery, of the Lowry Scouts, was one of them.

Montgomery had worked with nine other prisoners to build a 33-foot-long tunnel that took them out of the compound. In the early hours of 11 February 1864, just three days after they had begun digging, he and his close companion William Bell left the compound.

The two men agreed that if one was stopped en route, the other would deny all knowledge of him and would fend for himself. Bell was seen and stopped by a Union guard just minutes after they had emerged from the tunnel and started for the nearby train depot. Montgomery later recorded his feelings of relief that he was able to continue but also his sadness for his accomplice and perhaps even a streak of guilt that he had had to leave him behind.

See also: Andersonville; Columbia Prison; Conley, Capt. Edward

References: Denney, Robert E. *Civil War: Prisons and Escapes. A Day-by-Day Chronicle.* New York: Sterling, 1995.

CASANOVA, JACQUES (1725–1798)

Perhaps because his serial adultery had provided him with a thorough training, Jacques Casanova proved to be highly skilled at escaping from the imprisonment he was condemned to after being found guilty of "public outrages against their holy religion" (Villar 1892).

Sent to the notorious prison in Venice known as "the Leads" (after the lead that covered its roofs and walls) to serve his five-year sentence, Casanova was undeterred by the prison's reputation for being escape-proof and resolved to find a way out, writing in July 1755 that "it has always been my opinion that when a man sets himself determinedly to do something and thinks of nought but his design, he must succeed despite all the difficulties in all his path; such a person may make himself Pope or a Grand Vizier, he may overturn a line of kings—provided that he knows how to seize on his opportunity" (Villar 1892).

While exercising in the prison yard, he saw his opportunity and seized it: He found an iron bar in the yard that was large enough to be made into an excavating device but small enough for him to smuggle back to his cell.

Hiding it in his armchair when the guards were around, Casanova was able to dig a hole in the floor of his room and made a tunnel, though it took him several months. But just before he was ready to make his escape, the prison authorities moved him to another room, finding the tunnel and dashing his hopes of finding freedom.

Though as a result Casanova was now guarded much more heavily, the prison guards had failed to find the pike that he had used to dig the hole. He was once again able to hide it in his new room, and he prepared to try again. Knowing that he had no chance of building the tunnel himself without being seen, Casanova smuggled the pike—hidden inside the spine of a large Bible—to a prisoner in an adjacent cell, a monk named Balbi, telling him to dig a tunnel first between the two cells and then between Balbi's cell and the outside.

At last both tunnels were ready, and making their way onto the lead roof of the prison wing, the two men headed for an open window that they could see above the gutter they were precariously crossing. Casanova lowered Balbi on a rope through the window into the room some distance below, and then followed, finding a discarded workman's ladder nearby and forcing it through the window with some difficulty.

Neither of the escapees were sure where they were, and both assumed that they were still somewhere in the prison buildings. Wherever they were, they now had to make their way through a series of corridors and doorways to the main entrance, and once again they used the indispensable pike to force some of the locked doors that lay before them. Reaching the main entrance and seeing that it was far too big to force open, they waited. When the chief doorman arrived to open it, they raced into the streets outside before he had a chance to stop them.

After dashing out of town in the first coach they could find, the two men split up, knowing that separately they would have a better chance of evading the Venetian police, who would be in hot pursuit at any moment. But despite the risk, Casanova finished his escape in typically colorful and daring style, taking refuge at the house of one of the local police chiefs who was out pursuing him.

References: Villar, P. *The Escapes of Casanova and De Latude.* T. Fisher Unwin, 1892.

CATHOLIC CHURCH, RESCUE BY

Though if discovered it would have faced savage reprisals from the Germans, the Vatican saved a good many potential victims of the Nazis from gruesome fates. Sometimes this was a result of its own direct intervention, at other times it was through support for its clerics who set up special networks throughout Italy to aid their escape.

Soon after war broke out in 1939, the newly elected Pope Pius XII set up a chain of agents throughout Europe to gather information about the fate of prisoners of war (POWs), refugees, and other victims of war. One man who played a key role in this, spending a great deal of time visiting camps in Italy to inquire after the health and well-being of the POWs, was an Irish priest named Father Hugh O'Flaherty.

As the war progressed, there were also a few occasions when papal influence saved the lives of some of the Jews living in Rome. When in September 1943 the Nazis clamped down on the Jews of Rome and demanded a ransom of £2 million in gold from the city in return for their safety, the chief rabbi of Rome went straight to Pius XII and begged him to save his people. Within 24 hours papal influence ensured that the money was raised from the city's noble families, and Pius XII obtained more than 100 pounds of gold by ordering the Vatican's sacred vessels to be melted down. At the end of the war, the rabbi, who had lived in the Vatican during the duration of the war, converted to Catholicism.

The chief rabbi was in fact one of many Jews who lived inside the Vatican during the war. Since it was recognized as neutral territory, the Vatican was able to offer refuge to those who needed it, and one of its buildings, the College of Cardinals, was filled to the brink by refugee Jews. Many other escapees succeeded in slipping past the guards posted at the entrance to Vatican City, though as the numbers of asylum seekers increased and the Germans became uneasy, the Vatican authorities were forced to turn many away and leave their well-being to the priests who ran the escape line from Rome across Italy.

Father O'Flaherty, already well-accustomed to the ways of the Germans as a result of his many visits to POW camps, was a key player in this Catholic escape effort. When he came into contact with these escapees—most of whom were prisoners on the run—he would personally escort them to the homes of friends or to monasteries and convents. As the Nazis stepped up their searches for them during and after 1943, he increasingly took them to his own residence, to the German college behind the Holy Office, a training college that was soon crammed with an assortment of prisoners and Jews fleeing the Nazis. One of the places he liked to use, with typical audacity and a touch of humor, was a billet that was hidden behind the SS barracks but that remained undetected throughout the war. In all, he helped more than 4,000 POWs and many Jews evade the Nazis.

Of course O'Flaherty, like all his fellow rescuers, risked his life by undertaking such activities, and on several occasions he narrowly escaped arrest himself. When on one occasion the Gestapo raided the house of a leading sympathizer, O'Flaherty promptly fled to the cellar, removing his cassock and burying it under the sacks of coal around him. Smeared with soot and dressed in ordinary trousers and shirt, he casually walked past the SS soldiers outside, who could not easily have guessed that he was a highly regarded Catholic priest.

Outside Rome a great many priests and clerics also helped such fugitives keep one step ahead of the Germans, and one of the most senior clerics to organize an escape route for the country's Jews was the archbishop of Florence, Cardinal Elio della Costa. The archbishop was responsible for setting up and running a network of escape routes that was used by hundreds of fugitives who were fleeing to Switzerland. The escape organization was finally detected by the Gestapo in November 1943, and della Costa, protesting his innocence, only narrowly escaped execution.

The individual he turned to to help rebuild the escape routes was Padre Rufino Niccacci, who had also spent several months rescuing Italian Jews from arrest. Soon after the Germans had swooped down on the Jewish population of Rome, Niccacci had smuggled ten of them to the Swiss border by disguising them as monks, telling the German soldiers who stopped them that they were all a party of Christians returning home to Florence after a holy pilgrimage to Assisi. The first party he traveled with were able to avoid closer inspection from a wary German officer only because British planes appeared, with almost uncanny timing, and blasted the track further ahead, forcing the Germans to take cover.

After della Costa's organization was discovered, Niccacci became a key player in the rescue of Italy's Jewish population and was appointed chairman of Assisi's committee to aid Jews. On one occasion a group of 20 Jews who had escaped from the Nazi raid on the Jewish population at Trieste appeared in the city and begged its bishop to find them shelter. Niccacci, at the bishop's request, managed to persuade the nuns at a nearby cloister to hide the Jews behind their doors—an unprecedented act. When the Nazis came to search the building, the Jews were hurriedly hidden behind the sanctuary. Niccacci was able to persuade six monasteries as well as other nunneries to open their doors, and he was able to find a number of other shrines and holy places in the area that could provide shelter and accommodation if the need arose.

The young padre was also able to find an individual who was able to forge the identity papers that his candidates so sorely needed for escape. Luigi Brizi, one of the finest engravers and printers in Italy, was able to duplicate the passes, even though forging the intricate provincial emblems was one of the greatest challenges he had ever faced. Within days refugees were passing through German checkpoints without attracting even a second glance.

See also: Auschwitz; Koldyczewo Camp; Le Chambon; Schindler, Oscar; Sobibor Concentration Camp; Wallenberg, Raoul
References: Derry, Lt. Col. Sam, and David Macdonald. "The Vatican Pimpernel." In *True Stories of Great Escapes*, ed. Charles S. Verral. Pleasantville, NY: Reader's Digest Association, 1977.
Ramati, Alexander. *The Assisi Underground.* New York: Stein and Day, 1978.

CAVELL, EDITH (1865–1915)

During World War I a British nurse, Edith Cavell, helped to run an escape route for Allied soldiers who were on the run behind enemy lines, invoking both the wrath and admiration of her enemy.

From the Belgian hospital where she worked Cavell provided Allied escapees with new identities, adding their photos to stolen or lost passports, and found them places to stay en route to Holland. By April 1915, as Allied troops began to arrive in Brussels in increasing numbers, she had helped to establish a well-organized escape route that was run by a brave and devoted number of sympathizers.

There are many stories of the great personal risk she ran in order to help escapees. On one occasion she volunteered to find a guide for two British soldiers and had taken them to a house of a friendly local priest who was able to help them. The priest tore his visiting card in two, gave one half to Cavell, and told the three of them to wait at a particular time in a Brussels bar, where they were to use the half card as identification. Putting her half of the card down on a table, even though it was packed full of German soldiers, and waiting for her contact to place his own half next to it, Cavell was able to put the soldiers in touch with the guide who was waiting for her.

She also assisted escapees in finding places they could safely stay while they

Edith Cavell, a British nurse who helped run an escape route for Allied soldiers behind enemy lines during World War I, was convicted as a spy by the Germans and died before a firing squad. (Library of Congress)

waited to make the crossing. After the war two British soldiers, Harry Beaumont and Arthur Heath, recalled that she had met them in Brussels and taken them into a room at the top of a house near the clinic. Though the room was only 36 feet long and 9 feet wide and though it had no windows, they found a large group of other soldiers already there, eagerly awaiting their own turn to get back home. Another soldier was once hidden in a hole that was rapidly made in the floorboards of a sympathizer's house and covered with a laundry basket. When the Germans sent a search party shortly afterward to comb the house for escapees, they only looked in the basket, not underneath it. Another escapee was given temporary refuge inside a barrel over which a huge pile of apples was poured, once again providing effective cover from the German search party.

Though the soldiers were able to contact Cavell at the Brussels hospital where she

worked, they were not allowed to be treated there and usually remained hidden nearby. There were some occasions, however, when they were nearly discovered, which would have landed Cavell in front of a firing squad. When on one occasion the Germans arrived suddenly at the hospital, a British soldier was promptly whisked into bed, still wearing his army boots, and was described by Cavell as a Belgian peasant who was suffering from a chronic rheumatic condition, an illness that exactly fitted the effects of the shrapnel wounds from which he was really suffering. On another occasion the Germans arrived in the ward seconds after a British soldier jumped into bed and had a screen put round him for privacy.

But Cavell's luck could not hold. The Germans soon began to suspect her of collaboration and began to spy on her movements and her visitors. Arrested and tried in August 1915 on the charge of aiding and abetting Allied escapees, she was found guilty and sentenced to death. She died bravely before a German firing squad on 12 October 1915.

References: Hoeling, A. A. *Edith Cavell.* London: Cassell, 1958.

CEBEKHULU, KATIZA (1970–)

Although her husband publicly protested her innocence, during the apartheid era Winnie Mandela is alleged to have orchestrated crimes of violence and terror against her fellow black Africans and to have put together her own personal vigilante group, known as the Mandela United Football Club, to carry out her orders. In the early 1990s Katiza Cebekhulu narrowly escaped a death sentence that she had decreed, and he achieved worldwide fame in doing so.

The background to his escape from the "football club" lay in the mysterious deaths of several African National Congress (ANC) supporters during the late 1980s. Some— such as the deaths of Lolo Solo and Siboniso Tshabalala—attracted little attention even inside South Africa, but the murder of Stompie Moeketsi, a youth who had led several township protests against the government, soon made headlines across the world as accusations began to flow about who was responsible.

Having worked directly alongside Winnie Mandela as a member of the football club, Cebekhulu was in a better position than most to know the truth of the matter. Not only had he seen Mandela stab Stompie, but he could also give first-hand evidence about various other incidents, such as the capture and death of the ANC's most famous soldier, Sizwe Sithole, that would have been highly damaging to her.

In September 1990, soon after Winnie Mandela was formally charged in court with the murder of Stompie and three other young Africans, Pelo Mekgwe, Kenny Kgase, and Thabiso Mono, Cebekhulu heard that he was to play a key part in the proceedings as a witness, but he was warned by a fellow member of the football club that his life was in danger. Because the beginning of the trial had been delayed, his source said, Mandela would have much

more time to organize his execution, and he would have to run quickly if he was to escape with his life. Cebekhulu, well aware of the ruthlessness of the organization he had belonged to, did not need to be told twice. Hurriedly collecting what he could of his few possessions, he ran out of the back door, scaled the back fence, and disappeared into the night.

Over the next few weeks, as he ran from street to street in and around Soweto, living rough, he turned to the police for help, informing them of his predicament and begging for their help, but he was unable to persuade them that his story was not a hoax. He also turned to the courts, approaching a leading South African barrister at the Rand Court in Johannesburg, but again he received only a negative response. Cebekhulu, it seemed, was on his own.

He continued to move constantly among five different townships, breaking his bail conditions by failing to report at a police station twice daily. Instead he lived with the down-and-outs of the city and scrounged scraps of food. But this existence was safer than returning to his home territory, as he found out when he visited one of his Sowetan friends, Churi Mdanis. While he was there, ANC members combed the area searching for him and soon approached the house, brandishing assault rifles. Mdanis confronted them at the front door and saved his friend by putting on a brave face and convincing his pursuers that he had not seen him.

Cebekhulu had been on the run for nearly three months before he was finally recognized and picked up by the police in January 1991. His suspicions about Winnie Mandela's complicity with the police were confirmed when, instead of being given sanctuary, he was taken to his former leader and left for her to deal with. After trying so hard to elude her, he was once again face to face with Mandela and knew the fate that awaited him.

Beaten and tortured by members of the football club, he felt sure that his short life was already over. But when he was dumped in the back of a car and driven off, probably for execution, he was able to kick the trunk open and vanish once again, eventually reaching a hospital where he spent two weeks recovering from the injuries that had been inflicted on him during torture.

But again his luck failed, and, betrayed by acquaintances, he found himself back in the hands of Winnie Mandela. But perhaps because of the publicity that had by now become focused on him, his life was spared. Instead of being executed, Cebekhulu was sent across the border into Zambia to a camp of the ANC's armed wing, Umkhonto we Sizwe.

Still Cebekhulu feared for his life, unable to trust the assurances Winnie Mandela had give him and acutely conscious of the fact that he was one of the very few witnesses to the betrayal of Sizwe Sithole to the apartheid government. He ran off into the bush, sleeping rough and surviving on minimal food and water, and was eventually found and captured by the Zambian police. But once detained, he instantly felt much more secure inside prison than he had ever been during the last six months.

Cebekhulu was eventually released from jail in 1993, largely as a result of heavy diplomatic pressure, and currently lives in exile from his native South Africa.

See also: Mandela United Football Club
References: Bridgeland, Fred. *Katiza's Journey.* London: Sidgwick and Jackson, 1997.

CHANDOS, SYDNEY, EARL OF CARDIGAN (1904–)

During World War II, the earl of Cardigan "walked alone" from German captivity in Belgium to Spain, one of the most remarkable of all escape stories. But he owed his getaway to superb timing as well as good fortune.

Like other escapees, the earl found his long-awaited chance to make his escape when, together with a large number of fellow prisoners, he was moved from one camp near Boulogne to another. But he was well aware that the next camp would probably be far better guarded and thus far harder to escape from than the makeshift places they were being held in en route. It

was therefore essential, he reasoned, that he make his move before he got there.

At first he was too well guarded to attempt an escape, since a whole squad of men was deployed to guard each of the open trucks that were transporting them, but his luck changed soon after they had reached Lille. Because the Germans were unable to find accommodations for the number of prisoners involved, some were transferred to a nearby prison camp at Tournai in Belgium. But to his surprise, the earl saw that there were no German guards with the British prisoners of war packed into the back of the truck. The guards in the front merely watched them from their mirrors or turned around every so often. They mistakenly assumed that none of the prisoners would be able to get away during such a short, nonstop journey.

The earl knew that escaping would nonetheless be difficult, since the roads were full of German vehicles and soldiers. But when they were within a few minutes' drive of their destination, he judged the moment to be ripe. As the truck slowed down at a crossroads, he noticed that for almost the first time in the brief trip there was almost no one at all, German or Belgian, in sight. "With more agility than I knew myself to possess," he wrote, "I slipped over the tail-board of the lorry and took up a position in the roadway just behind it" (Cardigan 1974, 13). After a few seconds' pause the truck moved on, leaving him standing alone, scarcely believing his luck.

His journey back to Allied territory is a remarkable story of resource, daring, and determination. Reckoning that the Germans would concentrate all their troops in northwestern France, preparing for an invasion of England, he moved first into the center of the country and headed southward and made his way toward the Pyrenees. Over the next four months he walked most of the way to Spain, where he was briefly imprisoned by the Spanish police before being handed over to the British in Gibraltar.

There are a few particularly noteworthy occasions during this epic journey when the earl came closer to his enemy than he would have liked. Stopped by two German sentries two weeks after escaping, he knew he would have to muster all his acting abilities if he was to pass himself off as a Frenchman. He began by pretending he was unable to understand their poor French. *"Oh, les papiers!"* he eventually exclaimed, after the sentries had tried a dozen times to pronounce these words. Well aware that they would quickly notice his stumbling French, he feigned a stammer that would hide his lack of fluency.

He had another close shave some days later as he walked along a quiet rural lane in central France. A car suddenly appeared and stopped behind him, and he was only just able to hide his fear and surprise when a senior German officer offered him a lift. Pretending to be pleasantly surprised, the earl found himself speeding along the road alongside three German soldiers, one of whom spoke impeccable French and who would have picked up his slight linguistic discrepancies had he not managed to keep quiet during the journey.

It was not until November 1940, more than five months after he had leaped off a lorry in northern France, that the earl of Cardigan finally reached Gibraltar.

References: Cardigan, Earl of. *I Walked Alone.* London: White Lion Press, 1974.

CHARLES EDWARD STUART
(1720–1788)

Throughout his life Charles Edward Stuart—"Bonnie Prince Charlie"—claimed the British crown for himself as a direct descendant of the Stuart line, whose rule had been abruptly ended by the deposition of James II in 1689. But the failure of his bid for the crown forced the prince to spend months fleeing his enemy in the far north of Scotland, unfolding a story with all the ingredients of romance and legend: great daring and near capture, the glimmer of nostalgia for his doomed efforts, and of course the extreme beauty of the story's setting.

The prince began his attempt to overthrow George II in the summer of 1745. Arriving in northern Scotland from his exile in France, he tried to create maximum inconvenience for the British government, which was at that time entangled in the War of the Spanish Succession. Though he soon found a large Scottish following and was able to sweep southward to take Edinburgh and defeat the British at nearby Preston Pans, his army was eventually defeated at Culloden, near Inverness, in April 1746, and he was forced to flee.

Formidable difficulties lay ahead of him. He and his companions slipped away from his crumbling army at Culloden, but an enormous reward of £30,000 was immediately offered for his capture. It is a remarkable testimony to the loyalty that he was able to command from almost all who met him that he was never betrayed. Moreover, though he planned to move throughout the islands and wait for a French ship to pick him up, he knew that all the islands were regularly patrolled by the British fleet, which was ready and waiting for any move he or his Continental allies might make.

But Charles and his companions persisted and used all their resource and ingenuity to weave a path through the islands scattered along the western and northern coasts of Scotland. For several months they managed to keep one step ahead of the government forces by sailing in tiny, unobtrusive rowboats and by adopting a wide variety of disguises and stories to help them along the way.

But there were some close shaves. Two months after the defeat at Culloden, their pursuers, using all the means they could to close the net on their elusive prey, at one point managed to track Charles to South Uist, off the far northwestern coast. Though detachments of government soldiers were quickly deployed there and navy patrols around it stepped up, Charles still managed to slip away to a neighboring island. But within a few days his enemy was again on his heels, when a force of 700 led by Captain Caroline Scott, already notorious for his cold-blooded cruelty in hunting down Jacobites, landed nearby and forced the prince and his small party to embark in frantic haste, leaving most of their provisions behind them and even ducking rifle fire as they pulled their boat from its mooring to get away.

They had another near miss a few weeks later, in mid-July. They had managed to reach the south shore of Loch Nevis but were soon challenged by a group of militia, who ordered them to pull ashore. Charles's boat ignored the order and was pursued for some distance, though eventually they managed to out-row their pursuers. But word of his whereabouts soon spread. When they landed near Mallaig, they were told that a force of 500 men led by a General Campbell had anchored in Loch Nevis and were combing the area for him. Messengers gave them the even more alarming news that hundreds of Argyll militia were at the foot of every hill around them, waiting for them to make their move. But marching at night over the area, where the enemy's campfires were always within a half-mile of each other, and with the areas between campsites heavily patrolled, the prince's party nonetheless decided to make an effort to break through.

For several nights at the end of July, Charles and his companions very nearly fell into the hands of other enemies. On several occasions, wrote one of those who stood faithfully at his side, "they passed four lines of troops, creeping on their hands and feet betwixt the sentries, only just managing to slip through the net" (Maclean, 1988, 269–270).

In the most famous episode of his escape, Charles was forced to disguise himself as an Irish maid, Betty Burke, in order to make his way to the relative safety of Skye, further to the north, which offered him his only chance of obtaining a government permit to move through the area. At first his companion, Flora Macdonald, was reluctant to take part in such a dangerous plan, which would have brought a savage reprisal from the British authorities if they were caught. And when news filtered through that there were as many as 2,300 government soldiers on the island looking for them, the plan seemed even more foolhardy. But she was eventually won over by a simple argument: Her part in such an escape bid would bring

her not only lasting honor but would also make her name immortal. After hiding first under a rock and then in an abandoned hut, Charles managed once again to evade his enemies, though only just, for soon after he made his getaway his allies on the island, who had helped him prepare his escape, were arrested.

As he traveled across Skye, Charles assumed another identity, this time posing as Lewie Caw, the servant of Malcolm Macleod, the captain who was showing him the way. Macleod gave Charles instructions on how to play the part, and Charles walked at a respectful distance behind Malcolm, carrying the baggage and always ready, if they were stopped, to sit quietly a few paces away.

By the end of September, when Charles finally escaped to France, picked up by two French ships that had managed to find a way through the British lines, he had been on the run for six months and had endured not only constant danger but also very considerable physical hardship. He had often lived in the open and had traveled over some of the most arduous, if spectacular, terrain in western Europe. And he left behind a legend that has formed an indelible part of Scottish tradition and folklore.

References: Maclean, Fitzroy. *Bonnie Prince Charlie.* London: Weidenfeld and Nicholson, 1988.

CHARLES STUART (1630–1685)

During the political upheavals of England in the 1650s, the young Prince Charles Stuart, later Charles II, was forced to escape the Republican army whose rule he sought to challenge.

Charles's flight began after his army, made up mainly of Scots, was defeated by the revolutionary forces at the town of Worcester in January 1651. After being proclaimed king of Scotland at the beginning of the year, Charles led his army south of the border but failed to find the popular endorsement he had hoped for, finding instead that most people regarded his soldiers only as a foreign invasion force. After less than one day of battle, he

Before becoming king in 1660, Prince Charles Stuart, later Charles II, had a series of remarkable adventures and narrow escapes from the republican forces that were searching high and low for him. Here, he is welcomed back to England. (North Wind Picture Archives)

and the remnants of his army fled through the single city gate still under their control. He spent the next six weeks living off his wits in a desperate attempt to elude Oliver Cromwell's men, who were following in hot pursuit.

Though Cromwell offered a generous reward of £1,000 for his capture, Charles had to rely throughout this period on the refuge and guidance of total strangers. Charles spent his first day on the run in the hands of a local Catholic family in Shropshire, the Penderells, who took him to a desolate spot in the nearby Boscobel Wood while enemy soldiers combed the surrounding area for him. With Richard Penderell—one of the five brothers in the family—he then attempted to cross the Severn River but was thwarted by a miller who heard a noise and chased them off. "So we fell-a-running, both of us, up the lane as long as we could run, it being very deep and very dirty," (Falkus 1972, 48) Charles recalled years later

when, with a mixture of pride and nostalgia, he related some of his experiences.

His brief but famous sojourn in an oak tree came the following day when, having returned to the Penderells' house, it became clear that even more enemy soldiers were moving through the area searching for him. In desperation, his hosts mentioned that a nearby oak tree was large enough to hide two people, and within minutes Charles and a Royalist soldier he had met the previous night took shelter there, taking enough food and water with them to last two days. They hid just in time, since the soldiers arrived soon afterward, wholly unaware that they were being watched by their quarry.

When the soldiers had gone elsewhere to continue their search, the fugitives made their way to the home of another known Royalist sympathizer in the area, a Colonel Lane. It was possible, argued the colonel, that Charles would be able to travel part of the way in a simple disguise. The colonel's daughter, Jane Lane, was authorized by the Cromwell government to go as far as Bristol with a servant, and Charles could simply disguise himself as "Will Jackson" and go with her. From Bristol, Lane argued, it would then be possible for Charles to be taken to France.

Charles later described one unnerving experience that took place during his flight to Bristol. Though he was convinced that he was unrecognizable in his disguise, he wrote that he once found himself in conversation with one of his former soldiers who had fought at Worcester: "I asked him what kind of man (the King) was. To which he answered by describing exactly both my clothes and my horse; and then looking upon me he told me that the King was at least three fingers taller than I. Upon which, I made what haste I could out of the buttery for fear that he should indeed know me, as being more afraid when I knew he was one of our own soldiers than when I took him for one of his enemy."

Unable to find a boat in Bristol that could take him to the safety of the Continent, he continued his journey to Bridport in Dorset. But still he found himself in the midst of his enemies, and he even walked into an inn that was packed full of soldiers, forcing him to make a hurried exit and making the soldiers "very angry with me for my rudeness" as a consequence. It was only when he arrived in Brighton a few days later that he was at last able to find a sailor whom he could trust to take him out of the country.

Having been aided by so many English Catholics while he fled Cromwell's army and drawn to Catholicism during his years in exile, Charles later felt drawn to repay them by advocating a greater degree of toleration than they had hitherto enjoyed, a policy that was to sharply heighten political tensions.

References: Falkus, Christopher. *The Life and Times of Charles II*. London: Weidenfeld and Nicolson, 1972.

Fea, Allan. *The Flight of the King*. London: Methuen, 1908.

Hutton, Ronald. *Charles II*. Oxford: Oxford University Press, 1990.

Matthews, William. *Charles II's Escape from Worcester: A Collection of Narratives Assembled by Samual Pepys*. Berkeley and Los Angeles: University of California Press, 1966.

CHAVASSE, NOEL
(1884–1917)

Though the histories of both world wars are filled with stories of great heroism, the rescues undertaken by Noel Chavasse, one of the only three individuals to be twice awarded the Victoria Cross, are remarkable.

After an academically successful career at Magdalen College School, Oxford, Chavasse qualified as a doctor in Liverpool and ran for his country at the 1908 Olympic Games before volunteering to join the army at the outbreak of war in August 1914. He appears to have shared the views of many of his contemporaries: revulsion at the prospect of war but a sense of patriotism and duty toward what were at the time seen as his country's best interests.

As a member of the medical teams that accompanied the forward infantry units, Chavasse's task was to rescue wounded British soldiers. This was not just a case of waiting for others to bring them back from frontline positions to hospitals some distance away or of venturing out to them after military objectives had been secured. Instead it meant that, together with other members of his unit, whom he was required to organize, he had to venture into the battle zones—no man's land—often when fighting was at its height. The life expectancy of the unit's members, not surprisingly, was the same as that of every member of the infantry: only a few weeks.

Chavasse won a Military Cross in 1915 for exceptional gallantry in rescuing injured soldiers at the battle of Hooge. In the official history of his unit, the Liverpool Scottish, "special mention" was given to the stretcher bearers, especially to Chavasse's "inspiring example" and "untiring efforts." The following year his work received acknowledgment for its exceptional bravery. In August, at the battle of the Somme, one onlooker recorded how one night Chavasse had "carried and used his electric torch as he walked about between the trenches, whistling and calling out to the wounded men to indicate their whereabouts. . . . Ignoring the snipers' bullets and any sporadic fusillade, he carried on with his work of succour throughout the hours of darkness" (*London Gazette*, 23 October 1916).

Chavasse himself recorded some of the terrible suffering that he saw and tried to alleviate on the Western Front. In 1916 at Delville Wood, near Passchendaele, he noted that he came upon one injured soldier, and finding that "his arm was all but off and was only a source of danger, I cut it off with a pair of scissors and did the stump up. We had to do everything by the light of an electric torch and when we got a stretcher, it took two hours to get him out of the mud" (Clayton 1979, 163).

The citation for his first Victoria Cross gave an example of the exceptional courage that he had shown during more than a year at the front line. "During an attack," it ran, "he tended the wounded in the open all day, under heavy fire, frequently in view of the enemy" and on one occasion "carried an urgent case 500 yards into safety under heavy fire," though himself receiving a shrapnel wound in the process (*London Gazette,* 14 September 1917).

Chavasse was killed by incoming shellfire during the battle of Ypres in August 1917, aged 33, shortly after winning his second Victoria Cross. The remains of his body were buried and marked with a simple cross.

References: Clayton, Ann. *Noel Chavasse: Double VC.* London: Leo Cooper, 1979.

CHITRAL (1895)

At Chitral, in the far northwest corner of British India, a small garrison of British officers and their loyal Indian troops held out desperately against a savage enemy force, but were rescued at the last minute by relief forces that made extraordinary efforts to reach them.

Chitral had a clear strategic importance for the British governors of India. Because it was only a few miles from the Afghan border, in remote and inhospitable terrain, it presented the Russians with a clear opportunity to infiltrate hostile tribes from the surrounding regions to destabilize the whole of the Indian continent. So the British, always wary about Russian intentions, were alarmed when in the spring of 1895 the rebellious local rulers Sher, Umra Khan, and the Amir Nizam sought to pry the garrison from British rule and claim it for themselves.

The crisis broke out on 3 March when word reached the British fortress at Chitral that Sher was approaching them with a large party of followers prepared to take the garrison by storm. The officer in charge, Maj. George Robertson, sent out a reconnaissance party. The sheer ferocity of the enemy force quickly became apparent when the party was driven back into the fortress after 23 of its number had been killed and 33 wounded in a skirmish with an enemy force that they had gravely underestimated.

A rescue party from Gilgit, the nearest British garrison, also met an unfortunate fate. The party, made up of Kashmiri soldiers and led by two British officers, had been ambushed along the way but had managed to take up a defensive position and fight off their attackers. Seeing that the defenders were well trained and determined, the enemy commander decided to try to trick them. He sent a messenger under a white flag to tell the rescue party that a deal had been struck with Robertson and that they were guaranteed a safe passage to Chitral, and after being given the food and water they desperately needed, the two British officers reluctantly agreed to trust their enemy. But during a game of polo—a locally played game) that the Chitrali commander ordered as a celebration of the ostensible "accord"—the Kashmiri soldiers were caught off-guard and the two officers were kidnapped. Without officers and surrounded, the Kashmiris were soon overrun and slaughtered; the two Britons remained prisoners.

Meanwhile in Chitral, Robertson faced an increasingly difficult situation. There were nearly 400 Indian troops, five British officers, and a number of noncombatants all crammed into a fortress only 80 yards square, and he knew that the garrison's food supplies would last a month at most before they began to starve. The enemy was able to hide snipers in the tall, thick trees outside the fort, and a number of buildings near the fortress walls gave ample cover to any enemy attack. But though the odds were against them, Robertson defiantly gave the order to raise a makeshift Union Jack from one of the wooden towers and let it flutter splendidly in the winds for their enemy to see.

It was not long before Sher ordered an outright attack. Though all the assaults were beaten back, his forces inched closer and closer to the garrison walls until, on 5 April, they had managed to capture an old summerhouse that was only 50 yards from the main gate. This allowed them to make a particularly determined assault two days later, when a small party managed to creep from the summerhouse to the garrison wall wholly unobserved and to use firebombs to try to set the wooden fortress alight. But Robertson directed an equally determined effort to stop the fire from spreading that just managed to save the day. But after the Chitralis nearly succeeded in tunneling into the garrison from the summerhouse, Robertson knew that their days were numbered unless a relief force broke through soon.

Unknown to Robertson, two relief columns were now on their way, one from Gilgit in the east and the other from Peshawar to the south, to rescue Robertson from the same horrible fate that Gen. Charles Gordon had suffered in the Sudan only a decade earlier. Even in the spring, both rescue parties had to contend with formidable obstacles, mainly the deep snow over the perilous, mountain-top roads, none of which were free from the risk of ambush.

The Peshawar column, under Maj. Gen. Sir Robert Low, managed to storm the 3,500-foot high Malakand Pass, taking the 12,000-strong enemy force by surprise after a diversionary attack was made further to the west. Though 70 Britons died in this battle, huge numbers of their enemy were cut down, and the rest fled into the neighboring mountains, leaving the relief force with only one more major obstacle before they reached Chitral.

Hundred of miles away the Gilgit column, under Colonel James Kelly, had man-

aged to cross a 10,000-foot pass, sleeping in the open at night in atrocious conditions, but the real test—the 12,000-foot Shandur Pass, which they would have to cross with their two mountain guns—was still to come. At their first attempt the slopes and the snow, often more than six feet deep, proved too much for the men and their mules (two of which had already fallen down a 100-foot slope into deep snow) and they were driven back. But after a two-day effort, the heavy guns were at last dragged, sometimes carried in the arms of the soldiers, up and over the mountain pass. It was an astonishing feat, even though the following day Kelly's doctors had to treat 52 men for snow blindness and frostbite. As soon as word reached London, it was hailed as "one of the most remarkable marches in history" (Hopkirk 1990, 497).

As the two relief forces fought their way against the elements and the enemy forces, matters were desperate for the defenders of Chitral, who had no idea of the efforts were being made to rescue them. Many were ill or wounded, and all were reduced to eating horse meat in order to survive. The poor hygiene in the crowded garrison, and the rotting carcasses of dead people and animals, also presented a grave risk of disease. But just as matters were reaching the breaking point, their enemy suddenly and unexpectedly collapsed. On 18 April, Robertson wrote afterward, "word flashed through the fort that all our besiegers had fled" (Hopkirk 1990, 497). Having heard of the rapid advance of Kelly and Low, the attackers had quickly fled to the safety of the nearby mountains.

When Kelly's force marched into Chitral on 20 April, several days ahead of Low's, they found Robertson and his men to be "walking skeletons who could not have held out much more than a few days longer." But their shocking condition did not stop Robertson from greeting his rescuers in typically Victorian fashion, merely saluting them and apologizing that he could not offer them better hospitality.

Meanwhile, the British public had been set alight by the story of the dramatic rescue of Chitral, and a jubilant Queen Victoria was preparing to award numerous honors and titles to those who had taken part. Umra Khan was captured by the British, but with characteristic leniency they merely marched him off to exile in India. Sher fled to the safety of a hideout in Afghanistan, releasing the two British officers he had captured en route from Gilgit. The rescue of Chitral earned a place in the annals of British military history.

See also: Bailey, Lt. Col. Frederick; Kabul; Kandahār
References: Hopkirk, Peter. *The Great Game.* Oxford: Oxford University Press, 1990.

CHRASTNY, NIKOLAUS (C. 1945–)

In 1987 Nikolaus Chrastny, a criminal mastermind, escaped custody in Britain while awaiting trial because of his ability to forge friendships with those who were guarding him.

Chrastny, a German national of Czech origin, had been arrested in London in June 1987 as a result of police undercover surveillance work that had obtained evidence that he stood at the center of a massive, worldwide network of drug smuggling. Held first at Rotherham, he was then sent to a police cell at Dewsbury, in Yorkshire, where his presence was kept a strict secret to avoid any attempted rescues.

Left alone in his cell for long periods, Chrastny was able to saw through the inch-thick bars on his cell gate, which opened out onto one of the main thoroughfares in the cell blocks. He worked late at night and covered the noise with his television or radio, probably finishing in only a few days.

In order to make his escape Chrastny now used a great asset: charm. The police officers around him appear to have taken a liking to this international villain, and as a result they agreed to many of his requests. He obtained plasticine by claiming that he needed it to work on artistic models, and he used it to put the cut bars together again. He was even allowed out of his cell, into the corridor outside, and was able to get an idea of the layout of the compound where he was being held.

On the morning of 5 October 1987, the same day he was scheduled to go to London to make a court appearance, the police officers who arrived to fetch Chrastny found an empty cell. Their amazement was heightened because there was no obvious escape route, since the escapee had put the bars he had sawed off back with plasticine. In the cell they found only a note that stated that he "had not taken this step lightly" and that he apologized for "any inconvenience" he had caused. A phone call from the escapee to the police station later that day reiterated this message, and perhaps the escapee's sense of humor.

Nothing was ever heard of Nikolaus Chrastny ever again. A master of disguise and of many languages, and backed by very considerable wealth and contacts, he simply disappeared without trace.

References: Bean, J. P. *Over the Wall: True Stories of the Master Jail Breakers.* London: Headline, 1994.

CHURCHILL, SIR WINSTON L. S. (1874–1965)

Serving in the most remote and dangerous corners of the British Empire in his youth, Sir Winston Churchill had some lucky escapes from bitter and fanatical enemies.

In his memoirs Churchill recorded one narrow escape that took place during an Indian Army offensive against rebellious tribesmen in the Mamund Valley, near Chitral, in 1897. As he and his fellow soldiers fought pitched gun battles against the tribesmen, mostly native Indians, Churchill suddenly saw half a dozen Pathan swordsmen rushing out of cover and killing another soldier, and though he knew that his companions had fled at their approach he now "forgot everything else at this moment except a desire to kill this man" (Churchill 1990, 157) who had dealt the mortal blow.

Churchill, a champion fencer at school, drew his long cavalry sword and challenged the Pathan, who was now standing only some 20 yards away. As the tribesman waited for the young Churchill to mount his attack, he picked up a large stone and hurled it at him, narrowly missing, before drawing his own sword. At this moment

Sir Winston Churchill, shown in South Africa during the Boer War, served in the most remote and dangerous corners of the British Empire in his youth and had some lucky escapes from various enemies. (Archive Photos)

Churchill lost his enthusiasm for hand-to-hand combat, so he drew his pistol and fired, but to his astonishment he saw the tribesman still standing before him, as if nothing had happened. Again he fired, but still there was no result. After the third shot the Pathan ran back two or three yards and hid behind a rock, giving Churchill a chance to look around to see where his colleagues had gone. To his horror he suddenly realized he was all alone, facing a growing number of tribesmen who were only a very short distance in front of him. He turned and ran, and even though "there were bullets everywhere" (Churchill 1990, 157) he managed to reach some of his fellow soldiers, who were Sikh soldiers, further down the mountain slope. Together they managed to move slowly over a distance of nearly a mile toward the relative safety of their own lines.

Two years later, while working as a war correspondent, Churchill made a more dramatic escape from captivity by the other great enemy of the empire—the Boers. Captured after an ambush on an armored train as it moved through Natal and feeling deeply depressed by the boredom and sense of waste induced by captivity, he vowed to escape, having found the experience more "painful and humiliating" than any other he had experienced.

He was detained in a former state model school in Pretoria, and he put his escape plan into action on 12 December 1899, less than a month after his capture. After carefully watching the daily routines of the prison guards, he noticed that from a particular point on their regular patrols they were unable to see the top of a few yards of a section of the wall. If he could scale the wall just as they reached that crucial point, he reckoned, then he would be able to escape and head for the Portuguese frontier, 280 miles away, and from there back to the British lines.

On the night of 12 December the young Churchill strolled across the quadrangle before hiding himself in a small office by the perimeter wall. Carefully watching the sentries through a small window, he made his move when the two sentries, only 15 yards away, turned their backs and started chatting. Though he caught his waistcoat on the ornamental metal work on the top and had to pause to free himself, the sentries failed to see him.

Once over the wall he still had to get past another sentry, who was standing by a gate that opened onto a road. Knowing that he had virtually no chance of slipping by in the same way as before, he decided to bluff his way past. Putting his hat on, he strode straight past the sentry, less than five yards away, and walked straight out to the road, forcing himself to resist the impulse to look at the sentry as he walked past and to run when he reached the road.

But he still had a very long way to go. He was now in the heart of Boer territory, with no contacts; he spoke no Dutch or Afrikaans; and he knew that there would soon be a massive search for him. With more than 300 miles to go before he could reach Portuguese territory, the key to escape, he decided, was to contact some of the British citizens he knew lived within Boer territory, working in the mines as engineers and in other technical roles. Hungry, thirsty, and tired, he decided to take a considerable risk, and knocked on the door of one of the houses around the mining area he walked past, hoping he would get lucky.

Again Churchill was blessed with good fortune and by chance met John Howard, manager of the Transvaal Collieries, who had become a naturalized burgher of the Transvaal some years before but who was British by origin and had no real sympathy with the Boers in their war. While Howard and Churchill prepared the escape plan, Churchill was hidden at the bottom of one of the mines and generously supplied with candles, whisky, cigars, and good food.

On the morning of 19 December, several days after he had firstly broken free of his imprisonment, he was able to leave his hiding place and head for home. In the neighborhood of the mine was a Dutchman who was sending a consignment of wool into Portuguese territory on a train that would allow Churchill to hide himself as it headed toward his own lines.

As the train left Boer territory it was subjected to an extensive search that forced him to hide under a piece of sacking, scarcely daring to move. But after two and a half days on board, the train moved on into Portuguese territory, prompting the escapee to push his head out from under the tarpaulin "weary, dirty, hungry but free once more" (Churchill 1990, 205).

Churchill's escape from the Boers made him something of a national hero. "I was received," he wrote in his memoirs, "as if I had won a great victory. The harbour [in Durban] was decorated with flags. Bands and crowds thronged the quays. The Admiral, the General, the Mayor pressed on board to grasp my hand. I was nearly torn to pieces by enthusiastic kindness." He also noted how his escape had a highly positive effect on his career prospects. By escaping he gained a public reputation or notoriety that made him acceptable as a candidate in a great many constituencies.

See also: Haldane, Capt. Aylmer
References: Churchill, Winston L. S. *The Boer War: London to Ladysmith via Pretoria.* London: Mandarin, 1990.
————. *My Early Life.* London: Mandarin, 1990.

CODY, WILLIAM F. (1845–1917)

Better known as Buffalo Bill, William F. Cody was a miner in the Colorado gold fields, a Pony Express rider, a buffalo hunter for the railroad construction camps, an army scout, and the organizer and star of his own Wild West Show. During his long life of adventure, described with veracity in his memoirs, he made some remarkable escapes and rescues.

One day in 1860, before he had become well known in the American West, Cody escaped from a gang of horse dealers whom he happened to encounter and whom he instantly recognized as wanted men. They were, he wrote, "as rough and villainous

A 1900 lithograph of William F. Cody, better known as Buffalo Bill, one of the most famous figures of the Wild West, who made some remarkable escapes and rescues during his long life of adventure. (Library of Congress)

looking men as I ever saw in my life" (Cody, 1991), and he instantly felt that the quicker he got away from them the better.

He played innocent, giving no indication that he had recognized them, and told them he had to leave them to fetch his horse, which he had left a short distance away. The gang agreed, but sent two of their number to accompany him.

Fortunately the gang had not felt it necessary to search the young Cody, whose apparent innocence had misled them, and they did not realize that he was carrying two pistols. As he led the two men through the dusk toward his horse, he pulled out his Colt revolver and struck one of them on the back of the head, knocking him senseless to the ground. Turning around, he then had just enough time to shoot the other gangster dead before he fired his own gun. He then disappeared into the night on the back of his horse.

But Cody heard the rest of the gang in hot pursuit not far behind. He dismounted and gave his horse a good slap, sending it cantering on alone. Climbing quickly up the mountain he was passing, he watched the gangsters pursuing his horse, which they could hear in front of them.

A few years later he made another remarkable escape. Captured by Indians near Fort Larned and taken to their chief, Buffalo Bill explained that he had been looking for cattle when he was captured, knowing that the Indians had not had any supply of meat for several weeks and that they would undoubtedly be interested to know more. Just as he had hoped, the Indian chief allowed him to go and fetch the cattle, giving him the chance he needed to escape.

Though he was escorted by a group of 10 or 15 Indians, Cody managed to move a short distance ahead of them. When he was out of sight, he forced his mule to canter at top speed toward Fort Larned. But his escape was a close run thing because he was pursued by the Indians for nearly six miles and was never more than half a mile ahead of them.

Cody was also involved in the rescue of two Westerners who had been kidnapped by Indians. On this occasion he joined the forces of General Carr to raid an Indian camp that they knew harbored several white captives, whose footprints were unmistakable clues to their whereabouts. Cody's role on this mission was to secretly move several miles in advance of the main column in order to identify the key Indian positions and the Indians' subsequent movements once the attack started.

Following Cody's advice, the main force was able to advance within a mile of the Indian camp before starting their attack, killing many and forcing the others to flee. Soon after capturing the position, the company found two white women, both Swedish, one of whom had just been killed and the other wounded. It was the end of another dramatic episode in the extraordinary life of Buffalo Bill.

See also: Bonney, William H.; Logan, Harvey
References: Burke, John. Buffalo Bill: The Noblest Whiteskin. London: Cassell, 1974.
Cody, William. The Life of Buffalo Bill. London: Senate, 1994.

COLDITZ (1940–1945)

The prison camp at Colditz was, like Stalag Luft III, a *Sonderlager*—designed to be an inescapable prison to hold the undetainable. But even the most determined efforts of the German authorities could not stop some of the prisoners from getting away.

All of its prisoners, who were drawn from all over the world, had made previous bids for freedom and were felt to require extra supervision if they were to be kept in captivity. Unwittingly, the Germans put together a remarkable collection of talented and experienced would-be escapees, and by the time Colditz was finally liberated by the U.S. Army in April 1945, 27 prisoners—11 Frenchmen, 8 Britons, 6 Dutch, 1 Pole, and 1 Belgian—had made it back to Allied lines.

This was no mean feat. An entire German battalion of 500 men was deployed at Colditz, and extra security measures and roll calls were introduced. Overall, the task of escaping was infinitely hazardous, as

Michael Sinclair was to discover in September 1944. Sinclair had a formidable reputation for escaping, and at the time of his last attempt he had already made seven unsuccessful attempts, during one of which—an attempt to impersonate a German sergeant major—a sentry had shot him in the chest. His last effort was a brave but foolhardy attempt to scale the camp's barbed wire in broad daylight, using thick gloves to do so. Though he was nearly out of range by the time the German sentries could fire after him, a bullet struck him on the shoulder and was deflected into his heart.

The sheer difficulty of finding a way out required exceptional resources as well as daring. Some got out by feigning medical problems, usually gall-bladder trouble, which was difficult for the German doctors to disprove. In one particularly distressing escape attempt a prisoner feigned madness. He played the part so well that he convinced the prison doctors and the specialist consultants who were sent to examine him. But when he was taken from the camp and sent to a special hospital, as he had planned, his "escape" caused no jubilation among his fellow prisoners, who had realized that by pretending to be mad he had in fact driven himself insane. The senior officers at the camp forbade any similar attempts at escape.

Many other determined attempts to escape were made by Colditz prisoners. On the night of 29 May 1941 eight British and four Polish officers made their way through a tunnel that led from the prisoners' canteen. They bribed a German guard near the exit to overlook whatever he might see. Unhappily, the sentry kept the money he had been given but also told his superiors, and all were arrested as they crawled out of the tunnel onto the lawn.

A later escape bid by Major Pat Reid, head of the escape committee, was more successful. An engineer by training, Reid's practiced eye had located an unused passageway that ended in an attic over the Germans' guardhouse, and he recognized an opportunity to get out. Through this passage he sent Airey Neave, his deputy, and a

Dutch officer, Tony Luteyn. Both spoke impeccable German and both were dressed in homemade German officers' uniforms, which would not have stood up to a careful scrutiny but which looked convincing enough in the dark. With extraordinary self-confidence, Neave returned the salute of the sentry outside the guardroom door before strolling down a side path toward the married officers' quarters. Once out of the camp they traveled by train. The two men managed to survive a police check at Ulm by walking out of a government office through the back door, just as the Germans were getting suspicious. Soon afterward they bluffed their way past German officials at Singen, close to the Swiss frontier, and they reached Switzerland a mere 48 hours after leaving Colditz.

Another remarkable escape was made by Billie Stephens, an imprisoned naval officer captured after the Saint-Nazaire raid. On the night of 14 October 1942, together with Reid and two other officers, Johnny Wardle and Littledale, Stephens carried out a daring plan that kept the Germans at bay in the most ingenious way: by using the prisoners' orchestra. Conducted by the downed fighter pilot Douglas Bader, who was carefully watching the Germans' every move from a special vantage point, the orchestra would suddenly stop whenever he deemed it too dangerous for them to carry on with their escape attempt and would pick up again when it was safe.

After bending the bars of a window that overlooked the prison courtyard and crawling one by one onto a roof, the four men hid in a shed, using the musical signals as a guide, before finding their way into a cellar with an air vent just large enough for them to squeeze through. It was a case of "naked men being squeezed through a hole in the wall," Reid later said, "like toothpaste out of a tube." At 3:30 A.M., more than nine hours after they had begun their escape bid, they at last found their way to the outside of the fortress wall.

They made it past the next several obstacles—an 18-foot wall surrounded by a moat, the German barracks, and guard dogs—before reaching the final barrier to the outside, a 10-foot-tall outer wall with barbed wire coiled on top. By the time they had climbed over that it was 5:15 in the morning, and they had only a few hours to get out of the area before their absence was noted. To lessen the risks of being spotted en route, the men now split up, Reid going with Wardle and Stephens with Littledale. Using their immaculate forged papers, all the result of hours of hard work by their former colleagues, and a small-scale map and homemade compass, Reid and Wardle were able to make their way by foot and train to Singen, near the border with Switzerland. Stephens and Littledale crossed the border soon after.

At this point Stephens and Littledale had a narrow escape from the German sentries who were patrolling the border. Hiding in a wood only miles from their destination, they were found by a dog, which alerted a nearby German guard. But though they were both arrested at gunpoint, quick thinking and brilliant acting saved the day, for they pretended to be drunken Frenchmen, and the sentry left them to do what they wanted him to think they were doing: staggering back into Switzerland after a brief trip across the border. So on 20 October, a mere 24 hours after they had left the camp, Stephens and Littledale arrived on Swiss soil.

See also: The Great Escape; LeBrun, Lt. Pierre
References: Baybutt, Ron. *Colditz: The Great Escapes.* Boston: Little, Brown, 1982.

COLLET, CHARLES
(C. 1894–1951)

One prisoner of the Germans in World War I undertook what has been called "one of the cheekiest escapes" by concealing himself from his captors and hiding inside the prison camp for three whole weeks before making his getaway.

Charles Collet, a senior noncommissioned officer (NCO) of France's 119th Infantry regiment, knew that the success of his fourth escape bid was dependent upon his receipt of a parcel from friends in France who had sent him maps and other tools he needed to make his getaway. Unfortunately, while the parcel was on its way he was informed by the camp authorities that he was to be transferred to another place of detention from which, he feared, it would be much more difficult to escape, even if the parcel caught up with him there at all. So how could he avoid being sent away to the new quarters, while at the same time staying in the camp long enough for the parcel to reach him?

Collet's solution to the problem was simple but ingenious. If he could hide from the Germans but remain within the camp, then he would avoid being sent to the other quarters as his captors wanted but could have the parcel smuggled to him when it arrived. When he received it, he could then make his second getaway—out of the camp altogether.

Having received permission to leave his punishment cell—where he had been held since his last escape bid—to go to his hut to get some personal belongings, his fellow prisoners put a carefully arranged plan into action. They distracted his escort and positioned themselves in just the right places to screen Collet while he slipped through the hut window and ran to the latrines. Here he pulled up a plank that allowed him access to a cupboard in which he could just hide himself. After dark he made his way to another hiding place, under the floor of one of the huts, made comfortable with palliasses and blankets. He stayed there for a week, unseen by the Germans, who searched high and low for him and came to the conclusion that he had made his getaway.

Having completed his first "escape" successfully, Collet had to wait another 15 days for his parcel to arrive. As he had been promised, it contained two maps and detailed information about how to make his way back to France.

The day after the parcel had reached him Collet joined a party of prisoners in order to obtain access to a storehouse where they stored their tools. But when the time came for them to make their way back to their huts for evening roll call, he stayed behind and was locked inside. That night he got through a trap door and climbed the perimeter fence, nearly three weeks after the Germans had mistakenly assumed he had made his way outside. This was his fourth attempt to escape, and he was free at last.

References: Neave, Airey. *They Have Their Exits.* London: Hodder and Stoughton, 1969; New York: Beagle Books, 1971.

Reid, Pat. *The Colditz Story.* London: Hodder and Stoughton, 1952.

COLUMBIA PRISON (1865)

For those prisoners who were held by either side during the U.S. Civil War, the best chance of escape often came when they were being moved from one place to another. This was in part because of the difficulty of supervising very large numbers of prisoners over long distances but also because during their journey they were often guarded by troops of very poor quality.

One well-documented case concerns the evacuation of prisoners from the Confederate prison in Columbia, South Carolina, to another camp at Charlotte in February 1865. Although 1,185 prisoners were moved out on 14 February, only 1,003 reached their destination two days later. Nearly all of the rest had escaped, either by staying behind in Columbia, concealed in the prison roof, or by disappearing en route.

The officer in charge was instantly charged with inefficiency but vigorously protested his innocence. The camp at Charlotte, he argued, was a most inadequate and unsafe place to keep them, being just an old field that was guarded by wholly inadequate soldiers. Though he had taken "every diligence" to shake them up, he added, ordering them with "urgency" to maintain more vigilance, he could not stop them from taking the prisoners' bribes and disappearing into the night along with them. Nor could he punish any of those who remained, he said, because the remaining guards were all working double duties in order to make up for the numbers they lacked.

See also: Andersonville; Conley, Capt. Edward
References: Denney, Robert E. *Civil War: Prisons and Escapes. A Day-by-Day Chronicle.* New York: Sterling, 1995.

CONLEY, CAPT. EDWARD

One well-documented escape during the U.S. Civil War is that of Captain Conley, who in October 1864 was very lucky to have got away from Confederate captivity with his life.

An officer in the 101st Pennsylvanian Volunteers, Conley was on a train, en route to the prison in Columbia, South Carolina, when he seized his chance. Though the carriages seemed well guarded, each with one armed guard inside and another on top, he and an acquaintance saw an opportunity. Because the guard in his carriage was standing at the front and because the guard in the carriage behind was at its rear, there was a blind spot between them. So, standing at the back of his carriage, he and a few acquaintances waited until the train stopped before making their move.

When at last the train slowed down and halted, at the Congaree River, they slipped out of the carriage onto the track and waited at its side for the train to move off. In such a moment of crisis, recorded Conley, a few minutes seemed almost infinite, but when at last the train did move off, he was horrified to see an armed guard taking careful aim at him. But Conley just managed to dart away as the guard squeezed the trigger, allowing the bullet to tear through his leg but probably saving his life.

See also: Andersonville; Camp Morton; Columbia Prison

References: Denney, Robert E. *Civil War: Prisons and Escapes. A Day-by-Day Chronicle.* New York: Sterling, 1995.

"COOPER, D. B." (C. 1925–?)

The disappearance of the mysterious skyjacker known only by his alias, "D. B. Cooper," was made possible by the novel means he used to hijack a U.S. airliner and disappear midflight with more than $200,000 in his possession.

The story began on 24 November 1971 when a man about 45 years old got on board a Northwest Orient Airlines plane in Portland, Oregon, using a ticket that had been bought under the name Dan Cooper. By all accounts he appeared wholly innocuous, wearing a dark suit, dark tie, white shirt, and sunglasses and chain-smoking from the moment he got on board.

After ordering a drink, he calmly handed a note to the flight attendant, Flo Schaffner, that read, "Miss, I've got a bomb, come sit next to me—you're being hijacked." Opening his briefcase, he then showed the attendant a couple of red cylinders, some wires, and a battery, enough evidence to make the crew take his threats seriously. With great reluctance, the captain radioed the authorities, who agreed to meet Mr. Cooper's demand for $200,000 and four parachutes.

The aircraft landed at Seattle-Tacoma Airport, where the 36 passengers and two flight attendants were released and the money given to "D. B." The sole passenger then demanded that the plane be flown to Mexico, agreeing that it could stop at Reno to refuel.

About 40 minutes after the plane left Seattle Dan Cooper made his escape. Telling the remaining flight attendant to go to the front of the plane and pull the first-class curtain shut, he lowered the rear stairs of the Boeing 727 (the only plane on which this could be done) and disappeared. When the jet landed in Reno, the stairs were down and the passenger was gone, together with the money and two parachutes.

No one has discovered what happened to Dan Cooper after his dramatic exit from the plane or anything more about his true identity. No body has ever been found in the wilderness area over which he bailed out, although in 1980 $5,800 of his money was found by a boy playing on the banks of the Columbia River. Although some have called him one of the most audacious criminals of all time, others have called him the most foolish, arguing that his chances of surviving a drop, at night, of 10,000 feet, wearing only a business suit and loafers, were negligible, especially since he would have landed in a forest in midwinter with no food or survival gear. An extensive search was mounted, but no clues were ever found, and the FBI has admitted that the case, America's only unsolved skyjacking, will remain open "probably forever."

Dan Cooper's escape did have one last-ing legacy. Shortly afterward, Boeing changed the design of its rear stairway, adding a latching device that prevents it from being lowered in flight. But it was too late to stop Cooper, who had identified this weakness before the manufacturers and police authorities.

See also: Air, escape by

CORREGIDOR (1942)

After the Pacific island of Corregidor fell to the Japanese army in May 1942, a few of the 11,000 Americans who were captured and imprisoned managed to escape. Two of those who did so were 2d Lt. Edgar D. Whitcomb and Capt. William Harris, both of whom swam the eight miles to the Bataan Peninsula.

The two men left Corregidor with a great deal of confidence in their swimming prowess—both had practiced every day even while in captivity—but knowing the dangers ahead. During their crossing they swam into heavy seas, slowing them up and forcing them out of each other's sight for a time. They were also in constant danger of being attacked by sharks. But after several grueling hours they eventually reached the shore of Bataan and were able to head for U.S. lines.

See also: MacArthur, Douglas
References: Whitcomb, Edgar D. Escape from Corregidor. Chicago: Henry Regnery, 1958.

CORTÉS, HERNÁN (C. 1485–1547)

A sixteenth-century Spanish expeditionary force in South America was almost entirely annihilated by the native tribesmen who surrounded them. They were inspired to flee by the prophecies of an astrologer in their ranks. Their leader, Hernán Cortés, was one of the few to escape.

The Spanish armies of the sixteenth cen-tury sought to conquer much of Central and South America to find and exploit its reserves of gold. One such expeditionary force, under General Cortés, was sur-rounded and besieged in Tenochtitlán (in present-day Mexico) in the summer of 1520.

Before long casualties began to mount and supplies were depleted, and it became increasingly clear that the defenders would not be able to hold out much longer.

The Spanish leader's decision to escape from the city was prompted, at least in good measure, by the prophecies of one of his sol-diers, a man named Botello. Highly edu-cated and well versed in using complex fig-ures and astrology to demonstrate his predictions, Botello informed his leader that if they did not leave the city during one par-ticular night, they faced disaster. Hearing this, Cortés immediately ordered his men to construct a portable bridge, made from very strong forest timber, that could be placed over the canals to replace the bridges that their enemies had destroyed. Moving at night, he reckoned, would give them the best chance of not being seen.

Cortés's army, several hundred strong, set off at midnight, with each man carrying as much gold as he could. They moved as quietly as possible over the bridge and onto the bank opposite. But within minutes the enemy had seen them. One of their observers shouted at the top of his voice for his fellow tribesmen to join him in battle. "In an instant the enemy were upon us by land, and the lakes and canals were covered with canoes ... and attacked with redou-bled fury" (del Castillo 1928). Many of those who had managed to cross the river were caught in the hail of arrows fired by the natives. Others drowned, while some who launched a counterattack against the tribes suddenly found that their enemy had worked out an excellent tactic to counter their threat: They retreated into the water to escape the Spanish swords and then killed the Spaniards' horses with arrows.

Among those who did manage to escape was Cortés, together with his fellow senior officers, who spurred their horses on at full speed to escape the onslaught around them. As one survivor wrote: "The escape of such as were fortunate enough to effect it, was owing to God's mercy, who gave us force to do so. For the very sight of the number of the enemy who surrounded us, and carried off our companions in their canoes to sacri-fice was terrible" (del Castillo 1928).

References: del Castillo, Bernal Diaz. *The True Story of the Conquest of Mexico.* New York: Harper, 1928.

CRUMLIN ROAD PRISON (1971; 1981)

Two major breakouts of Irish Republican Army (IRA) terrorists have taken place in recent years from the maximum security prison in Crumlin Road, near Belfast.

In November 1971 seven prisoners escaped when they suddenly abandoned their game of soccer and ran toward the prison wall. With perfect timing, two rope ladders were thrown over the prison wall by their accomplices on the outside, and within minutes all of the seven men were over the wall and had been whisked away in the getaway cars, which were ready and waiting on the road outside.

Another escape, brutal and ruthless and in some ways similar to that made from the Maze Prison two years later, took place on 10 June 1981. The eight men who planned their getaway relied on a small number of firearms that were smuggled to them over a period of weeks by their visitors and with which they planned to seize several prison officers and steal their uniforms.

They made their move one afternoon when all eight men had gone to the visiting area to meet their lawyers. Paul Magee, one of the ringleaders, then took out a .25-caliber revolver and held it to the head of the prison officer who was escorting him, prompting his accomplice, Joe Dogherty, to do the same. The prisoners tied up the officers and the solicitors, took their uniforms, and headed for the two gates that were their last barriers to the outside.

At the first perimeter gate the officer on duty recognized one of the "officers" he saw walking toward him but found the barrel of a gun shoved into his stomach before he had a chance to raise the alarm. Nor was the guard at the second gate fooled, though he also was too late to do anything and was knocked unconscious by one of the escapees. But the suspicious behavior of the "officers" had prompted one other officer, watching nearby, to raise the alarm, forcing the prisoners to run as soon as they were past the second gate.

As the terrorists ran to a parking lot opposite the prison entrance, a fierce gunfight broke out between the IRA backup team, waiting to meet them, and the policemen who ran to stop them. But though the parking lot was soon surrounded and though the Royal Ulster Constabulary (RUC) riddled the IRA getaway car with submachine-gun bullets as it sped away, they could not stop them and, miraculously, did not even cause any casualties among the vehicle's desperate passengers. All eight of the prisoners escaped.

See also: Long Kesh Prison; Maze Prison

References: Bean, J. P. *Over the Wall: True Stories of the Master Jail Breakers.* London: Headline, 1994.

CUBA, ESCAPE FROM (1958–)

A fine line exists between audacious bravery and mere foolishness. But like some of those who fled the Iron Curtain, many Cuban dissidents have strayed perilously close to the dividing line in their determination to escape from their homeland.

Some have succeeded in escaping by sea, crossing the more than 90 miles of perilous water between Cuba and Florida. In August 1971 one family roped together six inner tubes to build a simple raft that allowed them to survive more than 11 days at sea before they were picked up by a passing oil tanker and taken to the United States. They were fortunate to have been found, since they were on the verge of collapsing from exhaustion, hunger, and hypothermia when they were discovered.

In the summer of 1969 one desperate teenager managed to escape by air. Armando Socarras Ramirez waited patiently in the grass at the end of the runway until an Iberian Airways DC8 was about to take off. He then ran to its wheels and hid inside its wheel well. He was well aware of the risks he was taking, feeling the scorching heat of the engines as he climbed inside and seeing that there would only be just enough room for him to squeeze in without being crushed. He had to contend not only with the extreme heat but also with temperatures of minus 41 degrees Celsius, and he soon realized that, dressed as he was only in summer shirts and trousers, he had not planned his escape properly. When the plane finally touched down at Madrid more than eight hours later, the ground crew found a nearly frozen body lying by the wheels. However, he was once again fit and well by the next day.

The most senior defector ever to flee from Cuba also flew out. On 29 May 1987 Gen. Raphael Del Pino put his wife and three children aboard a Cessna light aircraft in Havana for what seemed to be a routine flight. But the plane touched down 90 miles away at Key Largo, Florida. Cuba's leader, Fidel Castro, realized that the escape was a major blow both to morale and to his intelligence and military establishments, about which the defector knew almost everything. Already disillusioned by Castro's war in Angola—a war that seemed like an extravagant dream—Del Pino's patience had finally snapped when news reached him of his own son's death on the African battlefields.

One of the biggest single breakouts from Castro's Cuba took place in January 1969 when Eufemio Delgado hired a truck and, with 130 refugees packed in the back, headed toward the giant U.S. military base at Camanera. Though the perimeter was dotted with patrols and observation posts that would have daunted most people, Delgado drove up and down the road searching for the weakest point before making his move. Swerving the truck over the side of the road, he drove it full bore toward the perimeter fence. For a moment everything seemed to be going well, but when the vehicle plowed into a ditch and Cuban guards appeared on the horizon firing machine guns, the race to escape was plainly going to have a much closer finish. During the next few minutes, 40 of the refugees were captured, though 88 managed to climb over the fence.

See also: Berlin Wall; Iron Curtain

References: Reader's Digest Book of Escapes. See chapters by Armando Socarras Ramirez; William Schulz; Joseph Blank. Pleasantville, NY: Reader's Digest Association, 1995.

CURION, COELIUS SECUNDUS (C. 1600–1660)

Coelius Secundus Curion, a seventeenth-century Lutheran cleric, found a simple but highly ingenious method of escaping from prison in Turin.

Curion had been condemned to a very uncomfortable form of confinement, having his feet chained to huge pieces of wood. But he knew that if he could release himself from that, then escaping would be easy. The warders assumed that no one could free themselves from the wood and therefore that there was not much need to mount an effective guard of the prison and its surroundings.

After being held in this highly uncomfortable way for a week Curion begged his young warder to free one of his legs to make his punishment more bearable. When his left leg had been freed, Curion got straight to work, using his shirt and leggings to make a dummy leg that might fool the warder. The next day, when the warder appeared on his rounds, Curion begged him to lock up his left leg again and release his right leg, just for a day or two. Again the warder agreed. He failed to notice that the left leg his prisoner lifted and put into the chain was a dummy and that his real leg was concealed under his clothes.

After waiting for the whole day, Curion made his move. He threw aside his false leg, put his shirt and legging back on, and disappeared out of the window and over the wall, making an escape that left the prison authorities baffled for years afterwards.

References: All the Year Round, 21 September 1889.

CURRAGH (1941)

During World War II British soldiers and airmen escaped not only from the hands of their great national enemies but on occasion also from neutral territory. In 1941, for example, several British pilots escaped from their captivity in the Irish Republic.

All of the nine escapees were Royal Air Force Sunderland flying boat pilots who had been forced to crash-land their plane and who had been held at the Curragh, a bare plain 25 miles or so to the west of

Dublin, ever since. All quickly put their minds to the task of escaping, and since one of them was well acquainted with the code system that had been developed by MI9 it was not long before their outside contacts had arranged for several escape cars to pick them up close to the prison camp and set up a network of safe houses for the pilots to which they could make their way once they got outside.

The pilots managed to escape by using the simplest ruse of all: distraction. As a confederate diverted the attention of the guards by pretending to be drunk and then by vomiting within yards of the gate, the nine airmen made their getaway, confident that if they were seen the sentries would be much more likely than were the Germans to fire a warning shot rather than shooting to kill straightaway.

Two were recaptured almost immediately, picked up at an army checkpoint on the road. But the others managed to reach the house of a known sympathizer and were able to contact the MI9 agents nearby in order to pick up their forged papers. Before long, they had crossed the border into Northern Ireland and were on their way back to London.

The escapes did not make the relationship between the Irish Republic and Britain any easier. Dublin issued such an strong diplomatic complaint that MI9 refrained from organizing any more escapes, though they did send in escape equipment if anyone in the Curragh Camp requested it.

References: Foot, Michael R., and James M. Langley. *MI9: Escape and Evasion, 1939–45*. London: Book Club Associates, 1979; Boston, Little, Brown, 1980.

Neave, Airey. *Saturday at MI9: A History of Underground Escape Lines in North-West Europe, 1940–45*. London: Hodder and Stoughton, 1969.

Shoemaker, Lloyd R. *The Escape Factory: The Story of MIS-X*. New York: St. Martin's Press, 1990.

D

DALAI LAMA XIV OF TIBET
(1935–)

As Chinese Communist troops marched rapidly through his kingdom in 1959, the spiritual leader of Tibet, the Dalai Lama, was forced to make a sudden and dramatic exit, knowing that in all probability he would never return to a land that was about to lose its independence to Beijing.

Before he could set out he had to make his way through the crowds of local people who had gathered outside the palace gates. Earlier that day some other members of the royal family and several of the palace staff had already slipped though by hiding under the tarpaulin on the back of a truck or on a variety of pretexts. Now it was his turn.

Wearing a pair of laborer's trousers and a long black coat and carefully removing his glasses, which made him that much more recognizable, he stepped outside at the side of a faithful bodyguard. "For the first time I was truly afraid," he later wrote, "for if I was caught all would be lost" (Dalai Lama 1992, 152). Besides being concerned about the presence of Chinese spies, who he knew would be in the crowd somewhere, he was also aware that he could be taken for a Chinese soldier by Tibetan freedom fighters and killed. But perhaps because large crowds of people are easier to slip through than small groups, he was able to move outside without being stopped, and he headed out of the city. But he knew that there was still a real risk that Chinese soldiers, who numbered tens of thousands in the Lhasa area, could intercept them and cut them down at any moment.

But he and his party were not deterred and continued their perilous, if scenic, journey. While crossing the Kyichu River he nearly lost his balance on the stepping stones over its tributary, but he was taken over its main body in waiting boats. Reaching the mountains at last, the party climbed through the 16,000-foot Che La Pass. There, the Dalai Lama turned to take one last look at the ancient city of Lhasa before he finally left Tibet.

References: Dalai Lama XIV. *Freedom in Exile.* London: Abacus, 1992.

DAVAO PENAL COLONY, MINDANAO (1942–1945)

Though those involved risked savage retribution if caught, there were two major breakouts by U.S. prisoners held by the Japanese at Davao Penal Colony on the southern Philippine island of Mindanao.

The regime at Davao was considered by most Americans to be lax by the brutal and efficient standards of the Japanese army. Because the Japanese considered the surrounding jungle to be impenetrable, they made little effort to patrol the northern and eastern sides of the camp and did not always assign guards to the work parties that were often sent out for wood and other supplies. Such a setting was highly tempting to some of the prisoners, who were desperate to return to their own lines.

On the morning of 4 April 1943 a group of Americans and Filipinos left the camp to work on the surrounding land, as they had often done before, but, since they were unguarded, they instead headed for the dense jungle and tried desperately to hack their way through. Though the heat was ferocious and the jungle extremely dense, they were able to endure their ordeal for four days before making contact with a local partisan army that was dedicated to fighting the Japanese. Most later reached

Australia by submarine before returning home to the United States.

Nearly a year later, in March 1944, eight other prisoners, members of a similar work party, attacked their guards, killing two of them, before fleeing into the dense forest. All were very lucky to meet up with local Filipino natives who treated them with honor and respect rather than with the hostility that others in the region were inclined to harbor for runaways. Before long, these men had also rejoined their unit.

See also: Japanese army, prisoners of; Tall, Robert; Ward Road Prison, Shanghai

References: Lawton, Marion R. *Some Survived: An Epic Account of Japanese Captivity during World War II.* Chapel Hill, NC: Algonquian, 1984.

DE GAULLE, CHARLES (1890–1970)

In the autumn of 1961 President Charles de Gaulle narrowly escaped death at the hands of the Organisation Armée Secrète (OAS), whose leaders had sworn revenge against the president for his perceived betrayal of French interests in Algeria.

While being driven from the city center through a Parisian suburb near Pont-sur-Seine on his way to a military airfield, where he was to take a flight to his weekend retreat, de Gaulle suddenly saw flames shoot up across the road in front of him and caught a brief glimpse of figures crouching nearby at the roadside. In an instant the car was riddled with bullets, all fired from automatic weapons that the would-be assassins had hidden underneath their coats.

But de Gaulle's chauffeur was undeterred and calmly drove straight through the flames, though the tires' outer tubes had been hit and the car only kept going because the inner tubes were untouched. Though furious that the would-be assassins had opened fire while his wife was with him, the president, too, was reported to have looked entirely unruffled by the incident, and on arrival at the airfield he only brushed off the metal and plastic fragments that had dusted his suit before casually continuing with his journey.

See also: Algeria; Ben Bella, Ahmed; Egyptian embassy; Execution, escape from

References: Lacouture, Jean. *De Gaulle.* London: Harrill, 1993.

DE MARENCHES, ALEXANDRE

Euphoric because he had succeeded in crossing the border between occupied France and Spain during World War II, a French freedom fighter named Alexandre de Marenches gave himself away and was lucky not to fall back into German hands.

After crossing the Pyrenees and catching a train to Madrid, de Marenches felt confident enough to strike up a conversation with a well-dressed individual standing in the corridor and was euphoric enough to boast of his escape and to explain that he wanted to join the Free French. Only when the train reached Madrid and he saw this man being met on the platform by an important retinue did he realize that he had been talking to the German ambassador to Spain.

His knees shaking, de Marenches slunk away and looked for a hotel room where he could lie low until he had contacted the Free French. But by cruel misfortune he happened to move to the Hotel Floride, which was also the principal lodging for German intelligence officers in Spain. Disappearing once again, he was well aware that he had enjoyed far more good fortune than many of his former colleagues.

DE VALERA, EAMONN (1882–1975)

In 1918 the Irish republican leader Eamonn de Valera escaped British captivity. He was aware that he would almost certainly be free within weeks in any case but knew that his disappearance would inflict serious political embarrassment on his enemies at a time when the republicans wanted to put maximum political pressure on them.

Though many of those who had led the failed republican Easter Uprising of 1916 were executed, Eamonn de Valera, a leading figure in Sinn Fein, had been imprisoned by the British authorities, who feared an angry backlash from both his supporters in Ireland and from the United States if he was condemned to the gallows. Instead, he was sent to Lincoln Prison and put under heavy guard, where his thoughts soon turned to the possibility of escape.

In October 1918 he was sent some cakes for his birthday by his friends and followers outside. He realized that an escape tool, such as a key, could easily be hidden inside such a cake and would in all probability be overlooked by the prison guards, who tried to search everything and everyone that came inside but who were also badly overextended. A forged key might let him through one gate that would take him straight to the outer wall, avoiding several others that stood in the way. He smuggled a message to Michael Collins, his chief contact outside, and they planned to obtain a copy of the master key, smuggle it outside, and wait for a copy to be sent back to him, concealed within a cake.

With considerable ingenuity, he managed to obtain a copy of the master key. Having gone to mass as usual one day, he furtively took some wax from one of the candles and held it against the flame until it had melted enough to allow an imprint to be made. Then, as the priest was looking away, he went quickly to the sacristy and made a copy of the priest's key. The wax copy was soon smuggled outside, where Collins and his colleagues had a forged one made and sent back to their leader.

They were finally ready to make their escape bid on 3 February 1919. From the outside Collins and another sympathizer, Harry Boland, cut through the perimeter's wire and used a flashlight to give the prearranged signal at exactly 7:40 P.M. They received the answer, the glow of lighted matches, that told them that everything was going according to plan inside the prison.

As is true of most prison escapes, some things went badly wrong. After the rescuers had given their signal, they found to their horror that they were unable to switch the torch off and had to stuff it into a coat pocket. De Valera later noted that he had seen "too much" of the signal and had been sure that the warders would see the light, which should only have lasted a few seconds. But he enjoyed good luck in that no one heard the noise made by one of his two companions as they made their way through the prison corridors that night. For almost as soon as they left their cells the shoes worn by one of them fell apart, allowing the soles to flap noisily as they walked along.

For a very long moment it also looked as though their hopes would be dashed at the last minute. As they reached the perimeter Collins and Boland tried to use their own forged master key to open the last gate, but to their horror the key broke in two and jammed inside the lock. Arriving a few minutes later, de Valera produced his own master key, pushed the broken piece of the key out of the lock, and saw the gate swing open.

Though they were out of the prison they were still a long way from freedom, and they had to hope that none of the soldiers from the nearby barracks would see them running across the open fields. But again they were in luck, since all of the several soldiers who did see them were too preoccupied by the company of nurses from the nearby military hospital to take a second look. Just in case, the irrepressible Boland gave his heavy fur coat to de Valera, draped a light rain coat over himself, and linked arms with the escapee, hoping that in the dark the soldiers would be fooled. Moving briskly, they were unchallenged and were free to continue on.

Collins had gone to great trouble beforehand to arrange transport and a string of safe houses to which de Valera could now be moved. Moving first by taxi and then by train, De Valera was hidden in the presbytery of a Liverpool priest, Father Charles O'Manohy, within just four hours after he left the prison, and two weeks later he had been smuggled to Dublin, where he resumed active leadership of the republican movement.

Over the next few months, though he was really in hiding in Dublin, he was reputedly sighted in all sorts of different places the world over. The Dutch government on one occasion even issued a warrant for his arrest after such a sighting in their territory. But besides being a great story for the newspapers, his escape also devastated the British authorities and was a major boost to republican morale, just as he had hoped.

References: Coogan, Tim. *Eamonn de Valera: The Man Who Was Ireland*. New York: HarperCollins, 1995.

DEANE-DRUMMOND, ANTHONY (1917–)

Captured after the Allied debacle at Arnhem during World War II, the British officer Anthony Deane-Drummond was forced to rely on his exceptional ingenuity, determination, and stamina when things began to go wrong.

By 1944 he was already a veteran of two daring escapes from captivity in Italy, both made in 1941. On the first attempt he was captured near the Swiss border; while he later managed to squeeze under the barbed-wire fence that separated Italy and Switzerland, digging a small tunnel with his hands to do so. But as the Germans closed in on British positions at Arnhem, he knew how difficult it would be to get away.

With the enemy only a few hundred yards away Deane-Drummond ran to a nearby house to hide but, by sheer misfortune, the house he had chosen was soon taken over by a German squad, who placed their machine guns at all the top-floor windows only minutes after he arrived.

The only place that Deane-Drummond could now hide was in the lavatory. Dashing inside, he locked the door behind him and hoped that any German wanting to use it would assume that one of his colleagues had beaten him to it and would find another in the house. Miraculously, his ploy worked, and after staying locked inside for three days and nights he was able to creep away to freedom.

But his luck did not last. After he had swum 300 yards across the Rhine he fell into a German slit trench, only yards from no man's land, and was sent straight back into detention by the disgruntled German soldier he had stepped over and rudely woken. Deane-Drummond found himself joining 200 other prisoners marching from the Arnhem church to the grounds of a large home in the outlying district of the town.

But the energies of this irrepressible Englishman were still concentrated on escape, and he found another small place to hide. A cupboard seven feet high, one foot deep, and four feet wide was fitted exactly against one of the walls of the downstairs living room, and he felt sure that no one would notice if he reversed the lock on its door. If he took some provisions with him, he reckoned, then he would be able to hide in this cupboard for three days, with a good chance of not being found.

Again complications arose quickly, for the room in which he was now hiding was, quite unexpectedly, suddenly put to use by the German military police as an interrogation center, where Allied prisoners were taken and questioned. Listening to the interrogations from the cupboard, Deane-Drummond knew that he would have to choose his moment with the greatest possible care if he was to escape.

Even though he was extremely cramped, he managed to stay there for 13 days before he could find a suitable opportunity to move. Unable to sit down, he was forced to stand on one leg, then the other, to relieve the agony of his ordeal, and he also had to ration himself to four mouthfuls of water every five hours. Slowly eating the bread he had saved before hiding himself, he found that after nine days in the cupboard his mouth was too dry for him to swallow anything.

On the thirteenth day, noticing that the Germans had all left the room, he was at last able to flee. He stumbled out of the cupboard, feeling half-dead and blinded for several minutes by the brilliant daylight. Opening a french window and staggering outside, he fell into the shrubs, stretched out his tortured limbs, and cried with joy that his ordeal was finally over. His journey back to Allied lines had now begun.

See also: Arnhem
References: Deane-Drummond, Anthony. *Return Ticket*. London: Collins, 1953.

DENGLER, LT. DIETER (1942–)

Shot down over Laos on 1 February 1966 and captured by Communist insurgents, the

U.S. pilot Lt. Dieter Dengler was able to make a daring and extraordinary escape from his captors.

Dengler knew that unless he escaped he faced certain death. After nearly five months in captivity, both he and his fellow prisoners were close to starvation and on the brink of insanity, and they decided to mount an escape while they still enjoyed some semblance of their usual strength.

Watching his guards carefully, Dengler crept toward their hut and seized a rifle and some ammunition he saw in a corner. But he was suddenly seen by one of his captors and found himself under furious fire. Seeing one of the guards running at him with machete raised, Dengler opened fire, blasting his attacker and bringing him to the ground. Regaining his confidence, he continued firing at his enemies until a deathly hush fell over the camp.

With two other Americans, Gene Lebrun and Duane Martin, and a number of Thais, Dengler retreated into the dense jungle, knowing that the journey ahead would be arduous even for the fittest and that it would be made even more difficult by the constant threat of enemy soldiers searching for them. Before long, Lebrun disappeared into the jungle, never to be seen again, and Martin was shot dead by Communist guerrillas after a chase.

But left alone by the Thais, who went their own way, Dengler was able to find a place where he could be seen by U.S. pilots and was soon rescued by a Jolly Green Giant rescue helicopter.

See also: Rowe, James "Nick"; Saigon; Vietnam War
References: Dengler, Dieter. *Escape from Laos.* Novato, CA: Presidio, 1979.

DIKKO, UMARU (C. 1945–)

In 1984 Umaru Dikko, a Nigerian exile, was kidnapped and spirited away in the streets of central London by Israeli agents and eventually rescued at the last minute by British police at an Essex airport.

The background to the story lay in the Israeli government's ambition to gain favor with a new political regime that had taken power in Lagos. At the time almost all gov-

ernments had broken off ties with Israel after its invasion of Lebanon, Tel Aviv was eager to find new allies, especially if, like Nigeria, they were also a potential market for Israeli goods and a possible exporter of oil. An excellent way of promoting such links, Mossad bosses reckoned, would be to kidnap one of the leading supporters of the preceding Lagos regime who was wanted by the new government for his alleged part in economic crimes.

One July afternoon, just after noon, Dikko walked out of his pleasant house in Bayswater in central London and was attacked, forced into a van, and driven off. The only witness to this incident was his secretary, who quickly raised the alarm.

Within an hour of the kidnapping, Scotland Yard alerted special branch officers at all the ports and airports in Britain and ordered that Stansted Airport in Essex, where most freight was handled, be put on special alert. It was not long before two large wooden crates being loaded on board a Nigerian Airways 727 aroused the suspicions of customs officers. On closer inspection they heard the muffled sounds of someone trapped inside, and the police were instantly called in. Racing down the runway in their cars, they pulled up in front of the 727 just before it began its takeoff.

The crate was opened before a Nigerian diplomat who was hastily summoned from London. Dikko was found inside, bound and heavily drugged. He was watched over by another Nigerian who was ready to inject the prisoner with more sedative if he stirred. In the second crate were two Israeli agents, Alexander Barak and Felix Abithol, who had collaborated with the Nigerian secret service to hatch the plot.

See also: Mossad
References: Rayne, Ronald. *Mossad.* Transworld, 1990.

DITH PRAN (1945–)

Though in his library he proudly shelved a copy of Thomas Paine's classic work *The Rights of Man,* the Cambodian leader Pol Pot ranks with Hitler and Stalin among the perpetrators of the worst crimes of the twenti-

Dith Pran, a Cambodian journalist whose survival of and escape from Cambodia's killing fields was made famous in the book and film The Killing Fields. *(AP/Wide World Photos)*

eth century. But one who narrowly escaped the genocide he unleashed was a Cambodian journalist and interpreter, Dith Pran, whose story was later made famous in the book and film *The Killing Fields*.

As soon as his Khmer Rouge movement swept into power in 1975, Pol Pot started to use Stalinist methods to implement his extreme Maoist Communist principles. Perhaps as many as three million of his fellow Cambodians were exterminated because, in his estimation, they belonged to those classes of people—intellectuals, professionals, monks, those with foreign connections, even those who wore glasses—who were responsible for the perceived demise of their country.

At the time of the Communist takeover, Pran had been working as a journalist and interpreter alongside Sydney Schanberg, the *New York Times* correspondent in Phnom Penh. But after Schanberg and other Western journalists were allowed to leave the capital, he found himself alone under a fanatical and barbarous regime.

Pran quickly recognized their ruthlessness and quickly identified the types of individual they had begun to persecute. Throwing away his Western-style clothes, he put on sandals, shorts, and a dirty shirt and had his hair cut as short as possible. Claiming to have always worked as a city taxi driver and to being wholly ignorant of politics, he struck a very different figure from the professional and educated victims whose bodies littered whole sections of the roads outside the capital.

But though he was spared execution, Pran was nonetheless seized by the Khmer soldiers and taken to nearby rice paddies to work as a slave. Working 18-hour days at gunpoint, he quickly lost more than 50 pounds and watched many of his fellow prisoners die. He subsisted by supplementing his daily bowl of soup with termites, rats, and leaves. He survived four long years of this agony before, in 1979, he at last managed to escape.

His chance came courtesy of the U.S. Air Force. Because its B52s had struck deep into Cambodia a few years before, in a desperate attempt to stop Vietnamese Communists from moving their supplies southward, a great many unexploded bombs still littered the countryside. One afternoon a massive blast sent Pran hurtling threw the air, killing several of his fellow slaves as they worked in the paddy fields, and he quickly realized that they had stepped not on a land mine but on a 500-pound bomb.

In the confusion that followed, Pran lay low, making sure he had not been seen before sliding over the embankments around him and heading for the edge of the jungle, only 50 yards away. Remaining there until dark, he headed off into the night, relying on his sense of direction to guide him toward the Thai border and on his highly developed instincts of self-preservation to avoid the various dangers—mainly panthers, buffalo, and snakes—to stay alive.

Having passed through the "killing fields" on his journey, where he found himself to be the only living soul among the thousands of skulls and bones of Pol Pot's former enemies, Pran eventually reached a village not far from the Vietnamese border, Bat Dangkor. Having closely questioned him to ascertain that he really was who he claimed to be, the village chief temporarily employed Pran as a house servant, giving him the chance to recuperate and restore his shattered body in preparation for his next attempt to reach Thailand.

But Vietnam was at war with Cambodia, and as the Vietnamese Army started to advance rapidly, it looked briefly as though freedom might elude him. Because Vietnamese advance units were heading straight for the village, retreating Khmer soldiers rounded up all the villagers at gunpoint and ordered them to evacuate. But as they waived the villagers toward the waiting trucks with their rifles, Pran was once again rescued by events as dramatic as those at the paddy field. With almost prefect

timing, a Vietnamese MiG swooped over them at very low altitude, prompting everyone to dive for cover and the soldiers to open fire on it. Hiding under the house, Pran remained undiscovered until, very soon after, Vietnamese tanks rumbled into the village.

As he moved off into the mountains toward Thailand with new acquaintances, Pran was still some way from finding freedom. For he was well aware that the closer they got to the border, the more likely it became that they would encounter one of the many lethal traps that the Khmer had put down to stop fugitives from escaping. Sure enough, they soon unearthed a *punji* trap, a concealed hole dug deep into the path that contained long sharpened bamboo poles, which inflicted a slow agonizing death on its unfortunate victims; nevertheless, their vigilance did not prevent one member of their party from tripping a wire that exploded a grenade and killed him instantly.

But after several weeks on the run and four years in captivity, Dith Pran finally crossed the border, winning the freedom that eluded so many of his fellow countrymen.

See also: Khmer Rouge
References: Hudson, Christopher. *The Killing Fields.* London: Pan, 1984.
Pran, Dith. *Children of the Killing Fields.* New Haven, CT, and London: Yale University Press, 1998.

DODGE, JOHN (1894–1971)

One prisoner who enjoyed a legendary status for escape among his peers of World War II was a U.S. soldier, Johnny Dodge, who had a remarkable appetite for trying to break out of German captivity.

By the time he was sent to Stalag Luft III, Dodge had already led an extraordinary life. Though American by birth and upbringing, a member of the East Coast Dodge family that had made its wealth in copper, he had taken the first boat to England on the outbreak of World War I in 1914 and used the influence of his relative Winston Churchill to find a place in the British Army. After being seriously wounded at Gallipoli and surviving the horrors of the

Somme, he had later narrowly avoided execution by the Bolsheviks of revolutionary Russia, where his curiosity had taken him in 1919. Though well past fighting age at the outbreak of World War II in 1939, he had not been deterred from rejoining his former British comrades and holding off the Germans at the Dunkirk perimeter while Allied troops were evacuated. Captured by the Germans, he soon acquired a reputation as an irrepressible escapee who would try to disappear from almost every situation he found himself in.

When, on the night of 24 March 1944, Dodge participated in the Great Escape and left Stalag Luft III through the tunnel Harry, he was the least typical escapee of all. He was nearly 50 years old, and he was also the only one of their number not to have had any connection with the air force (his only experience with an airplane, it appears, was the prewar experience of sitting in a first class seat during a cross-Channel flight from London to Paris). But he was determined to escape and managed with difficulty to squeeze his large frame through the narrow tunnel entrance.

Though his escape got off to a good start as he and several other escapees traveled across the country by foot and train and reached the Czech border, he and his companion ran into trouble when a civilian entered their train compartment and demanded to see their documents. Neither his German nor that of his colleague was good enough for them to bluff through the situation, and both were soon arrested and handed over to the Gestapo.

But Dodge was one of the lucky ones. Though the names of 50 of the others were on the Gestapo death list, Dodge was recommended for *Aktion Kugel*, "special treatment." He and three others were sent not to the firing squad, nor to another prisoner of war camp, but to a concentration camp, Sachsenhausen. The horrors of Sachsenhausen shocked and sickened them. In this camp, run by the Gestapo and the SS to house the Reich's political enemies, the "Sachenhausen four" witnessed atrocities that they had never before imagined, as well as finding the barbed wire, sentries, and

German Shepherd dogs that they were more used to.

But Dodge and his three colleagues still proved that they were born escapers, though after hearing of the appalling fate of the 50 other escapees from Sagan, they had no illusions that they would live long if they were caught. Gestapo anger at the distraction caused by escapees had long since boiled over, and they had also showed an arrogant disdain toward the strongly worded Allied protests at the execution of the 50 escapees.

But almost as soon as they arrived at Sachsenhausen the four started digging a tunnel. It began under their hut but had to cross more than a 100 feet to reach outside the camp. Such was their desperation that they had it ready in just a few weeks, and prepared to move on 23 September.

Dressed in suits made for them by their sympathetic Italian orderlies, they deliberately left in bad weather, knowing that the Alsatians that usually sat on top of the guards' air-raid shelters just outside the wire would usually retreat inside with their handlers. Dodge was the last of the four to leave Sachenhausen that night, and very nearly paid heavily for it, since the tunnel started collapsing as he made his way through, forcing the three others to pull him out.

Once free Dodge lasted well, but not quite well enough to get home. He made contact with the French, and he was hidden in barns, pigsties, cowsheds, and cottages by civilians who risked their lives to help him. But he was eventually seen and betrayed to the Germans.

Yet his remarkable escape career brought him freedom in a way he could never have anticipated. When details about his family history and connections emerged during the interrogations that followed his recapture, the Germans were fascinated to learn about his distant kinship with the British prime minister, Winston Churchill. Desperate to strike a deal with the Western powers in an effort to stave off the Russian advance, the German High Command drew up a plan in which Dodge would be a key player. After spending some weeks in Sachsenhausen awaiting execution, Dodge was taken to Berlin and informed that he would be sent back to Britain to deliver a message to the prime minister, a message that detailed the terms of a conditional cease-fire.

And so it was that Johnny Dodge at last found his way out of German captivity, crossing the border into Switzerland and making his way to London, where he dined in style with Churchill.

See also: The Great Escape

References: Burgess, Alan. *The Longest Tunnel: The True Story of the Great Escape.* Bath: Chivers, 1991.

DUNKIRK (1940)

In an operation that was without doubt one of the most desperate and crucial of World War II, the British expeditionary army and other Allied soldiers numbering more than 300,000 were evacuated from the beaches at Dunkirk, France, in May and June 1940.

The British Expeditionary Force (BEF) had been sent across the channel in September 1939 to prepare for the German invasion, and though it contained some of the best units in the British Army, it was woefully underprepared for the dramatic onslaught that the Panzers would soon unleash. Many units were equipped only with a few World War I tanks and artillery, which were scarcely in working order. According to one officer, the 5th Battalion of the Green Howards had "only one weapon capable of making a loud bang, a 3 inch mortar" (Atkin 1990), while Sgt. Bill Brodie later remembered his dismay when his unit was given an antitank gun without a firing pin and "three ancient Lewis guns marked 1918" (Atkin 1990).

It was not surprising, then, that the British units and their French allies could only retreat when on 10 May 1940 the full fury of the German war machine was unleashed against them. They could do little more than try to hold back the advance of Wehrmacht, playing for time as they moved closer to the beaches and prepared to evacuate.

The chaos and terror of the evacuation at Dunkirk, which allowed more than 300,000 Allied troops to escape the advancing German army during World War II, is captured in this photograph. (Baldwin H. Ward/Corbis-Bettmann)

One of the most controversial decisions of the war, Hitler's Halt Order, ensured that the British were able to escape from the clutches of the Germans. Though his Panzers were a mere ten miles from Dunkirk and faced no natural obstacles or military opposition, Hitler halted their advance, depriving them of their one chance to finish off the Allied forces. Hitler and his generals seem to have been disproportionately alarmed by a counterattack made by British tanks at Arras on 21 May and felt that their own armored columns would be vulnerable if they raced ahead too quickly.

This crucial delay gave the BEF time to make its getaway, allowing the greatest rescue operation in military history to take place. Using three routes between the coast, the Navy mobilized every vessel it could muster. Minesweepers, destroyers, transports, steamers, ferries, lifeboats—all were seen on the Dunkirk beaches in the last few days of May and the beginning of June picking up the huge numbers of soldiers who were amassed, in some semblance of order, before them. Many of the smaller vessels involved had been requisitioned from the Thames without the permission or even the knowledge of their owners, although no one protested when they later found out what had happened. Regular Navy officers served alongside volunteers, pensioners alongside teenagers—aboard the tug *Sun 12* was a 14 year old, Albert Barnes—as a whole nation rallied to the rescue effort.

Inevitably, both rescuers and the rescued suffered losses, though not nearly as heavily as had been feared. The soldiers suffered badly from continual air attack and were virtually powerless as the Messerschmitts and Stukas strafed their positions from very low altitudes, often totally unchallenged by the Royal Air Force and even eliciting some sense of pity from the pilots who could see the suffering they had inflicted beneath them. Luftwaffe attacks on Allied shipping as it crossed the channel also cost about 2,000 lives. Particularly costly was the evening of 29 May, when several ships were bombed, among them the *Jaguar*, the *Grenade*, and the *Calvi*, in low-level attacks

that left hundreds dead. Only half the 600 soldiers aboard the *Waverly* were saved when it sank, and the *Crested Eagle* also lost half its passengers after it was hit near Bray-Dunes.

As the BEF was evacuated, the Germans were getting closer and closer. By the evening of 31 May a large area of beach had suddenly come under shellfire, controlled by an observation balloon hovering over Nieuport, and was too dangerous to use. And by the time the last troops pulled away from Dunkirk harbor, at 3 A.M. on 4 June, the sound of German machine-gun fire could clearly be heard in the streets of the town. Several areas in the defensive perimeter had also nearly crumbled to repeated German assaults, threatening to bring the entire operation to a sudden halt. The Belgian capitulation, for example, had meant that a major gap in the eastern perimeter was suddenly left exposed. But just as a German reconnaissance patrol appeared on the horizon, an armored car of the 12th Lancers arrived to challenge it, allowing time for troops to take up positions and fill in the gap.

References: Atkin, R. *Pillar of Fire.* London: Sidgwick and Jackson, 1990.

Barker, A. J. *Dunkirk: The Great Escape.* London: Dent, 1977.

Jackson, Robert. *Dunkirk: The British Evacuation.* London: A. Barker, 1976.

DUTCH TRAIN RESCUE (1977)

In the summer of 1977 a group of South Moluccans, all Dutch citizens, seized 55 passengers of a Dutch train at Assen and held them hostage in order to draw attention to the cause of South Moluccan nationalism.

After the siege had continued for nearly three weeks without any sign that the terrorists would back down, the Dutch government gave the order for a specially trained military unit to move in and bring the hostage crisis to a swift conclusion. In the early hours of 11 June, six Starfighter jets swooped over the train and dropped smoke bombs, allowing the units on the ground to move in undetected. A moment before they opened fire a loudspeaker broadcast an unmistakable message to the terrified passengers, urging them to lie on the floor until the shooting was over. In the ten-minute firefight that followed, six of the nine Moluccans were killed, together with two hostages.

As in the operations at Mogadishu, Entebbe, and the Iranian embassy in London, the success of the rescue missions was due to intricate planning, first-class intelligence, and the skill and professionalism of the units actively involved.

E

EGYPTIAN EMBASSY (1955)

Knowing that their capture would spark a serious diplomatic incident, two French secret service agents narrowly escaped capture during a surveillance operation that took place at the height of the Algerian war.

The Egyptians were known to be actively supporting the anti-French Front de Libération Nationale (FLN). Thus the French secret service, the Service de Documentation Extérieure et de Contre-espionnage (SDECE), focused its attention on the Egyptian embassy in Paris, bugging its telephones, bribing its employees, and finally sending in two agents to crack its safe and bring out the information they required.

After breaking in the two agents were surprised by the sudden approach of a security guard and were forced to run to the basement and hide behind a stack of papers bundled there. They then had to stay there for the rest of the night and the whole of the next day before they finally had a chance to escape.

Their hiding place proved a useful one, but not just because it allowed them to avoid the night watchman. Toward late morning, after they had already been there for some hours, a member of the embassy staff happened to come into the basement to throw onto the stack some more papers that, by sheer coincidence, contained details of all the payments made by the Egyptians to FLN operatives in France. Their escape therefore provided them with an unexpected windfall.

See also: Algeria; Ben Bella, Ahmed; De Gaulle, Charles
References: Porch, Douglas. *The French Secret Service.* London: Macmillan, 1996.

ENTEBBE (1976)

One of the most audacious rescue operations ever undertaken was made by Israeli commandos in an attempt to rescue their fellow nationals who were held hostage at Entebbe airport in Uganda in 1976.

The Entebbe incident began on 27 June when an Air France flight en route to Paris from Tel Aviv was hijacked during a stopover at Athens. The terrorists, two Germans from the Marxist Baader-Meinhof gang and two Palestinians from the Popular Front for the Liberation of Palestine, ordered the pilots to take the plane first to Benghazi in Libya and from there to Entebbe in Uganda. All 258 passengers and crew were then moved at gunpoint to the airport terminal and guarded by the hijackers, who were now joined by five accomplices who had waited there to join them and by the government troops of Uganda's President Idi Amin.

The Entebbe hijacking was at first an international affair, since the plane was French, the kidnappers were German and Palestinian, and the passengers came from all over the world. In addition, the terrorists demanded the release of a large number of their colleagues who were being held in Switzerland, Kenya, and Israel as well as in Western jails. But after a few days the hijackers released all their hostages except the 103 Israeli citizens on board, and the matter became essentially a matter for Tel Aviv.

The Israeli authorities' uncompromising attitude toward terrorism had become clear four years earlier after the kidnapping of Israeli athletes at the Olympic Games in Munich, and during the Entebbe crisis they had from the onset sharply differed from the Western governments by

An Israeli commando is taken to the hospital after taking part in the dramatic raid to rescue hostages at Entebbe airport in Uganda in 1976. (UPI/Corbis-Bettmann)

flatly refusing to compromise. Having been under terrorist attack throughout much of its 30-year existence and having themselves used terrorist tactics during the British Mandate in Palestine, the Israeli leaders were better placed than most to know the importance of intransigence in the face of orchestrated political violence. So as soon as the non-Israeli hostages were freed, the Israelis, no longer afraid of inflicting punishing casualties among other foreign nationals, began to consider the military options put forward by a force that specialized in counterterrorist operations, Unit 269, for securing the release of those held at Entebbe.

A number of different options were considered. The unit's chief commander, Jonathan Netanyahu, argued for a force that could land by parachute either at nearby Lake Victoria or in neighboring Kenya and then make its way by stealth to the airport. Others favored the much more audacious alternative, which was to land at the airport, unrecognized by the authorities. But whichever method was chosen there

would be formidable obstacles in their path, for quite apart from the distances involved, the terrorists and their Ugandan hosts—well aware of the hard-line Israeli position—would be ready, armed and waiting for just such an assault.

In the end, the Israeli chiefs decided to risk landing a rescue force at the airport. A unit that was dropped right on top of the airport probably faced just as much risk as one that was landed some distance away, it was argued, but nonetheless enjoyed one distinct advantage: Since the airport had been built by an Israeli firm that still had copies of its design plans, a full-scale mockup of the terminal could be constructed and used for practice.

The operation, named Operation Thunderball, that was approved by the Israeli cabinet on 2 July and that began at dawn the following day was by any standard extraordinarily audacious and enterprising. Flying below radar level over the Red Sea toward Ethiopia, four Hercules transports carrying the members of the rescue team were escorted by a Boeing 707 to Entebbe. The Boeing acted as the eyes and ears of the operation—the command, communication, control, and intelligence post—and was able to send a message to the Entebbe control tower that would enable one of the Hercules transports to land unchallenged. That message, extraordinarily, was that President Idi Amin was coming in to land.

The operation got off to a brilliant start. The Hercules was granted landing permission by controllers who did not have the time or the inclination to check the authenticity of the request, and as the plane came to a halt, a black Mercedes, identical to the one used by the Ugandan president, rolled out with two of its "escorts" and headed for the terminal ready to take the kidnappers by storm.

They got within yards of their target before they were finally challenged by the Ugandan guards. One guard was shot dead on the spot; the other was able to shout for help before he, too, was cut down.

The kidnappers in the terminal some 40 meters away had some idea that something was wrong but were still taken totally off guard when the first three members of the rescue mission burst through the glass doors and shouted at the hostages to lie down. Within three minutes the terrorists had been killed and the airfield secured by the other members of the rescue mission, who had been landed in the three other Hercules planes after receiving a ground signal. The hostages were now quickly put on board and flown back to Tel Aviv.

Like almost any such rescue mission, Operation Thunderball had not been without cost. One hostage had been killed by the terrorists, another had been killed by Israeli fire, and seven were injured in those crucial few minutes. Another hostage who had been taken to a nearby hospital and was still under Ugandan guard when the rescue mission took place was later executed by her guards. The Israeli commander, Jonathan Netanyahu, was shot dead by a sniper as he directed the assault from outside the terminal, and another soldier was wounded. But such remarkably light costs, and the sheer audacity of the raid, have ensured that the action at Entebbe has become legendary.

See also: Bangkok Airport; Dutch train rescue; Iranian embassy siege; Iranian hostage rescue operation; Mogadishu plane rescue; Munich
References: Hastings, Max. *Yoni, Hero of Entebbe*. London: Weidenfeld and Nicholson, 1979.

ESCAPE ATTEMPTS

It is ironic that many escape bids have failed even though they have been far more worthy of success than some of those that have succeeded.

Peter Allan was one prisoner whose attempt to escape from Colditz in 1941 was cruelly foiled, even though, strictly speaking, he did make it to freedom. Hidden inside a straw mattress, which was moved from the prison camp to the nearby town, Allan's bid for freedom started off well. He had an exceptional command of German, having studied before the war at Jena university, and he had been given an excellent disguise, courtesy of the camp's escape committee. On his way to Vienna, his acting ability even enabled him to hitch a ride for part of the journey in a car driven by an SS officer, and within a few days he reached his destination and made for the consulate of the United States, which at this time was still a neutral country.

It was only now, after having reached neutral ground, that by cruel misfortune his luck changed. The U.S. consul who met him was not sure about the identity of his visitor. Was this individual, he wondered, what he claimed to be, or was he really a Gestapo agent who wanted to know where the sympathies of the U.S. government lay? Unsure, he erred on the side of caution and sent his visitor packing. Quickly stopped by the Viennese police, Allan was arrested and returned to a long stretch in Colditz.

Another unfortunate escapee also managed to reach the safety of neutral territory in 1943 after bluffing his way out of a prison camp and making his way to Switzerland. But whereas Allan was deliberately turned away by his hosts, this particularly unfortunate individual crossed the border to safety without realizing it. Unaware that he was on Swiss territory, he continued walking and within a few hours had moved back into Germany, where he was quickly arrested by border guards. He had been unlucky enough to cross the frontier at the worst point: where a corner of Switzerland is surrounded on three sides by its neighbor.

Les Shorrock of the Royal Engineers must have experienced a similar sense of anguish at Dunkirk in the summer of 1940 as the German army overran the beaches and as he considered the long spell in captivity that awaited him. He had certainly come extremely close to reaching safety, for, clutching a broken attaché case full of military papers that he had been ordered to carry back to Britain, Shorrock had waited in line on the beach. But, as he put it after the war, "just as it would have been our rightful turn to board the next rowing boat, an officer, with drawn revolver, leapt into the water and ordered our party back, stating we had jumped the queue" (Atkin 1990). Though this charge was blatantly untrue, Shorrock and his colleagues had no choice but to obey and, whereas the others found alternative transport shortly afterward, he was injured by a bomb blast and had to be left behind.

Some Allied airmen who were on the run from the Germans in Provence in 1943 faced a similar predicament, although they were not destined to suffer so harshly. Having gone to great pains to reach the rendezvous where they expected to be picked up by a transport plane, the airmen duly assembled at the appointed hour. To their horror they found that far more escapees had turned up than had originally been expected. Since the Dakota was able to transport a maximum of only 18 people, 8 of those who turned up had to be left behind. But they did not spend as long as Les Shorrock in captivity, since Provence fell to the advancing Allied armies a few weeks later.

Escapees are particularly apt to fall victim to complacency if they succeed at the main hurdle and overlook the rest. This was perhaps the fatal mistake made by one prisoner in the Tower of London, Lord Capel, a close ally of Charles I who was captured and imprisoned during the English Civil War by Oliver Cromwell. Knowing that he faced life imprisonment for as long as Cromwell held power, Capel and his contacts outside devised a plan. It should be possible, they argued, to walk across the moat if he chose exactly the right spot, for there was one particular place that Londoners were apt to use as a dumping ground and where, as a consequence, it was far more shallow than elsewhere.

Capel was a desperate man and decided to risk drowning or, even worse, being dragged slowly underneath by quicksand. He made it out of his cell and got as far as the moat. There he cautiously stepped into the water at the carefully chosen spot that had been marked by his friends, waiting anxiously at the other side. Though he sank deeper and deeper into the mud beneath him until, for a few crucial minutes, it seemed that he had been lost, he managed to reach safety, though he was gasping desperately for breath as he did so.

But this remarkable feat seems to have taken his mind off the lesser obstacles that lay ahead, for shortly afterward they were betrayed by the boatman they had hired to ferry them across the Thames. In their jubilation they had almost certainly talked too

loudly of their achievement and let the ferryman scent the reward that he knew he would be given if he told all.

During World War II, Roger Bushell also seems to have fallen victim to complacency. Having escaped from Dulag Luft camp, he managed to make his way southwards toward the Swiss border disguised in a civilian suit and using the impeccable German that he had learned during his captivity. Throughout his escape he took immense care to evade the Nazi authorities—traveling, for example, only on minor trains rather than on the better-guarded main routes—until the very last stretch when, as he later freely admitted, he became a bit too reckless. As he wandered closer and closer to the Swiss border, he had one last decision to take. Should he wait until dark and move under the cover of darkness, even if this meant that he would have very little visibility as he moved over unfamiliar and perhaps dangerous terrain? Or should he move without delay and head straight for the border? Deciding upon the second of these options, he was arrested as he walked brazenly through Stuhlingen, only a few hundred yards from freedom. Bushell was sent to Stalag Luft III, where he organized the Great Escape.

Other escape bids have failed simply because they were too ambitious. For example, there are several recorded instances of Japanese prisoners of war (POWs) seeking to escape from Allied captivity during World War II by attempting mass breakouts that, against well-armed guards, were bound to end in mass slaughter. One riot, in March 1943, took place at an internment camp at Featherstone, east of Wellington, New Zealand, and left 464 prisoners dead and 66 wounded. Another attempt, in August the following year, resulted in 231 Japanese fatalities and 78 wounded. None of the POWs escaped.

One British spy's escape attempt was ambitious in a different way, because the would-be escapee assumed that he would not fall victim to the same tactics he was using against his captors. In 1918 Lieutenant Colonel Edward Noel was captured and held captive by a band of Jungalis, a Muslim tribe based near the Caucusus. Seeing his guards smoking opium one evening, Noel decided to try to encourage them to continue, hoping he could disappear when they began to succumb to its effects. He therefore started to smoke the pipe himself, thinking that it would make them more relaxed and that he could pretend he, too, was under its powerful influence. But his plan failed miserably, for though he saw his chance to escape, he had by that time started to feel too happy to want to.

Others have failed for more unusual reasons. The very unfortunate story of one would-be escapee can perhaps also be classified as an "escape bid." Captured in North Africa in 1942 and imprisoned in Italy with other senior officers, Brigadier David Miles, a New Zealander, escaped from Italian custody in March 1943. But though he managed to reach the safety of Switzerland after several hair-raising weeks, Miles appears to have been overwhelmed by posttraumatic emotional problems and took his own life shortly afterwards.

Two Irish prisoners paid heavily because they had been in prison long enough that they were unaware of some changes of circumstances, changes that meant they could not so easily copy earlier breakouts. During the troubles in Northern Ireland, two loyalist prisoners, Barry Redfern and Edward Pollock, sought to emulate another prisoner, Brendan Hughes, who had escaped some years earlier by hiding himself in a dustbin shortly before it was taken away by garbage collectors. As they had planned, the dustbins in which they had hidden themselves were shortly picked up and wheeled to the truck. Then disaster struck. Since Hughes had made his escape, methods of waste disposal had changed, and the two men were emptied onto the back of the truck and crushed by the compressor. One later died; the other was seriously hurt.

That some escape bids have failed is not altogether surprising. One Royal Air Force officer who had been sent to the hospital while a prisoner of the Germans in Frankfurt took advantage of an impromptu disguise when he saw a nurse's hat and cape hanging on one of the hospital walls.

He walked out of the hospital and into the street, but it did not take the police long to arrest this prisoner, who also sported a large mustache and flying boots.

Another attempt, made by Heinz Justus, a German prisoner of the British in 1917, was perhaps almost as futile. After several earlier attempts at escape had failed, Justus hit on the idea of simply walking through the main gate disguised as a Mr. Budd, the canteen manager who by chance was of similar size and shape. But he planned to travel on the British trains disguised as a female passenger, since he had been reliably informed that officials typically only checked the identity papers of male passengers.

The first stage of his plan went according to plan, as Justus strolled casually out of the camp and headed for the railway station, about two miles down the road. But soon after transforming himself into a woman, he ran into difficulties. He was lucky not to have aroused the suspicions of some British soldiers who bade him "good evening" but received no reply. Further along he was troubled by a shepherd's dog, which withdrew only when the escapee remembered his deterrent against such intrusion and reached for a box of pepper and sprinkled its contents around him, a well-known and proven canine repellent. But as he got closer and closer to the station, he was finally overtaken by some more British soldiers, who asked him if he had seen an escaped prisoner. Despite his best efforts of impersonation, it's not surprising that he quickly found himself behind bars.

References: Atkin, R. *Pillar of Fire.* London: Sidgwick and Jackson, 1990.

EXECUTION, ESCAPE FROM

Some dramatic escapes have been made by those who have nothing to lose and everything to gain if they succeed—those who are escaping from their execution.

A few prisoners have escaped death by breaking free just before their execution. Arthur Baxter of the Royal Warwickshire Regiment made a desperate bid for freedom from his German guards because he somehow sensed that he and his fellow prisoners were being taken to their deaths, though he had no way of knowing this. After his capture by a crack SS Panzer division at Wormhoudt, near Dunkirk, in May 1940, his gut feeling that danger lay ahead was so strong that he took the risk of running from his armed guard as he was marched away from the battle. Plunging through a gap in the hedge that alongside the road, he managed to survive the withering fire that was put down to stop him but was injured by a stick grenade that followed. Treated by a medical officer at an Allied artillery battery he stumbled across, he was put into an ambulance that was heading for the beaches and lived to tell the tale.

It proved to have been a risk well worth taking. He had noticed the sheer ferocity and brutality of the SS unit involved, the Adolf Hitler Regiment, and could see that their violence could easily spill over. Sure enough, only hours after he escaped his fellow prisoners were forced into a cramped barn and blown apart by SS grenades.

Several other prisoners have saved their skins by disappearing at just such an opportune moment. General Alexei Lukomsky, a White Russian general who fought the Bolsheviks during the Russian civil war, was captured by Russian villagers near Guliai-Borisov in February 1919, and though he vainly protested that he was just a traveling businessman, he was recognized and instantly brought before a revolutionary tribunal. Sentenced to death, Lukomsky watched his grave being dug and waited for the sentence to be carried out.

By chance, the villagers found and beat to death two other White Russians who had inadvertently strayed into the village, and as they fought among each other for possession of the dead men's boots, the general seized his chance and ran. He was scarcely able to believe his luck, not least since he had taken cyanide capsules some minutes before but—now to his relief—for some reason, they were having no effect at all.

In their desperation, some prisoners who face execution find a hidden strength that enables them to escape or at least to fight back. One British prisoner of war (POW) who was marched by the Germans to his place of execution in 1943 managed to wrestle a gun from the officer in charge of the execution squad and shoot him dead before being shot himself. And a British pilot named John Embry was determined to get away altogether when he was told that his days were numbered. Shot down over Europe, he was captured by the Germans and was held not as an airman disguised as a civilian but as a spy, whom, under the terms of the Geneva Convention, the Germans were entitled to execute. Embry was to be shot the day after his capture and was held under guard in a large farmhouse in northern France that was being used temporarily as the local German headquarters.

Realizing that he had nothing to lose, Embry put a hastily prepared plan into action. When a sentry brought him the glass of water that he had requested, the prisoner struck him as hard as he could on the jaw, seized his rifle, and made his way cautiously but quickly down the passage beyond. Just outside the exit into the courtyard was a second sentry. Luckily his back was turned. Hitting this sentry, too, very hard with the butt of the rifle, Embry now ran out of the courtyard, and with unusual presence of mind he then found a clever way of hiding by diving into a manure heap just outside the courtyard and digging a passage through the straw and into the muck. Just as the search for him began, he found himself in a place where no one thought anyone could hide and was able to make a full getaway after dark.

Other prisoners have been able to feign death and so escape before their death sentences could be carried out. During the Ardennes offensive in December 1944 one Belgian civilian, Monsieur Henri Geordin, was led from his home by the German soldier who had been instructed to execute him on the suspicion of harboring the enemy. Geordin took a deep breath and ran, knowing that he had nothing to lose. For what seemed like an age he heard no sound of rifle fire behind him and started to think he might get away, but then he felt an almighty crash that seemed to shatter his body and sent him rolling on the ground. Lying there motionless, he feigned death and fooled the German into thinking that he had been killed outright. He remained there, absolutely motionless, for five minutes or more. Geordin was one of the lucky members of a village, Stavelot, that lost 130 civilians to German terror that winter's day.

A very small number of prisoners have been spared execution as a result of the most unusual events. In March 1945 a number of Danish underground agents were awaiting execution at the Gestapo headquarters. They knew that because the Germans had built up an enormous dossier as a result of their interrogations, a similar fate awaited many of their former acquaintances on the outside. But just as further arrests and executions seemed imminent, the Royal Air Force raided the Gestapo building, blasting a hole in the roof. Many of the prisoners were able to break free and burn the files that the Germans had so painstakingly built up and that they were about to use to crack down on the entire underground movement. This was not without cost, however, since nine British airmen and eight prisoners lost their lives as a result of this daring operation.

See also: De Gaulle, Charles; Kashmir; Malmédy; McGartland, Martin

F

FANNING, DAVID (C. 1740–1800?)

During the American Revolution, David Fanning, a Loyalist governor of North Carolina, acquired a reputation not only for harsh cruelty toward his Patriot enemies but also for some dramatic escapes and rescues from their imprisonment.

To begin with he had worked alongside the Patriots, but when his sympathies had swung round to the British side he was imprisoned and tried for treason by his former comrades. He made his first dramatic escape, disappearing from his prison cell to join a party of Loyalist militia headed for east Florida. When the force stopped at the Savannah River and turned back, Fanning and a companion went on alone. They hid from the Colonial forces on their trail by lying low in nearby forests and eating only wild game, which they caught with their bare hands.

But the two were eventually caught some weeks later. This time escape would be harder for Fanning, who was stripped and chained to the floor. But somehow he again managed to free himself. He stole a horse from his captors and rode off into the night. This time, too, he hid in a nearby wood, eating nothing during the three days he was there apart from three eggs he found.

Now that he was free to fight the Patriot rebels, Fanning accomplished some remarkable rescues of captured Loyalists. In June 1781 he ordered his small force of 155 men to march to Cape Fear River to go to the rescue of 70 Loyalists who were in danger of being surrounded and captured on Drowning Creek. Though outnumbered by more than ten to one, his rapid and unorthodox military movements caught his enemy wholly by surprise, forcing them to flee,

after just one hour's fighting, with more than 100 casualties, against the 5 suffered by Fanning's men.

Even as his military prowess and his reputation for savage brutality grew, however, a few Patriots succeeded in escaping from him. In 1782 Fanning ordered the arrest of Andrew Hunter, who was suspected of supporting Patriot activity. When Hunter was captured, Fanning gave him 15 minutes to prepare for hanging. But with the energy typical of those who escape from execution, the prisoner broke free of his guards, jumped on Fanning's favorite horse, and bolted to freedom. It was an escape for which Fanning, despite his fury, may have harbored a secret admiration.

See also: Boston Massacre; Execution, escape from
References: Callahan, North. *Royal Raiders: The Tories of the American Revolution.* Indianapolis, IN: Bobs Merrill, 1963.

FOLEY, FRANK (1884–1958)

Though his deeds remained little known until long after the war, Frank Foley was responsible for saving perhaps more than 10,000 German Jews from persecution and extermination at the hands of the Nazis.

Foley was an officer in British Intelligence who was posted to the British Embassy in Berlin soon after Hitler rose to power in 1933. Though he ostensibly held an unimportant position at the embassy—he worked as its passport control officer—his work as a spy meant that he was more aware than most of the plight of the Jews, whom the Nazis began to persecute in earnest in the mid-1930s.

A man of great kindness, Foley used his authority at the embassy to evade regulations that restricted the issuing of passports to Jews who were desperate to leave the country and who approached him for help. Over a period of several years, he issued thousands of visas to Jews who wanted to go to Palestine as well as helping to provide documentation and access to escape routes out of the Reich for further thousands who would otherwise have undoubtedly perished. Some of these escapees he sheltered at his own home, and he found hiding places for others. These were acts of great bravery because he enjoyed no diplomatic immunity in his official position in Berlin and would have been executed as a spy if caught.

Foley's name later became well known in Israel. At the trial of Nazi war leader Adolf Eichmann in 1961, he was referred to as "the Scarlet Pimpernel." But he was mostly unknown elsewhere, largely because of his natural unobtrusiveness and because of the surreptitious nature of his work as a spy.

References: Smith, Michael. *Foley: The Spy Who Saved 10,000 Jews.* London: Hodder and Stoughton, 1999.

FORGERY AND IMPERSONATION

Many escapees have found their freedom by making good use of forgery and impersonation, using faked papers, often virtually indistinguishable from the real thing, and disguises.

During the Napoleonic Wars, a French soldier who was held by the British in Norman Cross managed to sew a complete uniform of the Hertfordshire Militia, which was then guarding the camp, and to make a wooden musket that was very convincingly colored and topped with a tin bayonet. Mingling with the British soldiers as the guard was changed one day, he was caught only when he placed his musket in the rack provided and found that it was slightly too big to fit. Since his colleagues immediately noticed, he was quickly found out and sent straight back to prison.

During the two world wars, similar audacious and inventive feats were carried out. At Stalag Luft III at Sagan—the setting for many escapes during its three-year occupation—the prison carpenters, all pris-

oners of war, were once asked by the Escape Committee to make some German rifles. It was not necessary for the rifles to work, they reassured them; the rifles only had to look the part. Though it seemed like a tall order, the carpenters quickly got to work, even creeping up behind German sentries on guard with measuring instruments to get a better idea of what they were supposed to be making. After a few weeks, they produced something very similar to the Germans' guns. The "rifles" were made of wood; to give them a metallic appearance, they were covered with pencil lead and then finely polished.

It is a testimony to their skill that the German soldiers who appeared out of the blue one day to escort some prisoners on a routine trip failed to attract a second glance from their "colleagues." All were in fact impostors who made a dash for the nearby woods as soon as they were out of sight. It was less fortunate that none of the three made it to freedom: Two were seized just as they started up a Junkers plane that they had bluffed their way to, and the third was recaptured in southern Germany.

At Colditz one attempt to design a German uniform so that a prisoner could bluff his way out met an unfortunate end. The plan was for the prisoner to disguise himself as the sergeant major in charge of the German battalion, and it could have worked brilliantly, since the prisoner's new uniform, appearance, mannerisms, and speech were almost indistinguishable from those of the real sergeant major. So it was particularly unfortunate that the real sergeant major happened to be looking just as his double was walking past. He put a quick stop to the escape attempt.

But forgery and imitation have nonetheless on occasion worked brilliantly. The story of "Albert RN"—a story that has become famous in escape history—is one example. "Albert" was the brainchild of Lt. D. P. James, imprisoned at a camp near Hamburg after his capture off the Dutch coast in February 1943. The question to which he turned his ingenious mind was simple: If the Germans regularly counted the number of prisoners under their command, how could he convince them he was there when in fact he had made a run for it? If he was to escape during one of his regular visits to the baths, at the far side of the prison compound, he knew his column would always be counted at the beginning of the trip and then again at the end.

James put his idea to the Escape Committee. Could not a papier-mâché head be made and painted to resemble his own? The guards always counted quickly and, if the head was properly designed, it was unlikely they would notice the substitution. And "Albert," he argued, could be assembled without too much difficulty in the bath house, from which he intended to make his escape, and carried out between the shoulders of two prisoners.

"Albert"—made within days by a professional artist, John Worsley—worked brilliantly, completely fooling the German sentries. Unfortunately James narrowly missed reaching a neutral ship at Lübeck docks. But the model had luckily gone undetected by the prison authorities, and James, never one to be easily dissuaded, made another attempt. Once again "Albert" was pressed into service, and once again he fooled the prison guards. This time James headed for Danzig and managed to board a Finnish ship.

One escapee from the Tower of London, George Kelly, assumed the identity of one of his guards, having studied their movements with great care, in order to find a way out of captivity. Imprisoned in 1716 for his part in the unsuccessful Jacobite Rebellion, Kelly made sure that he had become a popular and trusted figure among both the guards and his fellow prisoners before going into action, so that when he bought a horseman's heavy coat and claimed it was for the long winter nights no one suspected a thing. But his true motives were more devious, for he had noticed that at regular intervals he was guarded by soldiers of the Second Regiment of Foot Guards, all of whom were always dressed in long coats. When the sentries passed a man dressed almost indistinguishably from one of the Foot Guards, they thought nothing of it and allowed him to pass.

Escapees have also used all manner of disguises in order to hide their true identity. Wing Commander Sir Basil Embry was captured by the Germans in Flanders after baling out of his stricken fighter, escaped, was twice recaptured, and twice escaped again, leaving some dead sentries behind him in the process. But in order to find his way back to England on his last, successful attempt, he disguised himself as a country peasant, stealing the clothes off a scarecrow—top hat included—to do so.

An even simpler and more audacious disguise was adopted by two soldiers from the Argyll and Sutherland Highlanders, Privates Macfarlane and Goldie, who used a jimmy to break out of their Thuringian barracks in March 1942. Once free, they knew they would present an obvious target for the German soldiers and civilians who would soon be looking for them, since they were dressed in blue overalls whose backs were boldly marked "KG," for *Kriegsgefangenen*, "prisoners of war." So they took with them the simplest disguise—40-pound rucksacks, which completely covered the markings—and made sure they were never without when there was any possibility of being seen. Though they attracted a certain amount of attention on the road because of their large packs they were never stopped throughout their return journey to Britain, perhaps because they kept themselves scrupulously clean and tidy.

Forgery and imitation can be a matter not just of appearance and documentation, however, but also of linguistic skill, as Eric Loveluck proved while serving as an artillery officer in France in 1940. As the German advanced closer to his position, Loveluck and some colleagues began to retreat but they unwittingly ran into enemy soldiers who had taken up positions behind them.

Loveluck later recalled that, acting on impulse, he threw open the roof hatch of his tank and "yelled some choice abuse at the unsuspecting *Feldwebel* [who] leapt to attention and saluted as we swept through." He admitted that he was astonished by the reaction since "at the time I was wearing the service dress of a captain in the Royal

Northumberland Fusiliers, yet he swallowed it hook, line and sinker." Loveluck did, however, have one clear advantage: He had read German at Cambridge before the war and had a perfect accent.

One British soldier who narrowly missed being rescued at Dunkirk in May 1940 also made good use of his linguistic skills. Speaking excellent French and knowing the ways of the local people, Lieutenant Richard Doherty happened to stumble across a deserted farmhouse not far from Calais, which had just fallen to the Germans, and only had to change his clothes to carry out a convincing impersonation of a French farmer. When, shortly afterward, the German army arrived on his doorstep in search of British stragglers, Doherty was even able to sell them some farm produce at a good profit. He sailed back to Britain some weeks later.

Some British soldiers of the Fifty-First Division, also left behind after the evacuation, managed to walk from Calais to Spain, posing not as Frenchmen but as Russians. As Gaelic-speaking Scots, they baffled the Germans who stopped them to ask who they were, and since the German interpreters knew no better, they simply claimed to be Russians, fortunately at a time when there was a peace treaty between Hitler and Stalin.

See also: Alcatraz; Berlin Wall; Colditz; Iron Curtain; Wallenberg, Raoul

FRANCO-PRUSSIAN WAR (1870–1871)

Though the help of another escapee is often an essential ingredient in the success of an escape plan, one French runaway during the Franco-Prussian war of 1870–1871 gained his freedom at the deliberate expense of his fellow escapee.

The two soldiers, known as Loubet and Chouteau, were part of a column of captured French soldiers who were being moved along a road near the Belgian border. Seeing a thick wood only a short distance away, and since their Prussian guards had their backs turned, Loubet and Chouteau leaped over a hedge and into the field and headed straight for the safety of the woods.

Loubet was a good runner, and from the instant he headed off, it seemed he had a much better chance of getting away than Chouteau. But seeing that the Prussians were running after them and would soon catch up, Chouteau found a way—simple, devious, and malevolent—of making sure that it was his companion, not he, who was caught. "In one supreme effort," the narrator of the story says, "he dived between his companion's legs and brought him down; and while the two Prussians rushed to hold that man to the ground Chouteau darted into the wood and disappeared" (Zola 1972, 385).

Loubet was severely beaten by the Prussians as a punishment for attempting to escape, and he died shortly afterward. But though Chouteau had gained his freedom, he did so at a price: His name was now besmirched, for the other Frenchmen who had watched the scene "expressed their loathing of the criminal now running away in freedom, while they felt full of pity for his victim, poor devil" (Zola 1972, 385).

See also: Gambetta, Leon; Louis Napoleon
References: Zola, Emile. *Le Débâcle*. London: Penguin, 1972.

FRENCH GUIANA (C. 1880)

The islands of French Guiana, made infamous by the story of Papillon, were long used by the French government to detain their most ruthless criminals. But despite the brutal regime and their remote location, a sizable number of convicts were able to reach the South American mainland and start a new life.

A few escaped only with outside help, and one well-documented case of such a getaway occurred in the early 1920s. When one Frenchmen managed to sail away from one of the islands and reach Latin America, he did not forget his brother, who had also been convicted of the same murder in Montmartre and whom he had left behind at the colony. But with first-hand knowledge of the prison system, he was able to make his way back to rescue him.

He traveled first to Baltimore, where he spoke at length to some of the sailors from a freighter that traveled every two months to load minerals from some mines only 30 miles from St. Laurent, where his brother was being held. Having persuaded them to take him there, he then paid a native to find his brother and hand him a note that simply asked him to follow the Indian. When the convict received the note, he was quick to see its purpose, and, following the native as instructed, he was never seen by his captors again.

A few other runaways found ways of crossing the border into Dutch Guiana. Before 1923 the Dutch authorities had welcomed these runaways, making this a favorite goal of escapees, but the atrocious crimes committed by one fugitive when he arrived quickly ended their hospitality. Afterward, the only convicts who got away across this route were German nationals, who benefited from the special funds that the local German consul had at his disposal to help them get back to Europe.

One of the most risky means of escape, however, was to board a Brazilian contraband vessel, one of the few ships that passed the colonies at close range. Though a good number escaped by finding a hiding place on board, they risked being thrown overboard if they were unable to pay the Brazilians a hefty fee.

But, as the stories of Papillon and René Belbenoit show, a persistent and clever convict could conquer all these obstacles and reach the mainland.

See also: Belbenoit, René; Papillon
References: Belbenoit, René. *Dry Guillotine.* London: Jonathan Cape, 1971.

FUGITIVE SLAVE LAWS
(1850–1860)

The passage of the Fugitive Slave Laws by the U.S. Congress in 1850 meant that slaves who fled their owners could never relax their guard as long as they stayed on U.S. soil. Under the terms of the legislation their owners were entitled to reclaim possession if they were captured, and any well-wisher who tried to help them on their way to freedom was committing a criminal offense.

But though a great many slaves were returned to their owners, sometimes after getting within a whisker of reaching the Canadian border, a few were rescued after their discovery and arrest. Most of these incidents happened in the early 1850s, when resistance to the legislation was at its height.

Of the four most famous cases, the first concerned a slave called Frederick Jones, who had escaped from his owner in 1850, after working as a waiter at a coffee house in Boston. But before long he was tracked down, rearrested, and put in custody while his defense lawyers prepared his case.

Soon after he arrived at the Boston court, a large crowd gathered outside, loudly protesting his right to remain at liberty. As their protests became louder and louder, some of them pushed down the door and ran inside. One of the defense lawyers later wrote that he had seen two former slaves bearing the prisoner between them, running down the steps, bundling him into a nearby carriage, and driving him away before anyone could stop them. Jones soon made it to Canada to start a new life.

A more violent incident occurred the following year at Christiana in Pennsylvania when a farmer named Edward Gorsuch set out to pursue two of his missing slaves. When he finally tracked them down, he, Deputy U.S. Marshal Henry W. Kline, and some accomplices went to rearrest them. Almost instantly a group of blacks appeared at the fugitives' side, and violence soon broke out. Both sides were armed, and in the resulting shoot-out Gorsuch was killed and an accomplice injured, while three of the blacks were shot dead. The two escapees, in the meantime, fled into the night and were never apprehended.

By no means all of those who went to the rescue of fugitive slaves were blacks, however, and when a slave known as Jerry was arrested in Syracuse, New York, in 1851, most of those who went to his rescue were of European origin. When Jerry was taken to the courtroom, the group that gathered, made up mainly of abolitionist whites, soon became violent, and before long a group of them broke into the police station to secure his release. When, within minutes, the police had tracked down the small party of rescuers and rearrested Jerry, the rescuers were undeterred. Following him back to the police station, they quickly drew up a new plan of action. Twenty minutes later they had succeeded in breaking inside and putting the runaway onto a coach heading for the Canadian border.

Support for or opposition to the Fugitive Slave Laws was not determined by racial factors so much as by geographical lines. The laws had strong support from the South but met equally powerful opposition in the North, and it was inevitable that these rescue incidents severely soured relations between the North and South. As one correspondent for the *Savannah Republican* wrote prophetically, "These scenes are too common in the north and if persisted in will lead eventually from sectional jealousy to the bitterest hate and revenge."

References: Campbell, Stanley W. *The Slave Catchers.* Chapel Hill: University of North Carolina Press, 1970.

G

GAMBETTA, LEON
(1838–1882)

Besieged in Paris by the Prussian army in 1870, the French republican politician Leon Gambetta used a very simple way to escape his sophisticated enemy, slipping out of their grasp with a style and panache that have made his name famous.

Gambetta needed to escape from the capital to organize an effective war effort against the Prussian advance, whose rapidity had stunned the French high command. By the end of September the Prussians had already captured Toulon and Strasbourg, Tours was under threat, and Orléans had been invaded. French politicians and sol-

Leon Gambetta used a balloon to escape from besieged Paris in 1870 in legendary style. (Library of Congress)

diers were in a state of total disarray. The invaders were laying siege to the capital, which cut off their communications with the outside world and forced them to rely on carrier pigeons to get messages through.

Gambetta, a leader in the new republican movement that had swept away Napoleon III, wanted to stay in the capital, where he felt he was most needed. However, as minister of the interior and a highly dynamic and charismatic leader, he was widely seen as the individual best suited to the task of organizing the war effort. Despite his initial reluctance, he was soon inspired by a patriotic vision of saving the land of his birth: "I shall come back with an army and if I have the honour of saving France I shall ask no more of fate" (Deschanel 1920).

Shortly after 11 o'clock on 7 October 1870, two balloons, the *Armand Barbes* and the *George Sand*, rose from the Place Saint-Pierre at Montmartre in Paris. They took with them, among others, Leon Gambetta and his confidant, Francois Spuller. Though the flight began well—it was a fine day—before long they met trouble. As they approached the frontline positions outside Paris, they were attacked by Prussian troops, who fired guns and on some occasions even artillery at them as they passed overhead. They were already at a good altitude, about 2,000 feet above the ground, when they encountered this fearsome assault, but they were forced to climb even higher to avoid the bullets they could hear humming by.

They soon moved out of range, but worse followed. One of the balloons suddenly and unexpectedly lost altitude, and before long it had crash-landed on a stretch of open ground only a short distance from a Prussian position. As quickly as they could, the Frenchmen threw out some ballast to get the balloon off the ground and out of their enemy's reach.

The balloon was attacked again near Criel, this time by Würtemburger troops. Only good fortune prevented them from downing the balloon as it drifted at an uncomfortably low altitude of 600 feet. The only injury to the passengers was from a bullet that grazed Gambetta's hand as, once more, they struggled to gain height.

But at about 6 P.M. that evening, shortly before dark, the two balloons landed near Montdidier. Their passengers, relieved that the dangerous journey was over, reached Amiens shortly afterward and began to organize the war effort.

See also: Franco-Prussian War

References: Deschanel, Paul. *Gambetta.* London: Heinemann, 1920.

GAMBIAN RESCUE (1981)

In the summer of 1981 the British Special Air Service (SAS) was deployed to rescue about 30 people taken hostage in a coup attempt in Gambia. They managed both to free the hostages and to destroy the enemy with a bare minimum of force.

The coup took place while the country's president, Sir Dawda Jawara, was in London to attend the wedding of Prince Charles and Lady Diana. On 5 August a small but well-armed Marxist force backed by Libya and Angola seized key installations in the Gambian capital, Banjul, and announced that it had toppled the Jawara regime. At a military center not far from Banjul the insurrectionists also seized 30 hostages, including the wife and children of the former president. Partly because Gambia was its former colony, and partly because the Marxist-inspired coup took place at the height of the Cold War, the British government asked the SAS to step in to try to restore the former ruler.

By the time the three British officers assigned to the task arrived at nearby Daca to consider the situation on the ground, the rebels no longer held such a commanding position. Forces friendly to the deposed ruler had taken over much of the country, including the capital, confining the rebel force to the coastal areas. But the three officers, led by Major Ian Crooke, still had to consider the fate not only of the 30 hostages but also of an entire expatriate community of 400 Europeans, including British and U.S. embassy staff, whose residential areas had been overrun.

Crooke's plan to free them was twofold: To begin with, his team made a thorough reconnaissance of the entire coastal area in order to find any positions the rebel force had left relatively unguarded. They found a road that allowed them to move almost unseen directly to where the hostages were being held. He then selected a team of local soldiers, putting them through an intense training course specifically to take on the rebels and release their prisoners.

Before he deployed his new field force, Crooke and his two SAS colleagues probed their enemies' fighting skills, reconnoitering their positions from nearby. It quickly became apparent they were not of the highest caliber, so taking a small group of men, dressed in civilian clothes but heavily armed, across the front line he was able to make four soldiers who were guarding some of the hostages to lay down their weapons. Within minutes the deposed president's wife and child were back in safe hands.

If that experience was anything to go by, Crooke reasoned, then his enemy would be susceptible not just to the *use* of firepower but to the mere threat of it. So, lining up as much armor as he could muster, Crooke personally led a column that stormed through the front lines toward the rebel headquarters. The enemy soldiers fled in terror.

In an operation that lasted only two days, the SAS officers had managed to restore order and rescue all the hostages. Though the enemy they faced was not in the same league with others they had been trained to take on, the mission in Gambia had still been no small achievement.

References: Davies, Barry. *SAS Rescue.* London: Sidgewick and Jackson, 1996.

Geraghty, Tony. *Who Dares Wins.* London: Warner, 1993.

GARIBALDI, GIUSEPPE
(1807–1882)

In the true spirit of his deeply romantic image, the Italian nationalist revolutionary Giuseppe Garibaldi twice escaped the clutches of his enemies.

Garibaldi was a leader in the Young Italy movement—a group of idealistic nationalists who wanted to foment revolution in order to unify the separate Italian states. In his first dramatic escape he deserted from the Sardinian navy to help incite revolution

An 1860 engraving of General Giuseppe Garibaldi, the famous Italian revolutionary who twice escaped the clutches of his enemies. (Library of Congress)

in Genoa and then had to escape from the authorities of Genoa.

Garibaldi was serving on the *Eurydice* when, in February 1834, he heard news of impending revolution in Genoa, only a short distance from where the ship was docked. Desperate to get into the thick of action, he feigned sickness and obtained a permit to leave the ship and see a doctor on the mainland. Though on his arrival he found no sign of the revolution he had expected, he had no wish to turn back. Knowing the Sardinians would soon be searching for him, he set out to find a suitable hiding place.

He chose a dance hall, thinking that his pursuers would have difficulty barging through the festivities around him. He hid at the back and saw no sign of them all evening.

He made contact with members of the Young Italy movement during the evening and was able to find shelter at a house nearby. Now that there was no immediate prospect of political upheaval, he intended to go to Nice. But getting out of the city would not be easy. Government spies and police were on every street corner, and because he was a leader of the revolutionary movement, the government had also issued a detailed description of his appearance and offered a reward for information on his whereabouts.

Nevertheless, disguised by a cloak and large hat, the young Garibaldi was able to make his way through the streets of Genoa. He avoided the main highways and the busy but well-guarded port. Instead, he traveled along the quiet byways and footpaths, sometimes down small alleys, through back gardens and over walls and hedges until, on 5 February, a day after he had arrived, he slipped quietly out of Genoa. He had found the risk of discovery and arrest far more terrifying than the prospect of death on the battlefield, where his courage had already been well proven.

Some 15 years later, in July 1848, the revolutionary leader—by this time perhaps one of the most famous people in Europe—was forced to escape again, this time from the Austrians. Having suffered a heavy military defeat at their hands, Garibaldi fled with several hundred followers to the neutral town of San Marino in central Italy. But he knew they would not be able to stay there long, living off the goodwill of the governors while the Austrians surrounded them. They would have to escape.

Shortly after midnight he persuaded the porter to quietly open the town gates. Slipping through the Austrian lines, Garibaldi and his 200 followers headed west toward Venice, following dangerous mountain routes, usually in strict silence, with the help of a local guide. Though some got lost in the dark and were never seen again, the others safely reached the coast the next day and were able to continue with the rest of their journey towards their own lines.

References: Ridley, Jasper. *Garibaldi.* New York: Viking Press, 1976.

GERMAN SECRET SERVICE

Despite U.S. neutrality at the beginning of World War I, U.S. industry and financial organizations supplied Britain with huge amounts of materials that allowed it to wage war against Germany. In an attempt to win sympathy for the Kaiser's cause, the German secret service began to wage a covert war of intrigue, espionage, and sabotage.

The lucky escape of a U.S. spy, Frank Burke, helped prove the full extent of these operations. In May 1915, on the instructions of President Woodrow Wilson, the U.S. Secret Service began to investigate suspected German activities, in particular the activities of the German commercial attaché, Dr. Heinrich Albert. On 23 July Albert boarded a train in New York, shadowed by Burke. He inadvertently left his briefcase behind when he left the train at Fiftieth Street, but he saw Burke make off with it and instantly gave chase.

Burke just managed to escape, hurriedly boarding another train and telling the astonished conductor he was being followed by a lunatic. According to Burke's report on the incident, "the wild-eyed appearance of the Doctor corroborated my statement, and the conductor called to the motorman to pass the next corner without stopping so the nut could not get on" (McAdoo 1931).

As a result, the U.S. authorities obtained firsthand evidence of German covert activities, which caused an uproar when they were published shortly afterward.

References: McAdoo, William G. *Crowded Years*. New York: Houghton Mifflin, 1931.

Wilson, Arthur Link. *The Struggle for Neutrality*. Princeton, NJ: Princeton University Press, 1960.

GIRAUD, GEN. HENRI (1879–1949)

Though he succeeded in escaping from Nazi captivity, the French General Henri Giraud failed to find the freedom he had long craved.

At the outbreak of war in 1939 Giraud was already a veteran of one escape from the Germans, having fled a prisoner of war camp in World War I. Though he was 61 when he was captured in 1940, he was still not deterred from rappelling down the high walls of the castle where he was being held and making off into the night.

He traveled by train toward Vichy France, but he had no papers and realized that the German police, who were checking the papers of every passenger, would arrest him and discover who he really was. He was saved by his quick and clever thinking: Seeing an officer from Rommel's Afrikacorps in one of the compartments, he sat down and struck up a conversation about desert warfare. In his perfect German, he deployed his considerable knowledge of the desert to explain how Rommel could best defeat the Allied armies. When the ticket inspector arrived, the German officer snapped an order to be left alone, not wanting such a fascinating conversation to be interrupted.

At another railway station he was dismayed to see German officials laboriously inspecting the tickets of everyone boarding, but he once again worked out a way to evade them. Waiting until the very last moment, as the train was pulling out, he posed as a hassled German businessman, glasses halfway down his nose and cheeks puffed out, who had to catch the train to attend an important meeting. The officials not only let him pass but even helped him on board.

When he finally reached Marshal Philippe Pétain, his story made him something of a popular hero. But because the Germans wanted him back in prison, Giraud was forced to go into hiding and soon found that, far from finding his liberty, he had in fact merely swapped one form of prison for another. It was only some time later, when he was covertly taken to Britain, that he finally found the freedom he craved.

References: Bouscet, René. *De Gaulle–Giraud*. Paris: Flammarion, 1967.

GLASS, CHARLES (1951–)

In 1985 Charles Glass, an American journalist, escaped his captors in war-torn Beirut.

In the wake of the Israeli invasion of Lebanon in 1982, several radical Islamic groups had sought to draw the world's attention to their cause by kidnapping Western citizens. Most of those held were released unharmed, though some, like John MacCarthey and Terry Waite, endured very long periods of imprisonment, while others, such as the American expatriate Peter Kilburn, were murdered by their captors. Glass was one of the very few who managed to escape.

At the time of his kidnap he had been living in Beirut for some years, working as a journalist for a U.S. television channel. On 16 June 1985, while driving outside the city, his car was flagged down by a group of young men, all brandishing assault rifles. He had no option but to stop, and he was forced out of his car and bundled into a waiting van.

With a gun pointed straight at his head, Glass had no chance of emulating the escape bid of British correspondent David Hirst, who in a similar situation had jumped out of the car when it slowed down at an intersection and hidden in the back streets as the terrorists searched for him. Glass had no option but to let his captors take him to a succession of buildings and apartments in downtown Beirut, where he knew he would have no real chance of ever being found.

Like the other prisoners of the Lebanese radicals, Glass was held in very difficult conditions during the weeks that followed. Always chained, he was only rarely allowed to wash or shave and was fed only a meager diet that rapidly depleted his strength, if not his will to escape. Constantly interrogated by his captors, who tried to make him admit to being a CIA spy, he on occasion came close to complete psychological breakdown.

A few things kept his hopes alive. On the rare occasions he was allowed to visit the bathroom, he was able to cut his finger with his razor and write SOS messages in blood; he would then tear a hole in the blind and throw them out of the window. During the first few weeks he was able to send a good number of such messages, even though they were eventually found by his own guards rather than by any local citizen who might be drawn by his promises of a $10,000 reward.

After nearly two months of captivity Glass was able to work out a plan of escape. Held on one of the top floors of a Beirut hotel, he was able to slip off his blindfold while his guards slept and start picking at the chain attached to his ankle. To begin with he sawed away with a nail that he managed to remove from the wardrobe his guards used to block his access to the window blind, but he quickly realized that he was wasting his energies. Instead he ingeniously led his guards to misjudge the length of the chain wrapped around his ankle. The chain circling his ankle had 14 links. Glass reckoned that if there were just 4 more, he would be able to simply slip the chain off and disappear while his guards were asleep.

While the chain was attached to his ankle, Glass took thread from his discarded blindfold and sewed two links together, praying that when one of the guards came to unlock the padlock and take the chain off so that he could visit the bathroom, they would not notice what he had done. After he had washed and shaved, the guard would always wrap the chain around his ankle and lock it with the padlock. But this time, the guard unwittingly put the padlock into position not on the fourteenth link but

on the fifteenth. Glass was then able to repeat the process in order to create a sixteenth link and so on until he was able to cut the thread, release the four extra links and then slip his foot out of the chain.

At last his chance had come. He headed straight for the window and gently pushed aside the wardrobe to get at it. But when he reached the balcony outside, he found to his horror not only that he was far too high to be able to jump, but also that he had no chance of climbing onto any adjacent balcony to escape. His only option was to go back into the apartment, steal past his sleeping guards, and head for the door.

Moving as quietly as he could, Glass crept through the room, hearing only the loud snores of his captors, lying on the floor beneath him with their rifles at their sides. As he went through the main entrance, he was careful to take the key and lock the door behind him before he fled down the stairs.

All alone in the middle of the night, Glass moved cautiously through the back streets of Beirut, hiding every time a vehicle passed him in case his enemies were in pursuit. Though he was unable to trust most of the people he came across, he did eventually get a lift from local people to central Beirut, where he contacted the Syrian authorities. After 62 days in captivity, Charles Glass was free.

References: Glass, Charles. *Tribes with Flags: A Journey Curtailed.* London: Seckler Warburg, 1990.

GORDIEVSKY, OLEG (1938–)

Many of the Russian defectors who fled their homeland to the West in the days of postwar communism did so for mundane reasons. One left because he had lost a secret KGB document and did not want to face the consequences, another went in search of a more comfortable life, and another is known to have wanted only to escape his wife. But some fled for ideological reasons, perhaps because they genuinely hated the regime they were part of or perhaps because, like Oleg Gordievsky, they had passed secrets to the West and were forced to flee for their lives.

Gordievsky was the highest-ranking KGB officer ever to work for Britain. For 11 years, from 1974 to 1985, he acted as a secret agent for the British Secret Intelligence Service (SIS) while at the KGB bases in Copenhagen and London. Passing on many important Russian secrets, including the names of the moles within Western intelligence services, Gordievsky is widely considered to have done more than any other KGB officer to help bring about the collapse of communism.

But during the summer of 1985 the KGB net began to close around Gordievsky, who had been named by Aldrich Ames, a KGB agent working within the CIA, as the likely source of the first-class intelligence reaching the West. Though several other KGB traitors, also betrayed by Ames, were immediately sent to their deaths, the Soviets decided to move Gordievsky from London back to Moscow and to use covert surveillance to obtain the conclusive proof they needed to justify putting him to death. Like other trained spies, Gordievsky quickly realized that the KGB was preparing to move in for the kill and that it was therefore time to activate the escape plan prepared for him by the SIS.

The details of the escape plan had been bound into the covers of two English novels that he kept in his Moscow apartment. Afraid the KGB may have planted a secret camera in his Moscow flat—he knew for sure it was bugged—Gordievsky went into a small laundry room and by candlelight read what was written on the cellophane sheet hidden behind the flyleaf.

To warn the British that he was in danger, went the instructions, he would first of all have to appear on a certain street corner at 7 P.M. on the night of Tuesday, 16 June, and then stand by a lamppost on the edge of the pavement, holding a plastic shopping bag. Once he had given this message, the instructions went on, his escape would be set up for the following Saturday from a place in a forest near Viborg, on the border between the Soviet Union and Finland.

For a few agonizing minutes on the Tuesday evening, Gordievsky feared the escape plan had fallen through. As he waited on the pavement at seven o'clock that summer evening, he could see no one who resembled any of the British intelligence officers he had gotten to know over the last few years. As the minutes ticked away—5, 10, then 15 minutes past the appointed time—still there was no sign of anyone in the endless flow of faces, many of them KGB agents, that streamed passed him. But at last, at 25 minutes past the hour, Gordievsky saw his MI6 contact, "a man with an unmistakably British look, carrying a dark-green Harrods bag and eating a Mars bar." As they walked past each other, Gordievsky wrote, "he stared straight at me, and I gazed into his eyes, shouting silently 'Yes! It's me! I need urgent help!'" (Gordievsky 1995, 10). Though the contact lasted only seconds, Gordievsky knew that his message had made it through and that the escape plan would be activated.

His next task was to buy a railway ticket to Leningrad, and to do this he had to evade the KGB agents who he knew would be following him and who he was sure would arrest him if they saw him buying the ticket. So before setting out he was careful to change his shoes, knowing that one favorite KGB trick was to sprinkle their quarry's shoes with radioactive dust that allowed them to follow every move. As soon as he went round a corner he sprinted a short way into a block of flats and then looked back. He saw a car and a pedestrian searching frantically for him and knew he would probably have just enough time to buy the ticket before they caught up with him again. He headed for the station, weaving in and out of the crowds.

He had made a good start, and his journey to a remote spot outside Viborg, made by train, by bus, and on foot and helped along the way by a lift from a KGB official, was untroubled. But, as before, he wondered if his luck had run out, as he waited and anxiously watched the appointed time come and go—2:30, 2:40, 2:50. After he had waited half an hour, a car at last arrived and two Britons stepped out to greet him.

Hidden in the trunk, Gordievsky heard the car pass through five frontier barriers before it was finally stopped by frontier guards. He could hear his drivers talking with officials outside, and he heard the whining and sniffing of the dogs trained to search for hidden goods and defectors. At this point he thought the game was up, but the driver was using an old but effective tactic of diverting the dogs: feeding them potato chips when the guards looked away.

Finally, after six or seven minutes of waiting, the car engine suddenly started up again and they were on their way. From the trunk Gordievsky could hear Sibelius's *Finlandia* being suddenly blasted from the car radio, and knew that they had at last broken though.

See also: Berlin Wall; Blake, George; Iron Curtain; Kalbowski, Harry; Myagkov, Capt. Aleksei

References: Gordievsky, Oleg. *Next Stop Execution: The Autobiography of Oleg Gordievsky.* Basingstoke, Eng. Macmillan, 1995.

Gordievsky, Oleg, and Christopher Andrew. *KGB: The Inside Story of Its Foreign Operations from Lenin to Gorbachev.* London: Hodder and Stoughton, 1990.

THE GREAT ESCAPE (1944)

During World War II the Nazi authorities ordered that several thousand Allied airmen should be housed together at Stalag Luft III near Sagan. They had no idea that, far from making escape more difficult, they were pooling an astonishing array of escaping talent that made the "Great Escape" possible.

By the time the Great Escape took place, several remarkable escape attempts had already been made from Stalag Luft III. Within weeks of its opening, in the summer of 1942, three officers had walked out and made for the nearby airfield in the hope of requisitioning an aircraft for a flight home. They found nothing there, so they headed for the northern ports. They were finally arrested at Stettin, where they had hoped to stow away to Sweden. At about the same time, several teams had also collaborated on the construction of a tunnel—more than 300 feet long—that was discovered by the German authorities only shortly before it was ready to be used. And a year later, in October 1943, the camp was also the site of the famous "Wooden Horse," which allowed

three prisoners of war (POWs) to return to Britain. In all, it has been reckoned, about 60 tunneling projects were started during the three years the camp was occupied.

Like the others who contemplated escape by tunnel—notably, their contemporaries who used a wooden horse to conceal the tunnel—the Escape Committee, run by a South African–born airman named Roger Bushell, was confronted with formidable obstacles. The Germans had sunk seismographs nine feet into the ground, 33 feet apart, to detect any tunneling activity. They had raised the prison huts several feet off the ground so they could see anything going on underneath. And during 1943 an enormous trench, more than seven feet deep, was built around the entire compound, which made escaping even more difficult than it had been.

But because of the sheer size of the camp—nearly 10,000 strong by 1944—there was no shortage of skills that could be called on to find a way around these obstacles. A Canadian mining engineer, Wally Flood, assured the Escape Committee that there was no reason, given the time and materials, why a tunnel could not be dug deeper than the 25-foot range of the seismographic devices. And as another prisoner, a Polish officer with similar professional training, had already found out from his own researches, a tunnel could be built under the washrooms or stoves, the two places where the buildings could not be raised off the ground. There were also miners, carpenters, and engineers on site who were able and willing to join and try a new tunnel.

Bushell's plan, hatched in the spring of 1943, was nonetheless highly ambitious. There were to be three tunnels, "Tom," "Dick," and "Harry," that could be interchanged in the event of discovery. All three would run very deep—30 feet down—to evade the listening devices. The displaced sand was to be removed from the tunnel by trolley and then concealed inside the trousers of individual prisoners, who would drain it out of their trouser legs elsewhere in the camp, where it would be trodden into the ground. The tunnels would also be guarded by a number of prisoners who kept a constant watch on the German guards in case they made a spot-check on the prison huts.

Though their construction got off to a good start—it took just two months for Tom to reach the outside perimeter—there were also serious setbacks. The Germans, needing more timber, had cut down many of the trees in the adjacent forest that was supposed to provide the prisoners with cover. The extra 50 yards the tunnel would have to run to get there made the whole enterprise far more difficult. More seriously still, a German guard had by chance noticed more sand than he expected in some unlikely parts of the compound, and the thorough investigations that followed revealed Tom only days before it was to be used. But Bushell still had two other tunnels to play with, though it was to be several months before either was ready. It was not until 14 March 1944, eight months after Tom had been discovered and blown up, that its brother tunnel Harry was finally ready for action.

Though 200 men had been prepared to break out in a single night, only 76 were able to escape on the night of the break, 24 March 1944. Twenty prisoners got away in the first hour, but then the operation was brought to an abrupt halt when all the prison lights were turned off during an Allied air raid. It was impossible for the prisoners to see what they were doing in the dark. At last, after two hours, the lights came back on and another 40 were able to make their way out of the camp, but before long a routine German patrol caused yet another holdup, which meant that, with dawn approaching, only a few more could go.

But the breakout from the prison compound was nearly over. As the last three men left, a German guard saw one of them disappearing into the woods in the early morning light and raised the alarm. The guards instantly opened fire, and the compound was surrounded and sealed.

Of the 76 men who found their way out that March night, only 3 reached the safety of neutral territory. Another 15 were brought back to Sagan, and 8 others, who all survived, were sent to a concentration camp at Oranienburg. But after capture the remaining 50, Bushell included, were rounded up and machine-gunned on the orders of Hitler and his field marshall, Wilhelm Keitel, both infuriated by the distraction that the Great Escape had caused them and anxious to deter any other would-be escapees. The escapees ashes were scattered at Sagan by the other prisoners, and several of their killers, after the war, were tried and hanged. It was a tragic end to the greatest escape of all.

See also: Colditz; Wooden Horse

References: Brickhill, Paul. *The Great Escape*. New York: Norton, 1950.

Burgess, Alan. *The Longest Tunnel: The True Story of the Great Escape*. Bath: Chivers, 1991.

GRIMSON, GEORGE (1918–1944)

The outstanding bravery and resourcefulness of George Grimson, who escaped from German detention, was quickly acknowledged by fellow prisoners, who recognized his exceptional talents.

A Royal Air Force warrant officer whose Wellington was shot down over Germany early in World War II, Grimson quickly showed an extraordinary determination to get free, making several attempts to escape the various POW camps in which he was held before finally succeeding. On one occasion, while outside the compound, he caught a guard unaware, kicked him violently and fled into the nearby woods. On another occasion he impersonated a German corporal, to whom he bore a certain similarity, and walked brazenly past the main checkpoint wearing an imitation German uniform. A later attempt to fool the sentries by disguising himself as a Polish factory worker was also foiled.

His other attempts at escape showed equal ingenuity and determination. Disguising himself as one of the electrical engineers who had arrived in the camp to make repairs, Grimson deliberately dropped his pliers outside the highest barbed-wire fence while he was checking the insulation. He slipped past the sentry on the gate to fetch them and then, while an accomplice distracted the sentry, he ran off into the woods. But once again he was recaptured soon afterwards.

Grimson knew that to get out he would have to carry out a detailed surveillance of German movements in order to find the chinks in their armor. He saw that each morning, after the prisoners' parade, the sentries would casually hang around the camp gates while awaiting further orders. He reckoned that, wearing one of the imitation uniforms that were carefully prepared by the tailors in the camp, he could mingle with this group of guards as a prelude to making his escape.

On the morning of 21 January 1944 Grimson got out of his hiding place at the end of the parade, slung his dummy rifle across his shoulder, and wandered toward the gates, unnoticed by the real guards. Though 20 sentries had arrived on the parade ground half and hour before, 21 now left it.

Once outside the main gates, he moved quickly toward a small hut where the Germans kept incoming Red Cross parcels and used a duplicated key to get inside. He quickly changed into civilian clothes, with carefully prepared forged documents stuffed inside his briefcase, and left the camp, leaving behind his imitation uniform for other prisoners to pick up when they had the chance. Once they did so, he knew the Germans would have no real idea how he had managed to get free.

Grimson was then able to set up an escape line for other prisoners who were moving toward Sweden, although his efforts to help them to safety led to his detection and execution by the Gestapo only three months later.

References: Dominy, John. *The Sergeant Escapers.* London: Allan, 1974.

GROTIUS, HUGO (1583–1645)

One of the most famous escapes of the seventeenth century was made by the Dutch political philosopher Hugo Grotius, who was imprisoned by his enemies in the southern Netherlands in 1619.

In January 1621, after he had already been held in detention for more than a year and a half, Grotius's wife put her mind to carrying out an escape plan, and she saw a clear opportunity. For more than a year her husband had been allowed to borrow books from friends and colleagues on the outside, and she knew that the chest in which they were transported, together with spare linen, was moved in and out of the prison without attracting a second glance. Though it was little more than three and a half feet long, she bored some holes in the chest, which would enable him to breathe, and looked for the right moment to hide her husband in it and spirit him away.

Her chance came shortly afterward, when the governor of the prison left for Heusden to find recruits for his army against the rebels of the northern provinces. She introduced herself to the governor's wife and claimed not only that was her husband unwell but also that she wanted to remove a considerable number of books from his rooms, arguing that he might be tempted to read them and make his condi-

Hugo Grotius, the Dutch political philosopher who made one of the most famous escapes of the seventeenth century. (Library of Congress)

tion worse. So when the moment of escape came, the governor's wife might at least be fooled if any of the guards informed her that the chest was heavier than usual.

Shut up inside the chest, Grotius was carried out of his room by two soldiers who were supposed to be on guard. Both of these men noticed that the chest was much heavier than usual, and one went straight to the governor's wife to tell her that someone was probably inside it. But, for some reason that has never been known—some have said it was negligence, others that she overlooked it—she did nothing about it and merely told them to carry on lifting it out of the prison, assuring them that it was packed full of books.

In addition, after he was moved out of the prison, the other warders failed to notice that he was missing. Part of his wife's ploy had been to tell them that his illness would not only keep him in bed and out of sight but was also highly infectious, a claim that kept them well away from his room for some time. By the time the philosopher's absence was noticed, he had arrived in Brabant.

Inside the chest, Grotius now started a lengthy journey to freedom. He was put first on a boat to Gorkum and then on the back of a horse—a very uncomfortable experience—and taken to the house of a friend, David Dazalaer. Emerging from the chest, Grotius was taken through the streets to another boat that took him to Brabant and thereafter to the safety of Antwerp, where he arrived on 21 March.

His wife's story also has a happy ending. Questioned by the governor, she admitted that she had masterminded her husband's escape, and after giving him a detailed account of how she had done it she was herself sent to prison. But a few weeks after her husband reached Antwerp she was released, having gained the admiration of the government minsters whom she had petitioned for clemency.

See also: Brown, Henry

References: Burigny, Jean Lévesque de. The Life of Grotius. English translation, London. Printed for A. Millar. 1754.

H

HACKENSACK RIVER (1776)

When, in November 1776, George Washington ordered the evacuation of his men across the Hackensack River, he was forced to sacrifice a large quantity of arms and supplies.

When Washington received a dispatch that a strong British force had crossed the Hudson River and was approaching his stronghold at Fort Lee, Washington quickly ordered the evacuation of the fortress. But he knew there was only one avenue of escape, a single bridge across the Hackensack River, and unless they could reach it before the British force did, all would be lost.

His 2,000 soldiers assembled hastily and marched off, with Washington at the head of the column. But behind them they left most of their cannons, tents, and entrenching tools and nearly all their baggage. Though it was a loss Washington bitterly regretted, it was also inevitable, for leaving the arms and supplies behind allowed them to get to the bridge first, ahead of the British by just a few hours.

See also: Boston Massacre; New York; Valcour Island
References: Greene, J., and J. R. Pole. *Blackwell Encyclopaedia of the American Revolution.* Oxford: Blackwell, 1992.

HALDANE, CAPT. AYLMER (1862–1950)

Unlike his fellow British officer, Winston Churchill, Capt. Aylmer Haldane escaped from Boer captivity in 1899 not by going over the fence but, rather, by hiding inside the prison compound, waiting for the subsequent search for him to die down, and then finally making his move.

The hiding place that Haldane and a few fellow Britons chose lay in a gap underneath the floor of one of the rooms in which they were being held. The Boers had no idea that this gap existed because the building, a former school, had not long been in their possession and they had not had a chance to explore its every nook and cranny.

Lying low in their hiding place was no easy matter. The escapees had not dared to take much bedding with them, since its absence would have suggested they were still on site. Nor did they have much room to move in the cramped space, and they had only the barest amount of fresh air, food, and water. "Coughing, sneezing or talking above a whisper was absolutely forbidden" (Haldane 1900, 56), wrote Haldane later, adding that their inability to wash and the intense boredom, broken only by very occasional bouts of excitement, made the experience extremely trying.

Having hidden themselves in the compartments during the night of 26 February 1899, they waited for the inevitable commotion they knew would result as soon as their beds were found empty early the next morning. Sure enough, soon after the sentries noticed them missing, at 5:30 A.M., an extensive search began, and before long the escapees could hear the Boers' footsteps and voices as they hurriedly searched the room above them. But despite their guards' exhaustive efforts, they remained undiscovered, and by 11 A.M. the Boer authorities had called off the search inside the prison, assuming that they had escaped.

When the other prisoners heard the next day's newspaper reports, it was clear that the Boers had taken the bait. The *Volkstem* reported that the escapees were well on their way to Mafeking and that they had left clues—the remains of a roasted fowl and a hat—along their supposed trail. But though the escapees knew how effectively they had misled the Boers, they still waited two full weeks before finally moving. Haldane wrote later, "[We] fully recognised that each day that passed would give us a longer start when the time to emerge from the school came, for the officials had no idea that we were in Pretoria, and our having escaped was becoming ancient history" (Haldane 1900, 57). Waiting was to prove an astute move, and within a month of leaving the school they reached the British lines, having traveled across enemy territory on foot and by rail virtually undetected.

See also: Churchill, Sir Winston L. S.; Collet, Charles
References: Haldane, Aylmer. *How We Escaped from Pretoria.* Edinburgh: Blackwood and Sons, 1900.

"HARRIS, ELIZA"

Though it is a work of fiction, the classic story *Uncle Tom's Cabin* has a sound factual basis. When she wrote of the dramatic escape of the fictional character Eliza Harris from her owners, fleeing over an icy river into the arms of her rescuers, the author, Harriet Beecher Stowe, consciously had in mind two true stories of runaway slaves in nineteenth-century America.

The first inspiration for her story was the flight of a young slave—her name is unknown—who had been well treated by her owners but whose good fortune changed when their business began to fail, placing them in financial difficulty. Reluctantly, they decided to sell her to another business but to keep and raise her young child. The heartbroken slave determined to escape at any cost so that she would not have to suffer the trauma of separation.

She wrapped her child in a blanket and, very late one night, crept out of the house. Reaching the banks of the Ohio River early the next day, she persuaded the keeper of a small inn to provide temporary shelter. But when, a few hours later, she saw her owners in the distance, she knew she would have to take a desperate course of action.

Though the river was half-frozen, covered in large blocks of rapidly melting ice, she grabbed her child and ran across the ice,

nearly losing her footing and plunging to her death on more than one occasion but just managing to reach the other side. Turning around, she caught the anguished expression of her enemies, who were not desperate enough to follow her onto the ice, and she was free to accept the offer of shelter and support made by a kindly doctor who had seen her dramatic crossing and hurried over to help her.

At this point, Eliza Harris's story takes on elements of another true story, one in which the author was personally involved. In 1839 she had employed as a servant a young woman who had once been a slave but who had legally acquired her freedom. Though it was at this time illegal, the kidnapping of fugitive slaves was a lucrative trade, and word soon reached them that their young servant had been targeted.

Before long, Beecher Stowe had arranged for her servant to be taken to an individual named John Van Zandt (who appears in the book as a character called Van Tromp). At his remote farm in Kentucky, Van Zandt had already given his own slaves their freedom and was always happy to help others secure their freedom. With his help the fugitive was put on her way to Cincinnati, where she finally settled.

See also: Fugitive Slave Laws; Parker, John; Underground Railroad
References: Johnston, Johanna. *Runaway to Heaven: The Life of Harriet Beecher.* Garden City, NY: Doubleday, 1963.

HINDS, ALFIE (1918–1991)

Convicted of robbery in 1954, Alfie Hinds always claimed to have been motivated to escape from custody by a simple desire to protest his innocence and to bring the attention of the national press to his case. Escaping three times in the course of a single prison sentence, and always managing to make the headlines, he certainly succeeded in getting the attention he was so determined to attract.

Hinds's first break was made from Nottingham Prison in November 1955. As the other prisoners mingled, he and a fellow escapee, Patsy Fleming, were able to make their way into a cellar and to climb through a grate into the prison yard. They found an ingenious way of getting over the outer wall: They broke into the carpentry workshop, carried off two doors, propped them up against the wall, and shinned over. Hiding between orange boxes that were packed into the back of a truck, they were unnoticed by the police, who had set up road blocks all over the area within minutes of their breakout. Both men remained at large for three months before they were finally detected and resumed their sentence.

The following year, Hinds, now a prisoner at Pentonville, found another way out of captivity by making full use of his weekly visit to the London Law Courts. He got in touch with some of his contacts on the outside and arranged for a sympathizer to tape a padlock and key underneath the table in the tea room area of the law courts. He sat at the appropriate place, and when, a few hours later, he asked his officer escorts for permission to visit the toilet, they found the door slammed shut and padlocked behind them. Hinds fled while they could do nothing except shout for someone to come and release them. Following a prearranged getaway route, Hinds once again enjoyed several months of freedom before he was found and returned to jail to serve what was left of his sentence.

This time sent to Chelmsford Prison in Essex, Hinds still showed an irrepressible desire to escape. In the summer of 1958 he managed to find a way from the prison corridors into a store that gave him access to the grounds and the perimeter wall beyond. At an agreed-upon moment, a fellow prisoner started kicking and screaming, distracting the warders' attention. Hinds balanced two wheelbarrows one on top of the other and climbed over the wall. Though he ripped his hands on the barbed wire and nearly gave himself a concussion as he dropped some 25 feet to the ground, still he managed to get free of the area before the police arrived to look for him.

Hinds remained at large for some weeks, lying low with an acquaintance in Kent before, yet again, returning to custody. Though he was finally released shortly afterward, he ultimately failed to clear his name, well known though it had become as a result of so many escapes.

References: Bean, J. P. *Over the Wall: True Stories of the Master Jail Breakers.* London: Headline, 1994.

HOLZMINDEN (1918)

Probably the greatest tunnel escape of World War I took place at Holzminden in 1918, when a large number of Allied prisoners succeeded in breaking out of German captivity.

The leader of this great escape was Maj. H. G. Durnford, a British officer captured at the Ypres Salient in 1917. Appalled at the prospect of spending any length of time in captivity and greatly excited by the challenge of escape, he quickly set to work to organize a plan and implement it.

At first the prospect of building a tunnel, starting from the basement of one of the prison buildings and emerging outside, did not seem daunting, for the distance was less than 20 feet. Such a tunnel, he estimated conservatively, could probably be built in weeks, unless of course they were extremely unlucky and their path was blocked by rocks. In only a short time, a team had been put together and was preparing to start digging.

The prisoners used very basic materials, adapting them ingeniously to fit their needs. The tunnelers used trowels and chisels and relied only on bare candlelight. The ventilation system was simple: A homemade bellows, built from wood and leather from a flying coat, forced air into a pipe composed of several biscuit tins. The pipe was sunk into the floor of the tunnel, with its end as close to the tunneler's face as possible, like a simple oxygen mask. The threat of a collapse was kept at bay by wooden boards, which were taken from all over the camp, often from those who knew nothing of the real reason for their sudden disappearance, and which provided adequate support.

The use of such simple devices did not of course make the tunneler's job easy, and in his own account of the story Durnford noted that the romantic image of a tunnel escape obscures the less-appealing reality. The work of construction, he noted, was one of "damp clay and earth, mice, old clothes and much-breathed air." Work was always slow and frustrating, and the men had to be worked by well-considered rotas if they were to take the strain.

By cruel coincidence—an uncanny coincidence not unusual in escape stories— guards were suddenly and unaccountably introduced outside the perimeter fence, at almost exactly the point where the tunnel was designed to emerge. Knowing that a few months previously, at another camp at Schwarmstadt, other escapees had risked emerging from their own tunnel relatively close to the guards and had taken casualties as a result, Durnford ordered the tunnel to be extended another 50 yards, though underneath he felt bitter disappointment at the considerable amount of extra time that this would take. When, in the summer of 1918, the tunnel was at last ready to be used, it was nearly 60 yards long and had taken more than nine months to complete.

When, during the night of the 24 July, 29 prisoners used the tunnel to make their way out of the camp and into the German countryside, Durnford contemplated how fortunate they had been that the commandant, Hans Niemeyer, had not found the tunnel during the considerable time it had taken them to build it. Shortly before the break, some prisoners had asked to be transferred from their relatively luxurious rooms in one wing of the camp to a block near the tunnel entrance, and even though they gave no convincing reason, Niemeyer's suspicions were not aroused. On another occasion, an officer was found coming out of the basement, where prisoners were not allowed, but it was the sentry, unable to identify the particular individual, who was penalized. These, and several other clues that a more astute commandant would have detected, all went uninvestigated. And at no time during the long months that the tunnelers dug was the camp subjected to the sweeping and thorough searches that made similar escapes during the next world war so difficult. The reason for this glaring lack, Durnford felt, was complacency on the part of an individual who was sure the prisoners simply had insufficient means to get out of a compound that had been specifically designed to keep them in.

Of the 29 prisoners who fled into the darkness of that July night, 10 made it back to Allied territory. The rest were recaptured within days. But it was a spectacular break, and one that heralded the even more impressive digging feats of World War II.

See also: The Great Escape

References: Durnford, H. G. *The Tunnelers of Holzminden.* Cambridge: Cambridge University Press, 1930.

HOUDINI, HARRY (1874–1926)

Nearly a hundred years since his escapology astounded audiences throughout Europe and the United States, the name "Harry Houdini" today remains almost as famous as it was in his heyday, bearing testimony to his extraordinary powers.

Born Ehrich Weiss, the young Houdini changed his name at 17 after reading the

A contemporary billboard depicting Harry Houdini's extraordinary escape acts, which astonished audiences. (Library of Congress)

memoirs of Robert Houdi, the great French magician of the midnineteenth century whose story greatly inspired him. He later claimed that he had also derived many ideas after visiting an insane asylum, where he had seen some of the patients trussed up in straitjackets and struggling to free themselves.

Beginning his career as an escapologist in his late teens, the young Houdini quickly made a name for himself in the United States by performing his "substitution trick." For this feat, he would put himself in a large sack, which was sealed and put in a large trunk that was then tied and padlocked down. A screen was then put round the trunk while Houdini wrestled his way out, to emerge triumphantly after a few minutes.

He used his unusual skills to persuade skeptical theater managers to promote his shows. When he first visited Britain, in 1899, he claimed that he would escape from any handcuffs that any of his agents could find. He had himself locked in a pair of Scotland Yard handcuffs and freed himself within 20 minutes. The theatrical agents of London were soon begging him to sign a contract.

Over the next few years Houdini astounded vast crowds throughout Europe and America. He performed jail escapes, removing leg irons at a German prison in 1902 and escaping from an American death row cell in 1905. He jumped off bridges, fully bound, most famously from the Belle Isle Bridge near Detroit in 1906, and he wriggled free from straitjackets and special challenge containers. In Washington, he once broke out of a zinc-lined piano box, and in Boston in 1907 he got out of a coffin that was nailed shut by members of the audience. He broke free from an iron boiler and, in San Francisco, from a government mail-pouch. Nothing it seemed, could hold Harry Houdini.

During his career, there were of course several occasions when he was nearly defeated. At Blackburn in 1902 he offered £25 to anyone who was able to tie him down successfully, and one man, perhaps wanting to be as famous as Houdini, appeared with six sets of heavy irons, complete with chains

and padlocks, and spent considerable time attaching them. Behind a curtain, Houdini wrestled continuously in the hope of escape. After 20 minutes, to the dismay of his audience, he still seemed to be fully bound. Only after two hours did he finally manage to get free. Two years later, he took a full hour to release himself from a pair of handcuffs that had taken a blacksmith five years to make.

Over the course of his career Houdini became increasingly daring. In 1912, at the height of his powers and fame, he had himself lowered into the East River in New York, fully manacled and contained in an iron-weighted box that had been specially made for him. He emerged after 57 seconds, and the ecstatic press reports about his feat ensured that his subsequent performance at the city's Hammerstein Theatre was a sell-out. Shortly afterward he began performing another feat that daunted all the rival escape artists who tried to emulate him: He would be suspended from the top of a skyscraper, bound at his ankles and struggling to free himself from a straitjacket while upside down. Swinging around wildly in the strong winds, Houdini could not fail to impress the crowds below.

There have been many attempts to explain Houdini's powers of escape. Writing in 1930, for example, Sir Arthur Conan Doyle dismissed suggestions that he had relied on a pick-lock hidden under a plaster on the sole of his foot, not least because no one else had even come close to rivaling his feats using these same tricks. Doyle mentioned the instance of two unfortunate such rivals, one in the United States and the other in Germany, who had jumped into rivers in weighted packing cases and perished in the attempt. Others have argued that the members of the audience whom Houdini invited onto the stage to examine the locks and restraints were always specially selected individuals who were paid to say the right thing.

There is little doubt that some of his tricks can be explained. One of Houdini's most famous tricks was his escape from a large, solidly made trunk, like a giant milk bottle, that had no air holes and that was locked, roped, and submerged before he made his escape from it before an audience. Though he was always locked inside the trunk before an audience, he always managed to reappear within minutes of being submerged, and always without a trace of any water on him. The trick, according to one biographer, was that there was a secret compartment hidden inside the trunk, and that weights sank half the trunk to the bottom while Houdini escaped from the top.

But however one might try to explain his life and career, Houdini will almost certainly always be regarded as the greatest of all escapees.

References: Brandon, Ruth. The Life and Many Deaths of Harry Houdini. London: Mandarin, 1994.
Gibson, W. B. Houdini's Escapes. London: Phillip Allan and Co., 1931.

IRANIAN EMBASSY SIEGE
(1980)

When the Iranian embassy in London was taken over and its staff held hostage in the summer of 1980, neither the perpetrators nor the general public had ever heard of the organization that was shortly to conduct one of the most famous, and successful, rescue operations ever conducted in Western Europe.

The siege began on 30 April when a group of Iraqi terrorists forced their way into the embassy at Prince's Gate in Kensington, West London, and took 15 Iranians and one Briton hostage. Firing submachine guns and a Browning pistol as they arrived, nearly killing the policemen who guarded the entrance, it was obvious from the outset that this siege would be at least as difficult as any other faced by a Western government.

The terrorists were all members of a small Arab minority that lived under Iranian jurisdiction near the Iraqi border. The area had been under Iraqi sovereignty until only a few years earlier, changing hands in 1975, and by 1979 it was an obvious target for Saddam Hussein, who had seized power in Iraq in 1979 and who regarded territorial acquisition as a form of self-aggrandizement. By sponsoring the embassy siege Saddam sought to focus the world's attention on this corner of the world and to demand the release of the political prisoners held in Tehran, who had actively opposed Iranian rule over the region.

Entrusted with ending the siege and rescuing the hostages, the Special Air Service (SAS) faced no easy task. The Arabs were extremely well armed, with hand grenades, submachine guns, and large quantities of ammunition at their disposal. All the doors and windows were of course barricaded and constantly guarded, and any attempt to smash through them would have given the hijackers ample warning. With little to lose, they would in all likelihood kill as many of their hostages as they could if they started to lose ground to any rescue team trying to take the embassy by storm.

The SAS began by moving a small team to a nearby building a few hundred yards away. They were smuggled in inside moving vans to avoid press attention. If worst came to worst, military chiefs argued, and the captors started killing their hostages before any other plans had been made, the embassy could be raided by this forward team on a few minutes notice.

With these contingency plans in place, they then prepared for an assault on the embassy, an assault that they could mount at their own discretion. A full-scale model of the embassy was quickly but carefully put together at the nearby Regent's Park Barracks, based on photographs, architectural drawings, and witnesses' statements, and a plan of action was devised and rehearsed.

Their task was, however, facilitated by the use of some ingenious new surveillance devices, now being used for the first time. When some of the hostages began to complain about peculiar noises inside the walls, they could not have known that from the adjacent buildings a technical support team was quietly drilling holes in the wall and inserting miniature microphones and camera lenses to let them know exactly where the terrorists were. Though the Iraqis quickly became suspicious, they were reassured by the explanation of the British policeman present that it was only a

London mouse quietly making its way through the building, as it usually did.

The decision to end negotiations and use military force came when one of the hostages, the embassy's chief press officer, Abbas Lavasani, was murdered and his body dumped outside the front door, fulfilling the gunmen's promise to kill one of the captives if their demands were not met. Within minutes of Lavasani's body being picked up, the order was given committing the SAS to battle.

Two different teams were now put on ten-minute standby for a full-scale assault. Red Team took up positions on the embassy roof, masked and armed, and got ready to rappel down the wall and into the windows below to clear the top half of the building. The task of taking on the lower half was entrusted to the soldiers of Blue Team, who were waiting behind the walls in the garden and in adjacent buildings in order to blast a way in through the ground floor windows. Elsewhere snipers trained their telescopic sights on the embassy windows. Wearing individual headsets, each then waited for the order to make a move from a command unit that was stationed on the sixth floor of a nearby building.

When the the order was given Red Team began its speedy but silent descent by rope from the roof of the embassy, but they nearly met disaster: The team leader was trapped at a crucial moment when his rope became tangled in its harness, and his teammates, queuing behind him, accidentally broke a window as they tried to free him. Though the watching commanders had planned to pause the operation at this moment, there was now no time to delay, in case the terrorists had been alerted. Instead, they shouted through their microphones for the soldiers to go in straightaway and finish the operation.

Seconds later an explosive device, which had been carefully lowered from the roof to the windows, was detonated, rocking the entire building and bringing down some of the roof. The soldiers began to lob gas grenades inside. As they did so, Blue Team smashed through the ground floor windows and joined the assault.

At this point both rescuers and hostages had another near miss. While some of the soldiers were seeking to blow in a first-floor window, a terrorist armed with a machine gun appeared on the floor above and threw a hand grenade down at them. It was sheer good fortune that in the extreme stress of the moment he forgot to remove the pin. The grenade bounced away harmlessly. Instead, he was an easy target for the highly trained sniper teams watching and was dispatched by a single shot from an SAS soldier hiding in a nearby building.

As the SAS teams moved quickly through the building, luck once again came into play. One of the British soldiers had a gunman— Shakir Sultan Said—in the sights of his submachine gun, but it jammed at the crucial moment, allowing his prey to escape. Perhaps the best fortune of all was reserved for the hostages: Only one was killed and one other seriously wounded in the intense shoot-out that followed. For as the assault began, one of the terrorists opened fire with a submachine gun and another started shooting at them with a pistol. One of the embassy staff owed his life to a coin in his pocket; it deflected a bullet that would have gone straight through him. The firing suddenly stopped after a few moments as the terrorists lost their nerve and instead tried to melt in with the hostages in a last-ditch attempt to save their lives.

Another near miss was due more to the superb training of the rescuers than to good fortune. As one of the soldiers broke through the door to the room where most of the hostages were being kept, he was confronted by the terrorist Said, who had eluded him minutes before and who was now one of the few terrorists putting up armed resistance. With his finger on a grenade, Said was waiting for the SAS to arrive before blowing up everyone, himself included. But the British soldier proved to be fractionally faster than Said. He fired at the terrorist as soon as he broke through the door and hit him in the head.

The Iranian embassy siege remains one of the most successful antiterrorist operations ever mounted. It exacted only a modest toll from the rescuers and the rescued—

one SAS man was badly burned—but it gave a dire warning to other terrorist groups not to take similar risks on British soil. Only one of the terrorists—known only as Nejad—survived the siege; he was later given a life sentence for manslaughter. Having taken on an opposing force that was heavily armed with grenades, explosives, and automatic weapons, the Special Air Service, for the first time, attracted the admiration of the world.

> See also: Bangkok Airport; Entebbe; Iranian hostage rescue operation; Mogadishu plane rescue; Munich; Peruvian embassy siege
>
> References: Davies, Barry. SAS Rescue. London: Sidgewick and Jackson, 1996.
> Geraghty, Tony. Who Dares Wins. London: Warner, 1993.

IRANIAN HOSTAGE RESCUE OPERATION (1980)

The tragic consequences of Operation Rice Bowl, the attempt to free the U.S. hostages held by revolutionary forces in Tehran in 1980, revealed that complex rescue plans allow far more room for error than do simple plans of action.

The background to the seizure of the hostages lay in the virulent anti-Americanism of the radical Islamic militants, led by Ayatollah Ruholla Khomeini, who toppled the shah of Iran in February 1979. The source of their hostility lay not only in their perception that American materialism and secularism were antithetical to their own values and way of life but also in their belief that policymakers in Washington were actively trying to impose their influence and authority on other parts of the world, including their own.

On 4 November 1979, in this climate of fear and suspicion, the Ayatollah Khomeini's Revolutionary Guards broke into the American embassy compound in Tehran and seized 63 members of its staff. The hostage takers made their release conditional upon a single demand: that the U.S. government use its diplomatic weight to force the shah to return to Iran to face "revolutionary justice."

For President Jimmy Carter and his team—notably his National Security Adviser

Zbigniew Brzezinski—there was never any question of giving in to the Iranian demands. Besides the electoral cost of being seen to give way, such a policy gave encouragement to other would-be kidnappers and also failed to show any loyalty to a long-term ally. They decided to seek a military solution instead of a diplomatic solution and to try to rescue the hostages.

Operation Rice Bowl was planned by a small number of officials inside the Pentagon, including Charles Beckwith, a founder of the elite Delta Force; Brzezinski; Admiral Stansfield Turner, the director of the CIA; and General David Jones, the chairman of the Joint Chiefs of Staff. Having agreed upon the general aims and scope of the rescue mission, the more complex task of implementing it was delegated specifically to Beckwith and his associate, General James Vaught.

Beckwith and Vaught had only a limited amount of intelligence to rely on. Satellites and SR71 reconnaissance aircraft initially provided detailed pictures of the embassy grounds that were later augmented by a CIA agent, Dick Meadows, who had managed to infiltrate Tehran posing as an Irish businessman. The statements provided by the hostages who were released in late November also gave the planners some insight into the strength of the guard and the daily routines of the hostages, even though such information would probably be out of date by the time any assault took place.

By the end of November, despite the lack of detailed, up-to-date information, the picture that had emerged was not promising. Storming the embassy meant overrunning a much bigger area than other rescue missions—such as the raids on Entebbe or Son Tay—had had to contend with. The embassy compound covered some 27 acres and contained 14 buildings, and an assault would have to be perfectly timed if the guards were not to be alerted. To make matters worse, a few of the diplomats were being held separately from the others in a Foreign Ministry building some kilometers away.

By mid-January a complex plan had emerged. A 100-strong force of Delta sol-

The wreckage of one of the U.S. helicopters involved in the aborted attempt to rescue the hostages from the U.S. embassy in Tehran in 1979. (Corbis-Bettmann)

diers would be flown by C130 Hercules transport planes to a desert strip in southeast Iran—"Desert One"—which was to act as a stepping-stone for the rescue. They would then be joined by eight helicopters, flying from the USS *Nimitz* in the Persian Gulf, which would use the transports to refuel before taking the soldiers to another base, Desert Two, some 100 kilometers from the Iranian capital. After a few hours rest, they would then be driven by truck to a third site before being taken to the embassy and the foreign ministry to execute the assault. Having rescued the hostages, they would be picked up by the helicopters, which were to be kept under cover at Desert Two, and then flown to safety.

On 24 April 1980, eight days after President Carter had approved the plans, 132 men—soldiers, interpreters, and intelligence and communications experts— arrived at different U.S. bases across the Middle East and began the rescue mission they had spent months preparing for. Using

carefully plotted routes and timings to avoid being picked up by Iranian radar, the C130s left the Gulf. After eight hours of flying they arrived, almost on schedule, at the airstrip that a CIA mission had covertly laid out at Desert One a few weeks before. Using a prearranged radio signal, Dick Meadows, who had waited patiently for their arrival, at last acknowledged that everything had so far gone according to plan and that it was now time for the helicopters, bringing in the Delta soldiers, to move.

It was at this point that things began to go wrong. Of the eight helicopters that set off from the USS *Nimitz* that night, several quickly began to develop technical faults. Shortly after it crossed into Iranian airspace, the pilots of number 6 were forced to land their craft and board another when its warning lights signaled that one if its rotor blades was breaking up. Soon afterward, the instruments of number 5 began to fail, prompting the pilots—accused by some of mere cowardice—to renounce their part in the operation and return to base. Of the remaining six helicopters, two were seriously delayed when they flew into unexpected dust storms and were grounded while they waited for it to pass.

As soon as it became clear that two helicopters had already turned back and that two of the remaining six were several hours late, Beckwith contacted Vaught to recommend the cancellation of the mission. The request was put to the president, who agreed. But as the withdrawal began, even more mishaps occurred. As one of the helicopters flew close to the C130 in order to refuel, it was blown to the ground by a sudden gust of wind and ignited. In the deafening explosion that ensued, which sent flames hundreds of feet into the night sky, three of the helicopter pilots and the whole five-person crew of the transport plane died.

Though the fire could easily have exacted a higher toll, the aborted mission was a disaster for everyone involved, including the political authorities who had ordered it and the military personnel who had planned it. The Iranians, arriving on the scene the following day, found a considerable amount of classified material that had been left behind, including codes, maps, military and communications equipment, and even details about CIA agents inside Iran. Pictures of the downed helicopters and burned pilots were broadcast on television to the world and exhibited to the journalists they invited to tour the landing area. Recriminations in the military were far-reaching and bitter, as individual units and commanders pointed fingers at each other but denied responsibility themselves. And President Carter instantly became unelectable to a public that watched him admit responsibility for a full-scale national disaster, a disaster that was all the more painful for coming less than five years after the fall of Saigon.

After the event, military experts were quick to point out the reasons for the mission's failure. The plan was overly complex, since it depended on the rescue force moving to no fewer than three different bases before it even began its attack. This would have been difficult enough for any force to

contend with, but in addition, the assault team was made up of members of no fewer than 21 different agencies, including Delta Force, Rangers, Navy SEALS, Air Force pilots, and CIA, and therefore lacked any central chain of command. This had become painfully obvious, for example, at Desert One, where there were four different commanders, one each for the air control unit, the helicopters, Delta Force, and the security team, none of whom had absolute authority over the others. The operation was also undertaken by officers who were not only inexperienced in the unconventional warfare involved but who were also thrown into a new chain of command, rather than the existing one that had been proven to work.

The repercussions of the aborted mission were probably more serious for its planners than for the hostages, and the reputation of the U.S. military only began to recover with the later operations in Panama and the Gulf war.

See also: Iranian embassy siege; Tehran
References: McFadden, Robert. No Hiding Place. New York: Times Books, 1981.

IRIAN JAYA (1996)

In the summer of 1996 a team of conservationists, mainly Europeans, were rescued in the forests of Irian Jaya from the clutches of local rebels who had seized them as hostages some weeks before.

The conservationists had arrived on the island in January 1996 to study its cultural and natural landscape. But they had overlooked the fact that they were seen as legitimate targets by local members of the rebel OPM (Organisasi Papua Merdeka) movement, who recognized that their kidnap would attract the attention of the outside world to the plight of their organization.

The OPM's grievances were directed at the Indonesian government, which had semicolonized the eastern half of the island in order to exploit its natural resources and whose army terrorized any locals who protested. For more than 30 years, Indonesian jets had strafed and dropped napalm on the pockets of armed resistance that tried vainly to stop them. The focus of the local resistance was the giant U.S.-Indonesian installation at Freeport, which was situated next to a gold mine.

In February 1996 the expeditionary team was held hostage by armed gunmen and taken to a hiding place only 100 miles from Mapanduma. For more than four months the team was held under armed guard by the rebels, while diplomats and representatives of the Red Cross tried to secure their release. They were all well looked after during this time, mainly because the villagers nearby urged their captors to treat them as guests, not enemies, and they were not threatened with violence.

The end of their captivity came suddenly, when last-minute hopes of a peaceful outcome were dashed. The Red Cross had offered the rebels a deal that, if implemented by the Indonesians, would have given them a long-term health program and international support. The rebels unaccountably rejected the deal. The Indonesian army was ordered to move in, but as they did so the OPM guerrillas shot dead the two Indonesian members of the expedition before surrendering. In the confusion, the others managed to slip away and reach the safety of the Indonesian lines, bringing a sudden, and bloody, end to a protracted hostage saga.

References: Start, Daniel. *The Open Cage*. London: HarperCollins, 1998.

IRON CURTAIN (1945–1989)

The "Iron Curtain" that was drawn across Eastern Europe by the Soviet Army as it moved through Nazi-occupied territory in the latter stages of World War II was a material as well as a cultural and psychological barrier between different political ideologies. But despite the Soviet determination to stop their own people from escaping, a considerable number succeeded.

Those who were caught—whether they were citizens of the communist countries or not—could expect no mercy. Most went to prison for six or seven years, with no hope of early release, in prisons that made their Western equivalents seem like models of

luxury. The East German prisons in particular had the reputation as the roughest in the Eastern bloc, and many of those who served a term in them took a long time to recover their health afterward.

Some of those who sought to escape were smuggled out by sympathizers in the West. One such sympathizer was an Englishman, Peter Dupre, who became involved in "refugee smuggling" by chance. He answered an intriguing advertisement in the West German press that offered a "free holiday," all expenses paid, to a "clever" individual. Using a specially converted compartment hidden behind a bed in a trailer, Dupre succeeded in smuggling two East Germans to the West in the summer of 1982, crossing what was widely reckoned to be the least heavily guarded border in the Iron Curtain, the border between Austria and Hungary. A year later, while trying exactly the same thing, he proved less fortunate: The caravan was for some unapparent reason searched much more carefully by the border guards.

An East German family heads for the West German border in 1949, before Soviet authorities tightened the border defenses of the "Iron Curtain" throughout Eastern Europe. (UPI/Corbis-Bettmann)

A great many of those who crossed the Iron Curtain on their own initiative used forged documents. Phillip Hewitt, an Irishman who wanted to smuggle his fiancée out of East Germany to marry her, borrowed his parents' passport, which entitled them to travel together as a married couple. He stuck his own photo over his father's and changed the date of birth. Then he obtained a visa that would allow him to travel from East Germany to Prague, where regulations and checks were less stringent and where the authorities would not be aware that he had entered the Eastern bloc alone. Traveling from East Germany as two separate individuals, pretending not to know each other, they posed as Mr. and Mrs. Hewitt as soon as they crossed the border and the guards were changed. Then, taking seats in a compartment that was being used by several Western couples, mainly Austrians, who were returning to Vienna, they crossed the border and arrived on Western soil unchallenged.

Remarkably, one professional gang that organized escapes did not *copy* passports but daringly *invented* them. If they could make documents that resembled passports and copy only the stamps given to all incoming Western visitors, they argued, then escapees could cross the border claiming to be holding Spanish, Greek, or Turkish nationality. This worked for a short time. The East German police took longer to see through another deception devised by the same gang: With forged UN passports, refugees were able to get to the West by posing as UN delegates who were returning to the West after undertaking official business. To complete the effect, the gang always hired luxury cars for the escapees to travel in.

A few lucky individuals escaped to the West by sea. One East German who made a particularly dramatic escape by sea was Karl Bley. Bley spent all his savings to go on a holiday that he would never have taken had he not considered it to be his only real chance of escape: a cruise from the Baltic coast across the Atlantic to Havana, a focus both of the East's ideological sympathy and of its commercial interest, on a ship that was used by many vacationing East Germans. He wrote to his brother, a U.S. resident, telling him his plans and forthcoming movements, and sailed for Cuba, having no idea of exactly when he would have a chance to disappear.

Wandering around the deck as Cuba and the nearby U.S. coast appeared on the horizon, Bley realized that he was not alone. Bley knew enough about the system he was trying to escape to realize, when he saw three somewhat sinister men surreptitiously staring at him from the other side, trying to look innocent, that these were secret service men with orders to look out for escapees, or perhaps even to shadow him in particular. Getting to the United States, he now realized, would be much harder than he had at first thought.

But unknown to him, his brother, who had waited for the ship to arrive off the U.S. coast, was ready to come to his rescue. Knowing that Karl would almost certainly not be able to stow away a rowboat and that he would instead be forced to swim a considerable distance to get to shore, he made good use of his pilot's license and hired a small, light seaplane. If he could circle the ship, then Karl would hopefully realize his brother had come to rescue him and would jump into the sea so that he could be picked up.

As the plane flew low and circled the ship, all eyes on deck turned to watch it. Seeing his chance, Bley jumped overboard, heading for the U.S. coast, and he soon saw the plane land a short distance from him. He was whisked off to shore before the three secret service men, swimming furiously after him, could catch up.

There is one other known case of an East German escaping by sea, although she did so in a more cynical and unpleasant manner. Unable to get on board a holiday cruiser like the one Bley escaped from, Karin Kabofski introduced herself to lonely sailors, knowing that if she married one she would occasionally be granted permission to accompany her husband on long trips away: Married women, it was assumed, would not be likely to abandon their husbands and flee abroad.

But the calculating Kabofski was determined to do just that, and she sailed from Rostock in the summer of 1965 with that express intention. Unable to slip away at London, their first port of call, she waited patiently until they reached Havana before making her move. Still it proved too difficult to get away, and it was not until they arrived in Mexico that she was at last able to disappear. She played a determined but ruthless confidence trick on both the East German government and her heartbroken husband, who was told of her defection by the Mexican government a few days later and who never heard from her again.

See also: Berlin Wall; Cuba, escape from; Gordievsky, Oleg; Kalbowski, Harry; Myagkov, Capt. Aleksei

References: Dupre, Peter. *Caught in the Act: A True Story.* Tunbridge Wells, Eng.: Costello, 1988.

Gelb, Norman. *The Berlin Wall.* London: Michael Joseph, 1986.

Hildebrandt, Rainer. *It Happened at the Wall.* Berlin: Verlag Haus am Checkpoint Charlie, 1992.

Shadrake, Alan. *The Yellow Pimpernels: Escape Stories of the Berlin Wall.* London: Hale, 1974.

J

JAPANESE ARMY, PRISONERS OF (1942–1945)

There are many reasons why prisoners of the Germans were far more likely to attempt escape than their counterparts in the Far East. For although the Nazi authorities began to take a far harder line against captured escapees in the last stages of the war, killing 50 in cold blood after the "Great Escape," for example, the Japanese had never shied away from using savage violence against those they caught. Most of their victims were killed—usually bayoneted or beheaded—in front of other prisoners to make an example of them. And any prisoner contemplating escape knew that if he did disappear the Japanese would without hesitation keep their word and kill ten other prisoners.

Not surprisingly, such savage reprisals meant that there were very few escape attempts made by the prisoners of the Japanese. Most were in any case half-starved, suffered regularly from serious disease, and had almost no detailed knowledge of where to go in order to find their way to safety. The thick jungle around them would have seriously slowed down even the most determined escapee, as well as leaving clear tracks for the highly skilled trackers who would have quickly followed them. And any escapee—instantly recognizable by his skin—would probably have been found by one of the local tribes and either killed or handed back to his captors.

The fate shared by some of those who tried to break away from the infamous River Kwai railway was typical. There was one attempted escape from Tamarkan in Thailand by two British officers who were at large in the jungle for three weeks before being recaptured, interrogated, and then bayoneted. In December 1942 three Dutchmen were shot for trying to escape in the Burma sector, and a short while later an Australian who had escaped from the Wegale Camp and walked five miles to Thanbyuzayat in a bid to reach Rangoon gave himself up at a Japanese base and was also instantly put to death. It is likely that some of the people making these tragic and desperate efforts to escape had been made delirious by the deprivation and hardship of the captivity they were forced to endure.

Of those who were not prisoners but who found themselves on Japanese-held territory, perhaps several hundred got away. A group of ten Americans escaped from the Philippines, and a Dutch group got out of Burma and Thailand. A few others, mainly Australians, were also able to reach their homeland from Borneo and Ambon. On 25 October 1943, Privates Oscar B. Brown and Robert Lee Pease escaped from the Davao Penal Colony on Mindanao by killing a guard while working in a rice paddy and running off. One of the very few known instances of a prisoner escaping from a Japanese prison camp is that of a British soldier, Pvt. Ras Pagani, in 1942.

By the time Pagani escaped from the Japanese he was already a veteran of several similar attempts, some of them successful, made earlier in the war, notably at Dunkirk, Singapore, and Padang. He appears to have been planning his escape from the River Kwai from the moment of his arrival in Burma, and he had postponed his original plan to escape from the Burmese coastal area when he had heard that he was to be moved northward, the very direction he planned to take.

Pagani somehow managed to slip out of the camp unseen, perhaps because the guards assumed no one would try to escape, but he knew his real problems still lay ahead. "During my stay in the East," he later wrote, "I found that a European would always be detected, no matter how good his disguise, due to the lack of sway in his posterior. So of course this I had perfected whilst a POW, and I had hardened my feet by never wearing any footwear, as bad feet were the escaper's downfall." Dressed as a local, and with a good growth of beard, a traditional headband called a *pugri,* and a loincloth around his waist, he walked first to the coast and then to Thanbyuzayat, where he was befriended by local Indians who helped him along his way.

Pagani's adventures along the way were remarkable. As he came into the hands of the British-led Karen Christian community, Pagani was persuaded not to continue to head for the Allied lines but instead to make for the Karen hills to join a British army major who was operating the resistance there. After journeying through the roughest jungle he had ever seen, he finally met up with Maj. Hugh Seagrim. Seagrim encouraged him to join his band of warriors and then employed him as an envoy.

Though his Karen compatriots considered him "brave to the point of recklessness," a brush with Japanese troops made him decide to continue toward Allied lines rather than to stay with the Karen rebels. Assisted by four Gurkhas and an Indian servant, he moved from one Karen village to another but was finally betrayed by native Burmans as he tried to cross the Irrawaddy.

Shot, wounded, and sent back to a Japanese hospital in Rangoon, Pagani pretended to be a downed U.S. airman, managing to keep to his story despite being subjected to extended interrogation and torture from his captors. Because he was hundreds of miles from the camp he had escaped from and because he was readily accepted by the American prisoners of war (POWs) in Rangoon, who realized they were probably saving his life by doing so, he narrowly avoided the same fate that

had befallen so many of his fellow escapees. He later survived aerial attack by Hurricanes before being finally rescued by advancing Allied troops. Years later he still had no doubts that his efforts had been worthwhile, claiming that he had gained "earlier release from the hands of the Japanese, and the knowledge that I was a better man than they" (Kinvig 1992, 141).

There are a few other recorded instances of escapes from Japanese captivity during World War II. Like Pagani, U.S. Army Sgt. Howard G. R. Moore managed to escape on his own and also enjoyed an unusual amount of good fortune. Taken prisoner by the Japanese on Bataan at the age of 27, he soon managed to escape by boat, though he was soon recaptured at sea. Soon afterward he escaped again, killing a sentry in hand-to-hand combat, and organized an anti-Japanese guerrilla movement in the mountains where he took refuge. Captured a second time, and this time almost certainly facing immediate execution, he was beaten savagely during a month of brutal interrogation, though he later noted that because he managed, somehow, to keep smiling throughout the experience the Japanese treated him with more respect than he might otherwise have received. But extraordinarily, after four weeks of relentless pressure, his captors lowered their guard, thinking that they had broken their prisoner. Moore slipped back into the hills. He finally reached the safety of Australia in September 1944.

In the Philippines prisoners were usually organized into groups by their captors, who made it clear that if one member of a group should manage to escape, the rest of the group would be executed in reprisal. But a group of prisoners under the command of Maj. William E. Dyess of the Twenty-First Pursuit Squadron in Camp O'Donnell on Mindanao found a way around this problem: Forced to march to another camp and allowed almost no rest, food, or water during the march despite extreme temperatures, the whole group decided that the unknown horrors of the jungle were preferable to the proven horrors of Japanese captivity. So the whole group escaped en masse and there were no reprisals against the others that remained.

See also: Davao Penal Colony, Mindanao; Kennedy, John F.; Tall, Robert

References: Daws, Gavin. *Prisoners of the Japanese.* New York: William Morrow, 1994.

Kinvig, Clifford. *River Kwai Railway: The Story of the Burma-Siam Railroad.* London: Brasseys, 1992.

Perret, Geoffrey. *There's a War to Be Won: The United States Army in World War II.* New York: Random House, 1991.

K

KABUL (1928)

The first known organized escape by air took place on the frontiers of the British Empire where, in 1928, there were serious fears for the safety from tribal savagery of not just the British diplomatic contingent but also of all their Western counterparts.

The British government maintained a small diplomatic mission in Kabul, Afghanistan, to keep track of any developments that might threaten the security of India. Assignment among the cunning and volatile Afghans had always been difficult and dangerous, and there had been a great deal of serious trouble there before. When the Shinwari tribes, along the border with India, started to foment rebellion against King Amanullah it was apparent that this local difficulty could easily flare up into something much more serious.

At first the head of the mission, Lt. Col. Sir Francis Humphreys, had taken a fairly complacent view of the troubles, and even after the compound had been surrounded by the unruly tribesmen he still signaled to the reconnaissance aircraft above that there was no need for emergency procedures. But this was not a narrowly Afghan affair because the tribes were protesting, above all, at the increasing Westernization that they saw the king introducing. When the disturbance worsened, Humphreys finally requested evacuation.

On 23 December 1928, two Victoria aircraft took off from Peshawar, the nearest base in British India, and landed at a stretch of open ground at Sherpur, close to the compound. The Victorias were light aircraft, powered by two 50 horsepower engines that allowed them to travel at a maximum of 85 miles per hour and to carry a load of three-quarters of a ton, but the pilots were not deterred from braving the harsh winter weather and incoming sniper fire from the Afghan tribes. They made several trips to evacuate their countrymen.

Despite the sharp differences between their governments, diplomats from nine other Western countries now asked the Royal Air Force if they would help them evacuate their nationals as well. Temporarily united by a common danger, the British agreed and soon started to fly the diplomats and their families out of the tense situation in Kabul. Within three weeks of the first evacuations, more than 586 people and 12 tons of baggage had been rescued by air.

See also: Afghanistan: The flight of the Russian air crew; Air, escape by; Kandahār

References: Fellowes-Gordon, Ian, ed. *The World's Greatest Escapes.* London: Odhams, 1966.

KALBOWSKI, HARRY (1933–1966)

Harry Kalbowski, known to Berliners simply as "Harry the Wire," used his exceptional talents to repeatedly escape from under the noses of many East German guards.

Kalbowski fled East Berlin in August 1961, after the Communist authorities had suddenly tightened security along the border in an attempt to stem the constant and growing number of refugees. Although the Communist police had put down large quantities of barbed wire along all the rivers on the border to prevent people from swimming out, Kalbowski knew the canals and rivers better than did the police, and he was able to work out exactly how to get through their obstacles. Aware that the banks of the Berlin Canals were often very steep and would therefore hide him from the watchtowers, he was able to cut through the wire with a pair of pliers and cross the border.

Recognizing this weakness in the Communist armory, Kalbowski offered his services to refugees who were desperate to escape to the West. Unlike nearly all the others involved in helping people escape, he did not charge extortionate fees; he was motivated entirely by sympathy and goodwill. After traveling furtively from West to East Berlin, he would meet the refugees at a designated spot and lead them to the West along his chosen route. Within six weeks he had taken 12 East Berliners out.

But his luck could not last, and while escorting one refugee he was seen and stopped by a border guard. Tried and imprisoned by the Communist authorities, he was sent to a prison in Czechoslovakia in 1962. Though he soon managed to escape he was caught and sent back to prison. But this extraordinary man succeeded in escaping a second time, slipping into the waters of a lake during a bitterly cold night in January 1965 and making his way to the canal routes of East Berlin that he was so familiar with. Knowing that not many sentries would be on patrol in the subzero temperatures of the early morning hours, Kalbowski had once again succeeded in escaping Communist soil.

But his story has an unhappy ending. Only a few months after his return, Kalbowski was killed in a road collision in West Berlin, his death in a relatively minor accident a likely consequence of the trauma he suffered as a result of his experiences.

See also: Berlin Wall, Iron Curtain
References: Dupre, Peter. Caught in the Act: A True Story. Tunbridge Wells, Eng.: Costello, 1988.
Gelb, Norman. The Berlin Wall. London: Michael Joseph, 1986.
Hildebrandt, Rainer. It Happened at the Wall. Berlin: Verlag Haus am Checkpoint Charlie, 1992.
Shadrake, Alan. The Yellow Pimpernels: Escape Stories of the Berlin Wall. London: Hale, 1974.

KANDAHĀR (1880)

Like the rescue of the British garrison at Chitral, the relief of the British at Kandahār is a story of extraordinary physical endurance. An armed British force covered a long dis-

tance in very harsh conditions in order to save the lives of their besieged colleagues.

The crisis at Kandahār broke out in June 1880 after a maverick Afghan prince, Ayub Khan, began a campaign to drive the British out of Afghanistan altogether and to proclaim himself the new king of Afghanistan. With 8,000 men and considerable artillery at his disposal, he left his base at Herāt and marched eastward toward Kandahār, engaging and defeating a British force under Brig. General George Burrows which, though outnumbered and outgunned, had been sent to stop him at Maiwand. Although Burrows had lost nearly a thousand men in the battle, he decided to withdraw to Kandahār rather than surrender to a notoriously barbarous enemy.

From the moment it began, the siege of Kandahār was a desperate business. Because of the risk of treachery from within the city, Burrows took the drastic step of expelling all male Afghans of fighting age, knowing how easily they could hide knives under their flowing robes and act as a highly effective fifth column. The British general in charge of the Afghan expedition, Field Marshal Sir Frederick Roberts, heard of the desperate situation Burrows was in and immediately sent a 10,000-strong force from Kabul to rescue their fellow soldiers 300 miles to the south.

The march of the Seventy-Second Highlanders, with their Gurkha and Indian army escorts, to Kandahār is today recognized as one of the most rapid in military history. Though British planners had expected them to take a month to reach the south and though the soldiers traveled over difficult and hostile terrain in scorching summer temperatures that reached well over 100 degrees, the desperate garrison at Kandahār began to hear the distant strains of bagpipes in just 20 days and knew that they were safe at last.

Having heard that Roberts was on his way to rescue the garrison, Ayub Khan had withdrawn his men to mountain positions in the vicinity. But after relieving the town, Roberts's next priority was to destroy the enemy force that had already caused such trouble. Within hours of relieving Kandahār, 600 Afghan bodies lay strewn on a battlefield west of town, at the expense of only 35 dead among the British force. The British public was able to breathe a sigh of relief, and it proclaimed Roberts and his men heroes.

See also: Chitral
References: Hopkirk, Peter. *The Great Game*. Oxford: Oxford University Press, 1990.

KASHMIR (1995)

The life of a prisoner can sometimes depend on a split-second decision. Such was the case of a prisoner of the Kashmiri rebels who was kidnapped in the summer of 1995.

John Childs, an American, was captured, together with five other Westerners, by Al Faran, a Kashmiri militant group. He had a choice of either running off and risking being shot or staying put and risking a long term of captivity and possible execution. Soon after he was captured, he ran off down the mountains, seconds before his captors had a chance to shoot after him, and managed to reach the relative safety of mountain villages further downhill.

It proved to be the right decision. One of the hostages was beheaded a few weeks later and his body was dumped nearby, and almost no word has been heard of the other four since.

See also: Execution, escape from

KENNEDY, JOHN F. (1917–1963)

When his motor torpedo boat collided with a Japanese destroyer near the Solomon Islands in 1944, the young John F. Kennedy managed to evade capture before being eventually rescued by some of the natives of the islands.

A champion swimmer during his student days, Kennedy was able to save the lives of some of his colleagues who had been knocked into the water by the impact of the collision. He helped them swim to a small nearby island, one of the few stretches of land not occupied by the Japanese. By the time the group of survivors reached it, they had all swum for more than 5 hours, and

Kennedy had been in the water for more than 15 hours.

After spending four days exploring the neighboring islands in search of boats or of other Americans, the stranded sailors had a stroke of good fortune. Encountering several natives of the islands who seemed to understand his sign language, Kennedy pulled out his knife and scrawled a simple message on a coconut shell. It said simply, "eleven alive—natives know posit and reefs—Nauru Island—Kennedy." He repeated the name of the island—Rendova—where he wanted them to take the message, and he watched them disappear, hoping they would find friend, not foe.

Before long, four natives appeared, one of whom spoke impeccable English and who bore a note that had been written by a New Zealand patrol that had received and understood the message. Using several transport boats the natives had brought with them, Kennedy and his colleagues left their island and traveled to meet their fellow Americans at New Georgia.

See also: Japanese army, prisoners of
References: Donovan, Robert J. *The Wartime Adventures of President John F. Kennedy*. London: Anthony Gibbs and Phillips, 1962.

KERENSKY, ALEKSANDR (1881–1970)

It is paradoxical that those who conspire to foment revolution are noted both for their closely knit ties, forged by exposure to a common danger, and also for the ruthless rivalry that can exist between them. Though he had been a revolutionary leader during the February 1917 revolution, Aleksandr Kerensky was only just able to escape from the clutches of his former associates while he was serving as the prime minister of the revolutionary government.

Kerensky had soon begun to incur the wrath of the Bolsheviks by arguing that they should continue to fight in World War I. Viewing this as a deliberate distraction from the more pressing task of continuing the revolution in Russia, the Bolsheviks took offense, and during October Lenin unleashed a determined bid to oust Kerensky's administration by force and seize power for himself.

During the last few days of October, Kerensky and his allies had begun to think of ways of escaping from the Winter Palace, where they were besieged. Their spirits had briefly been raised by talk that their own troops were on their way to rescue them. Even if that was true, however, the appearance of a number of unfamiliar, hostile faces around them suggested that the Bolsheviks would get there first, using the same highly effective infiltration techniques they had already used in the February revolution. Kerensky and Lieutenant Vinner had resolved to take their own lives, but a last-minute chance encounter gave them an opportunity to escape.

That opportunity came with the arrival of a young soldier named Belensky, who was sympathetic to their cause. At his suggestion, Kerensky put on a military uniform that Belensky provided and a pair of aviator's goggles to mask his features from the Bolsheviks waiting for them. Belensky then led him through the crowds outside the palace.

Though the prime minister's disguise nearly succeeded in attracting attention rather than deflecting it, the quick thinking of another sympathizer, who could see what was going on, saved Kerensky's skin. Feigning a heart attack, he distracted the Bolshevik soldiers at the crucial moment, which allowed Kerensky to reach a car waiting for him nearby. He was driven off at high speed. His life was again saved by the bravery of his chauffeur, who offered to drive the Bolsheviks who were pursuing the getaway car and to simulate a mechanical breakdown after a mile or two.

When the Bolsheviks stormed the palace shortly afterward, they were furious to find their quarry gone. One of Kerensky's servants, who was suspected of helping him, was beaten and later executed, and a few months later his secretary, Boris Flekkel, was captured and shot, prompting the deputy head of the Cheka to state simply that "he admitted that he has been Kerensky's secretary—that's enough to be shot for." And when Tashkent fell to the

Bolsheviks in February 1919, Kerensky's brother Fyodor was also executed "in reprisal" for his escape. But it is easy to imagine the former prime minister's relief at having slipped through the net and his concern for those he left behind as he made his way to exile in the United States.

See also: Bailey, Lt. Col. Frederick; Russian Revolution and civil war; Stalin, Joseph; Trotsky Leon
References: Abraham, Richard. *Alexander Kerensky: The First Love of the Revolution*. London: Sidgwick and Jackson, 1987.

KHE SAHN (1968)

In 1968 one of the most famous battles of the Vietnam War, and certainly one of the bloodiest and most savage, was fought at remote and isolated Khe Sahn, only a short distance from the border with the Communist north. The garrison of U.S. soldiers fought desperately for survival while a massive rescue operation got underway to relieve them.

The rescue mission was of great importance. The fall of Khe Sahn would have meant the death or capture of the 5,000 men garrisoned there, a particularly devastating blow to confidence at a time when the Tet offensive had already seriously undermined morale. Moreover, its surrender would have greatly facilitated the movement of military supplies from North Vietnam to Vietcong bases in the south, since Khe Sahn had originally been established in 1962 by Green Berets to harass the Ho Chi Minh trail, along which these supplies were moved.

Communist pressure on the base had intensified considerably during 1966 as the Vietnamese army sought to remove a thorn in its side, but it did not begin in earnest until early 1968. In December 1967 General William Westmoreland's intelligence staff had detected two North Vietnamese divisions, each of about 7,000–10,000 men, massing around the base and preparing for an offensive that began on 21 January. For the next 77 days, the garrison—a mixture of Americans and South Vietnamese—endured constant shelling, sometimes more than 1,000 rounds a day, and hand-to-hand fighting in a struggle for survival.

A U.S. marine scrambles for cover during an encounter with North Vietnamese forces over an airstrip during the famous battle of Khe Sahn, in which a U.S. garrison fought desperately for survival while a massive rescue operation got under way. (Agence France Presse/Archive Photos)

The relief operation initially involved not only bombing runs but also supply drops by air, which were no minor task for a large, stranded garrison that had watched its water supply fall into enemy hands. Between 21 January and 14 April, up to 300 tactical air sorties were flown *each day* by the U.S. Air Force, as aircraft were guided in by radio to attack enemy positions to drop nearly 1,800 tons of explosive. By the end of the siege, the area around Khe Sahn had become the most heavily bombed target in military history, the target of approximately 100,000 tons of ordnance. In addition, hundreds of supply drops by transport planes had delivered more than 12,000 tons of food, ammunition, and other cargo essential to keeping the garrison in full working order.

Such efforts entailed enormous risks for the aircrews involved. In spite of constant air attacks, the besiegers were able to move antiaircraft guns into position and fire at the American transport planes. On 11 February a Marine C130—which happened to be carrying transport fuel—was hit by ground fire. It burst into flames as it landed, killing 6 of its 14 crew members. The level of danger prompted the commander of the Seventh Air Force, Gen. William Momyer, to withdraw the costly C130s from the rescue operation and put the smaller and cheaper C123K Provider in its place. He also tried to parachute supplies in rather than landing with them on the runway.

Minimizing these risks also called for a considerable amount of ingenuity from both rescuer and rescued. Dropping supplies by parachute proved very difficult under low cloud conditions, and its effectiveness depended critically on split-second timing by the pilots. In some cases, if cargo fell slightly outside the drop zone, Marines were brought within range of enemy fire. Nor could the pilots use the "cargo extraction" method, whereby cargo was dropped from the aircraft onto the runway as the plane flew over it at extremely low altitudes: This technique not only began to destroy the runway, repeatedly pounded by the heavy pallets, but it also required the pilots to fly perilously close to a transport plane that lay wrecked nearby, risking a nasty collision. The solution instead lay in the development of the Ground Proximity Extraction System (GPES), in which the transports swoop just over the runway and a hook connects the cargo to a giant net on the runway that snares it and pulls it to earth in exactly the right place.

Once the base was resupplied and had been supported during the most determined enemy assaults, Operation Pegasus, the second part of the rescue operation, was launched. On 1 April, Maj. Gen. John J. Tolson sent a task force to the garrison to link its defenders with the outside world, and the advance units of the force reached Khe Sahn on 6 April, pushing back the enemy and ending two months of bitter fighting.

See also: Vietnam War; Rowe, James "Nick"; Saigon

KHMER ROUGE (1975–1979)

After the Khmer Rouge assumed power in Cambodia in 1975 its cruelty and violence quickly caused a flight of refugees from the country. These were not just political activists but also many ordinary men, women, and children, who had good reason to fear the fanaticism of the new government and who were desperate to escape. One of them was later a best-selling writer, Var Hong Ashe, who fled the country with a group of other escapees in March 1979 and headed for the Thai border.

Their journey proved terrifying. As darkness fell and even the smallest noise became audible in the stillness of the night, they were forced to maintain a strict silence. Talking was forbidden, and every precaution was taken to stop babies from crying so that none of the Khmer Rouge patrols constantly patrolling the area would find them.

But despite their efforts, it was not long before they were detected. From far away, the wind carried the long, drawn-out cry of a wild animal that the Khmer Rouge used as a recognition signal. They would have to answer the signal if they were to avoid being mown down in cold blood. But luckily an inhabitant of a nearby village, who had joined the column shortly before, had once worked closely with the revolutionaries and knew the right reply. Cupping his hands together, he emitted a strange cry. The escapees waited breathlessly for the response, straining their ears to hear any sound from the eerie gloom of the forests around them. Again, in the distance, they heard the same animal-like cry, prompting the same response from the villager. They now felt it was safe to carry on.

There were other reminders that the Khmer Rouge was never far away. The threat of land mines and booby traps was real and constant, forcing them to stick carefully to the paths, and on one occasion they came across a cleared area that had been covered with sharpened bamboo spikes, each daubed with poison and specifically designed to stop people from crossing the area. There were also ample reminders of others who had tried to escape and had paid a heavy price: As dawn broke they could see skeletons all over the area and suddenly realized that the whole area stank of rotting flesh.

There were other, more natural obstacles in their way. Before long the trail disappeared altogether, leaving them to hack their way through bushes and undergrowth. Some of their number started to hallucinate, one thinking that the branches were really enemy rifles and armor, and one elderly refugee collapsed and died during this particularly arduous stage of the journey.

But because the Khmer Rouge did not have enough soldiers to mount an effective patrol of the entire border, they were at last able to reach the Thai border. They crossed to safety at 5 A.M. on Sunday, 11 March 1979. Though the first sounds they heard in Thailand were entirely familiar ones—"the sounds of dogs barking and cocks crowing"—the significance of those sounds was entirely different. "Then it had meant the start of another day of slavery under the Khmer Rouge," wrote Var Hong Ashe afterwards. "Now it signified that we were near

Shortly after the rise to power of the communist Khmer Rouge under Pol Pot, these Cambodians attempt to flee their country by motorcycle. (AP/Wide World Photos)

a Thai village and freedom" (Var Hong Ashe 1988, 169).

References: Var Hong Ashe. *From Phnom Penh to Paradise.* London: Hodder and Stoughton, 1988.

KING DAVID HOTEL (1946)

It is a curious irony that many of the loudest condemnations of Palestinian terrorism are voiced by Israeli leaders who themselves once deployed the same methods against their British and Arab targets during the days of the British Mandate in Palestine. Some remarkable escapes and rescues occurred during one such incident.

Shortly after midday on 22 July 1946, a bomb planted by the most barbarous Zionist terror group of all, the Stern Gang, caused a massive explosion at the King David Hotel in Jerusalem, destroying the entire building and killing 91 people. In the scenes of carnage and destruction that followed, acts of great heroism were under-taken by some of the rescuers, both civilians and soldiers, who dug through the rubble in search of those who were still alive.

One such was Police Sergeant "Blackie" Smith, who heard cries for help from a pile of concrete slabs near the remains of the canteen. He quickly jumped into what was left of the entrance and, with his bare hands, burrowed into the heap of bricks and rubble before him. Before long, he had made a makeshift tunnel and was inching closer toward the area where the cries for help had seemed to come from.

His colleagues outside, seeing that the tunnel was on the verge of collapse, shouted at him to return, but Smith refused to come back and carried on clawing through. When the tunnel collapsed moments later, it seemed for several dreadful minutes that he had become just one more victim of that terrible afternoon. But after five minutes he was able to crawl back to the entrance and prepare for his next attempt to get inside.

This time Smith rubbed his back with liniment to help him slide through the rubble and he took advantage of the efforts of an Arab welder who was able to cut away at several metal filing cabinets that were blocking the way. After half an hour, Smith finally reemerged, blackened and filthy from his efforts, followed by two wounded men.

For his efforts, Smith was awarded Britain's highest civilian award, the George Cross.

See also: Acre Castle; Palestine
References: Clarke, Thurston. *By Blood and Fire: The Bombing of the King David Hotel.* London: Hutchinson, 1981.

KLEMPERER, VICTOR (1881–1960)

One German Jewish academic, Victor Klemperer, was saved from deportation to a Nazi death camp by the almost uncanny arrival of the Royal Air Force in the skies above.

On 13 February 1945 Klemperer received notification that he would be deported to the Nazi death camps and that he was required to report at the Gestapo office in Dresden the following week so that arrangements could be made. Having eluded persecution for several years, he now knew that his time had come.

But he reckoned without the sudden arrival of the Royal Air Force. Suddenly and unexpectedly appearing over the night skies of Dresden, just hours after he had received his letter, their bombers flattened the city, inflicting hundreds of thousands of casualties.

In the ensuing chaos, Klemperer and his wife slipped quietly away, risking the bombs but knowing that they had nothing to lose. Walking day after day, they eventually reached American lines to the West.

References: Klemperer, Victor. *The Diaries of Victor Klemperer.* London: Weidenfeld and Nicholson, 1998.

KOLDYCZEWO CAMP (1944)

In 1944 a group of prisoners being held at Koldyczewo in Russia made a brave bid for freedom. They knew that as prisoners in a German concentration camp they had nothing to lose.

After having smuggled several pistols into the camp, the escape committee, headed by Leibel Zeger, set to work to draw up a plan. They found several members of the prison population with the specialist skills they needed. First, several holes were drilled in the barracks in which they were confined, which enabled them to make their way to the fence. Before long an electrician had short-circuited a small section of the compound wire, shutting off its powerful current and allowing a locksmith to cut through it.

On 22 March 1944 93 prisoners escaped, slipping silently past the tents that housed many of the guards and into the neighboring forests to join the partisans. They left unnoticed, but they left behind a nasty surprise for the German guards. Later that morning, when the Germans opened the doors to the suddenly silent barracks, a powerful explosive device went off and killed ten of them instantly.

See also: Auschwitz; Catholic church, rescue by; Le Chambon; Sobibor Concentration Camp
References: Suhl, Yuri. *They Fought Back: The Story of Jewish Resistance in Nazi Europe.* London: MacGibbon and Gee, 1968.

KOLWEZI (1978)

True to its reputation, the French Foreign Legion has on occasion carried out dramatic, even swashbuckling, rescue operations. Most recently, its soldiers descended on Kolwezi, a small, virtually unknown town in southern Zaire, to rescue Western residents from the clutches of rebel insurgents.

In mid-May 1978 armed militia of the Congolese National Front swept into the town, overran the garrison, and seized a large number of hostages from the community of European expatriates, mainly engineers, who were based there. After President Mobuto Sese Seko appealed to the Western governments to intervene, the French Foreign Legion was given the order to mount a rescue operation that had the backing of France, Belgium, and the United States.

The paratroopers were dropped above the town from C141 Starlifters and, though they were outnumbered by ten to one, they took the rebels completely by surprise, sending most of them fleeing back into the jungle in terror. Though a few of the insurgents took up positions around the Kolwezi police station and put up a determined fight, the rescuers' superior training quickly paid off, and they pacified the town after a few hours.

But the operation was only a partial success. The gunmen massacred 190 of their hostages and 200 native Africans, and the bodies of another 40 Europeans were later found in the bush, shot and left by the rebels as they fled. The rescuers—though killing about 250 of the rebels—lost five men and suffered an additional 25 casualties.

References: Geraghty, Tony. *March or Die*. London: Grafton, 1986.

KOREA (1950–1953)

During the three-year Korean war, U.S. soldiers and airmen—fighting for the United Nations—made some dramatic escapes and rescues from their North Korean and Chinese foes.

Of 1,690 airmen who were brought down by enemy fire, 175 were rescued immediately by the Air Rescue Service, which used tactics similar to those used later in Vietnam. Planes would pass over the site of a crash and, if it picked up a ground signal, it would radio headquarters that a helicopter was required for further reconnaissance.

Very few servicemen, however, escaped from captivity and safely reached the line of demarcation. One who did so was Capt. William D. Locke, who had been captured almost immediately after being shot down in 1951 but who escaped by moving quickly when his guards' backs were turned. He hid, with a supply of food, under the floor of a school house in Pyongyang, where he had been temporarily interned, until UN troops arrived. Another pilot also one day calmly walked out of a North Korean hospital where he had been held for three months. With the help of a Communist

defector whom he met soon after, he was able to signal his whereabouts to a passing U.S. plane, which then arranged a rescue operation on his behalf.

A third prisoner of war who managed to escape from Communist captivity was 1st Lt. Melvin J. Shaddock. He had avoided the Communists for several days after his plane was shot down, eluding enemy road blocks by swimming along a river and submerging himself as he passed them by, but he was finally captured by the Communists and taken to a small internment camp alongside several other UN soldiers. He was able to slip quietly away, take a mountain trail to a river nearby, and follow its course until he eventually reached and crossed the front line. Within hours a task force had been prepared that soon secured the release of the other Americans he had left behind.

In November 1950 a group of 19 GIs who knocked their guards unconscious before fleeing into the hills found their way home after being rescued from their pursuers. Their escape is noteworthy for the unusual and ingenious way they signaled their whereabouts to a U.S. reconnaissance aircraft that was hovering in the vicinity looking for enemy targets. Tearing down the wallpaper from a nearby—and hopefully deserted—house, they were able to lay it down in shifts to form the message "POW—19—RESCUE." Before long, several U.S. tanks had appeared on the horizon, ready to escort them back home.

There are also 12 known cases of military personnel who remained uncaptured by the enemy and were able to get back to their own lines. Two airmen who did so, Clinton D. Summerskill and Wayne Sawyer, patiently walked back to the front line and found during their long journey that their badly run-down condition worked to their advantage. When a passing patrol of Communist troops saw them, they resisted the temptation to run off. Instead, they kept walking, one in front of the other in the manner of village peasants. Seeing their ragged filthy clothes and bearded, unkempt appearance, the Communists merely walked on, wholly unsuspecting of their true identity.

References: Biderman, Albert D. *March to Calumny: The Story of American POWs in the Korean War.* New York: Macmillan, 1963.

Blair, Clay. *Beyond Courage.* New York: David Mackay, 1955.

Verral, Charles S., ed. *True Stories of Great Escapes.* Pleasantville, NY: Reader's Digest Association, 1977.

KOSOVO (1690)

One of the great myths of Serbian history is the story of the "Great Migration" of Serbs who fled the Balkan town of Kosovo in order to escape possible violence from the Turkish population there.

Kosovo had for centuries been a cosmopolitan mix of different ethnic groups and varied religious beliefs—Illyrians, Serbs, Albanians, and Turks. It was a town to which different peoples laid claim. When, in 1690, the Austrian army invaded the town and took control, they were welcomed as liberators by the Christian Serbs. But when, soon after, the Austrians were badly defeated by the Turks and chased away through Hungary, many Serbs fled the town, fearing Turkish reprisals.

Those who moved quickly, as soon as the Austrians withdrew, managed to escape, though a few did so only by the skin of their teeth, leaving all their belongings behind in their haste. In particular, the Patriarch bolted from his monastery on hearing the news of the Austrian defeat, leaving with "10 horse-loads of rich furnishings," of which he was robbed en route. But their flight was fortunate, since some of those who stayed behind were, in the words of a contemporary, "chopped to pieces" (Malcolm 1998, 158).

The national myth that has since surrounded the story of this great escape is not, however, quite so factual. The total number of escapees was probably no more than 10,000 families, rather than 50,000 families, as the myth holds. And there is no evidence that the Patriarch ever led a procession of refugees, as nineteenth-century paintings show him doing. His escape, like that of so many others, was in reality much more desperate and fearful.

References: Malcolm, Noel. *Kosovo.* London: Macmillan, 1998.

L

LATUDE, HENRI MASERS DE (1725–?)

Henri Masers de Latude was condemned to prison in 1749 for a trivial offense and was only rescued from atrocious conditions because a sympathetic outsider heard of his unfortunate fate and determined to rescue him.

Sent to prison after a youthful prank was misconstrued as part of a political conspiracy against the monarchy, Latude made several escape attempts, which gave him a taste of freedom, if not a lasting bite. On the first occasion, in June 1750, he waited until his guard opened his cell door, then rushed out, locked the guard in his cell behind him, and bluffed his way past four other sentries who were posted at several gates outside. He was captured soon afterward, even though his simple approach had taken him some considerable distance.

But this bid did not match the majestic escape attempt he made from the Bastille some years later, in February 1756. After making a rope, nearly 180 feet long, by tying shirts and sheets into one long chain, he climbed up the chimney inside his room to get onto the prison roof. Moving to a carefully chosen point, he lowered the rope to the ditch below and rappelled down, a task that he later described as being as terrifying as it was demanding. Together with a fellow escapee, he then submerged himself in the moat, more than four feet deep, and over the next nine hours they painstakingly removed stones in the outer prison wall to create a hole that allowed them to slip away into the Paris suburbs. Alas, after being on the run for more than a week, both men were finally caught near the Netherlands border.

But though he was punished severely for his escape bids, his will was not broken, and he turned his energies to finding an accomplice on the outside who might take pity on him. One winter's day in 1782, an obscure knitwear trader found a package near the prison. Inside was a message that described a "Monsieur de Latude, prisoner for 32 years . . . on bread and water, in a cell 10 feet underground." Latude had written the message for a government official who wanted to consider the fate of individual prisoners, but the messenger entrusted with its delivery happened to drop it nearby.

Deeply moved by his plight and desperation, the kindly French lady who had found the message spent three years trying to draw attention to his fate, circulating copies of the letter, contacting two attorneys at the Paris court, and finally interesting several grandees, such as the Marquis de la Villette, who had considerable influence over the king and his ministers. As a result of their influence a royal pardon was at last issued, and Latude was finally released in 1784, after enduring 35 years in the most terrible prison conditions.

See also: The Bastille

References: de Latude, Henri Masers. *Memoirs of the Bastille.* English translation. London: Routledge, 1927.

Villars, Paul, ed. *The Escapes of Casanova and Latude.* London: T. Fisher Unwin, 1892.

LAWRENCE, THOMAS EDWARD (1888–1935)

One of the most enigmatic of British heroes, T. E. Lawrence "of Arabia," made some remarkable escapes from his various enemies and also rescued some of those who served at his side.

Thomas Edward Lawrence, "Lawrence of Arabia," during the Hejaz campaign in 1917. (Imperial War Museum Q59075)

During his campaign in Hejaz against the Turkish army, Lawrence came within a whisker of being captured by his Turkish enemy on a great many occasions. The Turks had offered an enormous reward of £20,000 to anyone who was able to capture or kill the charismatic Englishman. In June 1917, while Lawrence was visiting tribal chiefs in an attempt to win their support for a coordinated offensive against the enemy, he was awakened one night by the "charged voice, whispering through a smoke-smelling beard into my ear" of Nawaf, the brother of the tribal leader, Fawaz el Faiz. Fawaz, his brother claimed, had secretly sent word to the Turks of Lawrence's whereabouts, and it would not be long before enemy troops arrived to arrest him. Sensing his urgency, Lawrence followed the Arab and crawled out of his tent, climbed onto the back of his camel, and retreated into the desert.

The Turks were not the only enemy of those who fought in the desert campaigns, however. In the *Seven Pillars of Wisdom,* Lawrence also recorded the rescue of a col-

league who was overcome by the intense heat of the sun in the Biseita desert, a heat that even Lawrence, renowned for his resilience, described as "purgatory," "deadly," and the "worst of my experience." In the late morning of 24 May he and his Bedouin colleagues suddenly realized that one member of their party, an Arab named Gasim, was missing, though his loaded camel was still alongside them. Though the caravan left no trace on the desert ground and mirages made it impossible for anyone to see far in the desert, it was obvious that someone had to turn back to find him. If not, Gasim would die.

Knowing that he could not put his legendary reputation among the Arabs at risk by asking one of the party to go back to search, Lawrence volunteered to go while the others continued. He would chart his exact route with his compass and catch up with them. After riding for a time he eventually found Gasim lying on the sand, half-crazed by the desert sun but soon able to continue his journey with the others.

Because of the legend that grew up around "Lawrence of Arabia," after World War I a few foreign officials feared he would stir rebellion in their own backyard. In 1929, while sailing back to Britain from India, where he had been posted as a serviceman, his journey was briefly disrupted at Port Said. An official in the local police, thinking that he was a dangerous spy, sent officers onboard to arrest him. Lawrence quickly hid and later wrote to a friend that "they were fair flummoxed, it seems, that night, and reported that I was probably not on the *Rajputana* at all" (Wilson 1989, 345).

Though Lawrence courted publicity, he also despised it. He often had to escape from peacetime "enemies," most notably the obsessive and intrusive press attention that tried to follow him everywhere. On one occasion he escaped through the rear window of his house at Clouds Hill and bicycled off, after punching one particularly insistent newsman in the eye. On another occasion his taxi was pursued across London by a posse of cars in a farcical chase that lasted more than an hour. Despite the "real Arabian fervour" (*Manchester Guar-*

dian, 4 February 1929) of his pursuers, Lawrence eventually got away and hid himself at Barton Street in central London, one of his favorite retreats.

References: Lawrence, Thomas E. *The Seven Pillars of Wisdom.* New York: Anchor, 1991.
Wilson, Jeremy. *Lawrence of Arabia.* London: Minerva 1989.

LE CHAMBON (1939–1945)

Some escapes and rescues have succeeded not just through the determination and cleverness of those evading capture but also through the secret complicity of their enemies. At Le Chambon, a remote village high in the mountains of southern France, the lives of a considerable number of Jews were saved as a result of the bravery of the local people and the covert sympathy of some of the Nazis in the area.

The village began to attract refugees, initially in very small numbers, in the late 1930s as a result of the pacifist preachings of the local cleric, Monsieur Daniel Trocme. When a few villagers started to actively defy some of the petty regulations of the Vichy authorities, the village acquired a reputation as a relatively safe haven for French Jews who were seeking to escape the dangers of deportation and who needed assistance to reach the Swiss border.

As the Vichy officers, acting under German pressure, became increasingly threatening, the villagers developed a plan of rescue for the Jews taking refuge there. When convoys of Vichy police arrived to search the village, the refugees were spirited away to cleverly concealed hiding places that had been prepared well in advance.

The villagers' success in rescuing the Jews was in part owing to the number of Vichy police who became actively involved in the rescue effort. Brief telephone calls were made to some of the villagers, informing them, sometimes in cryptic messages, of a planned raid.

But when, in November 1942, southern France was overrun by the Germans, the good fortune of both the rescuers and the rescued did not suddenly end. The Gestapo knew the village was the focal point of a rescue operation, but they never made as many raids on the village as had at first seemed likely. They did, however, place Daniel Trocme under arrest for a time.

Some years after the war Daniel Trocme and his wife met Julius Schmahling, who in 1942 had been an army major responsible for the region surrounding Le Chambon. Asked why the villagers were not arrested en masse and deported, he replied simply that, having been raised in the Catholic church, he had ignored some orders and had soon been touched by the quiet, brave resistance of the villagers of Le Chambon.

References: Pettit, Jayne. *A Place to Hide.* London: Piccolo, 1994.

LEBRUN, LT. PIERRE (1918–1968)

By escaping from Colditz castle in 1943, a French cavalry officer, Lt. Pierre Lebrun, proved that a blend of originality, daring, and speed of action is a highly effective formula for escape.

While undertaking his daily exercise in the prison, he watched his guards. When they had relaxed their guard, he gave a pre-arranged signal to two colleagues. They positioned themselves near the wire and formed a stirrup with their two hands; Lebrun then ran at them and was catapulted over the nine-foot wire in a brilliantly staged movement.

Because he still had another wall in front of him, he used an ingenious but near suicidal way of getting over. Instead of presenting himself as a slowly moving target, Lebrun deliberately drew the sentries' fire by dodging in and out of range. Knowing exactly when their magazines were emptied and how long it would take them to reload, he was able to get over the wall and drop to the other side just as a hail of bullets blasted the top of the wall. Not surprisingly, another prisoner later lost his life while trying to escape in just the same way.

He owed his getaway to some other highly original means of escape. Knowing that the Germans were hot on his trail, he hid in a field of wheat, walking into the field backward and rearranging the stalks as he went to escape detection. He then spent a whole afternoon watching a German reconnaissance plane circling above, desperately trying to spot him.

Lebrun's luck continued to hold, though only just. Taken prisoner by the Spaniards after crossing the Pyrenees, he made an overly audacious escape from the castle where he was held. Jumping from a window into the moat below him, he badly injured his back, and only immediate surgery by a local doctor saved his life. But even though he was permanently crippled, he was still able to make his way to Algeria and continue with the war effort.

His story has one charming postscript: Before he escaped from Colditz he had audaciously packed up his belongings and addressed them to himself in France. To his surprise, they were delivered some months later. They had been sent by the Colditz commander, who had learned of his escape. Like many other escapees, Lebrun viewed his adventures with a certain sense of mischief.

See also: Colditz
References: Reid, Pat. *The Colditz Story.* London: Hodder and Stoughton, 1952.

LEFEBRE, GEN. LOUIS (C. 1765–1825)

During the Napoleonic Wars, French officers in the captivity of the British were allowed considerable freedom because it was felt that an officer and a gentleman would never break his word and try to escape. But between 1810 and 1812 more than 462 officers broke parole and at least 307 managed to get back to France. One of them was General Louis Lefebre.

As a general, Lefebre did not take kindly to any restrictions being imposed on his lifestyle during his captivity. He used his considerable personal wealth and his command of the English language, as well as considerable cheek and self-assurance, to escape back to France while on parole in Cheltenham. After his wife joined him there, he posed as a German count with whom he happened to be acquainted; introduced his wife, dressed as a boy, as his son; and disguised his aide-de-camp as his valet.

The trio went first to London, where they stayed at a hotel in Jermyn Street while the British authorities prepared their travel documents. Before long they had boarded a suitable ship, and they reached France a few days later. The general then wrote an insolent letter to the British government explaining why he had had a "duty" to break his word, a polite but gloating touch that has characterized other "gentlemanly" escapees.

See also: Bitche Fortress; Napoleonic Wars; Press gangs, escape from
References: Reid, Pat. *Prisoner of War.* London and New York: Hamlyn, 1984.

LIBBY PRISON (1864)

The escape on the night of 9 February 1864 of several prisoners from the Confederate Libby Prison during the U.S. Civil War has become one of the most famous escape stories of all.

Though they possessed only the most basic tools, the escape committee in Libby Prison planned to dig a 60-foot tunnel from a basement to a cowshed that would give the escapees adequate cover when they made their move. Though, to their knowledge, such a long tunnel had never successfully been constructed before, they were willing to try.

The plan they drew up proved to contain all the elements necessary for a successful escape. Though there were more than 1,200 prisoners in Libby Prison, it was not until just before the break that anyone outside a closely knit group of 15 key persons knew of the existence of the tunnel, let alone its whereabouts. Such was their determination to stop mouths from chattering that one member of the group was even prepared to steal boots from a colleague rather than tell him the real reason why he needed them.

Organization and hard work were also key factors in their success. Over a period of two months, the tunnel was built according to a rigid code of conduct that had been drawn up to maximize the speed of construction and minimize the risk of detection. Always working at night, two men would take turns digging, while another two, per-

Escapees from the Confederate Libby Prison, the scene of some dramatic escape bids during the U.S. Civil War. (Library of Congress)

haps more, would remain at specific key points as lookouts.

Armed with only the most primitive tools, the diggers were forced to rely on determination. Lighting their work with a candle, they used clam shells or case knives to dig a tunnel 9 feet below the surface and about 16 inches in diameter. When, after they had covered 20 feet, the air became so foul that they were unable even to light a candle, one of the two diggers would stand at the tunnel entrance, using a fan to create an adequate air supply for his colleague.

The prisoners also used considerable ingenuity in making maximum use of limited resources to prepare themselves for their escape, knowing that once out of the prison compound they would need considerable physical fitness to keep one step ahead of their enemy. Wells and his partner in escape even walked 22 miles, round and round their prison cell in a never-ending circle.

Preparations aside, they also enjoyed an element of luck. On one occasion, a prisoner who had succeeded in digging nearly as far as the surface of the ground suddenly had his chisel break through the surface, in the full glare of a street lamp, only a few feet from one of the prison guards. Another guard, farther away, heard the noise it made and asked the first guard whether he, too, had heard anything. To the relief of the petrified prisoner, who overheard every word, they both dismissed it as the scurrying of rats.

Many of the escapees were recaptured before long. Some managed to steal a boat but then inadvertently steered a course toward the Confederate lines. Others tried to hide themselves in the surrounding swamps but were tracked down by dogs. But seven weeks after digging had commenced, more than a dozen prisoners made their way through the tunnel and headed for the front lines. In 1917 their story inspired six British officers imprisoned in a Turkish prison to make their own escape using similar means.

References: Johnston, Isaac N. *Four Months in Libby*; Cincinnati, OH: Methodist Book Concern, 1864.

LOGAN, HARVEY (18?–1904)

Though their crimes may be heinous, some criminals capture the public imagination with their adventurous lifestyles. The swashbuckling villain Harvey Logan was one such, partly because he was romantically identified as one of the last figures of the Wild West and partly because his escape from Knoxville jail in Tennessee in June 1903 was made in such remarkable style.

Logan was a well-established villain who had committed almost every type of offense by the time he was eventually tracked down and arrested in 1901. Found guilty on 20 counts, he was sentenced to 130 years in prison and was kept at a prison in Knoxville while his appeal of the sentence was heard. Logan felt that he would have to try and make his escape at this transitional stage, since he knew that the prison where he would be sent would be far harder to break from.

At first he tried to burrow through the wall of his cell with his kitchen knife, a near-impossible task even if he had not been discovered. Soon afterward, in a particularly desperate, even pathetic, attempt to break free, he attacked one of his escorts whose back was turned before trying to run for the door, but he managed to get only a few feet before being stopped. A fellow bandit on the outside also tried to smuggle a metal saw to him inside a long clay pipe, but this too was discovered when it was sent to the prisoner. It was not until June 1903, hours before he was due to be moved elsewhere to serve his sentence, that he finally broke free.

His stroke of good fortune came in his lucky acquisition of the seemingly innocuous: a small piece of wire. When the broom he used to sweep his cell suddenly fell apart one day, he noticed that it was held together by a piece of wire. He was forbidden to possess such items, which could easily be used to facilitate an escape, but he quickly hid it on his person and turned his mind to how best he could use it.

As he began to orchestrate a plan of action, he cleverly tried to mislead his guards into thinking he was resigned to his fate and had given up seeking to escape. Whereas during his previous imprisonment he had always been moody and depressed, he now sought to be upbeat and cheerful, knowing that the change of mood would be noticed straightaway by those around him.

To make his escape he planned to appeal to one of the most basic human weaknesses: greed. When one of his two guards left the prison corridor for his lunch, he called out to the other to come closer to the cell and talk with him. As the guard approached, Logan drew out a map, which, he said, showed clearly where he had hidden vast amounts of gold and money, the fruits of his remarkable criminal career. It would be of no use to him now, he said, because he was destined to spend the rest of his life behind bars.

The guard came closer, unable to resist such a temptation, and as he looked through the small window built into the cell door, Logan pounced. He whipped out the wire and nearly strangled the guard with it before grabbing the keys and unlocking his cell door. Within minutes the guard had been tied up and imprisoned. Logan, hiding his features with the guard's hat and brandishing the guard's revolver, was soon on his way outside. With one final stroke of audacity, he saddled the sheriff's own horse and rode it off into the wilderness at a furious speed.

Nearly an hour passed before the warder had freed himself and a posse was ready to follow. Though they spent a whole day searching desperately for the escapee, they found only his exhausted horse. He had found another and fled into the mountains.

The story of the escape quickly emerged and caused a sensation across several states. Extra copies of newspapers were printed to meet the surge in demand from a public that had long been fascinated by Logan. Before long, Sheriff James Fox, in charge of the prison, even admitted members of the public into the prison to see Logan's cell, the wire he had used to escape, and the horse so they could satisfy their curiosity.

However, he did not long enjoy his freedom. Almost exactly a year later, some bandits were killed during an attempted highway robbery. One of those found dead was identified as Harvey Logan. It was a suitably dramatic end to an extraordinary life.

References: Waller, Brown. *Harvey Logan: The Last of the Great Western Train Robbers*. South Brunswick, NJ: A. S. Barnes, 1968.

LONG KESH PRISON (1974)

Despite being held in conditions of maximum security, several Irish Republican Army (IRA) prisoners have succeeded in escaping from the prison at Long Kesh, eight miles from Belfast.

One bold attempt, which only narrowly failed, was made in 1974, when 35 prisoners made their way through a 65-yard-long tunnel that they had spent months digging with knives and spoons. Though all succeeded in getting outside the prison perimeter, all were picked up shortly afterward during the massive search that followed. A

few months earlier an attempt at escaping through a tunnel had been foiled at the last minute when a soldier chanced to walk over the tunnel, which collapsed underneath him.

But two years later another escape bid worked brilliantly. Despite their earlier setbacks, 12 members of the Irish Republican Socialist Party, a splinter group of the IRA, succeeded in building another tunnel, 44 feet long, under the noses of the prison authorities. But when at last the moment of escape arrived, they found to their dismay that they had miscalculated the length needed to get outside the perimeter. Now they would have to get through barbed wire and over a wall. After a desperate search, they managed at last to find some bolt cutters and a grappling iron, which enabled them to make it to the outside.

The escapees were also fortunate not to be picked up after they got beyond the wall. For although they had carefully planned their escape, their associates on the outside failed to turn up to meet them, and as a result they were forced to walk along the road outside to make their getaway. But despite this setback, only 3 of the 12 were recaptured.

See also: Crumlin Road Prison; Maze Prison
References: Bean, J. P. *Over the Wall: True Stories of the Master Jail Breakers*. London: Headline, 1994.

THE LONG MARCH (1934–1935)

The Long March of Mao Tse-tung's Communist army from the superior Nationalist forces led by General Chiang Kai-shek was a truly remarkable feat of endurance. Forced to evacuate the soviet republic that they had established in Kiangsi province of China, the Communists undertook a march of some 8,000 miles, heading northwestward for a year through difficult mountain country to Yen-an, on the Yellow River, where they were able to establish a stronger defensive position. Thousands died during this escape.

Much of the story of their journey is made up of feats not only of endurance but of deception, for Mao often misled his enemies about his true intentions in order to make his escape. In March 1934, for example, when he sought to move his army out of his enemy's reach, Mao wanted to make the Nationalist commanders think he wanted to cross the Yangtze River and thereby make them move their forces away from the more westerly route over "the River of Golden Sands," as the Yangtze was called, where he was secretly wanting to move his men.

Therefore, on 16 March, Mao first moved a force, large enough to look convincing and as ostentatiously as possible, across the Red River toward the Yangtze and within no time the KMT (the Nationalist army) had spotted them. Once his soldiers had crossed the river, Mao ordered one section of the force to continue in the same direction, prompting the newspapers to report that the strategic town of Guiyang was under threat. At the same time he brought most of this force back across the river, under cover of darkness, to prepare for the real escape that was going to take place over the westerly route.

As the remaining section of Mao's diversionary force moved further from the river, his strategy began to succeed. In a few days reports reached his enemies that his Red Army was moving east through Xifeng and K'ai-yüan and was now preparing to attack Guiyang, en route to the Yangtze. The KMT general, Chiang Kai-shek, immediately ordered that the town's defenses be strengthened and sent a telegraph to his top local commander to dispatch three crack brigades to do so. Mao's deception was so convincing that Chiang is known to have requested a whole team of guides and horses so that he could escape from the town before it fell to the Red Army.

But unwittingly, Chiang had given the order that allowed Mao and his army to make their escape. Mao had never had any intention of attacking Guiyang; instead, he had diverted his enemies at a carefully planned moment and opened his intended path over the River of Golden Sands. He had, as the KTM generals were to freely admit, succeeded brilliantly in deceiving his enemy.

See also: Aylward, Gladys
References: Salisbury, Harrison E. The Long March: The Untold Story. London: Macmillan, 1985.
Wilson, Dick. The Long March: The Epic of Chinese Communism's Survival. London: Penguin, 1977.

LOUIS XVIII (1755–1824)

Because their flight may worsen existing tensions, some who intend escape must choose their moment with great care. One individual who fled at the last minute, judging that the fine line between popular demonstration and public anarchy was dangerously close to being breached, was Louis-Xavier-Stanislas, who was the brother of King Louis XVI of France and who later became Louis XVIII. He left Paris just before the outbreak of a new wave of popular protest and turmoil in 1791.

Escape would not be easy, for he had few allies to help him along the way. The first three people he turned to for assistance were too frightened to help, for they knew they would be executed by the revolutionaries if caught. And Louis was also well aware that there were others he could not trust, since they had some sympathy for the revolution. But he was fortunate to find one person whom he was sure he could trust to help him escape, Comte d'Avaray, the son of one of his household servants.

One summer evening in June 1791 Louis and d'Avaray were at last ready to put their carefully planned idea into operation. Heavily disguised as English merchants, the pair slipped out of their quarters, taking immense care to avoid the patrols of the Garde Nationale, who were apt to stop and question passers-by at whim. Dutifully repeating a few phrases in English, such as "come along with me" and "I am ready," and speaking French with an English accent, they found their way out of the capital and reached the safety of the Austrian Netherlands.

As he crossed the border, Louis felt compelled to write: "pour la première fois depuis vingt mois et demi, je me couchai, sûr de n'être pas reveillé par quelque scène d'horreur [for the first time in over 20 months, I went to bed certain not to be woken up by a scene of horror]" (Mansel 1981, 54–55). Had he been caught, he would certainly have been imprisoned and, before long, sent to the guillotine.

See also: The Bastille; The Terror
References: Mansel, Philip. Louis XVIII. London: Bland and Briggs, 1981.

LOUIS NAPOLEON
(1808–1873)

Seeking to emulate the achievement of his uncle, Napoleon Bonaparte, Louis Napoleon was captured and imprisoned by his enemies. However, he was determined to escape their clutches.

The failure of his coup in 1840 was hardly surprising. Unable to obtain an eagle as a mascot, Louis had bought a vulture from London Zoo and tethered it to the mast of one of the small boats that he hired to transport a handful of sympathizers to France, where he hoped to foment revolution. The party landed at Boulogne, where Louis Napoleon walked calmly into a police station and announced the advent of revolution. As the sergeant in charge later described it, the Pretender had introduced himself by saying "Good Morning, my brave fellow. I hereby make you an offer— march with us to Paris" (Bierman 1988, 41). But though the revolutionaries were able to continue their march a bit farther down the road, they soon met armed resistance from an army unit whose barracks they entered in the same casual manner. Though some of the party escaped, Louis and others were captured after their boat capsized. The Pretender was banished to a gloomy fortress at Ham to serve a long prison sentence.

Though conditions in the prison were far from harsh, Louis became increasingly prone to depression as the months, and eventually the years, went by. "The years roll on with a depressing monotony," he wrote to a friend, "and it is only in the prompting of my heart and conscience that I find the strength to stand up against this leaden atmosphere" (Bierman 1988, 48). When, after five years of incarceration, there was still so sign of an amnesty, Louis knew he had to formulate a plan of escape.

In the spring of 1846 he at last found his chance. The fortress was to undergo much-needed repairs, and workmen had started to enter the castle. Louis knew that if he could disguise himself as one of them, he had a chance of finding a way out. By watching carefully, Louis and two acquaintances noticed that although the workers were all screened very carefully when they walked into the castle, they often left it unchecked in order to collect materials or tools from a site outside. This, they reckoned, presented the best chance of escape.

First of all, one of Louis's acquaintances managed to obtain a forged passport for him, since he planned to make a run for the Belgian border. Then he got hold of a set of workman's clothes before shaving off Louis's mustache and whiskers, blackening his eyebrows, and rouging his cheeks to cover the pallor left by five years' incarceration. Wearing a wig to complete the effect, Louis pulled apart a bookshelf in his rooms, slung a plank over his shoulder, and headed down the stairs for the exit.

The plank obscured his face as he passed two guards at the foot of the stairs, and the other soldiers paid him no attention as he headed for the gate and the drawbridge beyond. Nor did the sentry by the gate bother to look his way as he walked across the bridge to freedom, while two workmen whom he passed coming the other way took him for one of their own, knowing that casual laborers were coming and going on the site. Once out, Louis threw away the plank and headed for a cemetery two miles away where, as arranged, he was met by a cab and taken to Belgium.

Back at the prison another sympathizer had put a dummy in Louis's bed and told the prison governor that he was unwell. By the time the deception was uncovered, the prince was in Brussels, enjoying a celebration dinner.

When he arrived in London shortly afterward, Louis's escape caused something of a diplomatic stir. A British politician happened to meet a French diplomat at a dinner and asked casually, "I suppose you know that Louis Napoleon's in town?" His words made the diplomat drop his fork, leap to his feet, and leave hurriedly, mumbling some excuse.

References: Bierman, J. *Napoleon III and His Carnival Empire*. London: J. Murray, 1988.
Briffault, F. T. *The Prisoner of Ham: Authentic Details of the Captivity and Escape of Prince Louis Napoleon*. English translation. London, 1846.

LOUIS PHILLIPE (1773–1850)

In 1848 many parts of Europe were affected by violent political disorder, and it was from the unrest in Paris that Louis Phillipe, king of France during the postrevolutionary restoration, made his escape.

The king and his wife had slipped away from their Paris home amid the chaos and confusion that reigned as the 1848 revolution got underway. Traveling in unobtrusive carriages, with blinds drawn down, they made their way through the plundering mobs and headed not for Calais or Boulogne, which they knew would be swarming with enemy spies, but further south, to Normandy.

During the journey, they had several lucky escapes from recognition and capture. Passing through Versailles, at the very beginning of their journey, their driver saw six riders heading toward them. He slowed the horses so that the king could jump out and hide in the bushes. When the riders arrived and searched the carriage, minutes later, they found no one inside and moved on.

Further along the road, Louis Phillipe's party was forced on several occasions to bluff their way past gangs of militia who had blocked the road to trap them. But the king had made a great effort to disguise himself, dressing in shabby clothes, shaving his beard and hair, and wearing thick glasses, and he was now virtually unrecognizable to those who stopped them. Nonetheless, on a few occasions they were half-recognized by passers-by and were forced to race away at full speed before changing their horses and carriage in case word got around.

As they approached the Normandy coast, they headed not for Le Havre, which they knew would be well guarded, but for the nearby town of Honfleur. They sent a courier to the home of the British consul and were soon relieved to learn that Lord Palmerston, the British prime minister, had decreed that all British ships were to give as much assistance as they could to any royal refugees from the anarchy in France.

Boarding a small local vessel, the king was taken to HMS *Express*, which was harbored offshore, and arrived in London some days later.

See also: Garibaldi, Giuseppe; Wagner, Richard
References: Fellowes-Gordon, Ian, ed. *The World's Greatest Escapes*. London: Odhams, 1966.

LUCAN, LORD RICHARD JOHN (1934–)

Ordinary crimes committed by the rich and powerful inevitably attract more attention than shocking crimes committed by ordinary people, and when, in 1974, a member of the British aristocracy, Lord Richard John Lucan, committed murder and escaped the massive search that was subsequently conducted for him, he could not fail to attract the world's attention.

The story began late one November evening when the peace of the Plumbers Arms, in Lower Belgrave Street, was shattered by a blood-soaked woman who staggered inside toward the bar, screaming hysterically that she was trying to escape a murderer. By the time a police van arrived, it had been established that the semiconscious woman was Veronica Bingham, the 37-year-old Countess of Lucan, and that she had just run in her blood-soaked clothes from the Lucan family home up the road.

The police quickly discovered why she was in such a hysterical state. The body of Sandra Rivett, a 29-year-old nanny who had been employed by the Lucan family for only a few weeks, was found lying on the floor of the house. She had been savagely beaten to death. The perpetrator, according to Lady Lucan, was her husband, who had nearly succeeded in killing her as well.

Once Lady Lucan escaped to the Plumbers Arms, Lord Lucan began his own flight from the law. He drove south along the A27 to Sussex, where he stopped at the

Police in wetsuits scour Newhaven Harbor for the body of escaped murderer Lord Lucan, 15 November 1974. His fate remains a mystery. (Express Newspapers/Archive Photos)

home of some friends in Uckfield. He told them he had witnessed a struggle between his wife and an intruder and had stepped in to defend her. Using their telephone, he then called his mother to inquire after the health of his children, who had been asleep in the house at the time of the murder. After writing some letters to family, Lucan bid his hosts good night and drove off into the dark. That proved to be the last anyone would, with any certainty, see of him.

Only one thing is known about his subsequent movements: that he drove south from Uckfield to the nearest channel port, at Newhaven, where his car was discovered in a public place the following day. No one saw Lucan arrive, leave his car, or depart. He may have been met by someone and been driven away; he may have left the country; or he may have taken his own life, either by throwing himself into the sea or after wandering onto the neighboring downs.

The police exhaustively investigated each possibility. Teams of officers, using tracker dogs and infrared surveillance equipment, extensively combed the surrounding area for any signs of a body, pro-

fessional spelunkers descended into the caves and cliffs that abound in the area, and divers searched the sea. Interpol was alerted throughout Europe in case Lucan arrived on their territory, and search warrants gave police access to country estates from Kent to the Scottish Highlands, even those that belonged to the aristocracy, such as Holkham Hall, the seat of the earl of Leicester, and Warwick castle, which belonged to Lucan's cousin.

Some of those who knew him have claimed that he is still alive, having been offered sanctuary by rich and influential friends. Others say he would have committed suicide to escape pressing financial liabilities and to spare his children the ordeal of a murder trial. According to one rumor, his body was fed to lions in the zoo of an aristocratic friend at Howletts, in Kent. But though there have been claims that he has been seen as far afield as Riyadh and Rio de Janeiro, the fate of Lord Lucan remains a mystery.

See also: Cooper, D. B.
References: Ruddick, James. *Lord Lucan: What Really Happened.* London: Headline, 1994.

Lucknow (1857)

During the Indian Mutiny the rescue of the besieged garrison at Lucknow was made possible by the bravery of Thomas Henry Kavanagh, who was able to slip through enemy lines to give the rescuers first-hand information about the city's defenses, fortifications, and communications.

Kavanagh was a civil clerk working under Sir Henry Lawrence. Though he knew his mission was extremely hazardous, he later wrote that he was inspired to undertake the risks others had shunned by a strong sense of duty. He knew that the lives of all his colleagues might depend upon the success or failure of his mission. He was, however, also painfully conscious of how much would be lost if things went wrong, and before he left he would not look his wife in the eye lest she detect the anxiety he was unable to repress. Nevertheless, having made up his mind, he dressed himself in local garb, dyed his hair pitch black, and set off late at night.

In his account of his subsequent journey to the British lines, Kavanagh noted that the presence of his guide was indispensable to the successful completion of the mission. Had he traveled alone, he remarked, he would almost certainly have given up at the outset. Instead, he carried on so that he would not reveal his weaknesses. He also noted that the anarchy in the areas they walked through made their task very much easier: Because the street lights, always working when the British ruled, were now mostly broken, they were able to move at night with far less risk of being seen. At Kavanagh's insistence, the two men also traveled not along the back streets of the enemy-held towns but through the main streets. Because most of the locals were in the main streets, Kavanagh argued that it would appear far more suspicious if they were found in the less-crowded back streets.

When at last they reached Sir Colin Campbell's headquarters, both Kavanagh and his guide were well-rewarded, Kavanagh with the Victoria Cross. But, like many other escapees who have endured extremely stressful situations, he appears to have been badly affected by the trauma of his escape. He later had an uneven career before dying in 1883 at a relatively young age.

References: Kavanagh, T. H. *How I Won the Victoria Cross.* London: Ward and Lock, 1860.

Ludendorff, Erich (1865–1937)

After the cease-fire in November 1918, the political elite who had led Germany into war in 1914 and subsequently led the war effort were hailed as heroes by some but condemned as traitors and national enemies by others. It was from such violent condemnation that a top general, Erich Ludendorff, tried to escape in the winter of 1918.

Born and bred a soldier, Ludendorff was ill disposed toward running away from anything. At the end of the war, though he saw many of his fellow Germans clamor for revenge, he ignored the advice of friends and family who wanted him to find exile abroad. But as political order broke down suddenly in Berlin after the war and radical left-wing groups began to shout for revolution and vengeance against the war leaders, he made his move.

Sure that his enemies were following him everywhere, Ludendorff disguised himself with a false beard and a pair of thick spectacles and left his home in Berlin late one night, alone. Traveling by train, by taxi, and on foot, he soon reached the coast and boarded a passenger ship bound for Copenhagen. But his disguise was not adequate because not long after the ship set sail he was seen and recognized, and when they reached Denmark he found a huge crowd gathered at the dock to see him.

Ludendorff was not deterred from forcing his way past the crowd. He did his best to elude those who, mainly out of curiosity, tried to follow him through the streets. He met a kindly well-wisher along the way, a Swedish businessman who helped him find sanctuary at a large country house near Stockholm. He stayed there for two months before deeming it safe to return to Germany.

References: Goodspeed, D. J. *Ludendorff: Soldier, Dictator; Revolutionary.* London: Hart-Davis, 1966.

M

MacArthur, Douglas
(1880–1964)

When U.S. Field Marshall Douglas Mac-Arthur was ordered to evacuate his base in the Philippines and move further from the advancing Japanese troops, he felt torn between his duty to obey orders and his own wish to stand his ground.

MacArthur had moved his headquarters to Corregidor soon after the Japanese attack on Pearl Harbor in December 1941, but as the Japanese relentlessly advanced it was not long before his new base was also threatened. President Roosevelt was initially reluctant to order evacuation, which would have looked like a loss of nerve. "It

Douglas MacArthur, who escaped from the swift Japanese advance in 1942. (Library of Congress)

would mean that the whites would absolutely lose all face in the Far East. White men can go down fighting, but they can't run away" (Perret 1996), he commented wryly. But when a sudden crisis arose in U.S.-Australian relations, the president changed his mind, knowing that MacArthur's arrival in Australia would solve the problem by assuring its leaders that he was firmly committed to their defense.

Evacuation was anathema to MacArthur, who hated the idea of being seen to flee from his enemy and wanted to die fighting the Japanese on the frontline island of Bataan. He also knew that his own flight from the area could easily lead to a complete collapse of resistance to the enemy and that his men would blame him for abandoning them when they needed his leadership. And he had argued for nearly 20 years that in this kind of war the islands were well suited to a guerrilla campaign and could now be held against an enemy onslaught.

He was, then, devastated by the presidential order for evacuation. The color drained from his face when he heard the order and he is supposed to have walked around his house as if slightly crazed. "I am American Army born and bred and accustomed by a lifetime of discipline to the obedience of superior orders," he agonized aloud, "but this order I must disobey" (Perret 1996). But persuaded by his staff to follow the order, he sent a cable to the president that, instead of disputing the order altogether, requested only that he be allowed to choose the exact date of departure and his method of travel.

When Bataan looked ready to fall to the Japanese in March, MacArthur prepared to move. But he did not want to be evacuated by submarine, detesting the thought of being cooped up underwater in such a small space, and instead chose the far riskier option of leaving by boat. When on 11 March four torpedo boats arrived to pick up him and his staff, some soldiers were heard to comment that his chances of reaching Mindanao, nearly 500 miles away, were "maybe one in five."

The four boats set out at night, without lights and in radio silence. Their first obstacle was the minefield around Corregidor, and the sailors leaned over the sides to push away the floating mines that had been laid by the Japanese and that on occasion floated perilously close. But as their journey progressed they ran into other problems. After surviving some stormy seas, which had made them all violently seasick, they saw a Japanese cruiser on the horizon, some six miles away. But by making a fast turn to the right the torpedo boats made themselves virtually invisible by positioning themselves in such a way that the brilliant light of the setting sun made them invisible.

The following morning, MacArthur's torpedo boat arrived on the northern shore of Mindanao, shortly ahead of the three others that had also set off from Corregidor. But before boarding his flight to Australia, MacArthur turned and took one last look at the open seas and swore that one day he would recapture the islands that he had left so reluctantly.

See also: Corregidor
References: Perret, Geoffrey. Old Soldiers Never Die. New York: Random House, 1996.

MAGDEBURG PRISON (1916)

The escape of one young British officer, Lieutenant James Hardy, from German captivity at Magdeburg Prison in 1916 was made possible by his astute perceptions of those who guarded him.

One major obstacle confronting him was the numerous roll calls and bed checks of prisoners, which meant that camp guards quickly detected any absences. Like other prisoners during the next world war, some would-be escapees were able to get round this particular problem by placing a dummy in their bed to fool those counting the prisoners. But Hardy knew that the conscientiousness of the particular guard responsible for his own wing made this impossible, since this guard was renowned for taking extreme care to ensure that the figure in bed was a real, live man, not a dummy.

But by carefully watching the guard's every movement, Hardy managed to detect a flaw in his approach. Taking care and paying much attention to one thing, it seemed, did not necessarily entail efficiency with respect to another, for though the guard took such great care to inspect each bed before him, he did not make any effort to check the *number* of beds in the room, unless of course there was a very noticeable difference. So all he would have to do to avoid the count was to dismantle his own bed, perhaps slightly rearrange the layout of the others to disguise the change, and then hide until the head count was over.

A few days later this plan did the trick, and he and a fellow escapee made their way through a tunnel that they had spent several months excavating. But when they surfaced on the other side of the prison wall and stood up to see what lay around them, they turned around to see, at very close range, a sentry in charge of other prisoners working on a nearby railway; the sentry was staring at them in disbelief. Hardy had only a split second to decide if his cover was blown, in which case he would have been forced to dash off into the night and hide, or if he could bluff his way out of the situation.

Instinctively detecting that the sentry was in two minds about who they were, he decided upon the second of these options. Knowing that the guard would pick up even one sign of guilt or fear, he and his companion pretended to be searching for their lost dog, calling it in German, whistling, peering in every direction, and then moving off.

The two escapees appear to have been saved not only by the speed and precision of this response but also, it seems, by another miscalculation on the part of the sentry. Appearing to think that the two men could not possibly have entered this prohibited and well-patrolled piece of land without the permission of another guard, the guard gave them the benefit of the doubt and assumed that they had already been given approval to be there.

Both men eventually reached Allied lines, and Hardy rejoined the war effort in northern France, as he had hoped.

References: Hardy, J. L. *I Escape!* London: John Lane, 1927.

MALMÉDY (1944)

Battlefield atrocities are most often committed by the desperate, and when in the winter of 1944 Hitler launched an offensive in the Ardennes area of Belgium that was designed to cut through U.S. lines and capture Antwerp, his soldiers soon began to rely not on military success but rather on random terror and brutality to intimidate civilians and enemy soldiers.

Only hours after the offensive had been started, soldiers of the Kampfgruppe Peiper lined up 100 captured GIs in a field near Malmédy in Belgium before opening up with their machine-guns. Eighty-four were killed instantly, but a number were able to escape by feigning death, collapsing on the ground just before the guns opened fire. One of the men, Virgil Lacy, recalled the self-discipline he had to summon when he heard and saw several Germans searching through the pile of corpses for survivors, kicking the victims in the face to see if they flinched and dispatching those that did with pistol shots. Only after the Germans seemed to have left did he get up and run into the woods and lanes nearby, narrowly avoiding the bullets fired by a few remaining enemy soldiers and eventually reaching the U.S. lines half-frozen, dazed, and weeping in anger at what he had seen and endured.

See also: Execution, escape from
Whiting, C. *Massacre at Malmédy.* London: Leo Cooper, 1996.

MANDELA UNITED FOOTBALL CLUB (C. 1985–1989)

Two victims of the campaign of violence and terror that Winnie Mandela is thought to have unleashed against her fellow black South Africans during the last few years of the apartheid regime were the brothers Peter and Philip Makanda, who were arrested and tortured by the Mandela United Football Club but who managed to escape with their lives.

The two brothers were awakened one night in 1988 and forced at gunpoint to leave their uncle's house and accompany their captors to another building elsewhere in Soweto. They were both accused of being police informers and were brutally beaten as their torturers tried to make them confess to the betrayal of their comrades. Peter Makanda was even hanged by the neck with a piece of rope and only escaped death because the rope snapped when it was pulled.

Though the torturers were ready to continue their well-practiced routine, a guard suddenly burst through the door and shouted a warning. The police were in the area, he said, and they might make a surprise raid on the house. The brothers were then loaded into a van, driven to an accomplice's house some miles away, and locked in a garage.

The garage door, however, was not able to contain these desperate men, who in the past had seen the execution and torture of others suspected of being police informers and knew what lay in store for them. Before long they had discovered how to open the garage door from the inside and had freed themselves.

They raced to the nearest police station and reported their shocking stories to the officers, but to their astonishment they later found that their claims were never investigated or pursued, fueling accusations that Winnie Mandela was herself in fact a police spy.

See also: Cebekhulu, Katiza
References: Bridgeland, Fred. *Katiza's Journey.* Sidgwick and Jackson, 1997.

MAPLE LEAF (1863)

One of the largest and best organized breaks of the U.S. Civil War was carried out in 1863 by a number of Confederate prisoners from the Union steamer *Maple Leaf* in which they were being held.

The escapees appeared to have been motivated by their sudden realization that their high hopes of release were to be disappointed. Thinking at first that they were being taken north for exchange, they soon found that they were instead being shipped to the Union prison at Fort Delaware to join thousands of other captured Confederate officers. Broken and dispirited, and thinking that their captors had deceived them, they quickly drew up a plan of escape.

During the late afternoon of 10 June 1863, one of the prisoners sounded the prearranged call to his fellow officers that signaled the start of the attack. Immediately the other prisoners, who were allowed considerable freedom of movement on the ship, attacked the guards and seized their rifles, taking control of the vessel almost straightaway. Though some chose to stay behind, nearly 70 of the Confederate soldiers helped to lower the ship's boats and reached shore in Confederate Virginia.

News of the mass escape infuriated and embarrassed the senior Union officers who soon heard the news. When he heard of the escape, President Lincoln also dismissed from the army one of the unfortunate junior officers who had been in charge of the steamer that day, a 2nd Lieutenant William E. Dorsey, who had become a scapegoat for the whole affair.

References: Witt, Jerry V. *Escape from the Maple Leaf.* Bowie, MD: Heritage Press, 1993.

MAROON COMMUNITIES

Runaway slaves not only had to escape from their place of detention but also had to find a secure place to hide if they were to remain at liberty. "Maroon communities" were established by such slaves who knew that they had to be well organized if they were to keep one step ahead of their former slave masters who wanted to recapture them.

These Maroon communities had different characteristics throughout the many different imperial colonies where they existed. Some were founded and occupied by only a bare handful of runaways who had managed to creep away on their own, often as

soon as they had landed from Africa. Others were the creation of a huge exodus of escapees, occasionally numbering in the thousands, who had sometimes killed their masters before fleeing.

But despite their many differences, all of them were established in the most remote and inaccessible places the slaves could find. In America, this meant that the swamplands were the most popular hiding places; in Guyana, the thick and impenetrable jungle; and in Jamaica, the deep canyons. Paths to the settlements were always carefully covered, and in Guyana they were usually surrounded by lakes, rivers, and tracts of quicksand that would have deterred even the most audacious enemy. The runaways themselves often got around these obstacles by constructing hidden paths that, because they were submerged, were invisible to those who knew nothing of them.

But natives and settlers also occasionally had to be rescued from violence committed by some of the Maroon inhabitants. In Venezuela in the late 1760s, for example, a black slave named Guillermo Ribas attacked his owner, a magistrate named Marcos de Ribas, killed another fellow slave, and headed for the wilderness, where he established a series of Maroon communities and encouraged a great many other slaves to follow suit and join him. Over the next three years he led gangs of runaway slaves who plundered the homes of the inhabitants in search of food, money, arms, and women. He was captured in the small town of Chuspa, but he managed to escape after wounding eight men under the command of Nicholas de la Rosa. However, he was eventually caught and executed in 1771 after years of striking fear into the hearts of the settlers.

The support of some of the local peasant populations for the Maroon societies also began to dwindle when it became increasingly clear that some of the bandits were starting their own slave rings. At Kahola in Angola, for example, some of the native Africans were kidnapped by the Maroon settlers for this very purpose, helping to forge a new alliance between the Portuguese settlers and the local tribes.

See also: Brown, Henry; Fugitive Slave Laws;
   Parker, John; Underground Railroad
References: Buckmaster, H. *Out of the House of
   Bondage: Runaways, Resistance and Marronage in
   Africa and the New World.* London: Frank Cass,
   1986.
Price, Richard. *Maroon Societies.* Baltimore and
   London: Johns Hopkins University Press, 1996.

MARY, QUEEN OF SCOTS
(1542–1587)

As a descendant of Henry VII, Mary Stuart, known as Mary, Queen of Scots, was, for English Catholics, the legitimate heir to the throne that Elizabeth I assumed in 1558. She arrived in Scotland in 1561 from her exile in France, but her ambitions to find a secure political following there before claiming the English throne were dashed in 1567 by a rebellion of Scottish nobles, who had felt threatened by the scheming ambitions of her husband, Lord Darnley. Imprisoned at the remote castle of Lochleven by her enemies, Mary soon sought a means of escape.

Her motives are not hard to understand. She was only 24 years old, and the prospect of spending a long period in a remote captivity was bound to be torturous, especially for someone of her active temperament and political ambition. She was, as one historian famously described her, like a lioness pacing its cage. She wrote begging letters, all of them unanswered, to the French queen, Catherine de Medici, and even, in desperation, to Elizabeth, urging them to intervene to spare her a long ordeal. But it soon became evident that, for the moment at least, she would have to rely on her own devices if she was find a way out.

But escape from Lochleven demanded resource and cleverness. It was some miles offshore, and given the distance and the strength of the currents, it was out of the question for anyone, let alone for her, to swim to the mainland. Moreover, since she was the only prisoner on the island, there was a far greater risk of being seen and recognized by any boatman who ferried them across.

Nonetheless, Mary came close to succeeding at her first attempt, in March 1568. After her chief companion on the island, Lady Margaret Douglas, had given birth, Mary had been granted more freedom than before to move to and from her quarters. Disguising herself as a laundress, she sought to escape by boat while another of her companions, Mary Setton, took her place in the castle. But unluckily one of the boatmen was made suspicious by the way she turned her face away from him so shyly. He was prompted to take a closer look at his passenger and saw that her hands—white, slender, and elegant—were hardly those of a laundress. She was sent straight back to her quarters, although the boatman, with her best interests in mind, kept what he knew to himself.

Undeterred, Mary began to prepare for another escape bid. She possessed one gift that is often indispensable if any such attempt is likely to succeed: the ability to command loyalty. George Douglas, a young noble who also lived at the castle, was much taken with her, as was William, an orphan member of the Douglas household whom she appears to have won over with her charm and kindness. And two other members of the household, young girls of 14 and 15, soon began to hero worship the queen whom they had long heard so much about and whom they now found themselves alongside.

But the obstacles before her became more difficult for an unusual reason: There had been omens of her imminent escape. Not long before, the daughter of the lord of the castle had nightmares of a black raven swooping down and snatching the queen away to take her to freedom, and the girl became so distressed by what she saw in her dreams that she appears to have come very close to arousing the suspicion of the queen's captors. And the Laird of Markyston, a man renowned in the area as a wizard who was gifted with remarkable foresight, had begun to predict that the queen would escape by the beginning of May. As a result of his prophecy, her guard was stepped up. Furthermore, the lord of Lochleven, her captor, saw William putting pegs in the bottoms of all the boats—to stop anyone from stealing them—except one and became suspicious enough to keep a careful

A dramatic woodcut showing Mary Stuart defying Queen Elizabeth I. (North Wind Picture Archive)

watch over them during dinner the same day. But despite these setbacks, on 2 May Mary was given the prearranged signal that everything was ready for the escape and that she should prepare herself to go.

Well disguised, she boldly crossed the main courtyard, though it was full of servants going about their business, and went through the front gate to the boat waiting for them at the harbor. Several of the washerwomen who passed by recognized her, but William, who was not far behind, told them to keep what they had seen to themselves. Having already stolen the key to the main gate, William now locked it behind them to stop anyone from pursuing them and, in a famous gesture, put the keys into a cannon overlooking the sea.

By the time she was found missing, Mary had already arrived on the mainland and was traveling inland on her captor's best horses, all stolen from his stables. After ten and a half months of confinement on a tiny offshore island, she was free and enjoying the cheers and adulation of the country people who recognized her.

There is a certain irony to her escape. Forced to flee shortly afterward to England, she was again imprisoned by Elizabeth I. As the focus of a number of groups opposed to Elizabeth's regime, she became a source of political instability and was beheaded in 1587. She met her unfortunate end with the same courage she had shown during her escape from Lochleven 19 years earlier.

References: Fraser, Antonia. Mary Queen of Scots. London: Weidenfeld and Nicholson, 1994.

MASARYK, TOMAS
(1850–1937)

As a young politician representing the cause of Czech nationalism, Tomas Masaryk fled the Austrian authorities, who had long recognized him as an important political enemy.

Masaryk made his move in December 1914, wanting to take refuge in Italy before the Austrian authorities closed the border. But as he walked toward the train he was stopped by an official who questioned the validity of his identity passes. As the station master tried to telegraph his bosses in Prague for instructions, Masaryk took the law into his own hands and, seeing the train pulling away, sprinted toward it and jumped on board.

Perhaps because, with a philosopher's insight, he had foreseen the obstacles before him, Masaryk had traveled lightly and had wisely taken almost no luggage with him.

References: Lowrie, Donald. Masaryk of Czechoslovakia. Oxford: Oxford University Press, 1930.

MATILDA, EMPRESS
(C. 1102–1167)

As the daughter of King Henry I, the Empress Matilda enjoyed a stronger claim to the English throne than did King Stephen, Henry's nephew. The power struggle between Stephen and his challenger for the throne came to the fore in 1141, when armed conflict between their supporters broke out.

Matilda was forced to flee from one battle between the rival forces. Stephen's forces were besieging the city of Winchester, where Matilda had based her headquarters. When they suddenly started to advance, the queen was forced to escape; and while her own supporters fought a delaying action, she slipped out of the city under the escort of Reginald of Cornwall and Brian Fitz-Count, and made her way by horseback first to Ludgershall and then to Devizes. A rumor soon went round that she had escaped from Winchester by hiding in a coffin that was then carried out of town. What is certain, however, is that she was forced to ride to Ludgershall at such a brisk pace that she had to ride astride, like a man, which was at that time unheard of for any woman, let alone an empress.

Her enemies once again started to catch up with her, forcing another of her followers, Robert of Gloucester, to fight a rear guard action at the ford outside Stockbridge. Her enemies' advance was sufficiently delayed for her to disappear into the folds of Danesbury Down and find temporary sanctuary in the waterlogged marshes of the surrounding area. By the time she reached Ludgershall she was so exhausted that she had to be carried in a litter between two horses and, in the words of one historian is said to have arrived at her house more dead than alive.

But Matilda made her most famous escape from her enemies a few weeks later, in the autumn of the same year. She had made her way to Oxford, but before long her enemies followed her there and surrounded the castle where she had set up her base. Though the castle had formidable defenses, she knew that its supplies would start to run out before long and that, with winter well on its way, she would have to escape.

It was the harsh winter weather, however, that came to her rescue. Since the Thames River was frozen over, she knew her best chance would be to slip out from the castle and steal over the ice and out of her enemy's reach. Making her move late one night, she went unnoticed by Stephen's men, dressed as she was in a white cloak and concealed, it seems, by a blizzard that had already reduced visibility. According to one account of her escape, she was seen by one of King Stephen's guards who was persuaded to keep quiet about what he had seen.

Together with several companions, she walked another seven miles before they were able to obtain horses to take them as far as Wallingford. One contemporary felt moved to write that he had "never heard of any woman having such marvellous escapes from so many enemies threatening her life, and from such exceeding perils" (Davis 1992).

References: Davis, R. H. C. *King Stephen.* London: Longman, 1992.

MAZE PRISON (1983)

More usually known as the "H-Blocks" because of the distinctive shape of its cell buildings, the Maze Prison in Belfast is a formidably difficult prison for anyone to escape from. Built as a maximum security prison in the mid-1970s specifically to house Irish Republican Army (IRA) terrorists, it has an 18-foot-high outer wall, razor wire, watchtowers, and as many prison officers as prisoners. But on 25 September 1983, 38 of its inmates succeeded in breaking out by using the same considerable brutality and ruthlessness that had characterized the crimes for which they had been sent there.

The organizing spirit behind the break was Larry Marley, a leader of the IRA who had already succeeded in escaping Royal Ulster Constabulary (RUC) custody some

eight years before, having slipped through a toilet window with some accomplices while being held at a Newry courthouse. He arranged for visitors to smuggle handguns to his fellow prisoners and decided to stage the escape from Block number 7. He waited patiently until all those who were to go either moved into that block as residents or obtained some form of work or occupation there.

When they were ready, he planned the break to take place at the quietest time of the week, on a Sunday afternoon.

At shortly after 2:30 P.M. on that quiet September afternoon, a number of prisoners surrounded the officers who were supervising them and threatened them with the handguns, which they had cleverly concealed. After taking control of the block they were able to seize a kitchen truck that visited the prison every day, knowing that if they could hide themselves on the truck and force the driver to take them out, then they would have a real chance of escape. Since the truck almost always left the kitchens at 3 P.M., the terrorists knew they would avoid the prison guards' daily change of shift, when there were always double the usual number of officers.

Though their escape bid started off well, the terrorists had chosen the one day that the kitchen lorry happened to arrive later than usual. At just before 3:30, nearly an hour after they had taken over the wing and half an hour after they had expected it to arrive, the truck at last appeared. Almost as soon as it stopped, the driver and orderly were seized and ordered to take the vehicle back outside. The unfortunate driver was already taken wholly by surprise, but as a precaution the escapees tied his left foot to the clutch, jammed the door lock, and told him that a hand grenade had been tied to his seat. Though this last threat was just bluff, Gerry Kelly, one of the escapees, lay on the floor of the cab with his shotgun trained on the back of the driver's head.

Within minutes the truck had turned round and was on its way toward the gates, with Kelly in the cab and 37 others hidden in the back. At the first two gates the driver and his orderly were recognized by the officers on duty and the truck was allowed through without attracting even a flicker of suspicion. But as it approached the final, main gate, nearly half an hour later than planned, escape no longer looked so easy, since the shifts were now changing and there were far more officers around than the escapers had hoped.

But it was too late to turn back, and nine of the prisoners, who were all wearing prison officers' uniforms, jumped from the back of the truck and held up the five officers who were in the lodge and who were in no position to argue with the rifles being waved under their noses. Though one member of the security staff did manage to activate an alarm, prompting a telephone call from the control room, he was forced to report a false alarm by a gun pressed against his head. It was particularly unfortunate that the control center failed to notice his wavering tone as he spoke to them.

But the escapees' hopes that the gate would now be opened to them were dashed when one of the security staff suddenly broke under the pressure and tried to run out of the building in order to raise the alarm. But though 43-year-old James Ferris was stabbed through the heart and died soon afterward as a result, he gave one of his fellow officers a chance to contact the emergency control room and tell them what was happening. And at the same moment the control room received a call from a soldier, stationed in one of the perimeter watchtowers, reporting that a fight seemed to have broken out between prison officers.

Now it was each man for himself, as some prisoners and officers fled in opposite directions and others fought. In the resulting fracas—fighting, shouting, and screaming, with flying bullets and flashing knives—three other officers received serious stab wounds, while the prisoners abandoned their truck and fled on foot. Some of the escapees were caught in the perimeter wire, which was rolled around the ground outside, and others were caught some way outside by army patrols that scoured the area. One officer was shot in the leg by a terrorist gunman who was in turn shot by a soldier firing from the watchtower that overlooked the main gate.

The escape operation had not been as successful as the prisoners and the IRA had hoped. Before long, 17 of the 38 men who had tried to break out were back behind bars. But 21 convicted terrorists, all serving long terms for serious offenses, were able to see the outside of the H-Blocks far sooner than they had once imagined.

But the subsequent review of prison security did not render the Maze inescapable. On Wednesday, 10 December 1997, Liam Averill, who had served two years of a life sentence, escaped from the Maze in what was considered to be a meticulously planned operation. Averill had volunteered to help at the prison Christmas party, for which 150 wives, girlfriends, and children were allowed into the prison, and had then seized his chance. After changing into women's clothes and putting on a large amount of makeup, he slipped into the group that was waiting for a minibus to take them back to the visitors' parking lot outside and was for some reason missed by the security cameras in the block, which were probably disabled or obscured.

Averill's getaway was made possible by the flexible arrangements that had been introduced as a result of the cease-fire between the IRA and the British forces some weeks before. Head counts and cell checks had been in full force before the cease-fire but had then been slackened off, on the of orders of senior government figures.

References: Bean, J. P. *Over the Wall: True Stories of the Master Jail Breakers.* London: Headline, 1994.

MCGARTLAND, MARTIN
(1970–)

Throughout its history, traitors to the cause of Irish republicanism have faced a grim fate if caught. Many have been "kneecapped" (had their knees maimed), others have been repeatedly held under water until they were on the verge of drowning, and almost all of those who have been sentenced to death by the kangaroo courts of the Irish Republican Army (IRA) have been savagely beaten and tortured before being shot and unceremoniously dumped in the vicinity. One individual who narrowly managed to escape such a fate was the Royal Ulster Constabulary (RUC) spy Martin McGartland.

McGartland had been recruited into the IRA in 1987, aged just 17, but he soon became disillusioned with the savage brutality of his counterparts, especially with the violence that was directed toward innocent men, women, and children. Soon recognized as a possible "insider" by the RUC, he decided to thwart the terrorists' plans by using his first-hand knowledge to tip off the security forces about IRA plans.

Over the next two years, McGartland saved the lives of no fewer than 50 people, most of them employed by or associated with the RUC. Because he was employed as a member of its Belfast intelligence-gathering unit, which was responsible for finding and monitoring possible targets for assassination, he had a first-class knowledge of exactly who the republicans were going to target and when.

But he also knew that it would only be a matter of time before the IRA caught up with him. Each time one of their operations was inexplicably thwarted, the terrorists would obtain another clue to who was giving their game away, since they knew which of their members had had prior knowledge of it.

The net finally closed on McGartland in the summer of 1991. Arrested in Belfast at gunpoint by members of the IRA's Civil Administration Unit, which was responsible for tracking down those thought to be traitors to their cause, he was taken to a republican safe house in a Catholic area of the capital while his captors decided how to deal with him.

McGartland had lived in Northern Ireland all his life and had been involved with the IRA long enough to know the gruesome fate that lay ahead. He knew it was no use trying to bargain with his former colleagues, who were obviously absolutely sure of his complicity, and therefore realized that there was only one alternative to an ordeal of torture that his captors would make as long and agonizing as they could: He would have to jump out the window.

Though he was unable to see even the tops of the trees through the windowpanes, McGartland knew that he was at least 40 feet above ground. He had no idea what was underneath him or of the precise distance that he was going to fall. Bracing himself, he closed his eyes and threw himself head first through the glass, praying as he did so.

Some hours later he woke up on a hospital bed, remembering nothing of the citizens who had seen him fall to the street or of the army patrol that had rushed him to medical attention. He was spirited back to the British mainland soon afterward and given a new identity and secret residence in order to escape the IRA death squads who he knew would soon be looking for him. His dramatic life-and-death gamble had paid off.

See also: Execution, escape from
References: McGartland, Martin. *Fifty Dead Men Walking*. London: Jade Books, 1998.

McVICAR, JOHN (1939–)

Like the Kray twins and Walter Probyn, John McVicar was once notorious as a criminal mastermind, and for a time the popular press even labeled him Britain's "Public Enemy Number One." This reputation was forged not just by his criminal record, mainly as a mastermind of robbery, but also by his propensity to escape from custody.

McVicar made his first break in 1966, two years after he had been sent to prison for robbery. When, some weeks before, a fight had broken out between two prisoners in Parkhurst Prison, the authorities had had no reason to suspect anything and soon sent the two culprits to attend court proceedings at Winchester. What they had not realized was that the fight had been carefully planned so that McVicar, and several other prisoners, would have a chance to break out during the journey back from the court, where they had been asked to give evidence.

Soon after their bus pulled away from the courtroom, the 13 prisoners prepared to overwhelm the seven officers guarding them. Though most of the prisoners were handcuffed, they soon freed themselves, using the bus's high seats to shield their efforts from the guards. As the bus passed through Bishops Waltham, they jumped their seats, attacked the guards, and fled. Though seven of the nine who escaped were caught fairly soon afterward, McVicar and another got clean away.

McVicar was caught some months later, after returning to the life of crime that he had long been involved in. He was then sent to Durham Prison, where he met the infamous Walter Probyn, whose irrepressible aptitude for escape soon led McVicar to hope that he would soon be free.

Though Durham was a maximum security prison, both men knew that it had vulnerabilities. Probyn, not long a prisoner, soon set to work, walking along the prison corridors barefooted, hoping to detect currents of warm air that might reveal a possible ventilation shaft and escape route. He was not disappointed: He soon found such a place in one of the prison shower rooms, where they hoped to be able to build a tunnel.

Probyn and McVicar now started to smuggle the materials they needed from the prison workshops. With characteristic ingenuity, the two men managed to hide the long metal spikes they needed inside a hamster cage that they were allowed to move from their cells to the workshop and back. Boring a hole through the floor toward the ventilator shaft, they found a novel way of keeping the prison officers out when they wanted to work: They turned the showers' hot water on full to create steam that would have made a mess of the guards' clean uniforms.

At just after 7 P.M. on the evening of the 28 October 1968, McVicar and Probyn made their break. They went through the shower room, down the hole they had made in the floor, and along the air shaft; they then removed an iron grille, made their way onto the roof of one of the prison buildings, and headed for the main outer wall.

But unknown to them, their quick footsteps echoed along the corridors below them, and within minutes every prison officer in the building had been alerted and was trying his utmost to find them. The two escapees now went their separate ways, and Probyn was caught before he made it over the wall. But McVicar, who had stayed longer on the roof than Probyn, was able to get over the prison wall and drop into the gardens of a row of houses next door. He glimpsed members of the prison staff running full speed toward him before he turned and fled through the streets of Durham and hid first along the banks of the River Wear and then in the backyard of a student house nearby. Just as he was beginning to despair of evading capture, a car pulled up alongside him as he walked along the streets, and someone inside beckoned him in. Though he had no idea who the two men inside the car were and though he was destined never to find out, by taking a lift with them out of the area he was able to slip away from the massive search operation then underway.

McVicar had achieved what no one had thought possible: escape from a maximum security prison. Though he was recaptured again much later, in 1970, "the most dangerous man in Britain" had remained at large for much longer than the authorities had expected.

See also: Probyn, Walter

References: McVicar, John. McVicar: By Himself. London: Hutchinson, 1974.

MEDIEVAL ENGLAND, IMPRISONMENT IN

There are some recorded examples of prisoners who made their getaway from the extremely harsh conditions of the medieval prisons in which they were held.

One unusual escape story that has survived the centuries is that of a man who was sent to prison in Northampton some time during 1225. Perhaps because of the particularly hard life that prisoners then had to endure, he appears to have become demented. He started hallucinating, claiming that the devil had appeared before him in the guise of a monk. In order to defend himself from this powerful presence, it appears that the prisoner began to pull stones out of the prison wall. He eventually removed an entire section, a section big enough to allow him to make his getaway. An inquiry was held afterward to investigate how he had managed, unaided and undetected, to undertake a feat that no one had thought possible. According to the inquiry, he had managed to make three breaches in the wall, all of different sizes.

It was more typical for prisoners to work together in order to improve their chances of escaping. In 1347, for example, 12 prisoners in Old Salisbury Castle dug a pit four feet deep under the wall of the jail and were only prevented from leaving by a last-minute chance encounter with some warders. More successful were several convicts who were held in the archbishop of Dublin's prison at Swords. They managed to dig an underground passage to freedom. In 1455 some prisoners escaped by breaking the floor above the vaults in which they were held and climbing through. A few years before, in 1441, some prisoners stole the keys from one of the jailers' servants as he leaned over the stocks in which they were held in order to search them. The prisoners undid the stocks, assaulted the servant, and ran off.

The main prison for criminals of the time, Newgate, was also the setting for a number of escapes. In 1285 five prisoners made their way onto the prison roof and held several of their warders as hostages before making their getaway. Forty years later a prison warder was murdered by an escapee he was pursuing, and soon afterward ten prisoners escaped by cutting a hole in the prison wall. There are known escapes from other London prisons of the time, such as the mass breakout of those held in Marshalsea in 1504, during which nearly everyone in the prison is thought to have gotten away.

References: Pugh, R. B. *Imprisonment in Medieval England.* Cambridge: Cambridge University Press, 1968.

MIS-X, MI9

Many of the American and British pilots who managed to evade capture after being shot down over Europe or the Far East owed their success to the efforts of the secret U.S. organization MIS-X, and its British equivalent MI9.

Though both had roots in special departments set up during World War I to help prisoners escape, their role and importance were greatly expanded during World War II. In 1939 two Britons, Anthony Rawlinson and James Holland, both veterans of World War I, approached British High Command in London and presented a powerful case for widening the tasks of such bodies, entrusting them with the specific task of facilitating the escape of existing prisoners and helping downed airmen evade capture. Soon after the United States entered the war, the influence of W. Stull Holt, also a veteran of World War I and subsequently a professor at Johns Hopkins University, and U.S. Air Force chief "Tooey" Spaatz ensured that the Americans had an equivalent organization with a similar purpose.

Headed by Lt. Col. J. Edward Johnston, MIS-X enjoyed an annual budget (excluding wages) of around $160,000, which was spent on the development and production of all manner of devices designed to aid escape and evasion. One particular achievement of the two organizations during the war was the production of special maps for aircrews who risked being shot down while flying missions over enemy territory. Made by a small team from the technical design industry, finely printed maps were eventually produced on pieces of white silk, which were not only much smaller than their paper equivalents—each amounting to no more than about 18 inches square—but which were also much easier to carry and hide from enemy searches. They also designed and produced compasses that fitted neatly into their collars, cap badges, and pens. Nearly 2.5 million of these compasses were made during the war years and distributed to those who took part in active flying operations.

A whole host of other ingenious inventions were put forward or designed by one of the leading figures in this shadowy world: Clayton Hutton. Under his instruction, razor blades were magnetized to enable a pilot to find his bearings, bootlaces doubled as pieces of strong, serrated wire, and minute hacksaws, only 4.5 inches by .5 inch, were developed and manufactured. Later on in the war pilots sometimes traveled with a blanket that could be converted into a civilian overcoat and that when immersed in water would become a very different color from easily identifiable military fabrics. Tiny cameras, disguised as cigarette lighters, were also produced and smuggled into prison camps so that prison forgers could make copies of documents from which to work.

Hutton also designed the "escape box," which was packed with an enormous amount of material indispensable for anyone on the run. More than 10,000 cigarette boxes were acquired from the tobacco firm W. D. and H. O. Wills and packed with enough emergency rations for downed aircrew to survive for their first 48 hours, as well as with malted milk tablets, boiled sweets, and water purification tablets, a fishing line, and a razor. It was easy to carry and was enormously beneficial to the thousands of airmen who found themselves having to keep a low profile for the first few days deep inside enemy territory while the Germans or Japanese combed the area surrounding their crash site.

There was almost no end to the other gadgets that were sent out to Allied agents and prisoners of war on the Continent. Maps were hidden in the bowls of specially designed briar pipes with asbestos linings, and fountain pens, fake cigarettes, and even false teeth were all used to conceal items that might be of use to would-be escapees.

The two organizations also facilitated the escape of those who were already in German captivity. Prisoners were entitled under the terms of the Geneva Convention to receive parcels from their home country, and escape tools were hidden inside every conceivable object with extraordinary skill. Though prison guards always combed through these packages—and sometimes found what they were looking for inside such objects as gramophone records, board games, and bookbindings—MIS-X and MI9 were usually one step ahead, forcing the Germans to admit that they had little idea of what to look for and where.

Many airmen later testified to the effectiveness of the guidelines for escape that MIS-X and MI9 issued. On 1 November 1944, 2d Lt. Robert C. Lightfoot of the U.S. Air Force's Forty-First Squadron was shot down and baled out over Mindanao. As he fell he remembered MIS-X's advice not to pull the rip cord of his parachute until he got to within 3,000 feet of the ground, to lessen the chances of being seen by the wrong people. It was this, he later claimed, that allowed him to scramble away into the hills on landing and hide in the wilderness for two days before finding local anti-Japanese guerrillas and eventually be rescued.

But one pilot who touched down on an island in the Philippines and took MIS-X official advice was not so lucky. Advised to smile at the natives to demonstrate his lack of hostility toward them, he found merely that they all "only grunted" and sprinted off in the opposite direction as fast as they could.

References: Foot, Michael R., and James M. Langley. *MI9: Escape and Evasion, 1939–45.* London: Book Club Associates, 1979; Boston: Little, Brown, 1980.

Neave, Airey. *Saturday at MI9: A History of Underground Escape Lines in North-West Europe, 1940–45.* London: Hodder and Stoughton, 1969.

Shoemaker, Lloyd R. *The Escape Factory: The Story of MIS-X.* New York: St. Martin's Press, 1990.

MITCHELL, FRANK (1929–?)

One escape from British custody in 1966 illustrated how some prisoners can gain their freedom by using terror to pressure their guards into giving them certain freedoms. Frank Mitchell, who was classified as a dangerous psychopath, had a reputation for having an explosive temper and was unusually strong—on many occasions as many as seven or eight policemen or prison officers were required to hold him down—which daunted both prison guards and prisoners as soon as he arrived behind bars.

It was unfortunate that a man of such temperament and destructive power was also a determined jailbreaker, having twice broken out from Rampton Prison in Nottinghamshire, on one occasion by placing a dummy on his bed in an attempt to fool his guards. When he was sent to Dartmoor Prison in 1962, it was not long before he set to work in order to find an appropriate way of making his escape.

Mitchell found a way of obtaining undeserved prison freedoms, freedoms that were enjoyed only by a small minority of others but that he knew he would need in order to get free. Those few others had earned their privileges as a reward for good behavior and as a reflection of the trust they had won during their time inside. Mitchell, however, was given freedoms to prevent him from flying into the same terrifying rages that he had used while at Rampton to get the warders to give him almost anything he wanted. So in September 1966 he was allowed to join the work parties that left the prison compound to work, often daily, on nearby army rifle ranges and roads.

As it began to rain heavily at 11:30 on 16 December 1966, the party to which Mitchell belonged stopped work and headed for a nearby hut to find shelter. But after a few minutes in the hut Mitchell suddenly pulled the door open and ran off. Perhaps because the warders in charge were, with good reason, too afraid of the man to run after him, they left him alone and tried to contact their colleagues by radio, knowing that the moorlands would stop him from getting far. But unknown to them, Mitchell was quickly picked up by a car that had almost certainly been arranged for him by the Kray twins, the London gangsters with whom he had extensive contact and who were almost certainly heavily implicated in his jailbreak.

Mitchell is thought to have been murdered by the twins after disagreements with them. His body was never found, and his escape, like those of many other escapees, appears to have been in vain.

References: Bean, J. P. *Over the Wall: True Stories of the Master Jail Breakers.* London: Headline, 1994.

MODENA TRAIN BREAK (1944)

A "train break" was executed with great success by Allied prisoners of war (POWs) in Italy in 1943, even though it had a very adverse effect on those who remained behind in captivity.

The breakout took place at the time of the Italian capitulation, which forced the Germans to move the Allied prisoners under their control into their own hands. The detainees of one camp were moved from the camp to the railway station at Modena, where they were packed into cattle trucks and sent northward to a new place of internment.

The difficulties of finding a way to freedom were enormous. Not only were the compartments impossible to take apart with one's bare hands, but the Germans had also put an open truck in every fifth place, with machine guns at the ready, in order to pick off any prisoner who did manage to find his way outside of the trucks.

Quick reactions enabled Sherard Vaisey, a former commando, to get past the most immediate obstacle. As he was about to climb onto the train at Modena, he happened to notice an iron bar lying by the track. He dropped some of his load on it and managed to pick it up without his guards noticing. It was his best chance of knocking a hole in the truck and finding a way out.

Breaking open the floor turned out to be easier than he and the 29 other British soldiers in the cattle truck with him expected: After less than an hour of pounding, they made an opening wide enough for someone to get through. One of the officers in the truck, Peter McDowall, was able to climb onto the running board outside and unbolt the door for the others to get out.

The first to leap to freedom was Vaisey—the guiding force behind the escape. Even with the train traveling slowly, jumping out was dangerous. But despite the fears of his colleagues in the truck, he only injured a knee and was able to reach Switzerland with the aid of a deserter from the Italian army. He was the first of 50 POWs who were able to escape from under the noses of their guards that night. In one truck, all but 12 of the original occupants fled, and a second truck that McDowall had opened up was completely deserted by the time the train pulled in at Innsbruck and was inspected by the Germans. About half of these escapees made it to the safety of the nearby Swiss border.

But the success of the Modena escape had some unpleasant consequences for those unfortunate enough to still be in captivity. The Nazi authorities reasoned that the best way of preventing any more escapes was to debilitate their prisoners so that they were simply not in a fit enough state to be able to escape. Shortly afterward, therefore, an order was given to put even more prisoners in each cattle truck—now 40 were to be crammed in—and to deprive them of anything to drink for the whole of whatever journey they happened to be making. Another order decreed that prisoners would in future have their boots removed before making long journeys by train. Though a great many other POWs managed to slip free during the remainder of the war, the Modena break was, not surprisingly, the last "great escape" by train during the war.

References: Garrett, Richard. *Great Escapes.* London: Weidenfeld and Nicholson, 1989.

MOGADISHU PLANE RESCUE (1977)

Western governments were plunged into a state of crisis in October 1977 when a Lufthansa flight was hijacked by four of its passengers, two men and two women of Palestinian origin. Joining the flight at Majorca, where airport security was less stringent than in the Western capitals, the terrorists had been able to take on board all the weapons they needed to implement their plan to force the German government to release the Baader-Meinhof gang from prison and to exact a £9 million ransom.

As the aircraft hopped from one airport to another around the Middle East and Horn of Africa and the deadlock continued, two elite military units were given the order to prepare for the rescue of the hostages. One of the units was the German specialist antiterrorist force, the GSG-9, which had been set up in the aftermath of the 1972 kidnapping of Israeli athletes at the West German Olympic games at Munich; the other was its British military equivalent, the Special Air Service (SAS), which was familiar with working conditions in the Persian Gulf and which enjoyed very strong political and military connections to its governments and armed forces.

By the time the aircraft landed at Mogadishu in Ethiopia, the need for decisive action had become clear. At Aden the plane's captain, Jürgen Schumann, was shot dead by his captors, who suspected him of secretly being in contact with the security forces, and his body was dumped on the tarmac in full view of the 79 civilian passengers. Though the German government had hitherto considered meeting the terrorists' demands—the GSG-9 team had even set off with the ransom money—the murder of the captain made any compromise out of the question. The only option was to use military force to end the siege.

On the evening of 17 October two members of the British team, Maj. Alastair Morrison and Sgt. Barry Davies, threw specially designed "flash-bang" explosives, designed to stun the hijackers (as well as the unfortunate passengers) just at the crucial moment when the German assault team broke through the emergency doors on each side of the fuselage and started hand-to-hand fighting. During the eight-minute gun battle that ensued, three of the four terrorists were killed without loss among the passengers or rescuers.

The success of the operation was in large part due to the element of surprise. The terrorists had been led to believe, right up to the last minute, that their demands were being met, and at a crucial moment just before the operation was mounted, Somali soldiers lit a wood fire 100 yards or so in front of the plane in order to draw them into the cockpit and allow the GSG-9 men to approach the emergency exits without being seen.

The Mogadishu raid in this respect struck a clear contrast with the bloodiest rescue attempt ever made on a hijacked aircraft. When three gunmen seized Egyptair flight MS64 at Athens on 23 November 1985, the task of freeing the hostages fell to Force 777, an Egyptian special forces team that had been trained by Americans but that, by the time it undertook the operation, was hampered by outdated equipment and high turnover among the staff. At the end of the

Freed after a dramatic rescue operation by German and British soldiers, these passengers leave the hijacked Lufthansa 727 aircraft at Mogadishu. (UPI/Corbis-Bettmann)

operation, 57 passengers and one terrorist lay dead. The reason was not hard to see: The terrorists had been alerted to the prospect of an imminent attack when the airport lights were accidentally turned off, as if giving warning, and the Egyptian soldiers blew a hole in the airplane's roof and stormed it too long before the assault got fully under way. The element of surprise was lost essentially because the assault was made by a team that lacked the expertise of its Western, and some if its regional, equivalents.

But the Mogadishu operation had nonetheless been a close-run thing. The terrorists had very nearly wreaked havoc by rolling two hand grenades at the assault team. By sheer good fortune the hand grenades exploded under heavily padded passenger seats and did not do any harm. And the rescuers and passengers were equally fortunate that the aviation fuel and alcohol that the terrorists had scattered all over the aircraft, hoping to incinerate any rescuers, did not ignite.

The passengers' freedom did not come without a price. Six days after they were rescued, a leading West German industrialist, Hans-Martin Schleyer, was murdered and left in the trunk of an abandoned car. He had been kidnapped six weeks before the siege began by the Baader-Meinhof gang, which now exacted its bloody revenge for the defeat at Mogadishu.

References: Davies, Barry. *SAS Rescue.* London: Sidgewick and Jackson, 1996.
Geraghty, Tony. *Who Dares Wins.* London: HarperCollins, 1996.

MOHAMMED (570–632)

In A.D. 622 the founder of Islam escaped from his enemies in Mecca, who were sworn to put him to death if he was recaptured.

Though the rulers of Mecca allowed Mohammed to wander the streets of the city, he was in practice their prisoner. Everywhere he went he was followed and watched by their agents. He knew he would in all likelihood be arrested and executed if the rulers felt sure that his following was not strong enough to provoke demonstration and unrest.

To flee the city, Mohammed drew up a plan of escape with his friend and follower, Abu Bakr. They lay low at Abu Bakr's house in the city until they could quietly slip out of the city. Late one night they dashed through the city's deserted streets and headed by camel into the deserts toward Medina, where most of Mohammed's followers had gone.

Hiding themselves in the sand dunes, the two men constantly scanned the horizon for signs of pursuit. They did not have to wait long. In the distance they could see a huge cloud of dust, an unmistakable sign that a force of many thousands was making its way at a furious pace to stop them and place them under arrest.

As the Meccans closed in Mohammed and Abu Bakr took sanctuary in one of the caves they came across, and it was not long before they could even hear the voices of the men searching for them. But when one of the searchers began to enter their cave to look for the fugitives, he was stopped by his colleagues, who pointed to a spider's web that covered a section of the entrance and to a bird's nest just above it. There was no point in searching the cave, they said, because neither would be there if someone had gone into the cave recently.

Mohammed's escape is attributed to a miracle because there had been no sign of either the cobweb or the bird's nest when he and Abu Bakr had entered the cave. Instead, the nest and the cobweb had appeared just afterward, as if protecting the fugitives from the Meccans.

References: Andrae, Tor. *Mohammed: Man and Faith.* London: George Allen and Unwin, 1936.

MORGAN, GEN. JOHN

True to his reputation as a swashbuckling military adventurer of near legendary repute, the Confederate general John

Morgan made a remarkable escape from enemy detainment.

Morgan was captured in the summer of 1863 after conducting a series of lightning raids on Union forces, checking their rapid advance before pushing them back as far as the Ohio River. But though he was denied permission to continue the attack he blatantly ignored his orders. He was soon captured and imprisoned at a prisoner of war camp, formerly the Ohio State Penitentiary, at Columbus.

There were several hundred other prisoners of war at the camp. Morgan soon started to put together a team of dedicated escapees, and it was not long before one of them, Capt. Thomas Hines, found a possible way out. After carefully examining the walls of the cells, he concluded that the probable reason for their apparent dampness was an air passage behind the wall, a passage that might offer them a chance to escape. It was not long before Hines had begun digging a hole from his cell, using a stolen knife and moving his bed over to hide his work.

John Morgan, a Confederate general who made a brilliant escape from captivity during the U.S. Civil War. (Library of Congress)

The plan was carried out with all the ingenuity of the desperate. Spying a shovel lying abandoned in an isolated corner of the courtyard, the escapees staged a fight, of the half-serious variety that the guards were well accustomed to seeing. When one of the two combatants fell over at just the spot where the shovel lay, none of the guards noticed him hide it under his coat before he walked off.

The prisoners found an equally ingenious way of getting a better idea of the countryside around them, an essential task if they were to prepare their escape properly. Having heard that some years previously a prisoner had managed to climb up one of the walls onto a balcony—which would have given him a panoramic view—Morgan bet an unsuspecting warden that one of his fellow prisoners could repeat this feat. Minutes later, the prisoner had not only won the bet for him but had also obtained an excellent view of the area. He quickly drew a map that was to be indispensable during their escape.

Morgan also had large amounts of money smuggled to him, hidden inside the cover of a book, from his contacts outside. The money proved indispensable not only when they were on the run but also when they needed to bribe one of the guards to supply the information. Finding out exactly when the local trains departed, the escapees prepared to move at a precisely timed moment.

On the night of 27 November 1864, after their cell doors had been locked, Hines stuffed a shirt with straw, left it on his bed to deceive any guard who looked inside, and went into the tunnel he had so painstakingly prepared. When he reached Morgan's cell, he signaled his arrival and waited for the general to make his own way into the air passage, using the tunnel that he, too, had secretly prepared. Before long, these two men and five other escapees were all ready to leave the prison.

In the courtyard they found to their surprise and relief that the guards and their dogs had taken cover inside in order to escape the rain that was pouring down, and, unseen and unheard, they threw their home-made rope ladder over the wall and headed for the railway.

Knowing that news of their escape would spread quickly, Morgan and Hines, traveling together, leaped off the train and headed for the Ohio River. They linked up with an underground network of supporters in the region. Both men eventually reached the safety of their own lines, although Hines had a lucky escape from a group of enemy soldiers, jumping through a window into the darkness while they listened to the extraordinary story of his escape.

But Morgan's story, like that of so many other escapees, has an unhappy postscript. Having resumed fighting with the Union as soon as he returned, he was killed in action at Greenville, Tennessee, only weeks after his return.

References: Ramage, James A. *Rebel Raider: The Life of Gen. John Hunt Morgan.* Lexington: University Press of Kentucky, 1986.

MOSSAD (1951–)

Since its formation in the early 1950s the Israeli secret service, Mossad, has been involved in some remarkable escapes and rescues.

In its early days many of its leading personnel had first-class training and experience in such operations. One of its direct ancestors was the Mossad le Aliyah Bet, the Institute of Illegal Immigration, which took an active role in smuggling many Jews from Europe into Palestine. Though it had just ten active agents in Europe, this organization excelled at establishing escape routes, providing ships, and arranging safe houses and forged passports so that thousands of refugees could cross the border. Another ancestor was Shai, the information wing of the Haganah, a Zionist underground force, which also became expert in smuggling weapons and military supplies into Palestine.

After Israel achieved independence, the task of helping rescue stranded Jews from other parts of the world and bringing them to Israel continued to be an important role for Mossad. Building up contacts with pockets of Jews all over the world, Mossad was able to go to their aid whenever the need arose, and since 1953 is known to have sent teams to Iraq, Iran, South Yemen, and Algeria to arrange for the evacuation, either openly or in secret, of thousands of Jews. Probably the best known example occurred in Ethiopia, when 60,000 Falashas, black Jews who are reputed to be descended from one of the lost tribes of Israel, were airlifted first to Sudan and then to Tel Aviv.

But one of Mossad's most remarkable rescue operations involved not the seizure of people but of warships. In 1969 the French government had agreed to supply Tel Aviv with eight gunboats that, though they were to be supplied unarmed, were urgently needed by the Israeli navy. But when, in December, Israeli soldiers attacked Beirut airport and destroyed 13 airliners stationed there, Paris showed its disapproval by refusing to hand over the gunboats.

Mossad, however, came to the rescue. Within a week, skeleton crews were able to surreptitiously board three of the boats and ready them for use. The Israelis warmed up the engines, flew the Star of David, and headed out to sea before the astonished French officials had a chance to do anything.

Israel was still determined to get hold of the remaining five gunboats but chose a more subtle method. For when the director of the Norwegian shipping company Starboat arrived in Cherbourg to buy the five boats, the French civil servants saw nothing to suspect and quickly approved the sale. Had they made more careful checks, they would have realized that Starboat was a sham organization that had really been set up by Israel's biggest shipping company.

To make their plan all the more convincing, Mossad now arranged for 60 young Israelis, all Gallic or Norwegian in appearance, to be secretly flown to Cherbourg, where they posed as French or Norwegian employees of Starboat. When French vigilance was at its lowest, on Christmas Day 1969, the Israelis moved on board, started the motors, and raced the gunboats off the sea, the start of the long journey to Israel.

As President Georges Pompidou of France admitted, the rescue operation made the French authorities look "complete fools."

See also: Dikko, Umaru; Sadat, Anwar

References: Copeland, Miles. The Game of Nations: The Amorality of Power Politics. New York: London: Weidenfeld and Nicholson, 1976.
Payne, Ronald. Mossad. London: Bantam, 1990.
Posner, Steve. Israel Undercover. Syracuse, NY: Syracuse University Press, 1987.

MOUNDSVILLE PENITENTIARY, WEST VIRGINIA (1986)

Like those at Attica, New York, and Santa Fe, New Mexico, the penitentiary at Moundsville, West Virginia, has been the setting for explosive outbursts of violence that have ruined lives and reputations, as well as buildings.

When a prison riot broke out at Moundsville Penitentiary on New Year's Day 1986, three prison officers who were captured and held hostage in the dining rooms made a lucky escape. As the prisoners occupied themselves with the immediate task of knocking down a wall in order to gain access to another wing, which was strategically placed and home to the prison's most dangerous men, the three guards managed to slip away into the exercise yard outside, locking the door behind them. But having gotten this far, they were still not free from the clutches of the prisoners, since their path was now blocked by a 12-foot fence and a 15-foot metal wall topped by barbed wire.

Before they left the building they had managed to radio the prison's Control Center, requesting them to open the single door that would let them out of the yard. But to their astonishment, no one knew where the key was kept. Instead, standing at the foot of a watchtower and hearing the prisoners hammering at the door behind them, they could only shout at the solitary guard above to throw down some blankets that would enable them to crawl over the barbed wire or at least throw them some weapons or give them covering fire. But, again to their astonishment, the guard appeared petrified and refused to come out of his tower. Left to their own devices, the three desperate men braced themselves and clambered over the wire, ripping themselves badly on the barbed wire but escaping just as the prisoners succeeded in knocking down the door and chased after them.

Moundsville has also been the setting for some dramatic escapes. Probably the most violent, and infamous, took place in November 1979. Implementing a well-considered plan, a group of prisoners tricked a guard into opening their cell door. They then produced a handgun and forced him to open the security grills that let them outside to the streets. They threw a guard into the path of an oncoming car, forcing it to stop, and made its occupants hand it over. By chance, the driver was a soldier who shot and killed one of the escapees as they drove off, but who was himself killed by one of the others. This nasty incident prompted Governor Jay Rockefeller to warn of the grave danger to the safety of local people that was posed by conditions in the jail.

See also: Attica Prison; Santa Fe, New Mexico
References: Adams, R. Prison Riots in Britain and USA. New York: St. Martin's Press; London: Macmillan, 1992.
Atkins, Burton M. Prisons, Protests, and Politics. Englewood Cliffs, NJ: Prentice Hall, 1972.

MUNICH (1972)

The kidnapping of Israeli athletes at the West German Olympic Games at Munich in 1972 by the splinter Palestinian group "Black September" ended in a bold rescue operation by German police.

The terrorists, all armed with assault rifles, broke into the Olympic Village at Munich and burst into the apartments where the Israeli team was housed. Demanding the release of 234 prisoners held by the Israeli government and of several terrorists held by the West Germans, they threatened to execute the athletes unless their conditions were met.

At first it seemed as if they were going to get their way. After a day of negotiations, the kidnappers and their hostages were flown by helicopter to Fürstenfeldbruck. From there, they were told, they would be transported by plane to Cairo. It was only then, just as the hijackers started to relax

their guard, that a rescue attempt began, with unfortunate consequences for all.

As the terrorists left the helicopters, snipers who had taken up positions on the terminal roof opened fire and killed two of them. But almost immediately things began to go wrong. The other snipers who had their quarry in their sights lost their nerve and failed to open fire. They claimed afterward that the distance was too great and the light too poor to have justified firing.

This hesitation gave the six remaining terrorists a chance to barricade themselves in the helicopters, where they waited for the next German move. When it came, the Palestinians were well prepared to take them on, and in the face of an assault by armored car, they killed five of their hostages before blowing up both helicopters, together with nine Israeli hostages.

This bungled rescue attempt had important consequences not just for the West Germans but also for the rest of the world. In an age when terrorism had evidently become more international and more sophisticated, police and army units were plainly no longer enough to take them on. Instead, there was a clear case for the formation of specialist units with the expertise and experience to undertake tasks such as that attempted at Fürstenfeldbruck. Within weeks, the Grenzschutzgruppe (GSG-9) was set up in West Germany, while the French and British adapted their own police and army units to deal with the threat.

See also: Dutch train rescue; Entebbe; Iranian embassy siege; Mogadishu plane rescue
References: Adams, James. Secret Armies. London: Hutchinson, 1987.

MUSSOLINI, BENITO (1883–1945)

The rescue of the toppled Italian dictator Benito Mussolini during World War II by German commandos became a legend almost as soon as it took place.

Mussolini was deposed in July 1943 as dictator of Italy in a coup organized by King Victor Emmanuel III and Marshall Badoglio. He was imprisoned in a remote mountain area of the Apennines. His

Special SS commando leader Otto Skorzeny (left) and Benito Mussolini (right) after Mussolini's liberation by German forces during World War II (Archive Photos)

release was of considerable importance to his German allies, since without him there was no obvious figurehead to lead a puppet government in Italy and to fight the Allied armies, which were slowly advancing northward.

Specially selected to undertake the task of rescuing the Duce was Otto Skorzeny, a German parachutist whose abilities had won him fast promotion and the opportunity to form his own battalion to undertake such daring and dramatic missions. Taken to Hitler's headquarters, "the Wolf's Lair," in Poland, he was personally briefed by Hitler about the mission and its importance to the Axis war effort. Though he knew the dangers of the task involved, Skorzeny agreed to undertake the mission.

Over the next few weeks, German intelligence worked hard to find clues to the whereabouts of Italy's deposed dictator and eventually pinpointed his likely place of imprisonment: a remote mountain hotel in the Campo Imperatore area of the Apennines, where he was guarded by a carabiniere unit of about 150 men. Perched thousands of feet up, at the top of a mountain, it was a daunting place for any commando unit to reach.

Based on aerial reconnaissance photos and statements by a few isolated travelers who had become acquainted with the hotel during their prewar travels, the Germans were able to build up an accurate picture of the task before them. It would be far too difficult, they decided, to attempt an assault by climbing to the top, for they would easily be seen by the sentries and would have virtually no chance of overrunning their defenses. An assault by parachute was also out of the question, since such a high altitude would involve a descent far too rapid for safety. The only way was to use gliders.

Skorzeny's plan was to drop seven glid-ers on a meadow, a short distance from the former hotel where the Duce was being held, before whisking him away in a light plane. The soldiers would be able to descend the mountain to another airstrip for evacuation. Having specially selected a team of volunteers, Skorzeny had the glid-ers towed from their runway on 12 September 1943 and headed for the moun-tain top high in the Italian Apennines.

But the glider pilots who took their crafts toward the intended landing spot that night were in for a shock. The meadow was big enough to accommodate all seven of them, but the planners had overlooked one crucial fact: The air reconnaissance photos did not reveal how steeply they sloped, but the gra-dient made landing too risky. Frantically looking around for another suitable site, Skorzeny and his pilot could find only one other possibility: a small open space that was immediately adjacent to the hotel and where they were now forced to crash-land.

The landing was one of the most remark-able flying achievements in military history, for the first glider, carrying Skorzeny and his advance guard, landed a bare 15 yards from the lodge and only a few feet from some jagged rocks that could have easily torn them apart. The glider taxied a mere 20 yards before coming to an abrupt halt.

Though they had landed at a high speed—100 miles per hour was not unusual for incoming gliders—Skorzeny and his men instantly jumped from their glider and looked around. They were faced only by one Italian sentry, who, according to the German commander, merely stared at them, jaw dropped, lost in amazement.

The Germans had been trained not to fire until their leader had fired the first shot, and Skorzeny was careful not to alarm the entire garrison until he was forced to. With several colleagues at his side, Skorzeny charged up the hotel steps and stormed inside, and there, flanked by two sentries, was Mussolini. Outnumbered, the Italian guards lay down their arms and surren-dered their prisoner, only three minutes after the Germans had landed. Still no shots had been fired.

As planned, a signal was given to the Storch aircraft hovering above to come in to land and escort Skorzeny and Mussolini to safety. Though some fighting had by this time broken out and some men were lost when their glider crashed into rocks, every-thing had gone far more smoothly and quickly than the commander had ever dreamed. The German force made its way down the mountain to a prearranged evacu-ation spot. The operation had been astound-ingly successful.

Awarded the Knight's Cross, Skorzeny won the instant admiration of his *Führer* and even of the Allied leaders, who learned of his extraordinary exploit with near incredulity.

References: Skorzeny, Otto. *Skorzeny's Special Missions.* London: Greenhill, 1977.

MY LAI (1968)

During the Vietnam War, three U.S. soldiers rescued a group of Vietnamese civilians not from the Vietcong (VC) but from their fel-low Americans.

On 16 March 1968 an American patrol, led by Lt. William Calley, had swooped down on My Lai, a hamlet in South Vietnam that they wrongly suspected of harboring VC guerrillas. For several days their nerves had been worn down by the tactics of the Communist snipers, who picked them off one by one before disappearing into the jun-gle, and by the time they reached the village the strain of war had taken a heavy toll. Many of the GIs started firing randomly, and within minutes the village had become a frenzied scene as automatic fire raked murderously through it.

Hovering in the skies above, a U.S. heli-copter pilot, Hugh Thompson, watched the carnage unfold in horror and disbelief. "Every time we made a pass," he said years later, "there were more bodies. I saw one incident where an American just walked up to a woman and blew her away." But when he saw a group of ten women cowering in a bunker beneath him, Thompson and two colleagues, Lawrence Colburn and Glenn Andreotta, decided to take action.

Diving straight for the ground, Thompson landed the helicopter between the stricken women and a squad of GIs who were heading toward them. With his pistol drawn, Thompson asked the officer in charge for permission to take the villagers away but received a blunt reply: "with a hand grenade," growled the officer.

Thompson was undeterred. Brandishing his pistol, he ordered them to "hold your people right there. I think we can do better than that." Thompson and his two colleagues provided cover in case the GIs started firing, and Thompson called in another helicopter to evacuate the small group of terrified villagers.

Thompson's medal citation for heroism "above and beyond the call of duty" was followed, remarkably, by a blunt admission that he had landed his helicopter "in the line of fire between fleeing Vietnamese civilians and pursuing American troops to prevent their murder." The rescued had been the lucky inhabitants of a village where 450 civilians lost their lives to U.S. troops in a few hours of savage violence.

See also: Vietnam War

MYAGKOV, CAPT. ALEKSEI (1938?–1974)

During the Cold War the leaders of both NATO and the Warsaw Pact made a great deal of effort to obtain detailed and accurate intelligence about each other's military capabilities. The risks were considerable, especially for those who spied against their own side and who faced either long and arduous imprisonment or execution if caught.

One such individual was a KGB officer, Capt. Aleksei Myagkov. Based at Bernau, near Berlin, and attached to several battalions of the Soviet Eighty-Second Motorized Rifle Guards Regiment, his job involved the surveillance of his fellow officers in the regiment to ensure that they maintained proper levels of confidentiality and behavior. But motivated by what he claimed were pangs of conscience about the regime he was supporting, he became a Western agent in 1972 and supplied his spymasters with details about the movements, efficacy, and armaments of the units he was acquainted with.

His luck held for two years before his KGB colleagues began to close in. Having arranged a meeting in East Berlin with a Western agent, he noticed as he approached the rendezvous that agents of the Stasi— East German intelligence—were watching. They clearly knew the identity of his British contact and were waiting patiently for the traitor—not knowing it was he—to turn up. Myagkov saw them, just at the last moment, and quickly walked right by his British contact, pretending he had seen none of those waiting for him.

But the Stasi had seen him and became suspicious, though not suspicious enough to arrest him there and then, and spent the next five hours tailing him. Myagkov did not realize that KGB agents were tailing him again a few days later when he decided to make a dash for freedom by trying to cross the border into West Berlin. Loaded with top secret documents and wearing a rain-

Aleksei Myagkov, the KGB captain who dramatically escaped the communist East in 1974. (UPI/Corbis-Bettmann)

coat under his military greatcoat to use as a disguise, he joined the bus that ran from the military barracks into West Berlin. But he only noticed the Soviet agents behind him as the bus went into the British sector.

Myagkov knew that the KGB men were either waiting for any sign that he would step out of line before arresting him and returning him to the East or else that they would assassinate him on the spot. His only hope, he felt sure, was to make a run for it, and as the group of soldiers paused in front of the Charlottenburg Palace to take photographs, Myagkov seized his chance. He bolted inside the building, ran through the corridors inside, locked himself inside a small room at the back, and gasped at the nearest person to phone for the police. When, after a long wait, he was taken away by a British diplomatic team, his escort car was shadowed by KGB prowl cars that had been waiting for him outside.

Though he was now on Western soil, Myagkov was not free yet, for the British authorities—who were by now well aware of the defector's importance—still had to move him to an airfield and from there through East German airspace to the West. As Myagkov later wrote, "There was a very real risk of an attack by Soviet agents who might try and kidnap me" (Geraghty 1996, 182). Flying back to the West meant that there was also a real chance of being shot down by a Soviet missile fired "by accident." So Myagkov, in civilian clothes, was taken in an unmarked car, sitting between two British escorts, to the airfield at Gatow and was flown out in a Dakota.

As the plane finally crossed East Germany and reached Western airspace, Myagkov noted the sense of relief that he and his escorts felt. "At last the atmosphere in the aircraft brightened noticeably. Everyone began to smile. The captain congratulated me on my safe arrival in the West" (Geraghty 1996, 182). To the fury and embarrassment of Moscow, another KGB officer, with a swathe of secret papers, had managed to escape from its clutches.

See also: Berlin Wall; Cambridge Spy Ring; Gordievsky, Oleg; Iron Curtain; Kalbowski, Harry

References: Geraghty, Tony. *Beyond the Frontline.* London: HarperCollins, 1996.

N

NADIR, ASIL (1941–)

In May 1993 a leading businessman, Asil Nadir, broke bail and fled Britain for Cyprus, where he was out of the jurisdiction of the British legal authorities.

As head of the giant Polly Peck business empire, Nadir had been arrested on charges of fraud and was scheduled to stand trial in September. But he had little intention of doing so and soon found a way of leaving the country altogether.

Despite having to leave his wife and children behind, Nadir disguised himself in a hat and dark glasses, boarded a light aircraft at a remote country airfield, and was spirited off to Beauvais in northern France. Once there he boarded a jet and was flown to Cyprus, celebrating his newly won freedom with champagne and caviar en route.

References: The Daily Telegraph, 4 August 1998.

NAPOLEON BONAPARTE (1769–1821)

Defeated by his enemies at Leipzig in 1813 and exiled to the island of Elba, off the Italian coast, Napoleon Bonaparte made a desperate bid to escape his loneliness and regain his lost power as the ruler of much of Europe.

When he escaped in February 1815, he probably had a wide variety of other motives as well. He had not seen any sign of the two million francs he was entitled to as an annual stipend, and he may have heard rumors that Talleyrand and Castlereagh, the leaders of the alliance against him, were planning to remove him to a far more distant place on much harsher terms. Above all, Napoleon was an adventurer by inclination and experience, and captivity on Elba,

after years of war, was a torture that he could not endure.

In order to escape, Napoleon had to evade the extensive spy network around him, and to this end he acquired a vessel, the *Inconstant.* While his men secretly loaded the ship with all the provisions, arms, and ammunition he needed, mainly after dark and hiding their wares in barrels and under covers, it was painted in English colors to confuse any spies who saw it. And as he set off for the Continent, at the end of February 1815, he was careful to choose a landing place that his enemies would least suspect, stopping eventually at the bay of Jena where, with 1,200 men at his side, he planned to start his plans for reconquest.

Napoleon's efforts at concealment appear to have worked. Only at the last moment did Talleyrand's agents have any indication that the irrepressible Napoleon was once again on the warpath.

See also: Bitche Fortress; Lefebre, Gen. Louis;
    Napoleonic Wars
References: Campbell, Sir Neil. *Napoleon at*
    Fontainebleau and Elba, Being a Journal of
    Occurrences in 1814–15. London: J. Murray, 1869.

NAPOLEONIC WARS (1797)

Some French soldiers were captured soon after landing on the Welsh coast, near Fishguard, where they had been sent by Napoleon in 1797 to make a reconnaissance of British defenses. They used the love they inspired among local women to escape.

Like so many others who have managed to escape from enemy captivity, the soldiers were lucky to enjoy the loyal support of outsiders. The soldiers were permitted to pass the time by making toys and handicrafts, and thus they met two local girls, who brought them the bits and pieces they needed to make the toys. The girls had quickly become smitten by two of the soldiers and were only too keen to help them escape. The plan they devised was simple and made enterprising use of limited materials, for from a shin of beef the Frenchmen made digging tools with which they were eventually able to excavate a tunnel, while the two girls carried the soil away in their buckets.

Because the escapees would have to get hold of a boat that was big enough to accommodate all of them—there were 25 French soldiers waiting to escape—the two girls watched the harbor carefully, waiting for a suitably sized vessel to arrive. When at last they were able to make their move, the escapees seized the boat, a sloop carrying a load of anthracite to Stackpole, and tied up the crew. For a dreadful moment they thought that good fortune had left them, for they found they were unable to dislodge it from where it lay marooned high and dry on the beach. But they saw a yacht nearby that they were able to sail to a boat anchored a short distance away, which took them back to France.

The story of the failed invasion of Britain ends on a romantic note. Once safely back in France, the Welsh girls married the two French soldiers they had helped rescue and, as far as we know, lived happily ever after.

See also: Bitche Fortress; Lefebre, Gen. Louis; Napoleon Bonaparte

References: Reid, Pat. *Prisoner of War.* London and New York: Hamlyn, 1984.

NAZAROFF, PAUL (C. 1880–1942)

During the Russian civil war of 1918–1929, Paul Nazaroff accomplished some remarkable escapes from the Bolshevik enemies hunting him.

While working as a counterrevolutionary leader, Nazaroff had been the ringleader of a White Russian plot to overthrow the Tashkent Soviet and link up with the British forces farther to the West. But when, during the spring of 1919, the Bolsheviks' secret police, the Cheka, began a systematic hunt

to find him, Nazaroff knew that he faced certain torture and execution if caught.

Nazaroff was sheltering at the home in Tashkent of a sympathizer named Akbar when word reached him that Cheka officers and soldiers were combing every house in the area in search of him. With their patrols on every road and bridge, his chances of escaping seemed remote.

But just as Nazaroff began to despair, his host had an idea: Nazaroff could hide in a small cell in the house. Akbar would fill in its door with bricks, plaster it with mud, rub it over with dust, and finally smoke it with a lamp. With no time to waste, Nazaroff took enough food and water to sustain him for two days before he was bricked in.

Hours later the Cheka arrived to search the house, and Nazaroff could hear the soldiers moving through every room, questioning Akbar, his wife, and children about him. But to their relief, they totally overlooked the newly constructed wall. When Akbar was sure the last of the soldiers had left the village and would not be returning, he finally freed his "guest," who crawled out of his tiny cell into the daylight.

But Nazaroff still had to find his way out of Tashkent, out of the clutch of the Cheka, and if possible back to the White armies. He then began, in his own phrase, "the life of a hunted animal" (Hopkirk 1984, 74). Ever on the move, with the Cheka always close behind him, he traveled through the vast forests in the area, occasionally finding shelter with some of the families who lived in its isolated communities.

As he wandered across Turkestan Nazaroff had another lucky escape from his enemies. He had managed to obtain false papers that described him as one Nikolai Novikoff, an itinerant bee merchant. When a Red Army patrol saw him pass through a village and challenged him, Nazaroff shouted, "Comrades, do not come too close. If the bees escape, they will certainly sting you." The soldiers backed off and left him to carry on with his journey.

Like his contemporary Frederick Bailey, Nazaroff was able to escape the clutches of the dreaded Cheka. But by the time he escaped he was met by the news that the

White armies had been smashed by the Bolshevik forces, which by that time ruled supreme. Nazaroff eventually fled to South Africa to escape the threat of assassination by Stalin's secret police. He died there in 1942.

See also: Bailey, Lt. Col. Frederick; Russian
    Revolution and civil war
References: Hopkirk, Peter. *Setting the East Ablaze.*
    Oxford: Oxford University Press, 1984.

NEW YORK (1776)

The British invasion of New York during the American Revolution forced Gen. Israel Putnam to order his forces to beat a hasty retreat in order to avoid capture.

Putnam rushed his 3,000-strong force up the west side of the island, keeping as far as possible from the British beachhead during their 12-mile march. Dashing around on horseback, rounding up stragglers, and shouting encouragement to all, he was an inspiration to his weary troops, but despite his urgency it is doubtful if they could have eluded the British without the intervention of a Mrs. Murray, who lived on Inclenberg Hill.

At her invitation, Admiral Lord Howe, commanding the British forces in the area, and his fellow officers had taken refreshment at her home. Despite her husband's sympathy for the British, it appears that she was an ardent Patriot and knew that, by throwing a small party in celebration of their victory, she could slow their advance down to give Putnam and his men more time to escape.

Though the precise reason for his failure will never be known, Howe sent no troops from the beachhead to the west side of the island, and Putnam and his men were able to get away from the British unseen and unopposed.

See also: Brooklyn Heights

NIJMEGEN (1944)

In a desperate effort to rescue the British soldiers stranded at Arnhem, some U.S. soldiers made a remarkable crossing over the Nijmegen River. They defied their German enemy in a unique amphibious operation by airborne troops, an operation widely recognized as one of the most audacious feats of arms ever undertaken.

The crossing of the Nijmegen river was an unintended consequence of Operation Market Garden, which had started off as one of the most ambitious projects of the war. In a bid to force an early German surrender, General Bernard Montgomery had drawn up a plan of attack that would bring British and U.S. units over the Rhine and into the Ruhr valley, the industrial heartland of the German war effort. If the Ruhr could be captured, the Germans would be forced to surrender. For Montgomery, this plan had the added advantage of making him, rather than his great rival, Gen. George Patton, the architect of Allied victory on the Western Front.

The plan depended upon the capture of three key bridges, at Eindhoven, Nijmegen, and Arnhem, and three parachute units were dropped from transport planes and gliders—the U.S. 101st and 82nd Airborne Divisions, under Maxwell D. Taylor and James M. Gavin, and the British First Airborne at Arnhem, under Robert Urqhuart. Their task was to hold onto the bridges until the armored divisions had advanced from the Belgian border to relieve them.

Though the operation started off well, with the bridge at Eindhoven falling to the 101st after heavy fighting, it was not long before it turned into a rescue operation. By 19 September the Allied commanders further south knew that the First Airborne, lightly armed and deep within enemy territory, was in desperate straits. They had landed some miles from the bridge, and the main force had become divided and surrounded by superior German forces without ever having gotten close to their target. The British had also landed at the worst possible time because two elite German Panzer divisions happened to be in the Arnhem area, regrouping after serving in Russia, just when Market Garden began.

As fears for the trapped British force grew, the joint U.S.-British rescue operation further south got into full force. One of the first main obstacles was Nijmegen Bridge, for by the time the 82nd reached the town nearby the Germans had had time to rush reinforcements to hold the bridge. The Germans knew the British troops at Arnhem were almost certainly doomed if they could hold the bridge, and they made it virtually impregnable to assault. After both Americans and British suffered serious casualties in their attempt to take it, Gavin hit on an alternative: crossing the river by boat a mile downstream and taking the bridge from both ends.

Gavin's idea astonished the British commanders present. The river was too wide to allow whole boatloads of men to escape detection, and the opposite bank was so exposed that the Americans would have to cross more than 200 yards of flat ground. Beyond that was an embankment that gave the defenders excellent cover. Moreover, these soldiers were parachutists, hardly trained to undertake such an operation. But Gavin insisted, arguing that his assault would incur fewer casualties than any attempt to take the bridge head on, and General Frederick Browning, much impressed by the sheer audacity of the plan, gave it the go ahead.

Before long, 28 small boats made of canvass and plywood had been rushed to the front, while British tanks took up position to give covering fire to the Americans as they crossed the river. Against the deafening roar of British shellfire landing on the far shore, the first assault wave of 260 men assembled the boats, pulled them along the banks onto the river, and headed for the far side.

The crossing would have been daunting even for those experienced in using such boats. Some boats began to go round in circles, a few sank, some men fell overboard, others lost their paddles and were forced to use their rifles instead. Moreover, the brisk wind quickly blew away the smoke screen laid down by British shells, making them easy targets for German soldiers waiting on the shore for them to come into range.

As the German guns opened up, their fire became so intense that one of those present, 1st Lieutenant Patrick Mulloy, was sure that it was "the worst we had ever taken, even at Anzio," and the British, watching from the shore, spoke of the "horrible, horrible sight" before them. Another soldier, Second Lt. Virgil Carmichael, muttered "Hail Mary" with every stroke, followed by "grace of God" at the next. But no amount of prayer or covering fire from the British tanks seemed to stop the withering fire the Americans faced.

But nor did the German fire prevent half of the U.S. force from eventually reaching the far bank and their troops from storming through continued heavy fire to overrun the enemy positions, many of the them manned by teenagers and elderly men. With grenades, submachine guns, and extreme bravery, the men of the 82nd moved away from the bank and headed toward the bridges to the east.

At five o'clock, only a few hours after they had set off, a British officer on the southern bank watching the whole affair through binoculars, saw a GI standing on the railway bridge signaling to him. Within minutes, the Allied commanders of the units involved were informed of the astonishing news that the railway bridge had fallen and that the 82nd was heading toward the highway bridge, a few miles further east. Attacking the German flank and diverting their men and resources, the 82nd allowed the British armor and American troops, attacking from the south, to break through the German defenses and capture the bridge intact.

The way to Arnhem, 11 miles away, was now open, and the fall of Nijmegen made possible the rescue of the remnants of the trapped British forces, who were evacuated across the Rhine shortly after the Allied forces reached its southern banks on 25 September.

But the rescue operation had been undertaken at a heavy cost. Half of the two units deployed, 134 men, were killed in the action.

References: Ryan, Cornelius. *A Bridge Too Far.* London: Coronet, 1974.

NORWAY (1940)

The German forces that suddenly swept into Norway during the night of 9 April

1940 knew that defeating enemy forces on the battlefield was not their only objective. They would also have to capture and imprison or execute King Haakon, Crown Prince Olaf, and their ministers, who might otherwise become symbols of defiance and make ruling the occupied territory much more difficult.

But despite the extraordinary swiftness with which the German blitzkrieg raged, the king and his cabinet narrowly managed to keep one step ahead of them. With the enemy only a short distance away, they journeyed north to the capital, toward the town of Hamar. They owed their escape in large measure to the bravery of their small but determined navy, which laid down mines in the Oslo Fjord, obstructing the German warships trying to break through.

Over the next three weeks, the Norwegian government and royal family moved at breathtaking pace through their spectacular surroundings, constantly changing their plans to maintain their distance from the Nazis, only 20 miles or so behind them. Knowing their own country better than the Germans, and assisted by all the native people they encountered, they were at last able to safely reach the mountains.

The fugitives had agreed to meet an emissary of the puppet government set up by the Nazis, so the Nazis knew their whereabouts. Before long, German bombers appeared to flatten the buildings they suspected of harboring the Norwegian government and royal family, and it was only because they had a few minutes' warning that they were able to take cover at the edge of a nearby pine forest just as the planes roared over and blasted the buildings.

Still they journeyed on, finally reaching the coastal town of Molde. By now the Germans knew the fugitives had traveled far enough to be in a position to be rescued and form a focus for the hopes and aspirations of the Norwegian people. If they could not capture them, the Nazi leaders decided, then they would have to kill them. Within hours the Luftwaffe was on its way, seeking to raze the entire town and kill the king, his cabinet, and his supporters in the process.

But on 29 April, with the fires around him raging, the king dashed through the town's streets, heading for a rendezvous where he would be picked up and taken to HMS *Glasgow*, waiting offshore. Accompanied by British soldiers, who carried the large quantities of gold bullion that had accompanied him throughout his journey, he reached the ship and was taken to the safety of the Tromsö in the far north.

References: Fellowes-Gordon, Ian, ed. *The World's Greatest Escapes.* London: Odhams, 1966.

O'GRADY, SCOTT (1966–)

U.S. Air Force (USAF) pilots are intensively trained in the arts of escape, evasion, and survival, and the value of their training became clear in 1995, when Scott O'Grady managed to elude enemy capture for six days before being rescued.

Based at Aviano in Italy, O'Grady's unit, 555 Squadron, had begun to fly patrols over Serb-held Bosnia some weeks before. These missions, undertaken to back UN resolutions, were intended to warn the Serbs that their actions in the area were being carefully observed and that any violations of UN-brokered agreements about the sovereignty of the area would not go unpunished. But the Bosnian Serbs were determined to test Western resolve and harassed both the peacekeepers on the ground and NATO aircraft in the skies above.

Piloting a USAF F16, O'Grady was flying just such a routine mission on 2 June 1995 when his plane came under attack from a Bosnian Serb surface-to-air missile (SAM). Ordinarily such attacks did not cause insuperable difficulties for U.S. pilots, whose normal evasive procedure was to jam the missile's electronics before firing chaff decoy to draw the missile away. But for some technical reason this procedure failed, and the F16 was hit in the skies above Banja Luka, about 90 miles north of Sarajevo.

None of the other NATO pilots in the area saw O'Grady parachute to earth, and they soon feared for his safety. Even if he had managed to eject from the aircraft, he would inevitably have landed in the middle of Bosnian Serb territory and probably faced almost immediate capture. As U.S. satellites and reconnaissance scoured the entire region to find clues to his fate, the American people held their breath.

Before long, however, U.S. intelligence began to detect faint but spasmodic signals from the ground, and they sent aircraft overhead to investigate. Because they knew that these signals might merely be an enemy trap, they accorded more significance to the fact that the Bosnian Serbs had found O'Grady's parachute and other personal belongings in the area and had started a massive manhunt for him.

At 1:45 A.M. during the morning of 8 June, six days after O'Grady was shot down, a USAF F15 picked up a definite ground signal and realized they had found their man. A rescue operation started almost immediately, as soldiers from the Tactical Recovery of Aircraft and Personnel (TRAP) unit of the U.S. Marines scrambled on board the USS *Kearsarge* in the Adriatic and prepared to fly in and pick him up.

Little more than three hours later, a huge armada of NATO planes and helicopters escorted two CH33 helicopters that took 40 soldiers from this TRAP division to a pinpointed location 20 miles southeast of Bihać, a few miles from where O'Grady's plane had crashed. As they touched down, O'Grady fired a yellow flare to show he had seen them before he sprinted out of his forest shelter and was flown to safety, less than two minutes after the helicopters had touched down.

The rescue operation was a powerful testimony to the training of both U.S. pilots and specialist rescue teams. O'Grady, who had completed a 17-day survival course mandatory for all USAF pilots, had evaded an extensive enemy search by moving only at night, living off "bugs and rainwater," and sending only short, sporadic signals to NATO aircraft in order to conserve his beacon's battery. The rescue operation had also been accomplished to the highest standards by a well-trained specialist team, and the story of these "American heroes" sent waves of joy and relief through the people of the United States.

References: Vistica, Gregory. "An American Hero." *Newsweek,* 19 June 1995, 24–33.

P

PAINE, THOMAS (1739–1809)

Though his story has never been verified, the freethinker Thomas Paine claimed to have made a remarkable escape from execution, having been sent to prison while serving as a member of the Committee of the Constitution in Paris in the 1790s.

Paine was arrested together with another member of the committee. He was taken to a makeshift prison and put on death row, alongside three other prisoners who were also awaiting the guillotine. Every day prison guards would arrive, open one of the rooms, and take its occupants to immediate execution, referring to annotations chalked on the outside of the doors to identify those who were next in the queue.

It so happened that the door, when opened, not only swung *away* from the room, toward the corridor outside—which was most unusual in those days—but also could be pushed back flat against the wall. This meant that someone unfamiliar with the corridor could easily fail to notice that the door was open, not shut, and mistake the inside of the door for the outside.

When Paine had been in prison a short while, the official came along and marked his door with a chalk cross to signify that its prisoners were to be executed. However, he did not realize that he was in fact only marking the door's *inside*. Paine pulled the door back and erased the mark, hoping the official would assume they had been dealt with. He reckoned right, and very soon after this lucky escape Robespierre was deposed and an order for Paine's release was signed.

See also: Execution, escape from; The Terror
References: Aldridge, Alfred Owen. *Thomas Paine: Man of Reason.* London: Cresset Press, 1959.

PALESTINE (1937–1948)

In the summer of 1946, during the war for the independence of Palestine waged by Zionist groups against the British, the infamous Stern Gang kidnapped a senior British officer, a member of the intelligence corps. They knew that he would not only be a fruitful source of information but that he could also be traded for their own men held by the British. After forcing him into a car at gunpoint in the center of Jerusalem, they whisked him away to a safe house as the local Irgun commander triumphantly proclaimed the coup to his colleagues, listening on the radio.

But the officer managed to outwit his captors. After persuading his single guard to untie his hands, he found a hole in the ceiling of the room where he was held. As soon as the guard's back was turned, wrote Menachem Begin years later, the officer disappeared into the hole in one stupendous jump and reached the street outside. Though the guard gave chase, he could not stop the escapee, who sprinted ahead and jumped onto a bus.

News of the escape was heard with incredulity by Stern Gang leaders, who had always prided themselves on their efficiency and who now thought that the escape had been made possible only by outside support.

See also: Acre Castle; King David Hotel
References: Begin, Menachem. *The Revolt.* London: W. H. Allen, 1979.

PAPILLON (HENRI CHARRIERE) (1906–1973)

Like a handful of other places of detention, such as Colditz castle and Alcatraz, Devil's Island once had a well-deserved reputation

179

Henri Charriere, or Papillon, demonstrates his method of escape from Devil's Island. (Archive Photos)

for being impossible to escape. One of the few who got away was "Papillon"—a nickname for a Parisian criminal whose real name was Henri Charriere.

Papillon had fallen afoul of the French police as a gangster in the criminal underworld of the late 1920s. Though he always protested his innocence, he was arrested in 1931 on the charge of murdering a pimp and was sentenced to life imprisonment in the toughest detention area the French had at their disposal: their penal colonies in French Guiana.

From the outset Papillon was determined to escape, and his motives appear to have been more than just revulsion for the harsh life that awaited him. He also felt a strong sense of indignation at a system that had sentenced him, at the age of 25, to a life sentence with no hope of remission when there was no real evidence for a conviction.

He was convicted and sent to Guiana soon afterwards, but it did not take him long to make his first bid for freedom. After little more than a month, he knocked out the guards who were watching him while he

was in the hospital, and he traveled more than 1,000 miles in a stolen boat before being recaptured. Other attempts followed as the years passed: He tried, in vain, to blow a hole in the wall of his cell with dynamite, to start a rebellion among prisoners packed into a chapel, and to build a boat to sail away from one of the islands. In response to his escape attempts he was eventually sent to the island with the fearsome reputation of being the toughest and most brutal of all, Devil's Island. It was from Devil's Island that he finally managed to escape.

To reach the coast of Venezuela from Devil's Island was by any reckoning a daunting task. Quite apart from the sheer distance between them, more than 25 miles, it meant crossing deep and rough seas. But Papillon noticed that it would at least be possible to make a good start to such a crossing, for though the powerful incoming tides made launching very difficult, there was one—just one—isolated spot on the eastern coast where the tide, after hitting the rocks as it came in, was pushed back again, creating a powerful current that could help him move his craft out to sea. All he needed to do was to find some materials that would enable him to keep afloat, and he soon found a supply of coconuts that were well-suited to the task. As soon as he had hit on the idea, Papillon went in search of jute sacks that he could stuff with the coconuts to make a simple raft.

Papillon also discovered that this stretch of coast was the least heavily guarded, for though the island was a maximum security penal colony, there was one chink in its armor: complacency. Since the eastern coast of the island faced the Caribbean Sea, rather than the mainland, the guards assumed it was safe from any escape attempts and that there was no need to watch over it.

The prisoners knew not only that there were sharks in those waters but also that the powerful waves could break their flimsy rafts apart and leave them to drown. Papillon sent one such raft into the sea to test its resilience and was horrified to see it smashed to pieces almost immediately by one of the 15-foot waves he had often seen along the coast. But he also knew that, in the right weather, the powerful current would drive him to the mainland, although he reckoned that it would take two days to reach it.

Having hidden their craft in some caves on the coast, Papillon and his companion, Sylain, waited patiently on the shoreline until an incoming wave hit the rocks and rebounded away from the island giving them their chance. As planned, the current took them first away from Devil's Island and then toward the Venezuelan mainland.

Though they could neither eat nor drink throughout their journey (apart, that is, from the large doses of sea water they could not help but swallow) and though they were scorched by the ferocious midsummer sun, the two men managed to keep themselves going for more than 40 hours before the mainland appeared on the horizon. But despite the extreme physical and mental hardships they had endured, they were swept exhausted and severely sunburned onto the beach. Papillon later noted that he never regretted his decision to attempt the break.

The two men were eventually granted Venezuelan citizenship, allowing Papillon to settle down quietly in Caracas to write his famous account of his dramatic life.

References: Charriere, Henri. *Papillon.* London: Hart, Davis, 1970.

PARKER, JOHN (1827–1900)

Personal misfortune can engender sympathy as readily as indifference, and many of those who manned the Underground Railroad, which helped runaway slaves find their way to Canada, had once been in the same position as those they aided. One such was John Parker, who had bought his own freedom in 1845 and who subsequently devoted much of his energy to running the escape network. He recorded one particularly dramatic escape from slave catchers during this period in his memoirs.

Two runaways were brought to Parker's house by a group of former slaves, who had seen them in the company of a spy for one of the slave-catcher gangs and rescued them. Since daylight was rapidly approaching by the time they reached his house, making any journey outside far too risky, Parker hid the two men in his attic.

It was not long before he was awakened by a loud knock at his front door. Seeing a large, angry crowd outside, he realized that the spy they had escaped from had seen where they had gone and informed his enemies. Perhaps foolishly, he opened his front door, and within minutes the house was being searched.

Parker tried to delay the search party as much as he could, showing them places they overlooked in their haste, and he raised his voice as he called out to them in the hopes that the fugitives would hear them. But as they opened the attic door and looked in, he felt sure that the two men would be discovered.

To his astonishment, the searchers saw nothing, and after taking a careful look they merely came back down and left the house, swearing they would return and burn the house if they did not find the two slaves. When he took a look himself, Parker found that the ladder leading to the roof above

The flight of runaway slaves in nineteenth-century America was assisted by vigilante groups such as this one, led by John Parker, in Christiana, Pennsylvania. (North Wind Picture Archive)

was missing, and he realized that the slaves had taken it with them while they took cover above.

Their escape was not over yet, however, and Parker knew the gang would almost certainly be back later to conduct a more careful search of the house. He took them to the backyard of an acquaintance who was also involved in the Underground Railroad, but he failed to realize that once again they had been seen and that the same gang was now on its way to search the yard.

Only when he heard the loud knock at the front door did Parker realize what had happened and bolt for the back entrance with the two fugitives at his side. When he saw a guard, his back turned, straight in front of him he knew that there was no escape from the building and that they would have to find a hiding place inside.

Though he knew his new acquaintances were, like most slaves, deeply superstitious about such things, Parker beckoned them to jump into two empty coffins lying in the yard and to pull the tops over themselves.

Though they grimaced at the prospect, they both did so without protest, hiding just as their enemy started their search.

The slave catchers refrained from opening the coffins, fearful of finding corpses and contracting some disease, and assumed that their quarry had again managed to slip from their grasp. Within hours of their departure Parker was able to get the two runaways out of the town and along the Underground Railroad toward Canada. As in some other escapes, the cover of death had provided shelter for the living.

See also: Brown, Henry; Fugitive Slave Laws; Underground Railroad

References: Parker, John P. *His Promised Land, 1827–1900: The Autobiography of John P. Parker.* New York and London: Norton, 1996.

PERUVIAN EMBASSY SIEGE (1997)

The rescue of the staff of the Japanese embassy in Peru in 1997 is one of the most

The hostages held at the Japanese ambassador's residence in Lima were dramatically rescued by Peruvian special forces on 22 April 1997. (AP/Wide World Photos)

impressive examples of military force being employed to rescue hostages held by terrorist gunmen.

The saga began on 22 December 1996 as the ambassador, Morihisa Aoki, entertained 500 guests at his residence in Lima to mark the birthday of Emperor Akihito. Armed members of a left-wing terrorist group, Tupac Amaru, broke in through a hole in the wall and held the ambassador, his guests, and his staff at gunpoint. They quickly selected 72 hostages, all senior generals, politicians, businessmen, and relatives of the ruling elites in the country, and released the rest of the party guests.

As the siege began, Peruvian special forces quickly prepared for Chavin de Huantar, the rescue operation that seemed inevitable against intransigent and well-armed terrorists. Before long, a hand-picked team was sent to a building on the outskirts of Lima, which was virtually indistinguishable from the ambassador's residence and which was an ideal model upon which to practice the planned assault.

The ingenious plan that was drawn up was the product of cooperation between Peruvian soldiers and politicians and specialist advisers from the CIA and U.S. special forces, who offered advice on techniques and equipment. Using high-powered drills, several tunnels were dug underground, surfacing at specific points in the grounds, and sophisticated listening devices were employed to allow the military chiefs to monitor every move made by the terrorists. Above all, coded messages were sent to a particular hostage, who was informed exactly when the rescue attempt would be made and what the hostages were to do when the attack started.

The rescuers found a clever way of covering their rescue attempt: a brass band. As the engineers drilled underground, the military band played nationalistic marches outside the embassy compound, ostensibly to improve morale at such a difficult time but really to drown out the sound that was just audible from above. And when, during the afternoon of 22 April 1997, the band started playing, the terrorists could not have known that it was a prearranged signal to the hostages that the attack was about to commence.

The assault on the residency was put into effect when the military planners in charge were informed that 8 of the 12 terrorists were in one of the building's wings, not guarding the hostages but playing football. It was the right moment to strike, and within minutes of the signal the attack began.

The rescue began with a mighty explosion under the hall where the hostage takers were playing their game. One of the several tunnels had been packed with explosives, which were now exploded to devastating effect. As the explosion killed all of the 8 terrorists outright, Peruvian soldiers swarmed into the compound through the other tunnels and ran to engage the remaining gunmen; within minutes all the hostages had been freed and the gunmen killed.

The rescue was one of the most successful ever mounted, and, like some other escapes and rescues, it greatly augmented the political fortunes of those who stood—or were seen to stand—behind it.

PETERHEAD PRISON (1987)

At Peterhead Prison in Scotland the British Special Air Service (SAS) was once deployed to rescue a prison officer whose life was endangered during a siege by rebellious prisoners.

The riot broke out in September 1987 when 50 long-term prisoners seized control of one of the prison's wings. Though most of them surrendered fairly quickly, a small group continued to hold out and took a prison officer hostage, threatening to kill him if any rescue attempt was made. Though this would not have ordinarily provoked the government to request military action, the officer's deteriorating health—his kidney disorder demanded drugs and medical attention—made this siege an exception.

After the crisis had continued for a week or so, with no sign of the deadlock being broken, the government ministers at the Scottish and Home Ministry sent a two-man team to the prison to advise the police on the best way of bringing the crisis to a swift conclusion. But because the police no longer thought it was within their power to end it, the specialist services of the SAS were called for.

On the evening of 2 October, a small SAS team was secretly flown to the prison, ready to rescue the prison officer. From the roof of the prison they planned to steal toward the prisoners over a gutter and to enter the besieged area through a hole in the roof, a hole that the prisoners had made so they could climb outside and signal to the television cameras. The soldiers would then use riot gas and stun grenades to break the siege and rescue the prison guard. But walking through the gutter, on a high roof, was no easy task—especially since they would be wearing gas masks and moving at 5 A.M. on a dark October morning to avoid alerting anyone.

But they were seen by a prisoner in a nearby wing who managed to shout a warning to the guard's captors, and things very nearly went wrong. One of the prison rebels heard the warning shouts and appeared at the rooftop hole to confront the assault team, though not quite in time to stop the soldier from lobbing a stun grenade and CS cartridge inside and watching the prisoner reel as they exploded by his side. Having thus disarmed their opposition, the soldiers were able to snatch and spirit away the prison officer within six minutes of beginning the operation. Not far away, follow-up teams were able to put a swift end to the siege by blowing up the doors the prisoners had used as a barricade.

The Peterhead rescue was an exemplary operation, achieving its objectives with a minimum use of force, resulting in no casualties, and deterring any more prisoners from staging protests of their own.

See also: Attica Prison; Iranian embassy siege
References: Davies, Barry. *SAS Rescue.* London: Sidgewick and Jackson, 1996.
Geraghty, Tony. *Who Dares Wins.* Boston: Little, Brown, 1992.

PIGNATA, GIUSEPPE
(C. 1661–1725)

Giuseppe Pignata, a musician and composer, was detained in Rome by officers of
the Italian Inquisition in 1689 and imprisoned by Catholic inquisitors for his alleged
heresy. His subsequent escape became
famous in the Dutch Republic.

Though he would have been burned alive
if he had been caught trying to escape, the
young prisoner quickly started to draw up a
plan that he knew would take a long time to
set into action. To begin with, he managed to
obtain a prison room that was adjacent to the
city's streets, knowing that if he was given a
room that was next to the 20-foot-tall prison
walls or the deep ditch, he would have
almost no chance of getting over them. He
then took great pains to find out when the
Roman cleric who occupied the room above
would be absent, thereby allowing him to
drill a small hole through the ceiling and
escape through the window above to the
marketplace outside. Though the ceiling was
nearly 17 feet high, Pignata reached it by
stacking several chairs on top of each other.

To drill the hole, Pignata used a variety of
simple but effective tools. He extracted
vinegar from the salads he was often given
for his daily meal, knowing that it would
help dissolve the plaster, and, using a pair
of scissors, a penknife, and a nail, he was
soon able to cut through the plaster. With
considerable ingenuity, he also obtained
iron splinters which fastened the bandages
he asked the prison doctor to give him, and
used them to scrape away at the wall.

Once he had gotten into the priest's room
above, he lowered himself to the street on a
ladder that he had carefully made from
clothes and linen over the preceding weeks.
Nearly four years after he had first been
detained, Giuseppe Pignata was free and on
his way to the Netherlands.

References: Symons, Arthur. *The Adventures of
    Giuseppe Pignata.* English translation. London:
    Jonathan Cape, 1930.

PITMAN, HENRY

In his telling account of his escape from a
slave plantation in Barbados, where he had

been condemned to serve a prison sentence
for his involvement in a rebellion against
the monarchy in 1687, Henry Pitman made
some revealing references to the strength of
mind required in an escapee, who may be
tempted to turn back when difficulties arise.

Like many other slaves and prisoners
who had been detained on Barbados,
Pitman was able to acquire a boat and to
find several other prisoners who were eager
to join him. But after they set sail late one
night and headed for distant Curaçao, unexpected difficulties emerged that tested them
to the fullest.

Their boat was full of leaks, and all the
crew members struggled to throw out the
water that was seeping in. In addition, the
seas were rougher than they had anticipated
and it was not long before most began to
suffer from seasickness and were too debili-
tated to continue bailing. This situation,
Pitman noted, prompted a crisis of will
among the escapees. At this crucial point all
the others wanted to return to Barbados,
even if it meant facing punishment. Only
his leadership and persuasion kept them on
their planned path.

His determination not to give up was
rewarded. After sailing for a week in very
difficult weather conditions, the escape
party eventually reached dry land, allowing
Pitman and most of his colleagues to eventually return to their families in Europe.

See also: Sea, escape and rescue at

PLUSCHOW, GUNTHER
(1886–1931)

Though no German prisoners managed to
escape from the British mainland during
World War II, a few succeeded during
World War I. One of those who did was
Gunther Pluschow, in the summer of 1915.

Pluschow was a German pilot who had
been captured by the British in Gibraltar in
1915 and sent to a prison camp, Donington
Hall in Derbyshire, soon afterward. Having
spent a short time in Britain before the war,
he felt confident enough about his knowledge of England and about his command of
English to attempt an escape. He later
claimed that he was motivated to do so

chiefly because he suffered from the "prisoners' disease, home-sickness" as well as from "the apathy of most dreadful despair of entire hopelessness" (Pluschow 1922, 184).

Pluschow teamed up with a German naval officer, Oberleutnant Treffetz, in order to make his bid for freedom. Using as many maps of Britain as they could find, and obtaining information from their guards in exchange for cigarettes, they told some fellow officers what they intended to do and secured their cooperation before making their move on 4 July.

That morning, the two men reported themselves sick and lay in bed instead of attending the daily roll call. Then, late in the afternoon while a heavy storm limited visibility, they hid in the large gardens in a spot covered by shrubs and long grasses that could not easily be seen by the guards nearby. Eventually, after the camp had started to settle down for the night, they heard the prearranged signal from the other prisoners that all was clear and that it was safe for them to move.

Using their thick winter coats to protect themselves from the barbed wire, the two men quickly climbed the fences, carefully avoiding the alarms, which could be set off by a slight tremor, and ran along the route they had so carefully planned. They arrived in Derby before long and went their separate ways, thinking they had less chance of arousing suspicion if they traveled alone.

Treffetz did not last long before he was recaptured, but Pluschow, perhaps because he knew the country better, was more elusive. Having reached Leicester, he decided to head for London, where before the war he remembered seeing neutral ships heading to and from the docks. He knew that those ships would be very heavily guarded, but he could think of no better way of getting back home.

Though his escape had quickly become public knowledge and made instant headlines, Pluschow was able to escape recapture by living rough in all sorts of places in London, including churches, parks, cemeteries, and hiding places underneath discarded merchandise at Tilbury Docks. One of his most effective disguises was as one of the dock laborers—who were at that time on strike—a disguise he created by using coal dust to make his fair hair black and greasy and to change the color of the dark blue suit he had had worn since leaving the camp.

Pluschow later recorded one occasion when he thought he would be recognized and caught. Knowing that he had to get rid of his distinctive mackintosh to avoid being recognized, he walked into Blackfriars Station and handed the coat over to the attendant, having no intention of picking it up. "What's your name, sir?," asked the clerk casually, taking the German by complete surprise. "With shaking knees I asked '*Meinen*'?, answering in German as I naturally presumed the man had guessed my identity. 'Oh I see, Mr Mine' and he handed me a receipt in the name of Mr Mine. It was a miracle that this official had not noticed my terror, and I felt particularly uncomfortable when I had to pass the two policemen who stood on guard at the station and who scrutinised me sharply" (Pluschow 1922, 205).

But Pluschow's efforts were not in vain. After waiting for some weeks for a neutral ship to appear, he was at last able to make his way on board the *Princess Juliana*, hiding himself on board until, a few hours later, he woke up to see the Dutch port of Flushing on the horizon. Almost immediately his name and story were made famous by the German press, which loudly proclaimed his escape as if it had been a great victory.

See also: Werra, Franz von

References: Pluschow, Gunther. *My Escape from Donington Hall.* Translated by Pauline de Chary. London: John Lane, 1922.

POTTER, ARTHUR
(1905–1998)

Knowing the ruthlessness of his enemy, a young British colonial officer, Arthur Potter, went through enormous personal hardship in order to escape the clutches of the Japanese army in 1942.

Potter was the chief financial adviser to the Indian commander in chief. He was stationed at Myitkyina, a town in the north, with orders to destroy what was in effect the

Burmese national currency. As the Imperial Army advanced rapidly, he stayed at his quarters as long as he could to carry out the order. He had its coinage hauled by bullocks to the banks of the Irrawaddy and scattered the silver in the deep water channel; he then burned the banknotes. But the delay meant that the Japanese were by now almost on top of him.

With a small party, Potter set out to reach India on foot, some 200 miles away to the northwest. For a month they trekked through uninhabited jungle and across high passes, always hampered by deep mud and monsoon rains. Potter soon contracted malaria, often unable to tell if his shirt was soaked from the damp or from his high fever, but he forced himself on. By the time he reached Assam, he had lost over 40 pounds and was suffering from tropical ulcers, whose scars he carried for life.

See also: Japanese army, prisoners of; Tall, Robert

PRENDERGAST, SGT. JOHN (1912–)

Like many other escapees, Sgt. John Prendergast was able to break out of captivity in April 1942 by winning the trust of those who guarded him.

John Prendergast had been quick to recognize an escape opportunity that lay before him. Since the Germans were trying to recruit Irishmen among the prisoner of war (POW) population to join the Axis cause, thinking that they would be a fruitful source of extra troops, he claimed to be of Irish stock and said that he was willing to volunteer his services in the name of a free Ireland. Taken to Berlin from Salonika with another 190 men, he met another POW who had joined for similar reasons, John Bryan, and they drew up plans for escape.

They did not find it difficult to reach the outside, easily opening their huts' shutters from the inside and cutting some unlit wire. From a suburban railway station they then picked up a goods freight train heading for Antwerp and, having hidden themselves on board, managed to fake the seal on the door to make it seem unbroken.

Once in Antwerp Prendergast was careful not to fall into the traps that the Gestapo and other Nazi officials were always quick to lay. As he left the station a guard called out to him "Hello! Hello!" knowing that it was only too easy for a native English speaker to reply in the same terms, but by feigning puzzlement and walking on, he survived this first test.

But more was to come. Finding that the guard was clearly suspicious and had started to follow him, flashlight in one hand and revolver in the other, Prendergast was forced to resort to violence. He headed for a quiet spot near the station, turned sharply round a corner, and waited for the German to follow. He hit him on the chin, knocking him out, and left him in a dark corner of an air-raid shelter.

Free from this unwanted attention, Prendergast was able to find his way to freedom without difficulty, contacting the local underground and being spirited away along the Pat O'Leary line.

See also: Grimson, George

PRESS GANGS, ESCAPE FROM

One anonymous Frenchman had the particularly terrifying experience of having to escape from a ruthless gang whose enmity he could not understand. Though he did not realize it, his enemy was in fact a press-gang, headhunters for the Royal Navy who dragged unwilling recruits off the streets and forced them by threat of violence to enter its ranks and remain at sea.

This escapee had already managed to find his way out of his prison, in East Anglia, by slipping through the perimeter at a moment when he was sure the sentries could be caught off-guard. Knowing they began their shift at 9 P.M. and finished three hours later, he moved at 11 o'clock, when he reckoned their concentration would be at its lowest point. He left, moreover, in the middle of a rainstorm, sure that they would want to be indoors, and was soon on his way to the coast to find transport across the Channel.

Walking along a back street of a coastal town soon afterward, he noticed a group of six or seven men brush past him, casting furtive glances at him as they did so. Less than a minute later he felt several hands grab his collar from behind and pull him back. Though he did not realize it at the time, he had just been press-ganged into the British navy to serve against his own side.

Taken to a nearby house, the Frenchman was left alone in a ground-floor room with one member of the gang for company. The others, he assumed, were upstairs or elsewhere in the house and had entrusted this particular individual, a roughneck whom he knew he would have no chance of taking on by himself, to watch over him in the meantime.

As the hours ticked by, he hoped that his guard would fall asleep, allowing him to open the window a few feet away and jump through. But though the guard did not drift off, the prisoner's luck suddenly changed. In the room next door a shouting and scuffling began, and when someone started to shout for assistance the guard left the room to help.

Left alone, the Frenchman dashed for the window and succeeded in raising the sash high enough to get out. But just as he was about to dive through, he heard his guard returning and knew that he would be caught if he tried to do so. Thinking on his feet, he instead threw himself under the table, managing to conceal himself and hoping the guard would assume he had gone through the window and would run after him.

It worked brilliantly. The guard rushed out of the room in mistaken pursuit as soon as he saw the window open, allowing the escapee to double-back on him. But within minutes he had been seen and once again was being chased at furious pace down the town streets.

That he managed to evade them owed a great deal to sheer good fortune. Seeing a household door slightly ajar, he dashed inside and threw the door shut, hoping his enemies, only a few yards behind, had not seen him. To his relief, he heard them race past outside, oblivious of his hiding-place, and knew that, once again, he had managed to escape.

See also: Lefebre, Gen. Louis; Napoleonic Wars

PROBYN, WALTER (1931–)

Walter Probyn, a British criminal who was known in the London underworld of the 1960s simply as "Angel Face," appears to have become almost addicted to making escape bids during the many prison sentences he had to serve.

Until the age of 14, as he wrote in his memoirs, he *was* small enough to squeeze through the small hatches in the cell doors, using a clever ploy to do so: by repeatedly banging the cell door as if protesting his detention, he was able to make the catch of the closed hatch jump outward until he could get the hatch to slide down. Having squeezed himself through the hatch, Probyn was usually able to make his way into the air-shaft, only about a foot square, and then find his way onto the roof above. Though he admitted that he found such experiences terrifying, because of the claustrophobia and fear of being trapped that they induced, he was nonetheless able to escape from several police stations in London by using these methods.

As his reputation as an intrepid escapee grew, Probyn was forced to rely on different methods. Though he managed to steal some door keys during one stay at a remand center, he knew he was powerless to use them, since the staff watched his every movement remorselessly. He hit on an ingenious alternative: He took the keys to the governor, claiming he had found them and decided to hand them in. He was told to go to the kitchen to make himself a coffee as a reward for his "honesty." This gave him just the chance he had wanted, and minutes later he was out the kitchen windows and on the run.

Though he was recaptured some time later and sent to Rampton Prison in the autumn of 1949, Probyn escaped once again. After quickly climbing a drainpipe and making his way onto a roof one December evening, he leaped a 15-foot gap between roofs and made his getaway. He dived into a ditch and covered himself with vegetation in order to hide from the search parties that had been sent after him. Probyn also proved his determination to escape by surviving the severe, subzero temperatures of the winter night before he was able to find his way onto the back of a truck that took him to friends in London.

During another period of imprisonment, this time in Wandsworth, he was able to fake acute appendicitis by swallowing carbolic soap and rolling around in agony. Taken to the nearby St. James's Hospital, he soon hopped off the hospital bed in the casualty ward, dived though a window, and climbed the hospital gates to escape.

In 1963 he was sent to Dartmoor Prison, but he was not deterred from attempting escape by the prison's formidable reputation. Having been allowed to join a working party that was repairing some of the prison officers' homes, Probyn succeeded in stealing a compass and hiding it in one of the homes he was working in. When everyone's back was turned he took the compass and made off onto the moor, which was covered by a thick fog that hindered the search parties far more than it hindered him. Resting during the day and moving at night, he was able to reach Porton, near Salisbury, five days later and return, once again, to the criminal underworld.

He also proved himself highly adept at evading the police when they swooped down on his home to arrest him. On occasion they surrounded the house, knowing he was inside, only to see him leaving on the roofs of adjacent houses before disappearing altogether. Though the police felt sure he had used a secret passage between the houses, his real method of escape was not quite so elaborate: He would enter a trapdoor on the roof of one of the houses in the block and then lock it behind him, causing the police to think he could not have gotten inside.

Probyn recorded two occasions when he managed to escape from the police even though he was trapped in a block that was completely surrounded. On the first such occasion he hid under a large tarpaulin sheet that had been put on a roof that was being retiled. The policemen searched high and low for him; at one point one of them even stepped on him without realizing it. On the other occasion, he walked into someone's back entrance, through their hallway,

and out their front door, where the police were waiting for him. But though the policemen stared hard at him curiously as he boldly emerged from the house and shut the door firmly behind him, Proben later noted that his casual manner completely deceived them. It was not until he was outside the cordon that he was recognized, and by that time he was sprinting down the road and out of their grasp. Like other successful escapees, Probyn had used audacity and confidence to bluff his way out.

Probyn also joined forces with John McVicar to carry out a brilliant escape from the maximum security wing of Durham Prison. Probyn was recaptured but McVicar won his freedom. Placed in solitary confinement for several weeks as a punishment, Probyn never again attempted to escape before he was finally released in 1974.

See also: McVicar, John

References: Probyn, Walter. *Angel Face.* London: Allen and Unwin, 1977.

PYM, JOHN (1584–1643)

In 1642 King Charles I of England ordered the arrest of his chief antagonist, John Pym, from the House of Commons in an attempt to end the growing political crisis that was to soon allow civil war to break out.

Indicted in January 1642 on charges of depriving the king of his powers, alienating his subjects, and subverting the rights of Parliament, Pym had no intention of allowing himself to be detained at the king's pleasure. Instead, he sought to escape from the House of Commons together with his four companions, John Hampden, Arthur Haselrigg, William Strode, and Denzil Holles, who were indicted on the same charges.

As Charles left Whitehall and headed toward the House of Commons, a captain named Edward Langrish rushed inside to warn Pym and his colleagues that the king was on his way with 400 soldiers to implement the warrant of arrest and was only minutes away. Slipping through a back door, the five men jumped into a boat, waiting on the Thames outside, and sailed off for a hiding place in the City of London further downstream.

"The birds have flown," pronounced Charles in a famous phrase as he arrived with his soldiers to arrest them. Though he instantly ordered the ports to close and instructed the lord mayor to search the city for them, his enemies had hidden themselves too carefully to let themselves be captured, and they only emerged to take control of an emerging anti-Royalist party when Charles had left London shortly afterward. England was now well on the road to civil war.

Wade, C. E. *John Pym*. London: Sir Isaac Pitman and Sons, 1912.

RAWICZ, SLAVOMIR (1892–1957)

The escape of Slavomir Rawicz, a young Polish army officer who was arrested and imprisoned by the Red Army after the Soviet invasion of Poland in September 1939, is a story of extraordinary romance and adventure as well as of fear and discomfort.

Like most of the other Polish officers who shared his fate, Rawicz appears to have done little to provoke his arrest and imprisonment. Forced under duress to confess to a charge of espionage and sabotage against the Red Army, Rawicz was moved by cattle truck to a labor camp in Siberia to serve a 25-year sentence.

But the grueling daily routine of labor, near starvation, and cruelty at Camp 303 made Rawicz and several fellow prisoners absolutely determined to escape. But it was clear that leaving the camp would be the easy part. The camp was situated at Yautske, near the Arctic Circle in the middle of Siberia, and they would have to travel thousands of miles southward if they were to leave the Soviet Union. Though they planned to make their move in April 1941, they would have to cope with extreme cold and deep snow for the first part of their journey.

But ironically, the harsh conditions helped them escape. They waited until midnight before moving, knowing that the guards would not have more than 20 yards visibility through the heavy snow and that, without electricity, they had no searchlights to help them see. Moreover, even if the guards noticed they were missing, the snow would cover their tracks almost immediately.

The escapees headed southward. But when they reached the Gobi desert, in Mongolia, they were soon confronted by the possibility of dying in the extreme midsummer heat. Their rations were soon exhausted, and Rawicz later recalled the dark thoughts that they all shared. In the lifeless landscape, themselves pitifully run down by sunstroke and heat exhaustion, their movement reduced to "just a shuffle," their minds were haunted by the ubiquitous skeletons of people and animals that had met their ends in this harsh environment. It was only by eating desert snakes and by stumbling by chance over a water supply, just as their hopes of survival had started to fade, that they were able to keep going at all.

Two of the party fell victim to exhaustion. One, Sigmund Makowski, suddenly fell headfirst into the sand, making no effort to catch himself. His companions quickly noticed a telltale sign of heart problems—the soft, puffy flesh swelling over the top of his moccasins—and could do nothing to save him. The other collapsed and died soon after, though by cruel misfortune they were approaching the desert's end and soon reached Tibet.

It was now January 1942, nine months after they had left Camp 303. Once again they had to brave extreme cold, as they attempted to cross the Himalayas into Nepal over the lowest-altitude route they could find. Despite their ordeal in Siberia, the crossing brought "a new experience of intense physical discomfort," especially because of "the manner in which the cold struck at our foreheads until they seemed to be held in frigid bands of ice" (Rawicz 1995). Zaro, the lightest man in the group, now headed the mountain expedition, testing the holds with an ax, breaking through the ice crust on the snow, and blazing a trail for those following.

One peak they were forced to ascend proved to be the "very stuff of nightmares." From valley to valley, wrote Rawicz, its crossing took six days "and taxed our endurance to such a degree that for the first time we talked openly of the prospect that we might all perish." Just one blizzard of a few hours' duration, he continued, would have "wiped us out," and the temperatures plunged so low at night that "even attempting to doze would have courted death" (Rawicz 1995). Here another member of the escape party lost his life, falling suddenly into a crevice and leaving no trace.

Finally, after eight days without food, the remaining four men, who were by now little more than walking skeletons and were in filthy condition, at last saw the mountains give way to gentler, hilly, green slopes, and they knew they had reached the safety of British India. As the Russians shook hands with the amazed Gurkha soldiers who came to greet them, they had good reason to feel proud of themselves. They had survived a journey on foot of more than 2,500 miles through some of the world's most arduous terrain.

See also: Stalin, Joseph; Trotsky, Leon
References: Rawicz, Slavomir. *The Long Walk.* London: Longmans, 1995.

RESCUE ATTEMPTS

Despite immense preparation and calculation, some rescue bids have failed to achieve their ends because some essential ingredient is missing from the recipe for success.

One such ingredient is the need for accurate, detailed, and up-to-date intelligence about the movements of the enemy the rescuers face, and it was this that was missing during the failed raid on the SS *Mayaguez.* The U.S. merchant ship and its 40-strong crew was seized by unknown Cambodian gunmen en route to Thailand on 31 May 1975. U.S. planners feared this might be only the first instance of U.S. civilians being endangered by Communist insurgents, who were plainly winning the war for Southeast Asia. Without swift and decisive military action, the situation threatened to get much worse.

Though the rescue of the crew was planned and rehearsed with great care and in great detail by a special team, and though the ship was constantly watched by reconnaissance aircraft, military planners lacked the detailed intelligence necessary if any such rescue operation is to be successful. For not only had there been no clear sightings of the hostages or real clues to their whereabouts, but there was also no real idea about the strength of the Cambodian forces who were guarding Koh Tang, where the *Mayaguez* had anchored a few days after it was hijacked.

Because they were unsure about the crew's whereabouts, preemptive air and artillery strikes on Koh Tang were not carried out to smooth the path of the Marine force that raided it shortly before dawn on 15 May. Instead, the eight helicopters that were deployed to land the rescue force came under withering fire from a force that they had not known existed. The first helicopter had arrived at the landing zone and successfully landed its Marine force but had crashed into the sea shortly after leaving. The second and third were forced to return to base after being hit by small-arms fire en route. Another crash-landed on the beach, and the fifth burst into flames while moving inland. The last three waited offshore for several hours before leaving when the existing ground force had made the area safe.

At the same time that the land force was attempting to seize the ground, another force was landed by helicopter on the hijacked ship. In stark contrast to their fellow Marines on the mainland, they encountered no opposition at all, and within minutes it had become clear that the crew had been moved off the ship and were now somewhere on the mainland.

But during the morning of 15 May the ground attack force was in no position to carry out a rescue, for withdrawing from the unforeseen enemy fire took priority. In order to prevent the Cambodians from sending in troops or aircraft to cut off their retreat, U.S. aircraft struck mainland targets—notably Ream Airfield—as well as enemy positions in Koh Tang and flew in reinforcements. By nightfall, after more than

12 hours of heavy fighting, the Marine force was at last extricated.

It had become clear during the day that there had been no need to mount the operation at all, since the crew had not only been moved from the ship but also was released soon afterward. Their release was probably the result of the threat of military action—hard rhetoric and patrolling aircraft overhead—rather than its actual use. Nor, it appeared, would a rescue operation have been a blow to Cambodia's Communist regime, since the ship had been seized by local leaders who seemed to have nothing to do with the new rulers of Phnom Penh. The mission was launched without the most basic ingredient of success—intelligence about both the enemy and the crew—and 18 U.S. servicemen lost their lives.

Other attempts have failed because they have lacked the element of surprise that were so important a part of successful operations such as the raids at Entebbe, Mogadishu, and the Iranian embassy in London. One example is the bloody attempt by the Federal Bureau of Investigation (FBI) to "rescue" the members of an eccentric religious cult in Texas. For 51 days in the spring of 1993, U.S. officials laid siege to the heavily defended headquarters of the Branch Davidian sect at Mount Carmel, near Waco, Texas. Because its members were far more heavily armed than most other similar religious groups in the United States, the FBI presented a strong argument for moving inside, arresting its fanatical leader, David Koresh, and disarming the others. Many of the proponents of this policy saw this as a "rescue operation" as well because there was some evidence that some members were being kept in the fortress against their will. There were, without question, several children in the sect, who would have had no real comprehension of their strange surroundings.

An initial assault in March was beaten back by stiff resistance from cult members, resulting in the deaths of several FBI agents. The siege that followed was brought to an unfortunate climax on 20 April when FBI agents, acting under the orders of Attorney General Janet Reno,

attempted to flush the Branch Davidians out with tear gas and to destroy their compound with tanks and other armored vehicles. But some of the cult members had gas masks, and others were evacuated, perhaps at gunpoint, to specially prepared confines within the fortress that the gas could not penetrate. As the FBI agents moved in, they were unable to prevent Koresh from ordering his followers to commit mass suicide, though some of those who died were almost certainly shot. Seventy-two cult members were killed that day. Only nine survived.

See also: Iranian hostage rescue operation; Vietnam War

References: Rowan, Roy. *Four Days of the Mayaguez.* New York: Ballatine, 1971.

ROWE, JAMES "NICK"
Despite the exceptional physical and mental burden he suffered, James "Nick" Rowe, a U.S. Green Beret officer, survived more than five years of captivity by the Vietcong (VC) before finally escaping in December 1968.

Rowe had been captured by the VC at Le Coeur, a hamlet 140 miles southwest of Saigon, where he had been conducting a routine patrol mission. Over the next five years he was held in a series of prison camps, detention centers, and hideouts in South Vietnam and survived extreme malnutrition, mistreatment, and political indoctrination.

But like that of many other escapees his chance to escape came quite unexpectedly. One afternoon on New Year's Eve 1968, Rowe and his captors heard the distant noise of approaching helicopters. He instantly recognized them as those of American Huey Cobras. U.S. intelligence had obviously detected their position, and the helicopters now swooped overhead and started to machine-gun their position.

Rowe knew that he had little chance of getting away alive, not only because he was an obvious target for the U.S. gunners, who were too far away to recognize him as a prisoner, but also because his guards would rather kill him than let him escape. In desperation, he took advantage of the panic and chaos among his captors and, seizing a branch, struck his guard a violent blow, killing him instantly.

Running from cover into an open paddy field, he was at first nearly gunned down by a machine gunner who took him for a VC guerrilla. But his life was spared when another American ordered the gunner to hold his fire and take the "guerrilla" prisoner instead. When the Huey swept in, only feet away, the astonished crew recognized him as a fellow American and helped him on board.

After five years in captivity, Rowe was awarded the Silver and Bronze Stars before retiring from the army in 1974.

See also: Dengler, Lt. Dieter; Saigon; Vietnam War
References: Rowe, James. Five Years to Freedom. New York: Ballatine, 1971.

RUSSIAN REVOLUTION AND CIVIL WAR (1917–1920)

Characteristic of all revolutionary change, and perhaps also a manifestation of an ingrained trait of its peoples, acts of near savage destruction and cruel violence were committed in the climate of suspicion, rivalry, and anarchy that accompanied the outbreak of the Russian Revolution. Homes were ransacked, property was confiscated, individuals were arrested, often for no apparent reason, and thousands were executed. Many fled this state of terror.

A large number of those forced to leave their homeland had held high positions in the czarist regime. Many others were members of the privileged classes, who naturally identified with the status quo and whose wealth made them natural targets for the revolutionaries. One typical party that fled Russia in the winter of 1919, as the full extent of Bolshevik terror began to become apparent, consisted of very high ranking people, including generals and admirals and some young intellectuals, who had started their journey in Petrograd. Very few, if any, had ever experienced physical discomfort before, and because the majority of them had lived in isolated areas of a vast country, it is probable that few had any conception of much of their own homeland, let alone their eventual destination.

Their desperation is measured by the extraordinary hardships they were prepared to endure in exchange for their freedom. As they headed north toward Murmansk, for example, one escape party braved deep midwinter snow and subzero temperatures, even though they had with them only the most essential clothing and almost no provisions. It was, recalled a survivor, simply "a question of either walk and die on the railway or get caught by the Communists at certain points and get murdered" (Macaire 1997, 13). To make matters worse, they were unable to approach the villages and settlements along the way without putting themselves at grave risk, since there was a strong chance the inhabitants would be tempted by the generous reward for information and turn them in. Certainly the unfortunate members of one refugee party detected in this way were shown no mercy: The men were all shot, and the women and children given a choice of either continuing or returning home. All turned back, except one, Nadia Danilevitch, who wandered on alone, sleeping in the crooks of trees to escape prowling wolves and eventually reaching Norway after walking nearly 1,000 miles.

Such escapees often relied on the benevolence of those they met along the way. Fleeing the "butchery" of the Bolsheviks in 1918, one member of the royal family, the Grand Duchess Marie, managed to reach Ukraine after a long train journey from Petrograd and was given protection at the German diplomatic mission there. But she had traveled without the necessary documents, and she later described how she and her family had "trembled" every time the train was stopped and boarded by noisy, often violent, soldiers and officials. That they were able to reach the border at all was due in large measure to the influence of the sympathetic conductor they met en route. By standing outside their compartment for much of the journey and using a variety of excuses on their behalf, he was able to turn away anyone wanting to go inside.

Her own quick wits also helped her along the way. Stopped at the end of her journey by Bolshevik officials and asked for her papers, she kept a brave face and blurted out that they were in the possession of her husband, who had just walked off for a minute. Though such officials had a reputation for arresting anyone lacking the right papers and though they were not known to accept any excuses, they believed her. "We were alive, out of danger," she later recorded, "[and] he who has not lived through such a moment does not know what it actually means to enjoy life."

The civil war between the "Reds" and "Whites" was made possible by the White forces' escape from the Reds. In February 1919 the Reds had advanced to capture the remote town of Rostov, which had become a focal point for disaffected groups, but they failed to stop General Lavr Kornilov's force from leaving. Though the Reds pursued them, Kornilov and his army, only 4,000 strong, managed to keep ahead and were soon able to regroup and brace themselves for active operations.

This "Ice March," as it became known, has since become the most heroic epic of the Russian civil war, one that has entered popular mythology not least because of the terrible conditions the Whites endured as they trekked from Rostov into the steppes in midwinter. Many of them collapsed during the march and were left behind to die or to take their own lives. Some resorted to violence and terror to survive. Surrounded by a deeply hostile village population, they are known to have killed and threatened some of those they encountered in order to get the food and supplies they needed. But they survived the journey and were able to start the Russian civil war, dashing Lenin's hope that their flight into the wilderness was the beginning of their end.

Even some Western diplomats were forced to flee the Bolsheviks, for they knew they could expect no mercy if they were arrested as spies. In 1919 the head of the British intelligence station in Moscow, Sir Paul Dukes, escaped from Leningrad knowing that the Bolsheviks were closing in. Heading for the border with Finland, he started to cross the frozen waters between the two lands. Before long he realized that a Red Army patrol had seen him in the

moonlight and was moving rapidly toward him on horseback. But noticing the blackness of much of the ice around him, he abandoned his sledge and threw himself in the darkest patch of ice he could find. To his astonishment and relief, the patrol, though it passed very close by, failed to see him and soon disappeared again into the distance. A few hours later he arrived in Finland, although he had a great deal of difficulty getting past its immigration officials, who forced him to wait in prison until they knew who he was.

See also: Bailey, Lt. Col. Frederick; Kerensky, Aleksandr; Nazaroff, Paul

References: Dukes, Sir Paul. *Red Dusk and the Morrow.* London: Williams and Norgate, 1922.
Figes, Orlando. *The People's Tragedy: The Russian Revolution, 1891–1924.* London: Jonathan Cape, 1996.
Macaire, Tatiana. *Nadia.* London: Lithoflow Press, 1997.

RWANDAN GENOCIDE (1994)

One Rwandan, Venuste Karasira, had a lucky escape from the genocide that claimed the lives of at least half a million of his fellow citizens.

Taken away for execution, Karasira soon heard the cries of the people "who were in agony everywhere." Some of these prisoners were killed en route, though most were put to death at a specially designated place on a hilltop. "We accepted our fate to die," he wrote.

But as the killing started, he was able to survive by hiding among the dead. "I swam in their blood to survive," he recalled, and he was overlooked by the executioners as a consequence. Though terribly injured, he escaped with his life and later told the world of the shocking sights he had seen.

See also: Execution, escape from

"RYAN, CHRIS" (1961–)

While working behind Iraqi lines during the Gulf War, a British special forces soldier, known only by his literary pseudonym "Chris Ryan," was able to escape from a massive enemy search and make his way back to Saudi Arabia.

Ryan was a member of Bravo Two Zero, an eight-man reconnaissance patrol of the Special Air Service (SAS) that had been assembled for a specific purpose: to find the Scud missiles that Saddam Hussein's army had started firing at Israel and that threatened to provoke massive retaliation from Tel Aviv. Because such retaliation risked breaking up the alliance against Saddam, these long-range patrols were given urgent orders to locate the missiles, which satellites and aircraft had failed to find.

Moved secretly into Iraq in January 1991, the patrol headed toward the main supply route between Al-Hadithah, an important strategic town, and several nearby airfields along which the Scud missile carriers were thought to be moving. But things soon began to go wrong. Before long their positions were given away by a shepherd boy, and the SAS men were forced to flee.

On his long and grueling march back to Saudi Arabia, Ryan had some narrow escapes from the Iraqi forces. At one point, his last remaining colleague—the others had all become lost and had gone their separate ways—in desperation approached a shepherd and begged him for food and water. Trusting his instincts, Ryan stayed in the mountains. He waited for his fellow soldier to return but when, after a few hours, two Iraqi vehicles appeared on the horizon, he realized that his companion must have been captured and forced to tell the Iraqis of his own whereabouts.

Though he was already exhausted, Ryan raced away into the night in a frantic attempt to evade them. To his horror he found they were moving up a mountain pass onto the plain around him. As they approached, now only a few hundred yards away, Ryan reached a trembling hand for his rocket launcher and squeezed the trigger. In the carnage and destruction that followed he was able to flee into the night, his path lit up by the spiraling flames of the burning vehicles.

On another occasion his position was very nearly given away by dogs roaming the streets of a village, which he had approached in the hope of finding food and water. Ryan had noticed that if even one dog barked at him a terrible din would arise, since all the others would quickly follow suit. When he looked up and saw a whole pack of dogs running toward him barking, he felt sure that within minutes all the villagers would be awake and searching for him.

Acting almost on impulse, Ryan turned and ran a good 200 yards from the village, hoping the dogs would feel less threatened if he was at such a distance. He also knew that dogs were much less interested in someone who was not moving, so he then lay down and hoped they would turn back. Sure enough, to his immense relief, the dogs suddenly stopped, at a distance of just ten feet or so from where he lay, before wandering back to the village.

Ryan was to have at least one other close encounter with the Iraqis before reaching allied lines. He inadvertently wandered past a checkpoint into the grounds of a leading Iraqi soldier or politician, before being spotted by a figure that he could just make out in the dark. Seeing that he had almost certainly aroused suspicion, he ran and leaped into a ditch, seconds before searchlights were switched on and guards started to comb the area in search of him.

When he crept stealthily from his cover, he saw two Iraqis walking toward him. He reached for his knife and attacked each of the two men, killing both silently and instantly and disposing of the bodies in the nearby river.

After walking for a few more days, the SAS man was at last able to reach the border with Saudi Arabia, the only member of the original patrol group to evade capture.

References: Ryan, Chris [pseud.]. *The One That Got Away.* London: Century, 1995.

SADAT, ANWAR (1919–1981)

One of Mossad's more unusual missions astonished even its own leaders: a mission to rescue one of its sworn enemies, President Anwar Sadat of Egypt, from a Libyan assassination plot.

Libyan leader Colonel Mu'ammar Gadhafi's animosity toward the Egyptians stemmed from his advocacy of hard-line terrorism against Israel, a policy that had received a sharp rebuke from the Egyptians. The Colonel, always sensitive to personal slight, felt he had been treated contemptuously by his fellow Arabs and wanted revenge.

Soon Gadhafi's plot was unearthed by the Mossad surveillance teams operating in London, Paris, and Beirut. After raiding flats and intercepting communications they were able to deduce that a specially selected 20-man team was being trained to kill Sadat either at a military parade or at his Alexandria home, which would be covertly approached from the sea.

To the astonishment of Mossad chiefs, Israeli prime minister Menachem Begin and Israeli premier Yitzak Rabin now ordered their spy service to save the life of the Egyptian leader, thinking that his rescue would be seen as a gesture of goodwill at a time when talk of a peace settlement no longer seemed quite so unrealistic as it had in the past. Besides, they argued, if Sadat were killed he might be replaced by someone far more inimical toward their own interests.

Knowing that Sadat would be extremely wary of any information passed directly to him, the Israelis were able to persuade King Hussein of Jordan, with whom they already had some limited links, to act as an intermediary. Wisely, the Egyptian leader took no

chances and arrested all those who were named in the Israeli dossier. When their interrogation appeared to confirm the Israelis' information, several of the would-be assassins were executed and a punitive military strike was launched against Libya.

The rescue had a positive impact on the diplomatic relations between two countries that had been on frosty terms since the end of the 1973 war. Only a month later, Begin and Sadat agreed to meet secretly in Bucharest as a first step toward better relations between the two countries.

See also: Dikko, Umaru; Mossad

References: Copeland, Miles. *The Game of Nations: The Amorality of Power.* London: Weidenfeld and Nicholson, 1969.

Payne, Ronald. *Mossad.* London: Bantam, 1990.

Posner, Steve. *Israel Undercover.* Syracuse, NY: Syracuse University Press, 1987.

SAIGON (1975)

After the U.S. defeat in Vietnam, many people had to be rescued from the capital, Saigon, before Communist forces swept down from the north and captured it in 1975.

The North Vietnamese army (NVA) advanced from the north in a series of lightning military movements, and the sheer speed of their movement throughout South Vietnam took even the most pessimistic observers by surprise. Serious NVA inroads had not begun until March 1975, when a whole series of towns, cities, and provinces had fallen within the space of weeks: Banmethuot, Tuy Hoa, Nha Trang, Cam Ranh Bay, Hue, and Da Nang were all captured within four weeks of each other, their defenders outnumbered, outgunned, and painfully missing the awesome U.S. airpower that in earlier days had kept such

The final stages of the evacuation of the U.S. embassy in Saigon, 29 April 1975. (AP/Wide World Photos)

assaults at bay. By the end of March, the only real remaining target for the Communists was the capital, Saigon.

In such circumstances, it was not surprising that the evacuation of key personnel from the capital was a desperate, frantic, and often tragic affair. Even in the first two weeks of April, before the exodus turned into a flood, pilots worked under arduous conditions in which mishaps were bound to occur. For example, in one particularly tragic accident on 4 April during "Operation Babylift" (in which nearly 3,000 children of mixed U.S.-Vietnamese parentage were evacuated to new homes in the United States), a giant C5 transport crashed while attempting to return to its base after a rear door fell out and damaged the rudder and elevator control. The pilots and the 257 orphans on board were killed. Because of pressure for time, basic checks and maintenance were sometimes skimped, which made such accidents far more likely.

By 27 April, with thousands of military advisers still waiting to leave and with the evacuation now at fever pitch, the rescue had also become much more dangerous. Communist forces had suddenly swooped within striking distance of Saigon and were preparing for the final assault. Incoming transports were forced to brave incoming shells, antiaircraft fire, and, before long, the constant threat of NVA fighters—often captured U.S. planes—hovering in adjacent airspace. In the early hours of 29 April enemy fire made landings at the two main airports, Bien-hoa and Tan Son Nhut, so dangerous that the American ambassador, Graham Martin, was forced to send away the C130s that were circling above, waiting to land, and rely on helicopters instead.

Nonetheless, in the last 18 hours of the Vietnam War, with the fighting in its last stages, "Operation Frequent Wind" ensured the safety of the 1,373 U.S. citizens and 6,422 non-American personnel who had stayed in the capital as long as possible. Many were lifted from the roof of the U.S. embassy, others from scattered points across the city, often in darkness, sometimes under enemy fire. Finally at dawn on 30 April, six hours before President Thieu announced his government's formal surrender, the last Marines were airlifted from the roof of the embassy, formally ending not only "the night of the helicopters" but also nearly 20 years of U.S. involvement in a remote and distant corner of Southeast Asia.

But for many civilians the great escape from the Communist advance had only just begun. Tens of thousands left as boat people, sometimes using any vessel they could find to reach the U.S. ships a few miles offshore or to undertake extremely hazardous journeys to the Philippines or Thailand.

The images that remain of the Saigon evacuation are dramatic, occasionally shocking: soldiers brandishing rifles as a warning to the stricken crowds outside the U.S. embassy not to break down the gates and storm inside; officials using their fists to fight off those clambering on board; helicopters being pushed off carrier decks or crash-landed into the sea in order to make room for more essential equipment. One South Vietnamese soldier was crushed to death when he tried to escape by clinging to the wheels of a Boeing 727. Perhaps it was a fitting end to a desperate and tragic conflict.

See also: Khe Sahn; Rowe, James "Nick"; Vietnam War

SALADO PRISON, MEXICO (1846–1848)

During the U.S. war with Mexico (1846–1848), a spectacular mass breakout of 170 American prisoners took place from the Mexican prison compound at Salado.

The prisoners' plan was the most audacious and risky possible: They planned to overpower their guards and seize their rifles and armaments. Commencing their attack just as the Mexicans were at breakfast, the Texan prisoners succeeded brilliantly in overpowering their guards. Each armed himself with a musket and took a considerable cache of money and ammunition.

But the prisoners had concentrated so much of their planning on getting out of the compound that they overlooked the best way of reaching their own lines. Most of them were recaptured in the scorching desert, though four made it back home.

References: Haynes, Sam W. *Soldiers of Misfortune: The Somerwell and Mier Expedition.* Austin: University of Texas Press, 1990.

SALISBURY PRISON, VIRGINIA (1863)

In 1863 a group of Union prisoners held at the Confederate prison at Salisbury, Virginia, escaped in a bizarre fashion. They had been taken outside the compound to bury the dead. Unknown to the guards, one of the prisoners was a highly skilled ventriloquist. As one of the corpses was lowered into the ground and covered with soil, the guards were shocked to hear the dead man protest his own burial. Running off in fright, they left their prisoners unguarded, which allowed them to make their way back to Union lines.

References: Morton, Joseph. *Sparks from the Campfire.* Philadelphia: Keystone, 1892.

SAN QUENTIN (1862–)

Some of the escapes from the famous Californian prison San Quentin have been among the bloodiest and most dramatic in the United States. The two most famous breakouts took place in 1862 and 1935.

Like many other prison disturbances, the "battle of Ross Landing" in July 1862 was masterminded by a small but determined number of inmates. On the morning of 22 July ten men suddenly sprinted out of line and ran through the main prison gate toward the warden's office. Because they moved so quickly and knew exactly where to take cover from the sentries' rifle fire, it was clear immediately that this escape attempt had been planned well in advance.

Within minutes the prisoners had seized the governor and headed out of the camp, using him as a hostage to prevent the guards from intervening. As they left along the traditional escape route from the prison, which led westward along the shore toward Mount Tamalpais, the other 600 prisoners

took advantage of the general panic and disarray among the guards and produced
whatever they could as weapons—cleavers,
hammers, knives, and hatchets—to threaten
them and make their own escape. Though
estimates vary wildly, at least 300, and probably many more, escaped from the prison
compound on that summer day.

But the main group of escapees that left
the compound made one crucial mistake as
they were pursued by the police and soldiers of San Francisco: As the journey
became more and more arduous, the governor became exhausted and finally collapsed
on the ground. Unable to move his hefty
bulk, the convicts pressed on without him,
forfeiting their hostage and making them
easy prey for the mounted and heavily
armed soldiers. In the resulting shoot-outs,
seven prisoners lost their lives and nearly
all were rounded up and sent back to
prison. Only a few got away.

More than 70 years later, in 1935, there
was another big break from San Quentin.
On 16 January 1935 a meeting of the members of the prison parole board was interrupted by the sudden entry of four prisoners who shouted at them to keep quiet and
do as they were told. The prisoners were not
just violent; they also had a number of .45
Colt pistols, which had somehow been
smuggled through the rigorous checks
made on incoming personnel and parcels.

Though guards quickly surrounded the
building, they were helpless to stop the
men, who brandished their revolvers at the
governors' foreheads and commandeered
an official car. They traveled more than 25
miles west of the prison before police shot
their tires and forced them to stop. In the
pitched battle that ensued, the gang leader,
Rudolph Straight, was shot dead, though
the governors were all unharmed.

During the extensive inquiries that were
subsequently made into the episode, it
emerged that a former convict had smuggled the pistols to the gang by hiding them
under the dashboard of a car belonging to
an innocent civilian employee. Many people
also argued afterward that in any similar
situation in the future, the police should be
more willing to open fire on an escapee,

even if he was threatening a hostage at gunpoint. If the prison governor was killed in
the process, commented the Sacramento Bee
bitterly, it was a fate he deserved, since "the
keeper who cannot keep himself out of their
hands is no great shakes and ought not to be
spared."

All the other escapes made in San
Quentin's long history have been made by
individuals or small groups of prisoners
who have slipped away much more quietly.
A few are known to have nearly drowned
themselves by hiding in barrels of swill destined for the piggery; others have had themselves nailed up in boxes and sent outside;
some have tried setting fire to their cell,
hoping to disappear in the ensuing chaos;
most have made good use of the thick fogs
that cover the area to disappear over the sea.
But San Quentin, as many have found to
their cost, was never an easy place from
which to escape.

See also: Alcatraz; Attica Prison; Moundsville
    Penitentiary, West Virginia; Santa Fe, New
    Mexico; Sing Sing
References: Adams, R. Prison Riots in Britain and
    USA. New York: St. Martin's Press; London:
    Macmillan, 1992.
Lamott, Kenneth. Chronicles of San Quentin.
    London: John Long, 1963.

SANTA FE, NEW MEXICO (1980)

During the major disturbances at Santa Fe
Prison in New Mexico in February 1980 one
prison officer, held hostage by the rioters,
was able to escape because of the high
esteem in which he was held by most of the
inmates.

The guard was well liked and older than
most of the other guards, and some of the
prisoners sympathized with his plight.
Unknown to the other prisoners, a group of
three or four untied him in the early hours
of 3 February and allowed him to slip quietly past the other hostages and rioters and
cross back to the secure areas controlled by
the authorities.

See also: Attica Prison; Moundsville Penitentiary,
    West Virginia; Peterhead Prison; San Quentin
References: Adams, R. Prison Riots in Britain and
    USA. New York: St. Martin's Press; London:
    Macmillan, 1992.

Atkins, Burton M. *Prisons and Politics*. Englewood Cliffs, NJ: Prentice Hall, 1972.
Lamott, Kenneth. *Chronicles of San Quentin*. London: John Long, 1963.

SCHINDLER, OSCAR
(1908–1974)

Oscar Schindler was moved to rescue a considerable number of European Jews from extermination at the hands of the Nazis out of motives that have never been entirely clear, even to those who knew him closely at the time.

His story began in 1941 when Schindler, who had joined the Nazi Party in 1939, set up business in Krakow in occupied Poland. Taking over an enamelware business that

Oscar Schindler, who rescued hundreds of European Jews from the Nazis during World War II, in the grounds of his factory in Krakow-Zablocie. (Leopold Page Photographic Collection, courtesy of USHMM Photo Archives)

had previously been owned by a Jewish merchant, Abraham Bankier, who had been imprisoned by the Nazi authorities, Schindler renamed his company Deutsche Emailwaren Fabrik and began to manufacture various items needed by the German army.

Before long he began to man his business with Jewish labor, drawn from the ghettos of nearby Krakow. Though at first he recruited only a small number, it was not long before more than a thousand laborers were under his command at the Emailwaren. Among the local Jewish population, employment at Schindler's factory quickly acquired a reputation as a safe haven because their employer's influence warded off SS persecution.

But in 1944 Schindler was ordered to close down his business and send most of those working for him back to the ghettos, where they faced almost certain deportation to Auschwitz or to one of several other extermination camps. Seven hundred of the *Schindler Juden* ("Schindler's Jews") were sent back into captivity in August, but before long he was able to open a new factory at Brinnitz in Czechoslovakia, taking with him 300 of his original workforce together with another 700 to replace those who had been returned. Because their names were included on his "list," the members of this workforce were among the lucky few who escaped extermination.

Schindler was forced to fight for the welfare of his workforce as they moved southward toward Brinnitz. Forced to stop en route at several concentration camps, including Auschwitz, the *Schindler Juden* not only were horrified by the shocking sights and stories they came across but were also threatened with execution. Only by hard negotiation and bribery was Schindler able to get most of them free.

Schindler's motives have never been entirely clear. Some of those who owed their lives to him have argued that he was ultimately just an opportunist, a black marketeer who had joined the Nazi Party because it was commercially advantageous and who wanted free labor after 1942. Others have said that outwitting the SS was ultimately a great adventure for a man of intrepid and daring spirit, or that his later concern for the Jews was in part a way of forging contacts in a postwar world in which some of his talented workforce would find success and fortune. But no one has ever denied that Oscar Schindler also, somewhere in his heart, harbored sympathy for the people whose suffering he could see at first hand.

See also: Auschwitz; Koldyczewo Camp; Le Chambon; Sobibor Concentration Camp; Wallenberg, Raoul

References: Keneally, Thomas. *Schindler's List.* London: Sceptre, 1984.

SEA, ESCAPE AND RESCUE AT

Some escapees have walked to freedom, some have flown, and others have gone by sea, sometimes stowing away on neutral ships, on occasion even swimming.

In 1940, during World War II, two British officers being marched to a prisoner of war (POW) camp in the Reich slipped away from the column they were attached to and managed to find a small yacht on the Normandy coast. With the permission of its owner, a local teacher, they sailed it to England. Their passage would have been even easier had they been seen by two British destroyers that passed them but that somehow failed to notice their frantic efforts to attract attention.

Other prisoners were to do the same in the years that followed, and lines of escape were created not only overland to Switzerland and Gibraltar but also by boat to Britain. By 1943 Lucien Dumais and Ray Labrosse, two French naval officers who had escaped German captivity after the failed Dieppe raid of 1942, had established their own "Shelbourne line," which moved escapees from Brittany to Cornwall. After the passengers had been taken from special collection points in Paris and Rennes to a disembarkation point at Plouha, they were picked up by Royal Navy boats, which ran enormous risks to take them to safety. In all, 307 people were picked up and taken to Britain along this escape route.

It was more usual, however, for wartime escapees to head for the Baltic ports and then stow away to neutral Sweden. Two prisoners who tried this were Signalmen P. J. Harkin and J. B. O'Neill, who had slipped away from their working party in Silesia in April 1944 and hidden themselves in a deer-stalkers' hut, living only on bars of chocolate for several days. They found their way to the coast, where they ingeniously made contact with off-duty Swedish sailors by introducing themselves at the local brothels. Once they had been invited onto the Swedish ship, they hid from the Germans who came on board to search it. They eventually reached Stockholm four weeks later.

Escaping from enemy ports was just as difficult for German soldiers trying to make a getaway. During World War I, for example, Robert Neubau managed to escape from French captivity by absconding on a Swedish ship, but he had to use all his powers of ingenuity to avoid being captured by the sentries who were constantly on the look-out for prisoners on the run. Neubau, a German soldier, had been knocked off his bicycle and captured by the French in September 1914. After a brief spell spent building roads in Brittany, he was transferred to Rouen to unload coal from British ships. But though he was well guarded, his new role presented him with a tempting opportunity to find his way on board one of the Swedish boats that often came into the harbor, piloted by crewmen who were highly sympathetic to the plight of the prisoners they met at the docks.

When, during the night of 14 July 1915, Bastille Day, a dark storm brought heavy rain and severely limited visibility, Neubau took his chance. Making his way over two barbed-wire fences, catching and tearing his clothes as he did so, he was luckily not seen by a patrol that passed right by him. Within a few minutes he had reached the street outside the camp and then the harbor, which was only 100 yards or so beyond.

Neubau decided to avoid the ship he wanted until the last minute, though he was now in a position to keep it within his sights. All around him there were heaps of goods covered by tarpaulins. He dived under the covers and lay there for 31 hours, sleeping, dozing, watching, and listening.

When at last he judged the right moment to board had arrived, he jumped onto the boat's stern, and with the crew's help he was able to hide in the cable locker while the ship went first to England and then to the safety of Sweden.

Others have sailed enormous distances in order to escape. When Singapore fell to the Japanese in 1942, a group of British soldiers ran to some small boats, harbored nearby, and got away minutes before the Japanese arrived. Over the next few weeks they sailed more than 1,500 miles to reach friendly territory, braving extremely arduous weather conditions to do so. Because they were constantly harassed by enemy reconnaissance aircraft en route, they quickly perfected a technique that almost certainly prevented them from being shot: They would quickly dive under cover so that the enemy pilots would see only the two Malaysians who were traveling with them and assume that the boat was just a local fishing vessel.

One of the most daring escapes by sea took place in wartime Denmark when it became apparent that the country's Jewish population were facing persecution at the hands of the Nazis. For three months in the summer of 1943, more than 8,000 Jews were spirited away to Sweden by thousands of tiny boats of every description—motorboats, yachts, fishing boats, and even rowboats—by members of the underground. Always moving at night, the boats stole past German warships, sometimes at very close quarters.

The student Jorgen Kieler consulted several fishermen in order to map out several evacuation routes leading from Copenhagen. Having done so, he stationed himself at a hiding place on the shoreline and sheltered escaping Jews until a rescue boat arrived. Kieler alone saved 1,500 Jews from the Nazis.

Some of the most painless escapes made by American slaves were also undertaken by those who sailed to freedom. Knowing that he faced an extremely long and risky journey over land and would be easy prey to the dogs that were highly adept at picking up the trail of fugitives, one slave from Mississippi stole away in a 13-foot canoe with as much food and money as he could muster. He traveled along the rivers at night, hid in the willows during the day, and lived off the fish he managed to catch. Eventually reaching Wisconsin, he then sold his canoe and used the proceeds to pay for a journey by ship to Canada.

A few brave souls have on occasion made their way to freedom by swimming very long distances. In May 1943 Thomas Speed and a party of colleagues crawled out of a work camp near Erfurt. The group then split up to go their separate ways. Speed stole a bicycle en route and reached the banks of the Rhine, northwest of Zurich, where he took the plunge: "I tied my clothing on my back and swam to the opposite bank. I do not know how long I was in the river, but I was exhausted when I reached the other side," he said later. Found on the other side in an exhausted state by a Swiss peasant, he was given shelter until the police arrived.

In July 1971 an East German doctor, Peter Dobler, fled the Worker's Paradise by swimming for more than 26 hours from the holiday resort of Kuhlungsborn northwest to the West German island of Fehmarn. He followed a series of buoys that marked part of the route and used a map and emergency rations to survive the grueling journey, swimming almost the entire way before being found and picked up by a private boat.

See also: Alcatraz; Beniowski, Count Maurice; *Bounty;* Cuba, escape from; Dunkirk; French Guiana; Iron Curtain; Kennedy, John F.; Papillon; Tall, Robert; *Titanic*

SERVITUDE, ESCAPE INTO

Paradoxically, there are a few known instances of individuals who have tried to escape *into* servitude. In 1667, for example, the ruling Council of Barbados heard that seamen who did not want to fight against the Dutch had started deserting their ships while they were harbored offshore. They had hidden on the estates, begging the owners to take them on as servants. Although a great many servants and slaves envied the crews for the freedom they were perceived to enjoy, it was noted ironically that the sailors seemed to crave the security the servants and slaves were seen to possess. The problem became so serious that landowners were forbidden to employ the deserters.

SHEPPARD, JACK (1702–1725)

Jack Sheppard, probably the most legendary escapee of eighteenth-century England, threw away his hard-won freedom and allowed himself to be recaptured because he had developed a certain contempt for his adversaries.

During his short but dramatic life Sheppard had the distinction of twice escaping from Newgate Prison, the top-security prison of eighteenth-century England. First imprisoned there in 1724, Sheppard managed to break out on Sunday, 29 August, the day before he was due to go to the gallows. A girlfriend visiting him slipped a small file through the bars of his cell, and he wasted no time in cutting away at the window bars and slipping outside.

But sent back to Newgate soon afterward, he knew that another escape would be much harder. He was handcuffed and manacled with heavy leg irons that were attached to a staple fixed to the floor in the strongest cell in the prison, a room known as "the Castle," where he was to wait until his execution.

But there was no stopping this remarkable man. After quickly managing to snap off his handcuffs, he turned his attention to the chain that tied his legs together. Before long that, too, had been pulled apart. Though he was unable to remove the anklets that the chain had been attached to, he drew them as far up his legs as he could, to prevent them from making too much noise, and set about trying to find an escape route out of the room.

He started to climb through the fireplace and up the chimney but found his route blocked by an iron bar that had been built into the brickwork. Undeterred, he dug intensely at the brickwork with a broken link from his foot chain to pry the bar out of the wall.

He finished within an hour, having made a hole nearly three feet wide and six feet high, and was ready to continue his escape, now using the iron bar as a tool. Climbing through room after room, he eventually reached the leaden roof of the prison. From there he used a blanket rope to drop into the London streets below.

But he was not free yet. Not only was he still wearing prison clothes, which instantly identified him as an escapee, but he was also still unable to remove his heavy leg irons. Taking shelter in a cow house nearby, he struggled to free himself but got nowhere. The first blacksmith he contacted was entirely unsympathetic, recognizing him not only as an escapee from Newgate but as the legendary figure he had become. But he paid another with money he had saved, and it was not long before he was once again on his way.

In order to cross London to meet the friends and acquaintances who had no idea that he had escaped, he disguised himself as a beggar, tying a handkerchief around his head, tearing his woolen cap in several places, and moving from one poorhouse to the next until he finally got where he wanted.

But the jubilation he felt at escaping once more from Newgate proved to be his undoing. Insisting on driving past the prison gates in a horse-drawn carriage, with blinds drawn, it was clear that he enjoyed mocking his enemies. Not long after he had broken free he was recognized by a youth who worked in a public bar he was visiting nonchalantly. He died on the gallows on 16 November 1724, four weeks to the day since his escape.

References: Hibbert, Christian. *The Road to Tyburn: The Story of Jack Sheppard and the Underground.* London: Panther, 1959.

SING SING (1820–)

Built in the 1820s to house some of New York's most dangerous criminals, the giant prison at Sing Sing was also the setting for some audacious escapes.

Most of these were made by prisoners who hid themselves in the 20-acre yard in which they were allowed to take daily exercise and which allowed them access, if they were determined, to several old buildings, which potentially made excellent hiding places. There is a record of one prisoner, however, who found that he was unable to free himself from his hiding place and that it was too well concealed for anyone to bring him assistance. His skeleton was not found until ten years later.

Many escapees were also tempted to cross the Hudson River, which ran adjacent to the prison and which was cordoned off only by an iron fence. One particularly ingenious escapee even made a pair of rubber ducks that were fitted onto a headpiece, disguising a breathing apparatus that allowed him to stay underwater as he paddled away.

Like later prisoners in Alcatraz, some managed to escape by making dummies to fool guards, and there is one instance of a university student who took very little time to work out a way of picking apart his cell lock, using just a piece of wire and some parts from a pipe.

But on the whole successful escapes from this forbidding prison have been rare, and even those who have broken out have been quickly recaptured.

References: Lawes, Lewis E. *Life and Death in Sing Sing.* London: John Long, 1929.

SOBIBOR CONCENTRATION CAMP (1943)

Some prisoners are willing to try escape even though they know they will suffer extremely heavy casualties doing so. In 1943 the prisoners at the Nazi concentration camp at Sobibor in eastern Poland were so desperate that they were willing to brave the automatic fire of their captors in order to escape.

The escape plan was drawn up and organized by Alexander Pechersky, a Russian army officer who had been captured and imprisoned by the Germans some weeks before. Pechersky reasoned that a carefully orchestrated attack by a large number of inmates at just the right moment would have a chance against the camp guards, however well armed they might be. After making a careful surveillance of the camp and its routines, Pechersky arranged for a number of axes and hatchets to be made and smuggled to his acquaintances who were entrusted with putting the plan into action.

The first step of the plan was to dispatch the officer group that handled the everyday administration of the camp. The prisoners arranged that at 4 P.M. on the afternoon of 14 October, a senior officer, Unterscharführer Berg, would visit the tailor's shop in the camp to try on a uniform he had ordered; 15 minutes later two other senior offices would also visit the tailor. Several others were invited to the workshops for one reason or another, giving the 20 prisoners who were specially selected to carry out the killings their chance.

That afternoon, just as had been planned, the German officers entered the workshops and did not reappear. At quarter to five, Boris Tsibulsky, a prisoner who was entrusted with these first executions, returned to report to his fellow escapees that everything had gone as planned. The prisoners had also seized the officers' pistols and were now searching the dead officers' quarters to find more. Before long they also had six rifles with cartridges ready to use against the unsuspecting guards.

The prisoners now waited for the ringleaders to give the signal announcing it was time to head for the gates and march out of the camp. At the front of the approximately 600 prisoners who gathered in one of the camp yards was a group of 70 Soviet prisoners of war who had been hand-picked by Pechersky to lead an assault on the German arsenal. Their task was to seize the weapons needed to get out and to deprive the Germans of the weapons needed to stop them. At the same time, the others started to jostle and shove their way to the main gates.

Within minutes the attack on the German arsenal became a bloody failure, its attackers cut down by bursts of automatic fire from its defenders, who were by now well aware of what was going on. But this did not stop the others from breaking down the gates and fleeing, hurling stones at the guards they met and running as quickly as they could to the relative safety of the forests a few hundred yards away.

Many of the 600 escapees were killed or injured. Most were felled by automatic and rifle fire, though a minefield outside the camp also exacted heavy casualties. Even those who reached the forests were not safe from the massive search operation that was launched soon afterward to track them down. In all about 400 prisoners got away from Sobibor that autumn evening, leaving behind 48 dead guards in their wake.

See also: Auschwitz; Koldyczewo
References: Suhl, Yuri. *They Fought Back: The Story of Jewish Resistance in Nazi Europe.* London: MacGibbon and Gee, 1968.

SPARKS, JOHN (1902–1960)

In order to escape from Dartmoor, the British criminal John Sparks had to contend with more than just high walls and patrols. The prison is surrounded for miles by moors that demand great fitness and resource from those who flee.

Sparks was sent to Dartmoor in February 1939 with a track record of burglary, theft, and robbery. His plan to break out of Dartmoor was ingenious. Knowing that he had no chance of stealing the five keys he needed to get through the prison doors to the outside, he found an alternative: He memorized them. As the working parties to which he belonged were led back inside the prison, Sparks habitually engaged the officer in charge in conversation. This gave a chance to take a closer look at their shape before returning to his cell as quickly as he could in order to sketch what he had seen while his memory was still clear. He then stole some metal from the prison workshop in order to make replicas.

Sparks was brave as well as ingenious in the way he raised the money he knew he would need if he was to have any chance of keeping ahead of the law once he was outside. Aware that he faced a serious beating, possibly death, if he was caught, he began to gamble, using loaded dice, with some of the other prisoners. With the extra money he needed, and with a rope made from cloth and linen, he got ready to make his move.

One Wednesday evening in January 1940, when most of the other inmates were attending a choral class in the prison chapel, Sparks and two accomplices made it through all five of the gates. They used their rope, complete with a makeshift grappling hook, to climb over the 20-foot outer wall. Though their journey over the moors in midwinter was difficult—one of the escapees, Alex Marsh, nearly met his death in quicksand, and all suffered from frostbite—they were able to reach a railway line and escape first to Plymouth and then to London, where they found shelter with some of their acquaintances in the criminal underworld.

Involved in crime once again, Sparks was recaptured some months later. Perhaps he, like some other escapees, had become complacent after performing such an impressive feat as breaking out of Dartmoor.

References: Bean, J. P. *Over the Wall: True Stories of the Master Jail Breakers.* London: Headline, 1994.

SPARTACUS (C. 94–67 B.C.)

The acts of just one exceptional individual can sometimes change the course of history. The slaves' revolt against their masters that began in 71 B.C. and that nearly brought the entire Roman Empire, at the zenith of its power, to its knees was begun by just one remarkable slave, Spartacus.

Born into a slave family in approximately 94 B.C., Spartacus inherited from his parents not only their strength of will and physical prowess but also an intense desire to experience what they had never known: freedom from the Roman masters. Sent to the Nubian mines at a young age to excavate gold, he was determined to think the unthinkable and find a way of throwing aside the yoke of Roman rule.

His chance came in 71 B.C. when he was recognized by the Roman authorities as suitable material for gladiator training. Gladiators were chosen for their fighting ability and were trained to fight before vast crowds in Rome, either against each other in hand-to-hand combat or against lions. Though anything seemed better than the harsh life in the mines, Spartacus knew that the gladiators always fought to the death and that he would have a life expectancy of a few weeks, at most.

Wasting no time when he arrived at the gladiatorial training school, near Capua in central Italy, Spartacus quickly organized his fellow trainees and their wives, a mix of Gauls, Africans, and Thracians. Soon a plan had been developed that had a chance of succeeding against their guards, whom they outnumbered by five to one.

Arming themselves with knives, cleavers, spits, forks, and anything else that could conceivably be used as a weapon, the 200 slaves crept up on the sentries and killed them silently. But though they had moved as quietly as possible, they had not quite managed to hide from the remaining Roman soldiers, who now took up positions against them, closing ranks in the way that had worked against so many of the imperial enemies the Roman army had faced.

Seeing that the confrontation had reached a critical moment, Spartacus took charge of the situation and saw an opportunity to defeat the Romans. He ordered the other gladiators to circle the Roman position. They then began hurling rocks at them with all the force they could muster, and as the shocked soldiers shielded themselves, other slaves ran in and knifed them.

But though the slaves had won this particular engagement, they were not free yet. A nearby larger Roman force of several hundred men found out what had happened and was now on its way to crush them. Again Spartacus was quick to see what they would have to do if they were to have any chance of defeating this larger, better-armed, and better-trained force. He ordered his small army onto the mountain slopes that overlooked the road on which the soldiers were approaching at top speed, and the slaves again bombarded their enemy with all the rocks and boulders that they could find. Before long this relief column had been beaten back by slave army.

Against all the odds, Spartacus and his followers were now free to make their way across open countryside, gathering all the followers they could find and preparing to challenge Roman authority.

References: Ridley, Francis A. *Spartacus, the Leader of the Roman Slaves.* Ashford, UK: Maitland, 1963.

SPOONER, LT. COL. PAT
(1922–)

During World War II, a British soldier, Pat Spooner, showed exceptional determination and tenacity in order to rescue three senior military leaders from the Germans.

Because he had escaped from German captivity in central Italy and was still behind enemy lines, Spooner received a radio message from the British headquarters at Termoli, several hundred miles to the south, to contact two British generals, Sir Phillip Neame and Sir Richard O'Connor, and an air vice-marshall, Owen Boyd, who had all managed to escape from a prisoner of war camp for senior officers near Florence. Though they had all safely moved to a mountain hideaway, Spooner was ideally qualified for the job of leading them back to British lines.

The rescue plan was simple enough. Spooner would escort Neame, O'Connor, and Boyd across the Italian countryside to a rendezvous near Pesaro, on the Adriatic coast, where they would be picked up by a British submarine at 10 P.M. on 3 November 1943. Spooner was given the contact names of the British agents and sympathizers scattered throughout the countryside and was thoroughly briefed on the German counterespionage activities they would have to elude. He then set off for the monastery at Verna in the Apennines with high hopes, and it did not take long to find the three officers and to bring them to the coast as planned.

The party of escapees boarded a rowboat and made their way several hundred yards beyond the pier, signaling periodically with a flashlight to make contact with the submarine. Though at first they saw nothing, still they waited, straining their eyes in the dark for some sign of it. The waiting continued for one hour, then two hours, until they finally gave up hope and returned to base.

Though they had no idea of what could have gone wrong, Spooner was undeterred from rowing back to the meeting place the following night and continuing his vigil, this time in much colder and wetter conditions than the day before, for an answering signal from the submarine. For a few minutes, hearing the distant though unmistakable sound of an engine, they were sure their moment had come. But again their hopes were cruelly dashed, since its source proved to be only an Italian patrol boat. In fact, they were extremely lucky it had not seen them.

After renewing radio contact with British headquarters, arrangements were soon made for another, safer and more convenient, rendezvous, on the coastline near Cervia. But when the escape party once again made its way toward the coast to contact the submarine that was—supposedly—waiting offshore, good fortune continued to elude them. By chance, the place they had chosen was teeming with German military activity, and as they approached the coast they even walked straight through a full-scale mock battle. But even though enemy flares soared through the sky, shells burst, and small-arms fire crackled, they continued to the coast in order to find the submarine.

Incredibly, they were destined to continue waiting. After having struggled for several hours over arduous terrain and at great personal risk to a rowboat that took them offshore, they merely drifted for several hours in the freezing cold. Their signals went unanswered.

By now it was clear that they would have to take matters into their own hands, rather than relying on prearranged meetings, if they were to ever make it back safely to their own lines. It would be better, they decided, to find a boat of their own that could take them south to the British lines. But, extraordinarily, their plans were thwarted at the last minute. On 7 December, just before they were due to set sail, the Germans suddenly seized and impounded the fishing boat they planned to use. "Their suspicions had apparently been aroused," said Spooner years later, "though quite how we never knew" (Howard interview with Spooner).

It was not until 18 December that they finally managed to make some headway. Using the agent network to contact a sympathetic fisherman—who received 100,000 lire for his help—Spooner was able to find

another boat to take them south. Even this escape bid was fraught with dangers and risks: Rather than risking discovery and a firing squad, the fisherman could quite easily have kept his 100,000 lire and still handed them over to the German authorities, who would have generously rewarded him for doing so. And in mid-December they would have to brave stormy, rough weather that was daunting even in the most resilient vessels.

A few months later, one of the generals used his influence to find out what had happened to the promised submarine. It had, he learned, been diverted at the last moment "to another mission elsewhere"—a rather unflattering and unconvincing explanation for a rescue operation that could so easily have foundered as a result.

References: Howard, Roger. Interview with Pat Spooner.

STALIN, JOSEPH (1879–1953)

Like many other political activists of his day, the young Joseph Dzhugashvili—better known as Joseph Stalin—was exiled to Siberia for his revolutionary activities against the czarist regime in Russia. But he was determined to escape and resume the political struggle.

When Stalin was 24 he was arrested by the czar's secret police for stirring up political unrest and exiled for three years to Siberia. According to the official version of his life that was written and published during his years in power, Stalin escaped in January 1904, 14 months after arriving at the village of New Ula in Siberia. But there is some doubt as to whether he had in fact ever reached Siberia in the first place. It seems more likely that he had seized his chance during the long journey to the intended place of incarceration. Security during such journeys, which involved a great deal of discomfort for guards as well as to prisoners, is known to have been particularly lax.

The young Joseph Dzhugashvili was rearrested again in 1908 but he managed to slip away, although once again there are no reliable accounts of the details. What is certain, however, is that even when a prisoner did arrive in Siberia, it was not usually too hard for the really determined to escape, for though the czars enjoyed vast theoretical powers, in practice their rule extended over such enormous areas that the governments of particular regions had a great deal of scope to dissent from official policy. Many prisoners could also afford to bribe many of the guards and officials, not just with currency but also with alcohol and tobacco, and on occasion guards were also too inebriated to be able to watch over those who were supposed to be under their supervision.

Stalin certainly had little difficulty in executing his next escape attempt four years later. Arrested yet again in April 1912, he was sent to Narim in the Siberian province of Tomsk, a settlement of about 250 houses that had the heaviest concentration of political prisoners of any place in czarist Russia. He arrived there in the middle of July and had managed to escape by the beginning of September, apparently by simply walking

out of the main gate late one night and heading for Moscow.

The Siberian police, never noted for their efficiency, took some time to respond, for it was not until 3 November that the local officials ordered a general search for "the peasant of the village of Didi-Lilo, Joseph Vissarionovich Dzhugashvili." But the secret police in the capital were somewhat sharper. Having kept a careful watch on the political troublemakers whom Stalin visited on his return, they followed him not only through Moscow but also to St. Petersburg and the Baltic coast. But because they were anxious not to let his associates know of the surveillance, they acted too slowly. They failed to issue an order for his arrest in time to stop him from boarding a ship bound for Finland and thus allowed one of their greatest enemies to leave Russia at a critical time.

See also: Kerensky, Aleksandr; Russian Revolution and civil war; Trotsky, Leon
References: Radzinsky, Edward. *Stalin.* London: Hodder and Stoughton, 1996.

T

TALL, ROBERT (1922–)

In March 1942 a British soldier, Bob Tall, managed to elude his Japanese enemies and escape back to his own lines against overwhelming odds.

Bob Tall was a member of the Royal Engineers working at Senggarang in what is today Malaysia, when he and his company were surrounded by the Japanese Imperial Guard. Outgunned and outnumbered, resistance eventually crumbled, ranks broke, and men fled.

In the darkness Tall and a few colleagues were for a time able to evade the enemy by cutting a path through the thick jungle around them and using their well-practiced arts of jungle warfare to move silently, if slowly, away from their camp. But around midnight, just as they were beginning to think that they had escaped from the Japanese, they were suddenly challenged by an enemy patrol.

Tall was certainly quick thinking, even if his ploy seemed unrealistic. Suddenly raising his arm into the air, he screamed *"Heil Hitler"* and hoped they would give him the benefit of the doubt. But the Japanese were not fooled, and they opened up with a machine gun that, unknown to Tall, was already trained on their position.

Tall was shot through the leg, but he was just able to stagger away into the darkness, stepping over the bodies of his colleagues who had been either killed instantly or who were too seriously injured to move. The Japanese soldiers arrived quickly but in the pitch darkness and without flashlights they failed to notice him rolled up in a mud hole only a few feet from where they stood.

For the next six days Tall was entirely on his own as he limped toward the coast. He was able to dig most of the bullet fragments out of his wounds with his knife. He knew they would allow infection to set in fast if he failed to act as soon as possible. But though his leg was badly injured he reckoned he would still have the strength to sail from the island. When he at last reached the coast, he was able to make a simple sampan from a piece of wood, some rope, and some discarded pieces of sail. He set off and let the winds blow him away from the island.

After several days, beginning to be affected by delirium and extreme hunger, he was found by two Chinese fishermen, Lim Sim Guam and Lin Pie. They took him ashore and helped him recover before setting him off in the direction of Pekan Baru. There he would be able to link up with the Australian army. After a month of traveling from island to island Tall eventually reached friendly shores.

Not surprisingly, Tall's escape, which had revealed the highest levels of physical stamina, resource, and determination, amazed those of his former colleagues who survived the war. They were astonished to learn that he had not met the same unfortunate end as so many others in his unit.

See also: Japanese army, prisoners of; Sea, escape and rescue at

References: Daws, Gavin. *Prisoners of the Japanese.* New York: William Morrow, 1994.
Kinvig, Clifford. *River Kwai Railway: The Story of the Burma-Siam Railroad.* London: Brasseys, 1992.
Perret, Geoffrey. *There's a War to Be Won: The United States Army in World War II.* New York: Random House, 1991.

TCHERNAVIN FAMILY (1930)

While fleeing Stalin's secret police in 1930, a leading Russian professor and his family narrowly prevented their rescuers from becoming their enemy.

The Tchernavin family set off from the White Sea and walked more than 100 miles through thick forest and swamp toward the Finnish border. But as exhaustion set in and they lost their way, they decided to change their plans. The professor would go on and find help, they agreed, while his wife and children would stay behind and recuperate in an empty forest lodge they had come across.

After they had waited six days, the family started to fear the worst.

Thinking it was the only means he had of signaling to his lost father, the son stood outside the mountain hut and sang out loud, his clear voice reaching far into the area.

Though he had no way of knowing it, his voice was heard both by his father, some distance away, and by the two Finns who were escorting him. It could not have come at a better time because the Finnish men, having heard the professor's story, had agreed to walk with him to find the mountain hut and his family. However, fearing that Tchernavin might really be a Bolshevik leading them into a trap, they had allowed him just two hours to find his family. If they had not found them in that time, they said, they would kill him with the hunting rifles they were carrying. But at almost exactly the moment they became suspicious and barred his way, they heard his son's voice in the distance, carried by the wind.

Whether the boy's timing was coincidental, or whether he was inspired by the same intuition that has perhaps played a part in others stories of escapes and rescues, the family were at last able to continue their walk into exile, three weeks after leaving their homeland.

See also: Russian Revolution and civil war
References: Tchernavin, Tatiana. *Escape from the Soviets.* London: Hamish Hamilton, 1993.

TEHRAN (1953)

In 1953 a CIA venture in Tehran, Iran, led to a dramatic escape.

Because Dr. Mohammed Mossadiq, Iranian prime minister during the early 1950s, was more sympathetic to anti-American influences than they would have liked, the CIA conspired to remove him from power and replace him with their own choice, General Fazlollah Zahedi. But when Mossadiq got wind of the plot and forestalled it, some of those involved in the conspiracy were forced to take flight.

Playing a key role in the operation as head of CIA operations in the region, Kermit Roosevelt received a message late at night that things had gone badly wrong and that he would have to make urgent contact with Zahedi. Roosevelt drove to Zahedi's residence, where he found his fellow conspirator standing at the door, casually dressed and with suitcases at his side, all ready to go into hiding.

In what he later referred to as his "blanket routine," Roosevelt told the general to lie down in the back of the car before throwing a large blanket on top of him in case they were stopped at checkpoints. As quickly as he dared, he then drove him to the U.S. embassy compound, hiding him there until the situation cooled.

Two others who were rescued by Roosevelt in this way were the British intelligence officers, known by the pseudonyms Nossey and Cafron, responsible for the area. In the highly volatile political climate, with mobs starting to take to the streets in support of Mossadiq, they were delighted to have the support of their American opposite numbers.

References: Roosevelt, Kermit. *Countercoup.* New York: McGraw-Hill, 1979.

THE TERROR (1793)

After 1789 the leaders of the French Revolution sought to tighten their political grip over a country in turmoil, and all those deemed "suspect" were detained in prisons, and if they were thought—sometimes on a mere whim—to be a threat to the regime they were sent straight to the guillotine. Hundreds met their end in this grisly way.

Quite a few managed to escape execution by fleeing before they were arrested. At a time when all members of the nobility were considered suspect by the revolutionary authorities, many used all their resources, contacts, and ingenuity to avoid capture, often going into hiding or changing their identity altogether in order to do so. The easiest escapes were made by rich suspects who were placed under house arrest, even if they were forced to surrender most of their personal fortunes in order to bribe their guards for their lives.

There are also a few surviving records of escapes by people already in prison and awaiting execution. In the notes left by one prison warden, for example, there is an account of such a breakout in which a leading revolutionary prosecutor, Jean Jacques Fouquier-Tinville, unwittingly played a role.

Fouquier-Tinville was apt to take nocturnal walks through the prison corridors, as if to relish the power of life and death that he had over its unfortunate inmates. One night he caught a glimpse of a prison warden moving furtively through the shadows and called to ask him what he was doing.

From the shadows the guard replied that he had just finished work and was just leaving to have a minute's rest. His manner seemed a little nervous, but Fouquier-Tinville had no reason to question his story. Before moving on, the prosecutor told the guard to take a message to his house, close by, and shouted out to the guards at the gate to allow him out.

Fouquier-Tinville's order was transmitted from gate to gate, and the warden left the prison unchallenged. The porters had not recognized him, but they had assumed he was a new recruit, and in any case they did not want to be seen to question the orders of a revolutionary prosecutor who had a notorious reputation for bloody violence.

Fouquier-Tinville had asked the warden to take a note to his wife saying that he would not be back from the prison until late and so would not need anything to eat. But when he did finally return home, at 11 o'clock, he found to his fury that the message had not been delivered. And the next morning, when one of the prison guards complained that someone had stolen his best suit and it was found that a prisoner had gone missing, his worst fears were confirmed.

Ironically, Fouquier-Tinville had made the escape possible by arranging for the "sentry" to pass the prison gates. But, never one to admit to his own mistakes, he had the warder whose uniform was stolen punished: The guard should, argued Fouquier-Tinville, have noticed much earlier that the uniform was missing.

A few others condemned to the guillotine escaped. In his memoirs, Viennot de Vaublanc, a French nobleman, related the story of one such condemned man, Philippe de Chateaubrun, who managed to save his own life.

Having been taken to the Place de la Révolution with 20 or so others, de Chateaubrun was placed last in the queue lined up before the guillotine. But after a dozen or so had already met their deaths, he had a lucky reprieve: The guillotine broke and needed some considerable time to be repaired. The prisoner noticed that the enormous crowds gathered to watch the killings seemed mesmerized by the guillotine and scarcely noticed the condemned. He might, therefore, have a way of escaping in the failing light. So he leaned on those behind him, and the crowds "mechanically made way for him, til gradually, by no effort of his own, he came to the last ranks of the crowd" (dé Vaublanc 1833).

But de Chateaubrun was not free yet. He still had his hands tied behind his back, and he looked conspicuous without wearing a heat of the sort that everyone else was wearing. Going up to a workman, he claimed casually that some friends had played a practical joke on him by tying his hands up and taking his hat, and he begged the workman to cut the ropes. With his hands free, the escapee went into a shop and begged the owner to take a letter to a friend, who would lend him the hat he needed as well as bring him some money. Half an hour later, Monsieur de Chateaubrun was on his way, hat on head, having paid the shop owner for his trouble and having escaped a gruesome death.

See also: Louis XVIII; Paine, Thomas
References: Blanc, Olivier. *Last Letters: Prisons and Prisoners of the French Revolution.* London: A. Deutch, 1987.

dé Vaublanc, Viénot. *Mémoires*. Paris: G. A. Denta, 1833.

TITANIC (1912)

Shortly after midnight on 14 April 1912, the British-American liner *Titanic* struck an iceberg in the northern Atlantic and sank with the loss of 1,200 lives. Spectacular efforts were made to escape and to rescue from the sinking hulk, even though the event is also renowned for the infamous *failure* of some nearby ships to go to the assistance of the stricken liner.

There were only a small number of lifeboats on board. Most of those who got away from the liner that night were women and children, who were given priority by men who considered it their duty as gentlemen to stand aside. As word of the ship's fate spread to those who seemed to sense the seriousness of the situation, multimillionaires stood aside for women and children, no matter what class they were traveling, and wore their dinner jackets so that they could at least die bravely and with some honor. Though most who escaped had been given precedence in this way, a few found their way into the boats surreptitiously or through luck.

One lucky survivor was an Irish drunk from Belfast, Paddy Dillon, who is thought to have been under the influence of a large amount of brandy when he threw himself off the deck as it stood perpendicular in the water. Though he would not have survived in the freezing waters for more than a few minutes, he happened to land close to one of the lifeboats and was picked up almost immediately.

Another individual who had a lucky escape was a young officer named James Beesly. After lowering one of the lifeboats, packed with passengers, down the side of the massive ship to the water below, Beesly prepared to be hoisted back up again to lower the next one. But seeing that the next lifeboat was already on its way down, he suddenly realized, to his horror, that he was unable to release the fall ropes that had taken the boat down and that they would be crushed if they did not move off immediately. So he cut the ropes holding the boat in place and drifted out to sea with the other passengers.

There is also some doubt about the identity of some of those who claimed to be crew members and used their "official" position to get a place in the boats. One survivor, Marian Thayer, later testified that she saw one man in the boat, "who said he was a quartermaster," behaving in a way that was

Survivors from the Titanic *are hoisted aboard the* Carpathia *the morning after the sinking of the great liner. (UPI/Corbis-Bettmann)*

"absolutely inefficient." She added that "he could give us no directions or aid whatsoever and besides was most disagreeable. I do not think that he was a quartermaster" (Davie 1986, 51–53). Though some of those who tried to get away were turned back, occasionally at gunpoint, a number of men are also known to have hidden in the rowboats before they were used. When a Cornishwoman, Mrs. Davies, got into one of the lifeboats, she found a lot of men lying down in the bottom, several stretched out under its thwarts.

One of the officers who went to great personal effort to help others evacuate was lucky to find himself at their side. Charles Lightoller, a senior officer, had worked tirelessly to organize the flight of the rowboats and had gallantly refused to put himself on board the last one, a small collapsible boat. Soon after it had been lowered to the sea and started to move away, the *Titanic* suddenly plunged further into the ocean, still afloat but taking one more leap toward its complete immersion that was to follow minutes later. Lightoller was sucked by the sudden fierce rush of water into the vast forward funnel before him. He thought his hour had come, but after only a few seconds he was just as dramatically blown by a blast of hot air back out of the funnel into the water. Struggling to the surface, Lightoller found himself within range of the boat he had helped to launch shortly before, and he was able to cling to a rope its crew threw to him just as the mighty liner took its last plunge into the depths of the ocean.

Most of the lifeboats did not trouble to pick up those who were thrown off the decks of the *Titanic* as it rose vertically and sank below the waves, even though, in the starlight, the escapees could not fail to see the horrific scene before them—a mass of bodies and faces bobbing in the water—or hear the cries for help, cries that, years later, haunted the survivors more than anything else. Instead, most rowed on furiously, convinced, sometimes with justification, that their boats were already too full to cope with any more or that the sheer mass of people in the water would swamp the lifeboats or pull them under if they turned back.

The one exception was boat number 14, piloted by an officer named Harold Lowe. Lowe shouted to the boats around him to stop and take on his boat's passengers. He then turned his boat around and rowed, with his fellow crewmen, toward the scene of carnage. Though most of the passengers had frozen to death within minutes in waters that were well below freezing, Lowe and his crewmates saved the lives of four people that night. One of the women who traveled with him that night later recalled his exceptional efforts: "His bearing gave us great confidence. . . . as I look back now, he seems to me to personify the best traditions of the British sailor."

Despite such remarkable rescue efforts, the sinking of the *Titanic* is also infamous for the conspicuous absence of any attempt to rescue its unfortunate passengers by others who were in a position to help. One of the great mysteries of the story concerns the identity of a ship that a large number of those on board saw in the distance but that then just disappeared into the night. For a while, one of the lifeboats, number 8, steered toward what appeared to be a distant steamer: "There were two lights, not further than ten miles away," recalled one survivor, "everybody saw them, (including) all the ladies in the boat" (Davie 1986).

The other glaring failure was on the part of a nearby ship, the merchant ship *Californian*. Only a few hours before, the *Californian* had encountered the same ice field that was to trap the *Titanic*, and it was less than 100 miles away when tragedy struck. As the subsequent inquiry into the episode forcefully argued, its captain could have easily warned all other shipping in the area of the danger. And, when it saw distress signals emanating from the very area where the crew knew a ship might be in danger, the ship could have "pushed through the ice to the open water without any serious risk and come to the rescue of the *Titanic*. Had she done so, she might have saved many, if not all, of the lives that were lost," stated Lord Mersey.

Instead, the main rescue operation that night was undertaken not by the *Californian* or the passengers on board but by the

Carpathia, which picked up those who had managed to flee in lifeboats. When the liner's SOS reached the *Carpathia,* its captain rushed to the area at 17.5 knots, beating the many others that were also on their way to help. One of those who took credit for this rescue operation was the young wireless operator, who was supposed to have shut the radio down and gone to bed at midnight but whose enthusiasm for his job meant that he was able to receive the emergency message half an hour later.

Another who took part in the rescue operation was Rigel, a huge black Newfoundland dog that had belonged to a senior officer of the *Titanic* and that swam in the icy water for more than three and a half hours before the *Carpathia* approached. When the ship failed to see one of the lifeboats in front of it and looked set to plow straight into it, the dog was able to bring it to the attention of *Carpathia*'s crew by barking, sparing the *Titanic* survivors, too weary to shout loudly, from another disaster.

By virtue of its efforts, the *Carpathia* has since been one of the most famous names in the story of rescue operations.

References: Davie, Michael. *Titanic: The Full Story of a Tragedy.* London: Grafton, 1987.

Pellegrino, Charles. *Her Name, Titanic: The Untold Story of the Sinking and Finding of the Unsinkable Ship.* London: Robert Hale, 1990.

TOKYO, RAID ON (1942)

Some of the pilots who bailed out of their B25 after the first U.S. raid on the Japanese mainland, on 18 April 1942, had an unusually pleasant surprise.

The crew members of the 13 planes that took off in the Pacific from the aircraft carrier *Hornet* planned to raid specific targets in Tokyo with incendiary bombs before flying to a designated airfield in China to refuel. But since it was the first such mission, many of the pilots encountered serious navigational difficulties, and the crew of one plane, having gone seriously astray after raiding Tokyo, began to run out of fuel.

Forced to bail out, the airmen could tell only that they were somewhere on the Chinese mainland. But speaking not a word of Chinese, without maps or contacts who could help them, and wary that they might even be in an area controlled by the Japanese, they faced the prospect of a long, grueling journey over thousands of miles if they were to ever get back to their own lines.

But they were rescued in a manner they never anticipated. They boarded a train and when they had traveled more than 20 miles, they were greeted by an extraordinary sight. For gathered around the station at Yushan was a huge crowd of at least 5,000 Chinese, all carrying banners, smiling and greeting them like lost friends. "Welcome to Yushan," said one well-dressed individual in perfect English as he stepped forward, "I am the Mayor of Yushan, and this reception is to welcome you as American heroes." The pilots looked at each other in disbelief: "24 hours after we'd taken off from the carrier," wrote one afterward, "here we were, being welcomed by a crowd somewhere in the backwoods of China."

It later emerged that the U.S. Navy had broadcast news of their raid on Tokyo by radio throughout the whole region. The men were seen and recognized as downed U.S. pilots by a railway stationmaster.

See also: Japanese army, prisoners of

References: Daws, Gavin. *Prisoners of the Japanese.* New York: William Morrow, 1994.

Kinvig, Clifford. *River Kwai Railway: The Story of the Burma-Siam Railroad.* London: Brasseys, 1992.

Perret, Geoffrey. *There's a War to Be Won: The United States Army in World War II.* New York: Random House, 1991.

TOWER OF LONDON

A haunting epitaph is inscribed on the tombstone of one unfortunate prisoner of the Tower of London who tried to find a way out but failed: "Now do I thank thee, Death, and bless thy power that I have passed the guard and escaped the Tower." Surrounded by high walls and a deep moat and always heavily patrolled, the Tower of London was renowned as not only one of the most unpleasant places in which to be imprisoned but also one of the most difficult from which to escape. But during the 850 years in which it was used to house political

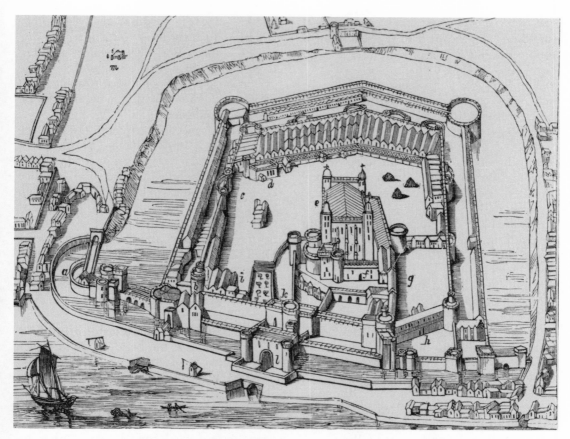

Despite its formidable defenses, a few ingenious and desperate prisoners succeeded in escaping from the Tower of London. (North Wind Picture Archives)

prisoners, spies, and traitors, a handful proved that its walls were not impregnable.

The first known successful escape was undertaken by Bishop Edward Flambard, who had enjoyed considerable influence at the court of William Rufus but who had suddenly fallen from grace on the accession of Henry I in 1100. Knowing that the bishop was unpopular with the people of London, whose goodwill he had to rely on, Henry had had him sent to the tower.

Affluent and influential, Flambard's chances of escape always looked good. He surrounded himself with his own servants in his prison quarters and sometimes held lavish parties. His warders were often invited, and he soon took advantage of their inebriated state. One of the wine jars secretly contained a rope. He quietly pulled it from the jar, carefully crawled out a prison window that overlooked the moat, and lowered himself down.

Cutting his hands to ribbons as he descended, the bishop found that the rope was a good 20 feet too short to reach the water below him. Since he had gone too far to be able to climb back up, he had to drop into the arms of his rescue party, who were waiting in a boat in the moat below and who now rowed him to safety.

Flambard's task was made easier by the fact that he had acted as the Tower's constable for two years prior to his arrest and therefore had a good idea about how to find his way outside. Moreover, during the Middle Ages security measures were gradually increased. The thickness of the towers' walls was increased to up to eight feet, its windows were barred, and patrols were stepped up. Draconian penalties against staff who misbehaved also ensured that candidates for escape had a great deal of trouble finding inside accomplices, even if they could reward them out of their own pocket. Every time someone escaped, suspects were rounded up, interrogated, and sometimes executed. But still there were a few who got away.

Most of these used disguise to escape. One such was the earl of Nithsdale, whose participation in the abortive Jacobite Rebellion of 1715 had condemned him to the tower. But when, late one February afternoon, his wife and three ladies in waiting paid him one of their regular visits, the warders had no idea that it was the opening move of an escape plan that had been carefully considered and that was now being calmly executed.

As soon as they reached the earl's chambers, one of the four women, a Mrs. Mills, quickly whipped out her own disguise and passed on the clothes she had been wearing to the earl, whose transformation into a new Mrs. Mills was as quick as it was dramatic. Surrounded by the three other women, the earl walked past the checkpoints. The sentries, watching the party in the failing light, saw nothing unusual. With the very considerable funds at their disposal, about £20,000, they were able to bribe their way by boat out of the country and into exile at Rome. The real Mrs. Mills was also able to flee before the alarm was raised.

William Seymour was imprisoned in the tower because, by marrying Arabella Stuart, he became an heir to the throne of James I and a possible source of conspiracy. He made his getaway by adopting the disguise of another visitor to the tower. From the natural vantage point of his rooms in St. Thomas's Tower, Seymour had carefully watched the comings and goings of prison visitors for weeks, and it did not take him long to see his opportunity: a carter who visited almost daily to pile his wagon with hay and firewood.

As a well-behaved prisoner, Seymour enjoyed relative freedom to move around the tower, and he soon used it to persuade the carter to accept a handsome bribe to let him ride on the cart to freedom outside. By late May 1611, he also had ready the other key ingredient essential to his plan: his disguise—a black wig, false beard, and battered hat—which was smuggled into the prison on the instructions of Arabella, and which made him indistinguishable from the real wagon-master.

Later that month the guards failed to see the carter hide himself behind the hay bales on his cart and a heavily disguised Seymour take his place. Nor did they notice Seymour's absence in time to stop him from being whisked downstream by a boat that was waiting for him on the Thames. Seymour escaped and lived happily ever after. But Arabella, without whom he could never have gotten free, was captured and executed shortly afterward. Seymour made no effort to help her escape, nor did he even appeal for clemency for her.

In 1597 John Gerard, a Jesuit priest who suffered badly at the hands of the tower's professional torturers and inquisitors, used another way of escaping their terrible clutches. He got out of his cell by chipping around the door's stonework, and, darting around quickly to avoid the patrols and sentries who guarded almost every corner, he was able to find his way onto the high wall that overlooked the moat. He had sent a message to contacts outside via a sympathetic prison warder who pitied him for the terrible injuries his inquisitors had inflicted. As he peered over the edge, he saw that his messenger had kept his word and delivered his messages. His contacts were now waiting to put their plan of action into effect.

In the middle of the moat, he could just see a boat whose occupants were hurling a small iron ball, with a rope attached, over the moat to the wall above. He secured the rope to a cannon and waited for the signal that would let him know the rope had also been fastened at the other end. Though his prison ordeal had badly sapped his strength, he somehow managed to slide across just before the guards heard the commotion and raised the alarm. Spirited away to a carefully chosen hiding place, Gerard was to die peacefully in 1637.

The last known escape from the tower happened more recently than most people suppose. The tower was used by the British authorities during World War I, when its prisoners included a British soldier who had been court-martialed for signing invalid checks. Feeling slightly bored one evening, the soldier decided he wanted an evening out in the West End, and he soon devised an escape plan. Since he had had quite a large number of visitors to his room, he simply waited until a new sentry was posted in the corridor and then calmly walked outside, overcoat wrapped around himself, as if he had just been visiting the prisoner. Having enjoyed a good night out in town, he casually arrived back at the tower and attempted to reimprison himself.

References: Abbot, Geoffrey. *Great Escapes from the Tower of London.* Nelson Lanes, UK: Hendon, 1988.

TRENCK, BARON FREDERICK VON DER (1726–1794)

Like his French contemporary Henri de Latude, the young Frederick Von Der Trenck unexpectedly found himself as the unfortunate victim of arbitrary royal displeasure and was determined to escape.

At the age of 19 he had already been a star officer in the Prussian Guards, a lover of the Princess Amelia, and a favorite of King Frederick, but to his astonishment he found himself under arrest, in May 1745, on a charge of treason. The real reason was simply that the king wanted Trenck out of the way so that Amelia's marriage to a Swedish prince, a marriage that suited wider Prussian interests during a time of great international tension, would remain intact.

Trenck now suddenly found himself out of love, stripped of rank, and in prison, facing whatever term of imprisonment the king decreed. Perhaps most importantly, his name and that of his family had been disgraced by the charges, even though they were wholly fictitious. Taken to a fortress near the town of Graz to serve his sentence, he soon determined to find some way out.

The unfortunate consequences of his first attempt would have deterred a lesser soul. Having filed through the bars of his win-

dow, he rappelled down the side of the prison, using (like de Latude) ropes made of linen sheets tied together. But when he tried to cross the ditch on the edge of the compound, he got stuck in its deep, thick mud. He was unable to free himself and was forced to call to the sentries for assistance. To punish him for trying to escape, the Prussian guards refused to help him and merely watched him rolling around in the mud for the rest of the day.

A second attempt to escape the castle at Graz also nearly succeeded. Though the commandant had ordered that Trenck be guarded at all times and at close quarters, this paradoxically had the opposite effect from what was intended. Because Trenck became well acquainted with many of the various soldiers who were sent to guard him, he was soon able to use his considerable powers of persuasion and financial resources to stir a rebellion in the ranks against the brutal discipline of the Prussian army. Before long there were 32 soldiers who were willing to rebel against the regime and who planned to release Trenck before fleeing to Bohemia. But a traitor betrayed the conspiracy and once again Trenck's high hopes were dashed. Most of those implicated fled at the last minute and reached Bohemian soil safely, but Trenck was left behind in his cell.

It was not until he met one Alexander von Schell, in December 1746, that his luck changed. Von Schell was an army officer who, like many accomplices to an escape, was seriously disaffected by his career and whose life, moreover, was becoming more and more difficult under the strain of gambling debts. Though he was a serving officer, not a prisoner, at the time when he met Trenck, the two men got along well and soon planned to escape.

Von Schell's method of escape was the most conspicuous imaginable. Dressed in a loud scarlet officer's cloak and carrying his sword, he marched the prisoner out of his room. "I am taking this prisoner to the Officer's Mess for a moment," he called out to the astonished sentry before him, "so stay there and wait." Quickly crossing the prison ramparts, along a highly precipitous route that none of the few who watched dared to follow, they leaped into the moat before them and headed into the mountains.

Minutes later they heard the sound that struck terror into the hearts of every deserter from the Prussian army: the sound of light artillery. Light artillery fired at distinct intervals was used as a signal to local people that deserters were on the run. They knew that almost immediately villagers would take to the streets searching for them, eagerly seeking the generous reward offered for their capture.

As a consequence, the two fugitives took a route opposite the one they thought everyone would anticipate. Instead of heading for Bohemia, they moved toward Silesia, crossing a frozen river and following its path until they felt sure they had slipped through the cordon of peasants who were undoubtedly all around them.

Before the two men finally crossed the border into safety, they had one very lucky escape from the clutches of the Prussians. Reliably informed that the army was conducting an intensive search of the area in pursuit of deserters, they felt sure that their capture was imminent. But when they did come face to face with their enemy, they saw, to their relief, only a single officer, who did not know their true identities but who took pity with their plight. Telling them exactly which route to take to avoid the search and to reach the border as quickly as possible, they narrowly managed to slip through the net.

Nearly half a century later, however, Trenck was unable to escape the imprisonment of the Jacobins, who detained him in Paris before executing him as a supposed enemy of the Revolution in 1794.

References: De Jeu, Vicomte. *A Prussian Casanova.* London: A. C. Black, 1924.

TROTSKY, LEON (1879–1940)

Though he was forced to leave his family behind him, the young revolutionary Leon Trotsky escaped czarist captivity in order to resume his political struggle.

The young Russian, originally named Lev Davidovich Bronstein, had been arrested as a revolutionary in 1898 and was sent to Siberia after enduring more than three months of solitary confinement. But his decision to escape was far from easy, for he was painfully aware that he would probably never see his wife and small children again and that they would face a deeply uncertain future without him. After a prolonged period of personal anguish, he concluded that his work toward the revolution should take priority.

He left the village of Verkhoyansk, where he was being held, concealed under a load of hay and headed for nearby Irtutsk. There he picked up the clothes that had been left for him by some fellow revolutionaries, whom he had contacted shortly before his escape, as well as a false passport that borrowed the name of one of the prison warders he had encountered: Trotsky. Using this passport, he was eventually able to cross the border into Austria in September 1902.

The experience of detainment in Siberia was not enough to deter him from further revolutionary activity on his native soil. Returning to Russia in February 1905, he was once again arrested, charged with organizing a soviet congress, and this time he was sentenced to lifelong exile in Siberia. But even as he left St. Petersburg to begin his sentence, Trotsky had already started to plan his next escape. Though this time he did not have to choose between his party and his family, he did have to consider his chances of survival on a daring journey that would take him first along the River Sosva and across the huge expanses of the Russian plains.

At first sight, his escape ambitions seemed unrealistic, for in the first place he and 13 fellow prisoners were escorted by more than 50 guards, and all the convicts were forced to carry leg irons that were clamped on if they were caught trying to escape. But Trotsky also knew that the regime in Siberia was lax, mainly because the authorities assumed that anyone who could escape from their remote exile and cross the extremely arduous terrain deserved to go free.

When the party stopped at the small town of Berezovo for a two-day rest, Trotsky put his plan into effect. Coached by a fellow prisoner who was a physician, he pretended to be suffering from heart problems and was allowed to remain behind with his two guards while the others went on. Assuming that their prisoner was in no fit state to run off, the guards relaxed and gave him the chance he wanted.

After a 500-mile week-long trek, and with the help of Siberian tribesmen in various tiny settlements who sold him a sleigh and reindeer, Trotsky at last reached the Urals. Claiming first to be a member of a polar expedition and then a government official, he finally reached the railway on horseback. At the station the secret police watched him dismount and take off the thick fur coats that had helped to keep him alive but made no attempt to stop him. Before long, he was back in St. Petersburg and was in contact with his fellow revolutionaries, Lenin and Martov.

References: Volkogonov, Dmitri. *Trotsky: The Eternal Revolutionary.* London: HarperCollins, 1996.

UNDERGROUND RAILROAD (1830–1863)

Though it lacked any formal structure, organization, or leadership, the Underground Railroad allowed a great many runaway slaves to reach the freedom of Canada.

The "railroad" was an escape route that facilitated the passage of runaway slaves, mainly from the South, through the northern states to freedom in Canada. The slaves traveled not just by train, although after the mid-1840s the railroads played a key role, but by horse and carriage, by steamer, and, for many, on foot. They were helped along the way by the spontaneous acts of many different individuals, such as John Parker, who acted independently as "conductors," guiding the runaways from one place to the next.

Many of these conductors were former slaves who wanted to help others escape. Many were whites, whose abolitionism was often based in their Quakerism or Methodism, and sometimes just in their sympathy and benevolence. But whatever their motives, all worked voluntarily and out of goodwill, and did their best to find others further along the route whom the fugitives could contact next.

A handful of individuals were prepared to go to much greater lengths to help unhappy slaves escape. For 12 years during the 1830s and 1840s John Fairfield regularly traveled from his home in Ohio to the southern states to help secure slaves' freedom. Posing as a slave merchant who was interested in buying slaves for his own needs, he was able to actively support their escape attempts or to supply would-be runaways with money and information about the conductors who would help spirit them away. During the 1850s Harriet Tubman, a former slave who in 1849 managed to escape from her harsh owners in Maryland, led more than 300 escapees north, managing to elude the enemies tempted by the huge $12,000 reward offered for her capture. Levi Cofin, a Quaker merchant from Ohio, was responsible for the escape of perhaps as many as 3,000 runaways.

Once they had slipped away from the immediate clutch of their owners, fugitives would usually try to turn to one of the known sympathizers in the region who would be willing to help them along the way. Word often spread fast from one slave to the other about these sympathizers, a few of whom were sometimes intrigued to know how they had acquired such a reputation. But perhaps because they had written newspaper articles against the practice of slavery, or because they had expressed such sentiments to those already working as "conductors," they would find themselves approached by desperate fugitives seeking shelter and wanting to be pointed toward the Canadian border.

Most of these runaways would arrive on a doorstep, already having traveled a considerable distance on foot or by carriage, and when they left they usually carried on in the same way. But though the road was well established before the 1840s, from the 1840s on many traveled by steamer over the seas and waterways. A good number of owners and crew members of the transport ships that often docked at southern ports to deliver and collect merchandise were sympathetic to their plight and were happy to help them along their way. Slaves often swam long distances to get on board their vessels. Others would pose as dock workers, carrying goods on board and then disappearing with the assistance of the crew.

Many runaway slaves found freedom with the assistance of the Underground Railroad, as depicted in this dramatic painting. (Library of Congress)

That they were allowed to stay on board is admirable testimony to the magnanimity of the owners and captains, who knew their insurance was void if they were caught carrying such unauthorized passengers and who risked financial ruin if something went wrong.

Other slaves walked alongside the canals. Because the towpaths were far emptier than ordinary roads, many runaways were guided by their conductors along the paths that ran alongside the many canals that were proliferating throughout central America. But with the construction of the railroads from the 1830s on, the railroads soon became the favorite mode of escape. A runaway could board a train that swiftly took the escapee considerable distances along their long journey.

Many of the "conductors" on the Underground Railroad were employees of the railroad companies. Typically, escapees would board freight trains—which were far less likely to be boarded by slave catchers—and relied on one or more of the employees

to watch over them during their journey. If word reached them that a slave catcher was waiting to board at the next station or stopping point, the train would stop or slow down so the fugitive passengers could disembark. In the same way, it was not uncommon for the trains to slow down to pick up fugitives who they had heard were waiting at a specific point. The engineers often knew nothing of these unofficial stopping points until the last minute, but they rarely refused the request of one or more of their staff. The officials in charge of the railway companies generally knew something of such goings-on, but they do not appear to have ever protested.

Some of the stationmasters became highly adept at the arts of disguise. The light skin of a mulatto could be made even whiter if the right makeup was worn, and if a wig and well-fitted suit were added, the runaway was virtually unrecognizable as a slave. Sympathetic Quakers could often disguise runaway women with the bonnet and heavy veil worn by their own womenfolk, and the wives of many Underground conductors are known to have organized sewing circles to maintain generous supplies of these and other disguises.

See also: Brown, Henry; Fugitive Slave Laws; Parker, John; Spartacus
References: Blassingame, Charles L. *The Underground Railroad.* New York: Prentice Hall, 1987.
Breyfogle, William A. *Make Free: The Story of the Underground Railroad.* Philadelphia: Lippincott, 1958.

U.S. PRISONER OF WAR CAMPS (1941–1945)

Of the many thousands of Nazi prisoners who were held in camps on the U.S. mainland, very few escapees ever succeeded in reaching the Canadian or Mexican borders and leaving the country. But paradoxically, the United States proved in at least one respect to be ideally suited to the purposes of many of the 2,803 runaway POWs who succeeded in escaping from their camps.

Whereas U.S. prisoners of the Vietnamese or the British prisoners of the Japanese were immediately recognized by the civilians who saw them, the Germans who did manage to escape captivity found that they usually aroused no suspicion at all from the Americans they met along the way. This was not just because word of an escape, or even of the presence of a POW camp, was slow to spread in a country of such size. Rather, it was also because in such a racially and culturally heterogeneous society no one thought twice about meeting someone with a strong German accent or even someone who spoke no English and would happily offer them their assistance. It was largely this heterogeneity, for example, that allowed one escapee from Camp Ellis in Washington, Illinois, to change his name and disappear into the anonymous masses of Chicago and evade detection until after the war. Hundreds, perhaps thousands, of others escaped in a similar way.

However, very few succeeded in crossing U.S. international borders. Two who escaped from Camp Scottsbluff in Nebraska, for example, came close but were caught in Philadelphia while trying to board a ship bound for Europe. Only one individual is known to have gotten back to Europe, an escapee from a camp in Oklahoma who moved to Baltimore before finding employment on a Lisbon-bound freighter and finally reaching the Portuguese shore. Most runaways, it appears, knew little of the country where they were being held and were astonished at its sheer size.

References: Gansberg, J. M. *Stalag USA.* New York: Thomas Y. Cromwell, 1994.

V

VALCOUR ISLAND (1776)

During the American War of Independence, some American sailors had a lucky escape from the British fleet, by which they had suddenly been surrounded.

The Americans had been cornered on the evening of 11 October by 22 ships of the British fleet, under Captain James Pringle, 20 miles north of Crown Point in a channel between Valcour Island and the west shore of Lake Champlain. As Pringle waited for dawn to break before going in for the kill, it looked as though escape was impossible, but Benedict Arnold, the American commander, was prepared to try.

During the night the American commander ordered his ships to slip through the British lines, using muffled oars and the cover of the thick fog to slip between the island and the enemy ships. Though only three of his boats got away—Arnold ordered that the remaining five be burned and beached—their escape won the admiration of the British, who saw and heard nothing and did not realize they were missing until dawn. "On the whole," wrote Arnold later to General Philip Schuyler, "I think we have had a very fortunate escape."

See also: Brooklyn Heights; Hackensack River
References: Greene, J., and J. R. Pole. *Blackwell Encyclopaedia of the American Revolution.* Oxford: Blackwell, 1992.

VIENNA (1683)

In July 1683 the dramatic arrival of a newly resurgent Ottoman army at the gates of Vienna prompted concern that the forces of Islam were on an unstoppable march across the rest of the continent. The competing powers of Europe were forced to cooperate and launch a rescue operation to save the city from the clutches of their common enemy.

The Ottoman army was led by a brilliant general, Kara Mustafa, and it was clear that Vienna was in as much danger as it had been five generations before, when the armies of Suleiman the Magnificent had nearly succeeded in breaking through its defenses. Now a huge army of 50,000 men, drawn from all the vassal provinces and client states of the Ottoman Empire, was at its door, and it was using sophisticated mining techniques to blow through the defenses of an exhausted and half-starved garrison.

The response to the plight of Vienna was a massive rescue operation that involved most, if not all, the European rulers. The Holy Roman Emperor, who had been forced to flee the city in the most unceremonious manner, raised an extensive force from the innumerable principalities that made up his kingdom. The papacy granted extensive funds from its own coffers and from those of its wealthy prelacies throughout Europe to help pay for the war effort. Charles V, the duke of Lorraine, raised a force of 10,000 men, which was surpassed in numbers by those sent by Saxony and, above all, by the effective leader of the rescue effort, John Sobieski of Poland. For a few weeks, even Louis XIV of France set aside his traditional Valois rivalry with the Holy Roman Emperor and informally agreed not to distract from the war effort against a common foe.

On 12 September, when Vienna had been besieged for nearly two months, the lookouts watching from St. Stephen's tower saw, in the far distance, the long-range rockets that the rescuers fired into the night sky to inform them that they had broken through the Ottoman lines and were now not far off.

News quickly filtered around the garrison, which was on the verge of starvation, that their ordeal was nearly over.

The unity among the victors did not last long, however, and the disagreements among them spared the retreating Ottomans from the complete annihilation that they would otherwise have faced. "Here we are on the Danube, like the Israelites on the Euphrates," sighed Sobieski wearily as the postvictory dissension began to emerge, "lamenting the loss of our horses and the ingratitude of those whom we have served" (Stoye 1964).

References: Stoye, John. *The Siege of Vienna, 1683.* London: Collins, 1964.

VIETNAM WAR (1964–1973)

Like the Allied prisoners of the Japanese 30 years before, the American prisoners of war (POWs) held by the Communist forces in North Vietnam during the Vietnam War had virtually no chance of escaping. Bearing no resemblance to the indigenous population, and without any underground network to turn to if they did break free, escapees faced certain recapture and serious punishment. Not surprisingly, only four prisoners held north of the border are known to have attempted escape during the 16-year U.S. involvement, and all were quickly recaptured.

Partly because escape from Communist captivity was a virtual impossibility and partly because of the ruthlessness of the captors toward their prisoners, American planners instead prioritized the rescue of downed airmen before they fell into enemy hands. "Search and rescue" operations were carried out for most of the war by "Jolly Green Giants"—the Sikorsky HH3 helicopters—which were mainly flown by a special rescue unit based in Thailand to wherever U.S. or South Vietnamese pilots had picked up radio signals indicating that a downed airman was still safe and awaiting rescue. The rescue helicopters, usually operating in pairs, then flew to the area and were guided toward the soldier's position by radio or any other form of ground signal, such as a mirror or fire.

These search and rescue operations sometimes created unfortunate dilemmas for the U.S. commanders, who had to weigh the risks of rescue attempts in Vietcong-infested territory against the welfare of the downed aircrew. The costs of making a mistake became clear, for example, on 6 November 1965, when an F105D Thunderchief was shot down near Hanoi, which was formidably well protected by Chinese and Soviet air defense systems. Despite the dangers involved, an A1 Skyraider was dispatched to patrol the area, allowing rescue helicopters to fly in and find the downed airman, but the A1 was itself shot down during the operation. As soon as the A1 pilot signaled his position, another rescue party came in to extract both the rescuer and the Thunderchief pilot. But again ill-fortune dogged the rescuer, for it was now the helicopter's turn to be shot down, and its four-man crew also waited for their own rescuers to appear on the scene. When another helicopter began to circle the area looking for them the next day, it too was hit by enemy fire and only managed to limp part of the way back to base before crash-landing. At the end of this rescue saga, its four-man team and the Skyraider pilot were eventually lifted to safety, but the Thunderchief pilot and the crew of the first downed helicopter fell into enemy hands. A determined attempt to rescue a single pilot had led instead to four other airmen being captured and to the loss of another plane and two helicopters.

A similar scenario occurred in April 1970 after Lt. Col. Iceal E. Hambleton's EB-66 plane was shot down just south of the North Vietnamese border. Once again, several helicopters were either crippled or shot down when rescue formations flew in to pick him up.

However, some attempts were made, in both North and South Vietnam, to rescue POWs who had already fallen into enemy hands. In 1965 television film of the treatment of U.S. prisoners held in Hanoi had shocked the U.S. public and much of the rest of the world, and rescue plans were drawn up to meet not only the concerns of the prisoners' families but also to give a much-needed boost to morale at a time when the war had become an extremely expensive commitment. But though 119 missions were made to rescue U.S. prisoners between 1966 and 1973, none was ever fully successful. During one such operation, a GI was rescued but died later from his wounds.

One operation, Operation Ivory Coast, was launched in the closing stages of the war, in November 1972, and illustrates that such failure was sometimes due just as much to bad U.S. practice as to the determination and abilities of the enemy. After intelligence photographs had identified a considerable number of Americans—estimated to be about 50 or 55—in the Son Tay compound not far from Hanoi, a hand-picked team was prepared for a rescue mission. An assault was rehearsed time and time again—altogether about 170 times—at an exact, full-scale replica of the Son Tay compound at Eglin Air Force Base in Florida. The force landed with almost exact timing, avoiding Hanoi's radar dishes by flying along precise routes, and killed between 100 and 200 enemy soldiers without loss. But the mission failed for the simple reason that there were no longer any prisoners to free. At fault was a Pentagon official: Photographic experts had told him a month earlier that there were no longer any prisoners to be released, but he had refused to accept the report and failed to inform his commanders.

The large number of GIs who were still unaccounted for by the end of the war—2,497—could not fail to arouse the interest of many of their countrymen, and isolated reports and rumors that many of them were still alive inside Vietnam and were being kept in captivity inevitably attracted the interest of would-be rescuers. In 1979 Lt. Col. James "Bo" Gritz, a Vietnam veteran with a great deal of special forces experience, was approached by two retired officers and asked if he would undertake investigations into the fate of some of the missing personnel and, if possible, organize a rescue operation. The site of particular interest to them was a rice field in Laos in which, according to a air reconnaissance photo, some 30 Caucasians appeared to be working.

Gritz started to prepare for Operation Velvet Hammer in the spring of 1981, hiring 25 former Green Berets, all Vietnam veterans, to form a force that could take a closer look, but he was acting purely on his own initiative and on that of his sponsors. Because they were seeking to carry out this independent, maverick enterprise without the approval of the White House, it never looked like it had a realistic chance of success. Before long Pentagon officials intervened on the grounds that such a rescue bid could have far-reaching and highly damaging diplomatic repercussions if it went ahead and would also endanger the success of other similar enterprises they claimed to be planning. So, like so many other plans and operations to rescue U.S. soldiers in Vietnam, Velvet Hammer was a fruitless venture.

See also: Khe Sahn; Rowe, James "Nick"; Saigon
References: Anderson, William C. Bat–21. Reprint, New York: Bantam. 1983.
Brown, John M. G. Moscow Bound: Policy, Politics, and the POW/MIA Dilemma. Eureka, CA: Veteran Press, 1993.
Freith, J. Code-Name Bright Light. The Untold Story of US POW Rescue Efforts During the Vietnam War. New York, London: Free Press, 1997.
Hemmingway, Al. "Daring Raid on Son Tay." VFW Magazine, November, 1995. Pp. 20–23.

VON TRAPP FAMILY SINGERS (1938)

The Nazi invasion of Austria in March 1938 prompted one of the most famous escapes ever made—the flight of the Von Trapp singers over the Alps to Italy—though the manner of their escape was rather different from what was depicted in The Sound of Music.

Georg Von Trapp knew that, as a former senior naval commander, he would be forced into the German Navy, so he and his wife, Maria, drew up their escape plans soon after the Nazi takeover. To behave as inconspicuously as possible, they decided to disappear by doing what they often did: strolling into the mountains for a day's hike. But this time they would secretly be carrying enough food and water to keep going until they reached the Italian border.

In her memoirs, Maria Von Trapp recorded the conflict of emotions that were aroused by their escape. On the one hand they were overjoyed by their success in slipping out of the Nazi grasp, she wrote, but their spirits were also depressed by the knowledge that overnight they had become refugees and had gone from riches to rags.

References: Von Trapp, Maria. *Maria.* London: Coverdale, 1973.

WAGNER, RICHARD
(1813–1883)

The early life of the great composer Richard Wagner was colored by a fleeting involvement with radical politics in the tumultuous 1840s, when much of Europe was affected by political unrest.

At the time he perceived a relationship between political liberty on the one hand and artistic and cultural renewal on the other. The young Wagner thus began to involve himself with radical groups then active in Prussia. Most were not opposed to monarchical rule but, rather, wanted to extend individual freedom and expression and sought to invoke popular protest and demonstration in order to get their message across.

After the Prussian king dissolved the Saxon parliamentary body in May 1849, riots and disorder spread throughout the kingdom. Though it was always said that he fired shots from a barricade against the local soldiers, it is much more likely that Wagner's involvement was limited to organizing the movement of men and materials to and from Dresden, though he probably did carry a musket when doing so.

But when Prussian troops moved in to arrest the demonstrators and their ringleaders, Wagner was forced to flee, knowing that his growing reputation as a composer would not bring him any special leniency from the authorities. He managed to reach Weimar, where he went into hiding under the wing of his fellow musician, guide, friend, and father-in-law, Franz Liszt.

But still he was not safe. During his stay in Weimar he heard that the police had issued a warrant for his arrest and were searching for him, issuing a description to all local inhabitants.

Wagner's escape from the city was so hasty that, according to a letter Liszt wrote to an acquaintance, he left Weimar without hearing a performance of his own opera *Tannhäuser*, which he had much looked forward to.

But after safely reaching Zurich, Wagner was once again at liberty to continue composing.

See also: Garibaldi, Giuseppe; Louis Napoleon
References: Anderson, Robert. *Wagner: A Biography.* London: Linnet, 1980.

WALLENBERG, RAOUL
(1912–1947?)

Perhaps because he valued the lives of others more than his own, the story of the Swedish diplomat Raoul Wallenberg, one of the most famous rescuers of World War II, is tainted with sadness and a certain mystery as well as heroism.

Wallenberg arrived at Sweden's embassy in Budapest at a time when the liquidation of Hungary's 750,000 Jews—about half of its Jewish population—had just begun in earnest. German soldiers and local collaborators were rounding them up and either deporting them to concentration and extermination camps elsewhere in Europe or imprisoning them in specific quarters of the capital. Wallenberg had gone to Hungary expecting trouble, having accepted requests from Jewish organizations in the United States and from a few Jewish individuals in Stockholm to alleviate the sufferings caused by the occupation, but he had not expected persecution on such a scale. But as a diplomat of a neutral country that the Nazis were anxious not to antagonize, he had freedoms that the representatives of the Allied countries did

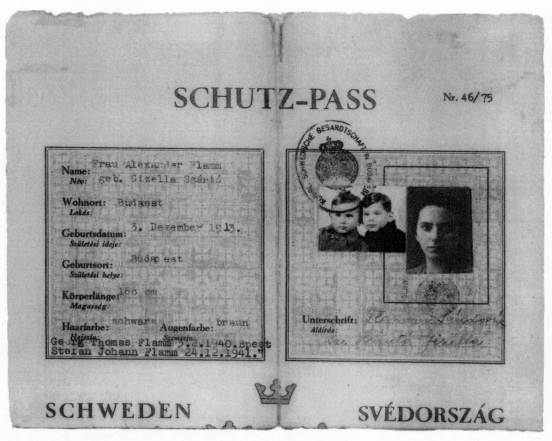

One of the official documents that Swedish diplomat Raoul Wallenberg was responsible for producing, allowing possibly thousands of Jews to escape from occupied Hungary during World War II. (Ferenc Flamm, courtesy of USHMM Photo Archives)

not and was therefore well placed to help the Jews of Budapest.

Though he was not able to simply hand out Swedish citizenship to the Jews, he nonetheless hit on an idea almost as good. He set up a special unit at the embassy to design and manufacture a document that looked official and was very impressive, the *Schützpass*, which had no legal status at all but whose design and presentation commanded instant respect from the Nazis. This cleverly manipulated a weakness in the German armor, for Wallenberg had noticed that the Germans were inclined to respect any form that had some seal of authority.

At first the Hungarian Foreign Ministry gave permission for 1,500 of these passes to be manufactured, but Wallenberg, mainly by bribing and blackmailing officials, was able to have the number increased to 4,500. Eventually he merely increased the number he manufactured regardless, though later he simply issued signed letters and papers to avoid attracting the full wrath of the authorities. Both through couriers and personally, he arranged for all of them to be handed out to Jews he was able to meet in Budapest.

Wallenberg also found other methods of saving Budapest's Jews. He established a series of safe houses across the capital, where pass holders could go and find refuge before they fled the country. And in stark defiance of the Nazis and their Hungarian sympathizers, he even arranged for the Star of David to be flown from these houses alongside the Swedish flag.

One of his last single great acts of rescue took place in 1945 after he was tipped off by a contact in the Hungarian police that an SS unit had been ordered by Adolf Eichmann, who was in overall charge of organizing deportations, to execute the Jews in the capital's ghetto. Wallenberg instantly rushed to the scene in order to personally confront the German officer in charge. Since the Red Army was moving rapidly toward Hungary, he was quick to seize on the officer's secret fears. He threatened to have him hanged by the Russians if he gave the order for his troops to open fire. The German backed down, and the Jews were spared.

The fate of Raoul Wallenberg remains a mystery. All that is known is that in the last chaotic days after the Germans had pulled out of the capital and before the Russians moved in, he and an escort bravely went toward the Russian lines to meet the main Soviet commander. What seems certain is that he was arrested and locked up in Moscow's Lubianka Prison, probably because he had been taken for a Nazi sympathizer. There are unconfirmed reports that he was executed by the Russians in the prison in 1947.

References: Smith, Danny. *Wallenberg: The Lost Hero.* Basingstoke, Eng.: Pickering, 1986.

WARBURG (1942)

Some prisoners tunnel under the barriers, and others forge identity documents or uniforms to go through a main entrance, but a few go over, scaling a wall or climbing over wire at a well-chosen moment. The most celebrated attempt to put this third option into practice—always very risky—occurred at a German prisoner of war (POW) camp, Oflag VIB, in Warburg in 1942.

The plan for escape that was put into effect that summer enjoyed the support of 91 of the prisoners, who were being held in a camp with a particularly unenviable reputation. The plan called for a large number of POWs to create a distraction in one corner of the camp, thereby allowing others the chance to use ladders and duckboards, specially made out of the hut roofing, to get over the wire fence to freedom. This was nonetheless extremely hazardous, since prisoners caught in the act of escaping

risked being shot dead on sight. Several others, often acting on impulse and without the meticulous planning that effective wartime escapes depended upon, had already been shot while making the attempt.

But the escape plan worked remarkably well. In the three minutes that the commotion lasted, 41 prisoners scaled the wire and made a dash for freedom. Most of them were recaptured within days, but the first three over made their way to Holland. There they were put in touch with the local underground, which operated the "Comet" line of escape through Paris to Madrid and Gibraltar, and they eventually reached Britain.

One of these three had to think particularly quickly during his getaway. While he was traveling by train through Lille, an official took an unusual interest in his forged papers, as if noting something not quite in order. The official seemed to be on the point of asking some searching questions, but a further glance at the escapee stopped him. For at the crucial moment, the escapee posed as a lunatic, feigning a look of madness and blabbering away at the guard at top speed. The official decided that questioning him was more trouble than it was worth and stamped his papers, letting him carry on.

References: Reid, Pat. *Prisoner of War.* London and New York: Hamlyn, 1984.

WARD ROAD PRISON, SHANGHAI (1944)

Drawing up plans to escape from Ward Road Prison in Shanghai, where he had been held since 1942, a Shanghai pilot who had been inducted into the U.S. Navy, Comdr. C. D. Smith, soon discovered that his attempt to escape would test far more than his ability to saw through the window bars of his cell and avoid being seen by his guards.

One such difficulty was keeping the plans confined to the individuals involved. This was not because any of his fellow escapees were inclined to chatter unnecessarily, he later noted, but rather because the prisoners' close proximity meant that they could almost read each other's thoughts. After dinner, on 6 October 1944, as he and his accomplices waited to make their move, "it seemed as though the whole prison was waiting," such was the "tenseness and expectancy in the air." This was in part because, although the prisoners usually whispered to each other from cell to cell or corridor to corridor, the escapees now kept a sudden and suggestive silence. "You can't keep secrets in a prison," he commented wryly later (Reynolds 1973).

Smith also learned the importance of self-control in avoiding suspicion. As he took a brief rest from sawing at the bars of his window one night, he suddenly found a bright light beamed at him by someone standing only three or four feet outside his cell. The jail superintendent, quite by chance, had arrived to investigate why the electric light in the hangman's room, next door, had been left on. Hiding the hacksaw blade in his pocket, Harris possessed just enough self-control to hide the tremors of fear running through him and to play innocent.

It is possible, too, that a more defensive reaction from the escapees a few days later might have cost them their necks. They scaled the prison wall with a rope made from sheets and blankets, and many passers-by in the street saw them lower themselves down into the street below. But though their sudden appearance drew gasps of surprise, to Smith's astonishment people merely stopped and looked, making no attempt to hinder them or to inform any of the guards. Had the prisoners reacted more defensively, showing signs of guilt or fear, then the outcome might have been entirely different.

Smith had also quickly realized that he would need to make some extremely difficult choices, choices that would require an accurate reading of his enemy's mentality: Once free of the prison compound, should they head north, almost straight out of Shanghai into a wilderness; east toward the Huang-p'u River; or west, through the city?

Smith decided to take the route the Japanese would least expect. No one would think they would have the audacity to walk right through the center of the city, over well-lighted highways, he reasoned. Instead, they would surely expect the escapees to take the quickest route out of the city and would therefore concentrate their search toward the north and east. Smith also knew that crossing either an open plain or a river, which was almost certainly heavily defended, would make them extremely vulnerable.

The decision to go through the city proved to be right. Within a day, Smith and his two companions had crossed Shanghai, and they soon met up with Chinese Nationalist soldiers. Smith reached American lines long after he had been presumed dead, and he eventually reached San Francisco and was reunited with his family.

References: Reynolds, Quentin. *Officially Dead*. New York: Random House, 1973.

WERRA, FRANZ VON (1918–1941)

A few very rare individuals are born escapees who would flee any form of captivity, no matter how tolerable its conditions. Franz von Werra was unusual not just because his escape attempts were so audacious but because he made them at all: Almost all the other German prisoners of the British during World War II merely accepted their fate and showed no propensity to even try to escape.

Von Werra was a decorated Luftwaffe pilot who had already earned considerable distinction by the time he was shot down over the southern counties of England in September 1940, in the closing stages of the Battle of Britain. He was taken for interrogation to a military center at Cockfosters, but it did not take him long to turn his mind toward thoughts of escape, and he even offered to bet the British officer he met there—a magnum of champagne against his own ten cigarettes—that he would escape within six months. (His offer was turned down.)

Such an immediate declaration of intent shows that, unlike for many prisoners of war, it was not boredom or deprivation that lay behind von Werra's fanatical ambition to escape. Nor is there any evidence that he held the strong ideological beliefs that made some others regard escape as the duty of a good Nazi. Instead, von Werra appears to have been a man in search of constant challenge and adventure, like those he had already had in his year of active service flying a Messerschmidt. The statements he later made to the world's press, after his escape, also reveal a man who lived his life in the imagination—one journalist even compared his story to the *Arabian Nights*—and who may therefore have always strongly romanticized the adventure of escape.

His first escape attempt followed only a month after his capture. At Grizedale Hall in the Lake District, where they were held, they were often taken on walks along the neighboring roads. He quickly noticed that an agile prisoner could slip away during the walks if the others were to surround him to shield him from the guards. And though the prisoners were always counted on departure and arrival, an escapee could probably confuse the soldiers long enough to disappear.

This first stage of his plan worked, though he never got close to reaching the coast and stowing away on board a neutral ship, as he and his fellow officers had hoped. Instead, he was eventually recaptured five days later, half-starved and exhausted, by a party of police, soldiers, and dogs.

The lenient treatment he received afterward—very different from that meted out to Allied prisoners in Germany or the Far East who tried to escape—would hardly have discouraged a man such as von Werra from having another go. He was initially taken to a nearby inn and given a cup of tea and a cigarette, before being sentenced to 21 days in the prison "cooler," whose spartan, solitary conditions were relieved by the friendliness of a prison guard who smuggled in some extra rations.

He certainly wasted no time in making his next escape attempt. This time, again with the full cooperation of the camp's escape committee, he decided to tunnel out. Using a chisel, crowbar, and scoops, he and his team of accomplices set up the Swanwich Tiefbau AG ("Swanwick Construction Company"), which took only a few weeks to reach the outside.

Of the five who broke free on 12 December 1940, four were recaptured almost straightaway. But von Werra, who spoke far better English than his colleagues and who had an unusually strong nerve, fared far better. With astonishing audacity, he planned to head for an airfield and steal a plane to take him to Ireland. Wearing his flying suit, stripped of all badges, he adopted the identity of a Dutch flying officer, Capt. Albert William van Loft—a character entirely his own invention—and asked local people of the whereabouts of the nearest Royal Air Force (RAF) base, claiming, improbably, that his aircraft had crash-landed a few miles away after returning from the Continent.

That he arrived at Hucknall, the nearby RAF base, at all seems in retrospect almost miraculous. On a brief train journey two local policemen who had been tipped off by a suspicious guard tried their best to trip him up. Like the German police, who would address British escapees in German before suddenly asking a question in English, they tried to elicit a German reply from the "Dutch pilot." Their efforts only received the reply in English that, yes, he did speak a little German. He also deliberately used RAF slang—using phrases such as "pancaking the Wimpey" and others he had picked up from the newspapers and prison guards—and he rightly pointed out that he could not produce any identity papers because it was forbidden for aircrew to carry them on active operations. Though they had initially been highly suspicious about van Loft, the policemen allowed the staff at Hucknall to send a car to pick him up and take him to the base, and by the time the police went to search the fields of the area for the wreck of the aircraft von Werra had claimed to have crash-landed, the German was already at the RAF base, trying his best to get an aircraft.

While the adjutant was trying to call the RAF authorities to verify his story—on a very bad telephone line—von Werra was told by a mechanic that he would have to sign the visitors' book and fill out some forms before he was allowed to requisition one of the Hurricanes, parked only a 100 yards or so away. He filled out the papers and made his way over to the aircraft on the pretext of needing to familiarize himself with the controls before taking off. He climbed into the cockpit and pressed the starter button, and only one thing stopped him from taking off: a flat battery, which the mechanic said could be changed in minutes.

The mechanic was not quite quick enough for von Werra. The sudden arrival of the duty officer, who had been unable to verify his story on the telephone and who now brandished a revolver as he shouted at him to leave the cockpit, brought his second, and extraordinary, escape bid to an abrupt end.

A few weeks after he was recaptured, when his camp was moved to Canada, von Werra had a chance to make his third attempt to escape internment. After being shipped across the Atlantic in January 1941, he and his fellow Germans were put on a train bound for their new camp on the northern shore of Lake Superior in Ontario. The United States, then still neutral, was not too far from the railway he was traveling on. Though it was midwinter when he arrived, von Werra knew that if he could slip from under the eye of his guards, then he might be able to reach the United States.

His departure revealed, once again, a mixture of audacity and simplicity. While his guards watched other prisoners go to and from the toilet, von Werra simply raised the carriage window and disappeared headfirst through it, his escape effectively shielded by a fellow German who had conveniently held up a blanket just at the crucial moment. Perhaps because they found it hard to believe that any of the prisoners would have wanted to leave their warm surroundings and generous rations for the harsh conditions outside, none of the guards even noticed, or said anything, until the following afternoon.

He left the train about 40 miles southwest of Ottawa, and he only had 30 miles to travel to reach the banks of the St. Lawrence river. From there, in the distance, he was able to see the distant lights of Ogdensburg

in the United States. Though the river is wide, and though there were no bridges across it, because it was midwinter von Werra was able to walk over its thick ice to freedom. Using a boat to cross a channel on the U.S. side of the river, he at last arrived on American soil and therefore on neutral territory.

Yet his efforts were to prove tragically futile. After returning to Germany and rejoining his unit, von Werra survived a spell at the Russian front and was even credited with shooting down another eight aircraft. But in October 1941, barely eight months after he had broken out of Allied captivity, he was killed on a routine patrol over Holland. It is even possible that this was an indirect consequence of his earlier adventures, which may have nurtured a touch of arrogance: A Court of Inquiry concluded that the crash had been caused by engine failure and *by the pilot's carelessness*. It hardly seemed a fitting end for an individual whose extraordinary career had won him the admiration of all who knew him.

See also: Pluschow, Gunther

References: Burt, Kendal, and James Leasor. *The One That Got Away.* New York: Ballatine, 1957.

Wenzel, Fritz. *Single or Return? The Story of a German POW in British Camps and the Escape of Lieutenant Franz von Werra.* London: William Kimber, 1954.

WILSON, CHARLIE
(1931–1990)

One of the most infamous British criminals of his time, Charlie Wilson was able to stage a dramatic escape from the prison sentence he had been given for his key role in the Great Train Robbery of 1963.

Only a year after the robbery, three men are known to have used a rope ladder to get over the wall of Winson Green Prison in Birmingham in order to spring Wilson. They had come well prepared, for they had in their possession several forged keys that took them into the prison corridor where Wilson, along with 500 others, was being held. After hitting the unfortunate prison guard who was on duty (and giving him a concussion), they did not take long to locate Wilson, finding his cell by looking on the list of those who were considered by the prison authorities to be "an escape risk." In very little time the four men had made their way through the bathhouse, into the grounds outside, back over the wall, and into the street outside.

While the police searched for Wilson, pursuing, in their desperation, all sorts of unlikely clues, their quarry was using a forged passport to board a ferry at Dover and make his way first to France and then to Canada. It was a very long time before the police had any clue at all to his whereabouts.

Although Wilson enjoyed high-level contacts in the criminal underworld, he was able to make his getaway only because of the duplicity of a prison officer who was bribed to make copies of the keys that his rescuers were then able to forge. This became clear in the extensive investigation that followed, when traces of soap were detected on the original key. That clue led to the arrest and imprisonment of the prison officer.

Wilson was not found and rearrested until 1968. In 1990, more than a decade after his release, he died a violent death, probably at the hands of rival criminals.

See also: Biggs, Ronald
References: Bean, J. P. Over the Wall: True Stories of the Master Jail Breakers. London: Headline, 1994.

WOODEN HORSE (1943)

Like a few other wartime escapes—notably the Great Escape and the Colditz breakouts—the story of the Wooden Horse has long captured the public imagination. It was made famous by the best-selling book published shortly after the war.

The setting was Stalag Luft III, at Sagan in Silesia, a camp for Allied airmen who had been shot down over the Reich. Stalag Luft III was not an easy place from which to escape, for the huts were all built on special stilts, which made it easy to spot any burrowing beneath them, and were regularly inspected by "ferrets," Germans who were specially trained to find concealed tunnels underneath the hut floors. The Nazi authorities had even planted seismographs in the ground, ordinarily used in mining operations, in order to detect any digging.

Since tunneling under the huts was not a realistic option, the prisoners had to look elsewhere for a way out. The plan this group came up with, reputedly inspired by the musings of one prisoner on the ancient Greek story of the Trojan Horse, was to dig not under the huts but instead under a wooden gymnasium exercise horse, moving it as close to the perimeter as they dared. The seismographs would not be a problem, it was argued, because tunneling would only take place when the men were using the horse for exercise. The machines would record the noise they made exercising, which would mask that of the burrowing. It was just possible, the plan's advocates argued, to build a horse from the wood in the huts.

The escape attempt was carefully planned. The horse was used by the prisoners for exercise for several weeks before tunneling began, so that the novelty would wear off and the curiosity—and suspicions—of the Germans who constantly watched over them would diminish. The length of tunnel needed was precisely calculated to be about 120 feet, and it was to be dug several feet underground.

With a prisoner hidden inside, the Wooden Horse was taken from the huts each morning, and the tunnel was uncovered. Maps, forged documents, and civilian clothes were also prepared long in advance for those who were preparing to go, a feat made possible because one prisoner had been able to persuade a German guard in the prison hospital to show him one of the permits that allowed foreign laborers to travel by train.

The tunnel was begun in June 1943 and took four and a half months to build before it was finally ready for use. On its last journey, the horse was taken to its usual place. This time, however, it contained not more tunnelers but three men intending to escape. Waiting until early evening, they made their way through the dark tunnel and arrived on the other side of the fence at six o'clock, exactly as planned. At the same time, as arranged, some other prisoners created a major disturbance in order to distract the guards at the crucial moment when the three escapees were ready to dash from the tunnel exit to the relative safety of the nearby woods.

All three men made it to freedom. One went alone by train to Danzig and managed to stow away on a Swedish ship almost immediately. The other two, traveling together, also managed to board a ship—with the assistance of some French laborers they met—and made it first to Copenhagen, then to Sweden.

But this was not the last breakout from the camp at Sagan. Not long after, it was also the setting for another at least as extraordinary: the Great Escape.

References: Williams, Eric. *The Wooden Horse.* London: Collins, 1979.

Z

ZWICKAU PRISON (1952)

During the postwar years of Communist rule in Eastern Europe, a young bureaucrat, Hans Lindemann, organized one of the most remarkable and audacious escapes ever carried out from East German territory.

While working in a government ministry in 1952, Lindemann felt intense sympathy for two prisoners at Zwickau Prison because he knew the true reason for their imprisonment. They were in prison not because they were guilty of various economic crimes, as the authorities claimed, but because the government wanted to take over their successful businesses. But, knowing how the release procedures worked, Lindemann reckoned he might just be able to help them escape.

The usual procedure to release a prisoner started with the issue of a release order that was drawn up in Leipzig and then signed by the city's attorney. The form was sent by post to the prison governor, who then made a brief phone call directly to the attorney to verify its authenticity.

Because a new attorney had just been appointed when he drew up his plan, Lindemann had to wait three months before he was able to obtain a specimen of the signature he sought to forge. When the documents were at last ready, he traveled to Leipzig to post the letter from the same post office that was used by the attorney's office.

Lindemann knew that a moment's delay could wreck the plan because the governor might phone Leipzig as soon as he received the letter. An acquaintance of Lindemann's, whose voice and elocution were a good match for those of the real attorney, telephoned the prison governor and barked a simple order in the imperious tones for which Communist bureaucrats were renowned: "This is *Oberstaatsanwalt* Adam," he announced. "No return call is necessary for verification." The governor did not question the validity of the call, and arrangements were made for the release of the prisoners.

When, the next day, West Berlin radio announced the extraordinary stories of the two arrivals who had been spirited out of East Berlin almost as quickly as they had been released from prison, it caused a mixture of incredulity, outrage, and fury among the East German ministers. They had been sure their elaborate procedures were escape proof.

See also: Berlin Wall; Iron Curtain
References: Dupre, Peter. *Caught in the Act: A True Story*. Tunbridge Wells, England: Costello, 1988.
Gelb, Norman. *The Berlin Wall*. London: Michael Joseph, 1986.
Hildebrandt, Reiner. *It Happened at the Wall*. Berlin: Verlag Haus am Checkpoint Charlie, 1992.
Shadrake, Alan. *The Yellow Pimpernels: Escape Stories of the Berlin Wall*. London: Hale, 1974.

BIBLIOGRAPHY

Abbott, Geoffrey. *Great Escape from the Tower of London.* Hendon: Nelson Lancj, 1988.

Abell, Francis. *Prisoners of War in Britain 1756–1815.* Oxford: Oxford University Press, 1914.

Abraham, Richard. *Alexander Kerensky: The First Love of the Revolution.* London: Sidgwick and Jackson, 1987.

Ackerley, J. R. *Escapers All: Being the Personal Narratives of 15 Escapers from War-Time Prison Camps, 1914–18.* London: John Lane, the Bodley Head, 1932.

Adams, James. *Secret Armies.* London: Hutchinson, 1987.

Adams, R. *Prison Riots in Britain and USA.* New York: St. Martin's Press; London: Macmillan, 1992.

Aldridge, Alfred Owen. *Thomas Paine: Man of Reason.* London: Cresset Press, 1959.

Anderson, Robert. *Wagner: A Biography.* London: Linnet, 1980.

Anderson, William C. *Bat–21.* Reprint, New York: Bantam, 1983.

Andrae, Tor. *Mohammed: Man and Faith.* London: George Allen and Unwin, 1936.

Armstrong, H. C. *Escape.* New York: Robert M. McBride, 1935.

Arnold-Foster, Mark. *The Siege of Berlin.* London: Collins, 1979.

Atkins, Burton M. *Prisons, Protests, and Politics.* Englewood Cliffs, NJ: Prentice Hall, 1972.

Atkin, R. *Pillar of Fire.* London: Sidgwick and Jackson, 1990.

Aylward, Gladys. *Gladys Aylward: Her Personal Story.* London, Coverdale House, 1970.

Bailey, Ronald H. *Prisoners of War.* Alexandria, VA: Time-Life Books, 1981.

Barker, A. J. *Dunkirk: the Great Escape.* London: Dent, 1977.

Barney, Mary, ed. *A Biographical Memoir of Commodore Joshua Barney.* Boston: Gray and Bowen, 1832.

Baybutt, Ron. *Colditz: The Great Escapes.* Boston: Little, Brown, 1982.

Bean, J. P. *Over the Wall: True Stories of the Master Jail Breakers.* London: Headline, 1994.

Begin, Menachem. *The Revolt.* London: W. H. Allen, 1979.

Belbenoit, René. *Dry Guillotine.* London: Jonathan Cape, 1971.

Biderman, Albert D. *March to Calumny: The Story of American POWs in the Korean War.* New York: Macmillan, 1963.

Bierman, J. *Napoleon III and his Carnival Empire.* London: J. Murray, 1988.

Biggs, Ronald. *Odd Man Out: My Life on the Loose and the Truth about the Great Train Robbery.* London: Pan, 1984.

Blair, Clay. *Beyond Courage.* New York: David Mackay, 1955.

Blanc, Olivier. *Last Letters: Prisons and Prisoners of the French Revolution.* London: A. Deutsch, 1987.

Bland, Elizabeth, ed. *Escape Stories.* London: Octopus Books, 1980.

Blassingame, Charles L. *The Underground Railroad.* New York: Prentice Hall, 1987.

Bligh, William. *A Narrative of the Mutiny on Board His Majesty's Ship "Bounty."* London, 1790; reprint 1901.

Bourke, Sean. *The Springing of George Blake.* London: Mayflower, 1971.

Bouscet, René. *De Gaulle–Giraud.* Paris: Flammarion, 1967.

Brandon, Ruth. *The Life and Many Deaths of Harry Houdini.* London: Mandarin, 1994.

Brett, Sidney. *John Pym.* London: John Murray, 1940.

Breuer, William B. *The Great Raid on Cabanatuan: Rescuing the Doomed Ghosts of Bataan and Cabanatuan.* New York: Wiley, 1994.

Breyfogle, William A. *Make Free: The Story of the Underground Railroad.* Philadelphia: Lippincott, 1958.

Brickhill, Paul. *Escape or Die: Authentic Stories of the RAF Escape Society.* New York: Norton, 1952.

———. *The Great Escape.* New York: Norton, 1950.

Bridgeland, Fred. *Katiza's Journey.* London: Sidgwick and Jackson, 1997.

Briffault, F. T. *The Prisoner of Ham: Authentic Details of the Captivity and Escape of Prince Louis Napoleon.* English translation. London, 1846.

Brown, John M. G. *Moscow Bound: Policy, Politics, and the POW/MIA Dilemma*. Eureka, CA: Veteran Press, 1993.

Bruce, John C. *Escape from Alcatraz: A Farewell to the Rock*. London: Hammond, 1984.

Buckmaster, H. *Out of the House of Bondage: Runaways, Resistance and Marronage in Africa and the New World*. London: Frank Cass, 1986.

Burgess, Alan. *The Longest Tunnel: The True Story of the Great Escape*. Bath: Chivers, 1991.

Burigny, Jean Lévesque de. *The Life of Grotius*. English translation. London: Printed for A. Millar, 1754.

Burke, John. *Buffalo Bill: The Noblest Whiteskin*. London: Cassell, 1974.

Burns, Robert. *I Am a Fugitive from a Georgia Chain Gang*. New York: Vanguard, 1932.

Burt, Kendal, and James Leasor. *The One That Got Away*. London: Mayflower, 1978.

Butt, Sidney. *John Pym*. London: John Murray, 1940.

Callahan, North. *Royal Raiders: The Tories of the American Revolution*. Indianapolis, IN: Bobs Merrill, 1963.

Campbell, Sir Neil. *Napoleon at Fontainebleau and Elba, Being a Journal of Occurrences in 1814–15*. London: J. Murray, 1869.

Campbell, Stanley W. *The Slave Catchers*. Chapel Hill: University of North Carolina Press, 1970.

Cangemi, Joseph P., and Casimir J. Kowalski. *Andersonville Prison: Lessons in Organizational Failure*. Lanham, MD: University Press of America, 1992.

Cardigan, Earl of. *I Walked Alone*. London: White Lion Press, 1974.

Cecil, Robert. *A Divided Life: A Biography of Donald Maclean*. London: Coronet, 1990.

Charriere, Henri. *Papillon*. London: Hart, Davis, 1970.

Churchill, Winston S. *The Boer War: London to Ladysmith via Pretoria*. London: Mandarin, 1990.
———. *My Early Life*. London: Mandarin, 1990.

Clarke, Thurston. *By Blood and Fire: The Bombing of the King David Hotel*. London: Hutchinson, 1981.

Clayton, Ann. *Noel Chavasse: Double VC*. London: Leo Cooper, 1979.

Cody, William. *The Life of Buffalo Bill*. London: Senate, 1994.

Coogan, Tim Pat. *Eamonn de Valera: The Man Who Was Ireland*. New York: HarperCollins, 1995.

Cooper, H. S. F. *The Flight That Failed*. London, Baltimore: Johns Hopkins University Press, 1995.

Copeland, Miles. *The Game of Nations: The Amorality of Power Politics*. London: Weidenfeld and Nicholson, 1969.

Crawley, Aidan. *Escape from Germany: A History of RAF Escapes during the War*. London: Collins, 1956.

Cumming, W. P. *The Fate of a Nation*. London and New York: Phaidon, 1975.

Dalai Lama XIV. *Freedom in Exile*. London: Abacus, 1992.

Darell, William. *Mr. Blount's Escape out of His Father's House*. London, 1598.

Davenport, Basil. *Great Escapes*. New York, Sloane, 1952.

Davie, Michael. *Titanic: The Full Story of a Tragedy*. London: Grafton, 1987.

Davies, Barry. *SAS Rescue*. London: Sidgwick and Jackson, 1996.

Davis, R. H. C. *King Stephen*. London: Longman, 1992.

Daws, Gavin. *Prisoners of the Japanese*. New York: William Morrow, 1994.

De Jeu, Vicomte. *A Prussian Casanova*. London: A. C. Black, 1924.

Deane-Drummond, Anthony. *Return Ticket*. London: Collins, 1953.

del Castillo, Bernal Diaz. *The True Story of the Conquest of Mexico*. New York: Harper, 1928.

Dengler, Dieter. *Escape from Laos*. Novato, CA: Presidio, 1979.

Dennett, Carl P. *Prisoners of the Great War*. Boston: Houghton Mifflin Riverside Press, 1919.

Denney, Robert E. *Civil War: Prisons and Escapes. A Day-by-Day Chronicle*. New York: Sterling, 1995.

Deschanel, Paul. *Gambetta*. London: Heinemann, 1920.

Dominy, John. *The Sergeant Escapers*. London: Allan, 1974.

Donovan, Robert J. *The Wartime Adventures of President John F. Kennedy*. London: Anthony Gibbs and Phillips, 1962.

Doyle, Robert C. *A Prisoner's Duty: Great Escapes in U.S. Military History*. Annapolis, MD: The Naval Institute, 1998.

Dukes, Sir Paul. *Red Dusk and the Morrow*. London: Williams and Norgate, 1922.

Dupre, Peter. *Caught in the Act: A True Story*. Tunbridge Wells, England: Costello, 1988.

Durnford, H. G. *The Tunnelers of Holzminden*. Cambridge: Cambridge University Press, 1990.

Earl, Lawrence. *Yangtze Incident*. London: White Lion, 1973.

Evans, A. J. *Escape and Liberation, 1940–45*. London: Hodder and Stoughton, 1945.

Falkus, Christopher. *The Life and Times of Charles II*. London: Weidenfeld and Nicolson, 1972.

Fea, Allan. *The Flight of the King*. London: Methuen, 1908.

Fellowes-Gordon, Ian, ed. *The World's Greatest Escapes*. London: Odhams, 1966.

Figes, Orlando. *The People's Tragedy: The Russian Revolution, 1891–1924*. London: Jonathan Cape, 1996.

Foot, Michael R., and James M. Langley. *MI9: Escape and Evasion, 1939–45*. London: Book Club Associates, 1979; Boston: Little, Brown, 1980.

Fraser, Antonia. *Mary Queen of Scots*. London: Weidenfeld and Nicholson, 1994.

Fraser, Ian. *Escape from Al Ould*. London: Frederick Muller, 1983.

Freith, J. *Code-Name Bright Light. The Untold Story of US POW Rescue Efforts During the Vietnam War*. New York, London: Free Press, 1997.

Gansberg, J. M. *Stalag USA*. New York: Thomas Y. Cromwell, 1994.

Garrett, Richard. *Great Escapes*. London: Weidenfeld and Nicholson, 1989.

Gelb, Norman. *The Berlin Wall*. London: Michael Joseph, 1986.

Geraghty, Tony. *Beyond the Frontline*. London: HarperCollins, 1996.

———. *March or Die*. London: Grafton, 1986.

———. *Who Dares Wins.* London: Warner, 1993.

Gibson, W. B. *Houdini's Escapes*. London: Phillip Allan and Co., 1931.

Gilbert, Martin. *Auschwitz and the Allies*. London: Mandarin, 1991.

Glass, Charles. *Tribes with Flags: A Journey Curtailed*. London: Seckler Warburg, 1990.

Goodspeed, D. J. *Ludendorff: Soldier, Dictator, Revolutionary*. London: Hart-Davis, 1996.

Gordievsky, Oleg, and Christopher Andrew. *KGB: The Inside Story of Its Foreign Operations from Lenin to Gorbachev*. London: Hodder and Stoughton, 1990.

Greene, J., and J. R. Pole. *Blackwell Encyclopaedia of the American Revolution*. Oxford: Blackwell, 1992.

Haldane, Aylmer. *How We Escaped from Pretoria*. Edinburgh: Blackwood and Sons, 1900.

Hardy, J. L. *I Escape!* London: John Lane, 1927.

Hastings, Max. *Yomi, Hero of Entebbe*. London: Weidenfeld and Nicholson, 1979.

Haynes, Sam W. *Soldiers of Misfortune: The Somerwell and Mier Expedition*. Austin: University of Texas Press, 1990.

Heaps, Leo. *The Grey Goose of Arnhem*. London: Futura, 1977.

Hemmingway, Al. "Daring Raid on Son Tay." *VFW Magazine*, November 1995, 20–23.

Heuman, Ged J. *Out of the House of Bondage*. London: Cass, 1986.

Hibbert, Christian. *The Road to Tyburn: The Story of Jack Sheppard and the Underground*. London: Panther, 1959.

Hildebrandt, Rainer. *It Happened at the Wall*. Berlin: Verlag Haus am Checkpoint Charlie, 1992.

Hoeling, A. A. *Edith Cavell*. London: Cassell, 1958.

Hopkirk, Peter. *The Great Game*. Oxford: Oxford University Press, 1990.

———. *Setting the East Ablaze*. Oxford: Oxford University Press, 1984.

Horne, Alistair. *A Savage War of Peace: Algeria 1954–62*. London: Macmillan, 1977.

Hudson, Christopher. *The Killing Fields*. London: Pan, 1984.

Hutton, Ronald. *Charles II*. Oxford: Oxford University Press, 1990.

Jackson, Robert. *Dunkirk: The British Evacuation*. London: A. Barker, 1976.

Jerrome, Edward. *Tales of Escape*. Belmont, CA: Fearon-Pitman, 1959; reprint 1970.

Johnson, Forrest Bryant. *Hour of Redemption: The Ranger Raid on Cabanatuan*. New York: Manor Books, 1978.

Johnston, Isaac N. *Four Months in Libby*. Cincinnati, OH: Methodist Book Concern, 1864.

Johnston, Johanna. *Runaway to Heaven: The Life of Harriet Beecher*. Garden City, NY: Doubleday, 1963.

Kavanagh, T. H. *How I Won the Victoria Cross*. London: Ward and Lock, 1860.

Keneally, Thomas. *Schindler's List*. London: Sceptre, 1992.

Kinvig, Clifford. *River Kwai Railway: The Story of the Burma-Siam Railroad*. London: Brasseys, 1992.

Klemperer, Victor. *The Diaries of Victor Klemperer*. London: Weidenfeld and Nicholson, 1998.

Lacouture, Jean. *De Gaulle*. London: Harrill, 1993.

Lamott, Kenneth. *Chronicles of San Quentin*. London: John Long, 1963.

Latude, Henri Masers de. *Memoirs of the Bastille*. English translation. London: Routledge, 1927.

Lawes, Lewis E. *Life and Death in Sing Sing*. London: John Long, 1929.

Lawrence, Thomas E. *The Seven Pillars of Wisdom*. New York: Anchor, 1991.

Lawton, Marion R. *Some Survived: An Epic Account of Japanese Captivity during World War II*. Chapel Hill, NC: Algonquian, 1984.

Lovell Jim. *Lost Moon*. London: Coronet, 1995.

Lowrie, Donald. *Masaryk of Czechoslovakia*. Oxford: Oxford University Press, 1990.

Lusebank Hans-Jürgen, and Rolf Reichardt. *The Bastille: A History of a Symbol of Despotism and Freedom*. Durham, NC: Duke University Press 1997.

Macaire, Tatiana. *Nadia*. London: Lithoflow Press, 1997.

Mack Smith, Dennis. *Garibaldi*. London: Hutchinson, 1957.

Maclean, Fitzroy. *Bonnie Prince Charlie*. London: Weidenfeld and Nicholson, 1988.

Malcolm, Noel. *Kosovo*. London: Macmillan, 1998.

Mansel, Philip. *Louis XVIII*. London: Bland and Briggs, 1981.

Marvel, William. *Andersonville: The Last Depot*. Chapel Hill: University of North Carolina Press, 1994.

Massingberg, Hugh, ed. *Daily Telegraph Book of Obituaries*. London: Fontana, 1996.

Matthews, William. *Charles II's Escape from Worcester: A Collection of Narratives Assembled by Samuel Pepys*. Berkeley and Los Angeles: University of California Press, 1966.

McAdoo, William G. *Crowded Years*. New York: Houghton Mifflin, 1931.

McFadden, Robert. *No Hiding Place*. New York: Times Books, 1981.

McGartland, Martin. *Fifty Dead Men Walking*. London: Jade Books, 1998.

McVicar, John. *McVicar: By Himself*. London: Hutchinson, 1974.

Messimer, Dwight R. *Escape*. Annapolis, MD: Naval Institute Press, 1994.

Morton, Joseph. *Sparks from the Campfire*. Philadelphia: Keystone, 1892.

Neave, Airey. *Saturday at MI9: A History of Underground Escape Lines in North-West Europe, 1940–45*. London: Hodder and Stoughton 1969.

———. *They Have Their Exits*. London: Hodder and Stoughton, 1969; New York: Beagle Books, 1971.

O'Brien, Donat Henchy. *My Adventures during the Late Wars*. London: John Lane, 1932.

O'Donnell, James. *The Berlin Bunker*. London: Dent, 1979.

O'Faolain, Sean. *The Life Story of Eamonn De Valera*. Dublin, London: Talbot, 1933.

Parker, John P. *His Promised Land, 1827–1900: The Autobiography of John P. Parker*. New York and London: Norton, 1996.

Payne, Ronald. *Mossad*. London: Bantam, 1990.

Pellegrino, Charles. *Her Name, Titanic: The Untold Story of the Sinking and Finding of the Unsinkable Ship*. London: Robert Hale, 1990.

Perret, Geoffrey. *Old Soldiers Never Die*. New York: Random House, 1996.

———. *There's a War to Be Won: The United States Army in World War II*. New York: Random House, 1991.

Pettit, Jayne. *A Place to Hide*. London: Piccolo, 1994.

Pluschow, Gunther. *My Escape from Donington Hall*. Translated by Pauline de Chary. London: John Lane, 1922.

Porch, Douglas. *The French Secret Service*. London: Macmillan, 1996.

Posner, Steve. *Israel Undercover*. Syracuse, NY: Syracuse University Press, 1987.

Pottle, Pat, and Michael Randall. *The Blake Escape*. London: Harrap, 1989.

Pran, Dith. *Children of the Killing Fields*. New Haven, CT, and London: Yale University Press, 1998.

Price, Richard. *Maroon Societies*. Baltimore and London: Johns Hopkins University Press, 1996.

Probyn, Walter. *Angel Face*. London: Allen and Unwin, 1977.

Pugh, R. D. *Imprisonment in Medieval England*. Cambridge: Cambridge University Press, 1968.

Radzinsky, Edward. *Stalin*. London: Hodder and Stoughton, 1996.

Ramage, James A. *Rebel Raider: The Life of Gen. John Hunt Morgan*. Lexington: University Press of Kentucky, 1986.

Ramati, Alexander. *The Assisi Underground*. New York: Stein and Day, 1978.

Ransom, John L. *Andersonville Diary: Escape and List of Dead*. Auburn, NY, 1881.

Rawicz, Slavomir. *The Long Walk*. London: Longmans, 1995.

Rayne, Ronald. *Mossad*. Transworld, 1990.

Read, A., and D. Fisher. *The Fall of Berlin*. London: Hutchinson, 1992.

Reader's Digest Book of Escapes. Pleasantville, NY: Reader's Digest Association, 1995.

Reid, Pat. *The Colditz Story*. London: Hodder and Stoughton, 1952.

———. *Prisoner of War*. London and New York: Hamlyn, 1984.

Reynolds, Quentin. *Officially Dead*. New York: Random House, 1973.

Ridley, Francis A. *Spartacus, the Leader of the Roman Slaves*. Ashford, Eng.: Maitland, 1963.

Ridley, Jasper. *Garibaldi*. New York: Viking Press, 1976.

Ripley, C. Peter, ed. *The Black Abolitionist Papers: The British Isles, 1830–1865*. Chapel Hill: University of North Carolina Press, 1985.

Roosevelt, Kermit. *Countercoup*. New York: McGraw-Hill, 1979.

Roskey, Bill. "Great Escapes: POWs Break Through the Wire." *Soldier of Fortune*, May 1991, 68.

Rowan, Roy. *Four Days of the Mayaguez*. New York: Ballantine, 1971.

Rowe, James. *Five Years to Freedom.* New York: Ballantine, 1971.

Ruddick, James. *Lord Lucan: What Really Happened.* London: Headline, 1994.

Ryan, Chris [pseud.]. *The One That Got Away.* London: Century, 1995.

Ryan, Cornelius. *A Bridge Too Far.* London: Coronet, 1974.

Salisbury, Harrison E. *The Long March: The Untold Story.* London: Macmillan, 1985.

Shadrake, Alan. *The Yellow Pimpernels: Escape Stories of the Berlin Wall.* London: Hale, 1974.

Shipwrecks and Disasters at Sea. Vol. 3. Edinburgh: A. Constable, 1812.

Shoemaker, Lloyd R. *The Escape Factory: The Story of MIS-X.* New York: St. Martin's Press, 1990.

Shuster, A. I. *Great Civil War Escapes.* New York: G. P. Putnam and Sons, 1967.

Skorzeny, Otto. *Skorzeny's Special Missions.* London: Greenhill, 1977.

Smith, Danny. *Wallenberg: The Lost Hero.* Basingstoke, Eng.: Pickering, 1986.

Smith, Michael. *Foley: The Man Who Saved 10,000 Jews.* London: Hodder and Stoughton, 1999.

Start, Daniel. *The Open Cage.* London: HarperCollins, 1998.

Stearns, Charles. *Narrative of Henry Box Brown.* Philadelphia: Rhetoric, 1969.

Stoye, John. *The Siege of Vienna, 1683.* London: Collins, 1964.

Suhl, Yuri. *They Fought Back: The Story of Jewish Resistance in Nazi Europe.* MacGibbon and Gee, 1968.

Swift, Catherine M. *Gladys Aylward.* Basingstoke, Eng.: Marshalls, 1984.

Symons, Arthur. *The Adventures of Giuseppe Pignata.* English translation. London: Jonathan Cape, 1930.

Tchernavin, Tatiana. *Escape from the Soviets.* London: Hamish Hamilton, 1933.

Utley, Robert M. *Billy the Kid: A Short and Violent Life.* London: Tauris, 1990.

Var Hong Ashe. *From Phnom Penh to Paradise.* London: Hodder and Stoughton, 1988.

Vaublanc, Vincent de. *Mémoires.* Paris: G. A. Denta, 1833.

Verral, Charles S., ed. *True Stories of Great Escapes.* Pleasantville, NY: Reader's Digest Association, 1977.

Villar, Paul, ed. *The Escapes of Casanova and De Latude.* London: T. Fisher Unwin, 1892.

Vistica, Gregory. "An American Hero." *Newsweek,* 19 June 1995, 24–33.

Volkogonov, Dmitri. *Trotsky: The Eternal Revolutionary.* London: HarperCollins, 1996.

Von Trapp, Maria. *Maria.* London: Coverdale, 1973.

Wade, C. E. *John Pym.* London: Sir Isaac Pitman and Sons, 1912.

Waller, Brown. *Harvey Logan: The Last of the Great Western Train Robbers.* South Brunswick, NJ: A. S. Barnes, 1968.

Wenzel, Fritz. *Single or Return: The Story of a German POW in British Camps and the Escape of Lieutenant Franz von Werra.* London: William Kimber, 1954.

Whitcomb, Edgar D. *Escape from Corregidor.* Chicago: Henry Regnery, 1958.

Whiting, C. *Massacre at Malmedy.* London: Leo Cooper, 1996.

Williams, Eric. *The Book of Famous Escapes.* New York: Harper, 1958.

———. *The Wooden Horse.* London: Collins, 1979.

Wilson, Arthur Link. *The Struggle for Neutrality.* Princeton, NJ: Princeton University Press, 1960.

Wilson, Dick. *The Long March: The Epic of Chinese Communism's Survival.* London: Penguin, 1977.

Wilson, Jeremy. *Lawrence of Arabia.* London: Minerva, 1989.

Witt, Jerry V. *Escape from the Maple Leaf.* Bowie, MD: Heritage Press, 1993.

Zola, Emile. *Le Débâcle.* London: Penguin, 1972.

INDEX

247